BOSNIA AFTER DAYTON

In memory of my father
Dr SISIR K. BOSE
(February 2, 1920-September 30, 2000)
who would have read this book
with great interest

SUMANTRA BOSE

Bosnia after Dayton

*Nationalist Partition and
International Intervention*

HURST & COMPANY, LONDON

First published in the United Kingdom by
C. Hurst & Co. (Publishers) Ltd.,
38 King Street, London WC2E 8JZ
© 2002 by Sumantra Bose
All rights reserved.

The right of Sumantra Bose to be identified as the
author of this work has been asserted by him in accordance
with the Copyright, Designs and Patents Act, 1988

A British Library Cataloguing-in-Publication
Data Record is available for this book.

Printed in Scotland

ISBNs
1-85065-585-5   *paperback*
1-85065-645-2   *casebound*

CONTENTS

Acknowledgements   *page* vii

Chapters
1. An Important and Complex Place: Bosnia
    after Dayton   1
    The importance of Bosnia   2
    The complexity of Bosnia   10
    Epilogue and prologue: a Bosnian Story   38

2. A State by International Design? Liberal
    Internationalism and the Balkans   41
    A question of legitimacy   42
    Foundations of the Dayton peace   52
    Structure of the Dayton state   60
    Conclusion: dilemmas of liberal internationalism   89

3. Mostar, 1994–2001: Nationalist Partition and
    International Intervention in a Bosnian Town   95
    The city that was   99
    War and partition   100
    *A tenuous bridge: international intervention in
       partitioned Mostar, 1994-2001*   106
    Politics: the persistence of polarization   116
    *Other dimensions of partition: economy, education,
       culture, symbols*   131
    Conclusion: lessons of Mostar   142

4. Bosnia and the Partition Debate — an
    Intervention   149
    Untangling the debate   161
    Beyond the partition debate   199

v

5. Democracy amid Division: the Institutional
   Architecture of the Dayton State   204
   Bosnia's party system   206
   Electoral integration   215
   Federalism, federation and the Bosnian state   241
   Consociational present, consociational future?   246

6. Post-Yugoslav Futures: Lessons from (and for)
   International Intervention   253

Select Bibliography   283

Index   291

MAPS

1. Political Geography of Bosnia & Herzegovina, 1991
   (with inset for Sarajevo area)   *facing p. 2*

2. Political Geography of Bosnia & Herzegovina, 2000
                                                facing p. 3

3. Bosnia & Herzegovina after Dayton: Cantons and
   Regions   *facing p. 42*

4. City of Mostar   *facing p. 96*

FIGURE

Political Structure of Bosnia & Herzegovina under the
Dayton Regime   *facing p. 60*

ACKNOWLEDGEMENTS

Writing this book has been an immensely inspiring experience, but it has also been quite challenging. It is a pleasure to record my gratitude to the family, friends, colleagues and institutions whose support and encouragement have sustained me along the way: Dr Aida Velic in Mostar, 1998, and in Florida, 2000, for her affection and enthusiasm; Professor Lisa Anderson, Dean of the School of International and Public Affairs at Columbia University, New York; Professor Brendan O'Leary of the Department of Government at the London School of Economics and Political Science; Kishore Mandhyan of the United Nations for all his help and generosity in Mostar, Sarajevo and, before that, in western Slavonia, Croatia; Gordon N. Bardos, assistant director of the Harriman Institute, Columbia University; Professor Peter Loizos of the Department of Anthropology and Professor Dominic Lieven of the Department of Government at the LSE; Lejla Mrkonja in Sarajevo; Lara Jane Nettelfield, also in Sarajevo; Rubina Khan of the UN in Mostar; Dejan Djokic, Jasna Dragovic-Soso and Nebojsa Vladisavljevic in London; the late Professor John Petropoulos of the Department of History, Amherst College, USA, who twelve years ago introduced me to Eastern Europe and to what was then still a country called Yugoslavia; Professor Mark Kesselman of the Department of Political Science, Columbia University and Professor William Taubman of the Department of Political Science, Amherst College, for their continuing support; Michael Dwyer, director of Hurst and Co., London, for contracting me to write this book before I had written a word of it; and at home in India, my mother Professor Krishna Bose, MP; my brother Sugata, sister Sarmila, brother-in-law Alan, nephews Aidan (Tipu), Kieran (Tunku) and Euan (Puchku).

Preliminary research in Bosnia and Herzegovina in 1998 was made possible by a grant from the International Peace and Security Program of the Social Science Research Council, New York, using funds provided by the MacArthur Foundation. In 2000 a generous award from the social sciences division of the Nuffield Foundation, London, towards further research in BiH enabled me to carry the project to fruition, and boosted morale and energy.

While I was gradually developing this book, opportunities to test my ideas and arguments before sophisticated audiences were provided by invitations to speak at the Harriman Institute's international conference 'From Dayton to Kosovo' at Columbia University in November 1999, at the School of Slavonic and East European Studies (SSEES) annual conference on 'Balkan Security' in London in June 2000, and at smaller seminars organized by the East-Central Europe Centre of the Harriman Institute in October 1998 and by the LSE's European Institute in March 2000.

London, January 2002   SUMANTRA BOSE

1

AN IMPORTANT AND COMPLEX PLACE: BOSNIA AFTER DAYTON

'The peace agreement for Bosnia is the most ambitious document of its kind in modern history, perhaps in history as a whole. A traditional peace treaty aims at ending a war between nations and coalitions of nations, while here it is a question of setting up a state on the basis of little more than the ruins and rivalries of a bitter war. There are often calls for a revision of the peace agreement, either to break up Bosnia further or to pave the way for a more unitary state. Neither is realistic, and both are irresponsible in view of the fears that would be unleashed by any attempt to remake the peace, in effect opening up all the questions of the war. The peace agreement balances the reality of division with structures of cooperation and integration, and is based on the hope that over time the imperative of integration in the country and the region will be the dominant factor.'—*Carl Bildt, the first international 'high representative' in Bosnia & Herzegovina after the Dayton Peace Agreement*[1]

'On paper, Dayton was a good agreement; it ended the war and established a single, multiethnic country. But countless peace agreements have survived only in history books as case studies in failed expectations. The results of the international effort to implement Dayton would determine its true place in history.'—*Richard Holbrooke, principal representative of the US government at the Dayton peace negotiations*[2]

'If protection rackets represent organized crime at its smoothest, then war-making and state-making—quintessential protection rackets with the advantage of legitimacy—qualify as our largest examples of organized crime. Without branding all generals and statesmen as murderers or thieves, I want to encourage the value of that analogy... A portrait of war-makers and state-makers as coercive and self-seeking entrepreneurs bears a far greater resemblance to the facts than do its chief alternatives...

---

[1] Carl Bildt, *Peace Journey: The Struggle for Peace in Bosnia*, London, 1998, p. 392.
[2] Richard Holbrooke, *To End a War*, New York, 1998, p. 335.

To the extent that the threats against which a government protects its citizens are imaginary, or are the consequences of its own activities, the government has organized a protection racket. Since governments themselves simulate, stimulate and even fabricate threats of external war, and since the repressive and extractive activities of governments often constitute the largest threats to their own citizens, many governments operate in essentially the same way as racketeers. There is, of course, a difference: racketeers, by conventional definition, operate without the sanctity of governments.'—*Charles Tilly, scholar*[3]

'We must finally realize that Bosnia & Herzegovina is not only not the centre of the world, but not even the centre of the region any more either. In fact, Bosnia has become a side-issue.'—*Zlatko Lagumdzija, leader of the Social Democratic Party of Bosnia & Herzegovina (SDP-BiH), the country's largest non-nationalist party, on the fifth anniversary of the Dayton Peace Agreement, November 2000*[4]

The importance of Bosnia

For almost four years between April 1992 and January 1996, the war in Bosnia & Herzegovina dominated global headlines and soundbites. Since then, BiH may have ceased to be 'the centre of the world', as Zlatko Lagumdzija caustically reminds its citizens. Yet this small country of perhaps 3.5 million people, located geographically and otherwise on the margins of Europe, remains an important place to know and understand.

At the end of 1995, a controversial peace agreement reached after heavy American arm-twisting on a nondescript air force base in a remote town in the American Midwest ended the Bosnian war. That accord, initialled in Dayton, Ohio, on November 21, 1995, was formally signed almost a month later, on December 14, in the somewhat more hallowed precincts of the Versailles palace near Paris. But 'Bosnia' and 'Dayton' have ever since come to be used as thoroughly entangled, almost interchangeable expressions. Every Bosnian child knows about 'Dayton', and one of Sarajevo's more enterprising companies is called 'Dayton Import-Export'. For the past six years, the merits and demerits of 'Dayton' have been the topic of spirited debate not just among Bosnians and

---

[3]   Charles Tilly, 'War-making and state-making as organized crime' in P. Evans, D. Rueschemeyer and T. Skocpol (eds), *Bringing the State Back in*, Cambridge, 1985, pp. 169-71.
[4]   Interview with TV BiH, November 20, 2000.

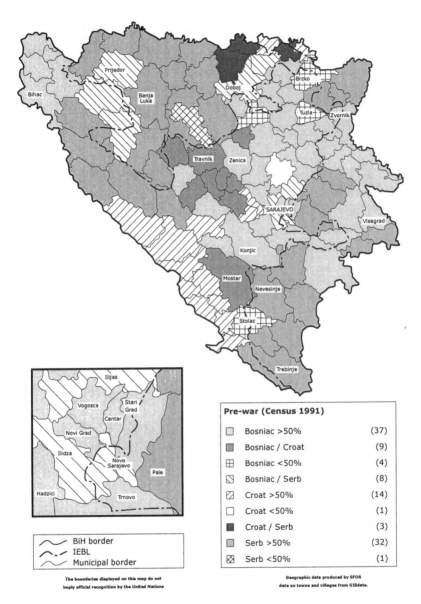

Pre-war (Census 1991)

☐	Bosniac >50%	(37)
◼	Bosniac / Croat	(9)
⊞	Bosniac <50%	(4)
◨	Bosniac / Serb	(8)
◩	Croat >50%	(14)
☐	Croat <50%	(1)
◼	Croat / Serb	(3)
▦	Serb >50%	(32)
⊠	Serb <50%	(1)

BiH border
IEBL
Municipal border

The boundaries displayed on this map do not
imply official recognition by the United Nations

Geographic data produced by SFOR
data on towns and villages from GISdata.

**Map 1: Political Geography of Bosnia &
Herzegovina, 1991 (with inset
for Sarajevo area)**

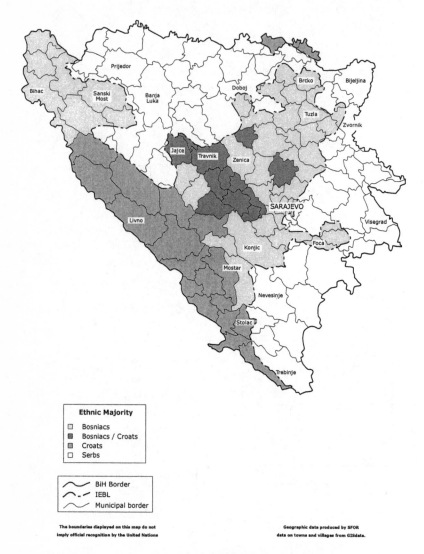

Ethnic Majority

- ☐ Bosniacs
- ◼ Bosniacs / Croats
- ◼ Croats
- ☐ Serbs

- BiH Border
- IEBL
- Municipal border

Geographic data produced by SFOR
data on towns and villages from GISdata.

Map 2: Political Geography of Bosnia & Herzegovina, 2000

other former Yugoslavs, but among scholars, politicians, diplomats and assorted 'experts' throughout the Western world. With good reason. Since the beginning of 1996, 'Dayton Bosnia' has been the site of internationally sponsored political engineering on a remarkable scale. This endeavour seeks to utterly transform a society that was at war with itself for forty-three months, which emerged from the fighting with its territory effectively partitioned into three national(ist) statelets, and whose population continues to be deeply divided on fundamental issues of identity and allegiance.

Tens of thousands of military and civilian staff deployed by a consortium of international organizations—the North Atlantic Treaty Organization (NATO), the Organization for Security and Cooperation in Europe (OSCE), the United Nations (UN) and its agencies, the World Bank and International Monetary Fund (IMF), among others—have been engaged in the arduous mission of transforming this fractured society into a economically and politically viable state. They are strongly backed by the governments of the United States and most other significant Western countries.

The task for would-be state-builders and democratizers is daunting. Bosnia is not just a society divided but a society polarized on the most basic of issues—the question of legitimacy of the state, its common institutions and its borders. In 1997, 91 per cent of BiH Serbs and 84 per cent of BiH Croats opposed a united Bosnian state, while 98 per cent of Bosnian Muslims supported such a state.[5] Political scientists generally believe that a minimal consensus on borders and national unity is necessary for sustainable democratization in any society. In the words of one such scholar, 'the vast majority of citizens in a democracy-to-be must have no doubts or mental reservations as to which political community they belong to'.[6]

Six years on, the degree of effectiveness of the enormously ambitious international experiment in state-making and democracy-building in Bosnia—necessarily in uneasy collusion with

[5]   Susan L. Woodward, 'Bosnia and Herzegovina: How Not To End Civil War' in B.F. Walter and J. Snyder (eds), *Civil Wars, Insecurity and Intervention*, New York, 1999, p. 96.
[6]   Dankwart Rustow, 'Transitions to Democracy: Toward a Dynamic Model' in L. Anderson (ed.), *Transitions to Democracy*, New York, 1999, p. 26.

local political interests who, for the most part, act and operate like racketeer syndicates—is a matter of some dispute. But it is generally agreed, among people with widely divergent perspectives on wartime and post-war Bosnia, that the situation of BiH remains precarious in almost every sense, and that the shape of the future is uncertain.

This book is about the political dimensions of the internationally led reconstruction process in Bosnia since the Dayton Peace Agreement (DPA). I argue that the post-war experience of Bosnia & Herzegovina is important and relevant far beyond that tragically divided society's contested borders. This is not only because the international intervention in Bosnia since Dayton 'has become a highly visible testing ground for post-Cold War interventions in general, for the re-direction of European and transatlantic security organizations, and for the new agenda of development agencies in regard to post-conflict reconstruction'. The case of Bosnia is worthy of attention in its own right, because it involves dilemmas that go to the heart of an unsettled post-Cold War international order.

Is the preservation of a multinational state desirable in a situation where the vast majority of citizens belonging to two of the three constituent communities of that state only reluctantly acknowledge its legitimacy? Even if desirable, is it possible in a context where those two groups taken together constitute around half the state's population,[8] control some 70% of the state's territory, almost all its 'international' borders, and have contiguous 'mother states' to support their claims and act as an alternative focus of loyalty? Or is a formal partition not just the more realistic but the more just alternative in these circumstances, where communitarian claims to 'self-determination' are not just in con-

[7]   Susan L. Woodward, 'Transitional Elections and the Dilemmas of International Assistance to Bosnia & Herzegovina' in S. Riskin (ed.), *Three Dimensions of Peacebuilding in Bosnia: Findings from USIP-sponsored Research and Field Projects*, Washington, DC, 1999, pp. 5-6.
[8]   On the eve of war in 1992, Bosnia's population of 4.4 million was roughly 45% Muslim, 35% Serb, and 18% Croat. No reliable statistics are yet available on the current population and its composition, in the wake of wartime losses, post-war emigration, and large-scale displacements within and outside the country. Bosnia-based officers of international agencies such as UNHCR, working on return and rehabilitation of refugees and internally displaced persons (DPs), estimated to this author in 2000 that the population is now approximately 48%

flict but mutually incompatible? If the answer to the first two questions is a carefully qualified affirmative—as this book will argue—the problem only becomes more complicated. First of all, it has to be demonstrated why a joint state, upholding the principle of multinational coexistence, is in the longer term an option preferable to the partition of Bosnia, not only because that denies the preferences of most BiH Serbs and BiH Croats, but because the overwhelming and at least partially internationally sanctioned tendency throughout the former Yugoslavia since 1991 has been progressive decomposition and the emergence of national states (and statelets). The longer-term desirability of preserving Bosnia as a single, albeit highly decentralized state cannot be taken as an axiomatic proposition at all—it has to be established through argumentative dialogue with the proponents of alternative perspectives and solutions.

Once that is accomplished (if it is), the problem moves on to another plane. What sorts of political processes, and frameworks of rights and representation, can (or cannot) mitigate such intense disagreements over the fundamentals of sovereignty and statehood? This dimension of the Bosnian crucible goes to the heart of debates over power-sharing and consociational democracy, federalism and the functioning of federated states, party-system formation and the role of national(ist) parties therein, the priority given to elections in post-conflict peace-building, the prospects of encouraging inter-group cooperation through design of electoral systems, and so on. There are many reasons why even those not specifically interested in 'southeastern Europe', 'the former Yugoslavia' or 'the Balkans' should find contemporary Bosnia compelling. The challenge of balancing realities of division with the longer-term imperative of cooperation is probably the principal challenge of the post-Cold War global order.

The role of the 'international community' (IC) vis-à-vis this

Bosniac (Bosnian Muslim), 39% Serb and 12% Croat. The precise national breakup of the population is a politically sensitive question in this deeply divided society. See Drazen Simic, 'How Many Inhabitants Does Bosnia Have? The Only Country Without a Population Census', AIM, Sarajevo, April 28, 2001. Simic suggests that the absence of a proper count serves the manipulative agendas of a variety of 'political and quasi-national interests', including those that exaggerate the population of Republika Srpska, and those that deliberately under-estimate the number of Croats still living in BiH.

torn society remains of paramount importance. At the height of the Bosnian war, it was observed that in addition to the three belligerents who were tearing the place apart, 'the international community has itself unwittingly become a fourth constituent part of that tragic place'.[9] In 1992, with the comprehensive collapse of the structures of Titoist Yugoslavia and the demise of conventional modes of doing politics, Bosnia's politicians resorted to war—the continuation of politics by other means. Since late 1995 they have stopped fighting but the early years of post-war politics can accurately be described as the continuation of war by other means. For most of the war period, the 'international community'—shorthand for Western governments and multilateral institutions controlled by those governments—appeared impotent. Its harassed mediators, poring over maps, calculating percentages and shuttling ineffectually between the warring factions, did not present an impressive sight, the 'peace-keeping' contingents on the ground with no peace to keep even less so. However, since late 1995, the decisive role of IC elements—especially the United States—in the making and subsequently the enforcement of the Dayton settlement has made the IC a serious player in the Bosnian drama, indeed the pivotal factor in the weak, disunited and dysfunctional state that is post-Dayton Bosnia. Indeed, it has become increasingly obvious that the main faultline of conflict in post-Dayton Bosnia has not been between the three Bosnian national groups, but that the 'main line of confrontation has been between Bosnians [of all three groups] and [representatives of] the international community'.[10]

The IC in Bosnia sees itself as the flagbearer of a vision of liberal internationalism in a place destroyed by competing particularist nationalisms. The standard international perception of the problem posed by contending particularist factions is basically accurate. 'Nationalists' in the post-war Bosnian context are often wartime racketeer networks, grown rich on an abnormal political and economic situation, who manipulate the fears of the impoverished people of their respective groups in an effort to preserve their own dominance, and profit-making. Their apparent espous-

[9]   Mihailo Crnobrnja, *The Yugoslav Drama*, Montreal and London, 1994, p. 188.
[10] Susan Woodward, 'Transitional Elections', p. 9.

al of the collective identity and common interests of their national group is often simply a superficial ideological camouflage for their racketeering activities. However, many dimensions of international involvement in Dayton Bosnia are themselves problematic, and call for serious scrutiny and assessment.

The indifferent results, after six years of intensive engagement, in such crucial areas as refugee and DP returns, is one obvious concern that raises questions about the ultimate capacity of even the most ambitious international intervention to build *and* democratize a state in a severely divided society, on the basis of little more than the ruins and rivalries of a murderous war. Deeper questions and dilemmas underlie indifferent performance, however. Since 1997 the international community in Bosnia has arrogated to itself more and more powers of direct intervention in Bosnia's public life, especially through the person of the civilian head of mission who coordinates the multi-agency international effort, the 'high representative' (HR). The HR has summarily dismissed elected Bosnian officials deemed 'obstructionist', and imposed legislation on institutions deadlocked by political feuding (and more than occasionally, by sheer incompetence). IC agencies have become involved in fundamentally reforming Bosnia's educational, media and judicial systems. Yet, despite enhanced powers of intervention and control, frustration has on balance outweighed progress. A pattern has emerged instead of the IC becoming drawn into acrimonious confrontations with the political class of all three Bosnian communities. A series of ding-dong battles has ensued between the heavy guns of the IC elite and the lethal snipers among the local elites.

The outcome of this war of attrition has hinged ultimately on one factor: the degree of popular support the snipers are able to continue to demonstrate among their respective constituencies. A foundational assumption of international engagement in post-war Bosnia is that the international community is there to do good for the people of Bosnia, whose lives and future are being held to ransom by venal and sectarian leaderships. The venality and sectarianism of many of those leaders is in itself not in doubt. The problem is that venal and sectarian as they are, they have in the end been able withstand international sound and fury because they have repeatedly proved the resilience of their popular base in a

series of competitive elections between September 1996 and
November 2000. A tacit expectation that 'wartime' parties would
gradually wither on the vine has proved to be unfounded. Open
exhortations from high international officials to reject 'nationalists' and vote in more 'moderate' alternatives have largely fallen on
deaf ears among the Bosnian public. In 1997 the IC embarked
upon a strategy designed to irrevocably undermine the Serbian
Democratic Party (SDS) in the Republika Srpska (RS). Four years
later, the SDS, in a superficially reformed incarnation, is resurgent,
way and ahead the single largest party in the RS's (somewhat lib-
eralized) political space and the pivotal player, notwithstanding
Western (particularly American) disapproval, in its institutions.
During 2000-1, the IC has been involved in an explosive stand-
off with the Croatian Democratic Union in Bosnia (HDZ-BiH).
The rub, once again, is that the HDZ has proven beyond reasonable doubt, in the most recent set of elections in November 2000,
that it continues to enjoy overwhelming support among Croats in
BiH. It is only in the Muslim zones of the country that the SDP-
BiH, a party of genuinely social-democratic, cross-national orientation, has been able to displace the sectarian Party of Democratic
Action (SDA) as the most popular choice, and that too only in
larger urban centres. Moreover the SDP, Bosnia's only major party
of unambiguously non-nationalist orientation, has negligible support among Serbs and Croats, although it does have some Serbs
and Croats in its leadership cadre. In Bosniac politics, the SDA is,
despite a significant erosion of its base, still a major player, and will
continue to be so.

The contentious, indeed adversarial relationship between the
international community and much of Bosnia's political spectrum
is therefore, actually, also a contentious and adversarial relationship
between the international community and vast segments of the
Bosnian electorate. This situation inevitably raises uncomfortable
questions about the premise of the IC that corrupt and authoritarian local elites are the sole obstacle to the successful 'implementation of Dayton'. When given a choice between corrupt and
authoritarian leaders and 'moderates' favoured by the IC—i.e.
implicitly between the local and international elites who co-gov-
ern Bosnia in a fraught relationship—most ordinary Bosnians
seem to prefer the homegrown devil that they know. In the mean-

time, incessant IC chatter about improving 'transparency' and 'accountability' of Bosnian leaders and structures leads to uncomfortable questions about what sort of transparency characterizes the IC's own decisionmaking processes which have an impact on so many spheres of Bosnian life, and what sort of accountability increasingly authoritarian, decree-prone IC leaders themselves have to the constituency on whose behalf and in whose interests they are supposedly working—the people of Bosnia.

The international predicament in Bosnia is perhaps best described by a paradoxical phrase—*power and powerlessness*. An increasingly intrusive international presence has not produced the expected breakthroughs. The inability to change the balance of power between local and international elites decisively in the latter's favour—because of the support troublemaking local elites continue to command *at the mass level*—is a source of severe frustration. As a Council of Europe spokesman expressed it after the November 2000 elections, 'we are disappointed and mystified that people [in Bosnia] want a better life and financial support from the West, but are not prepared to vote for the parties that could make it happen'.[11] It has dawned on some internationals that it is far too simplistic to blame racketeering elites for all the IC's woes in Bosnia, and that the crucial source of blockage is actually the reinforcement such elites receive from the mass level of Bosnian society. Does this mean that ordinary Bosnians have a herd-mentality with no conception of where their 'real' interests lie, that they do not appreciate the international community's enormous investment in rebuilding Bosnia from rubble, and that they are intent on actively sabotaging their own future? Many in the IC in Bosnia would undoubtedly say yes, but my answer would be—no, not really. There is a genuine puzzle here, the unravelling of which requires problematizing and critically examining the assumptions, premises, strategies and objectives of the international mission in Bosnia & Herzegovina. This book will argue that many of those assumptions, premises, strategies and objectives fail to take sufficient account of the extraordinary complexity of this small but important place.

---

[11] Zeljko Cvijanovic, 'Bosnia Poll Sparks International Row', *Balkan Crisis Reports* 197, November 21, 2000.

The complexity of Bosnia

Understanding Bosnia necessarily involves an appreciation of complexity. The debate over Bosnia's past, present and future is dominated by essentialized images and binary dichotomies which do enormous violence to complex Bosnian realities. In the following pages we take a critical look at three of the most prevalent dichotomies—tolerance or hatred? civil war or aggression? integration or partition?—in an effort to take the debate at least one step beyond these categories of understanding. If there is one attribute that is indeed intrinsic to Bosnia's past, present and, most probably, future—it is complexity and the fluidities, ambiguities and uncertainties that a complex historical legacy brings in its wake. A society shaped on the crossroads of empires for four centuries and on the cusp of competing modern nationalisms during a fifth, Bosnia defies simplistic categorization.

Tolerance or hatred?

'Bosnia… was in a sense a microcosm of the country as a whole… It had been fought over repeatedly by Turks, Austrians and Serbs, and most of the national trends and tendencies were represented there, all at their most violent. The population was made up of violently Catholic Croats and no less violently Orthodox Serbs, with a strong admixture of equally fanatical local Moslems. It is hard to imagine the savage intensity of the passions that were aroused or the extremes of bitterness which they engendered. Magnified and revitalized by the war… the latent tradition of violence revived. The lesson we were having was an object lesson, illustrated by burned villages, desecrated churches, massacred hostages and mutilated corpses'.

This is a description of Bosnia in 1943, not 1993. It features in the memoirs of Fitzroy Maclean, a Scotsman parachuted into Bosnia by British intelligence to establish the facts about conditions inside Axis-occupied Yugoslavia and find out more about the strength of the Yugoslav Partisans led by Tito's communists. Maclean dropped into Bosnia somewhere close to the town of Mrkonjic Grad, on the cusp of central and northwestern Bosnia, then travelled to nearby Jajce to meet Tito and take up his duties as Allied liaison officer with the Partisans. He is an important figure in his own right in modern Yugoslav history, who subsequently was to cultivate a lifelong association with the country lasting until his death in 1996. Maclean's first few months in Bosnia were quite enough to persuade him about 'the violence and fanaticism of this Balkan war'.[12] To those familiar with Fitzroy Maclean's memoirs it must have seemed that history was repeating itself in Yugoslavia and in Bosnia in the 1990s. The issue is central to understanding Bosnia, and was one of several polarizing arguments to have emerged during the latest Bosnian war that have remained unresolved since. Has Bosnia historically been a haven of tolerance, a mosaic of nations, religions and cultures where people and communities generally got along happily? Or is it, in the memorable phrase of Warren Christopher, United States Secretary of State during the 1992-5 war, a 'problem from hell',[13] a place where atavistic hatreds simmer not far below the surface and bubble up at regular intervals?

The popular image of Bosnia is probably more influenced by the second stereotype. The Bosnian war received massive attention in the international media throughout its duration. Journalists looking for stories—the more lurid and macabre the better—could find a virtually inexhaustible supply in this place which seemed to have imploded and exploded at the same time. This type of coverage made a powerful impression on people's minds, and its effects linger long after the end of the armed conflict. Throughout the world—not just the Western world—'Bosnia' still evokes images of brutality, of emaciated, abused prisoners behind barbed wire with that chillingly hollow, unfocused glaze in their eyes, of merciless shelling of civilian centres, and most notoriously, of the 'cleansing' of populations that had become undesirables overnight. War journalism ran out of current material in late 1995, but sensational narratives that can only be classified as war-voyeurism continued to appear even several years later.[14]

This fascination with the violent ways of primal 'Balkan' peoples has a long lineage in a variety of 'Western' representations of the region in modern times. In deconstructing such egregious works as Robert Kaplan's 1993 publication *Balkan Ghosts* (which

[12] Fitzroy Maclean, *Eastern Approaches*, London, 1949, 1991, pp. 337-8.
[13] Ivo Daalder, *Getting to Dayton: The Making of America's Bosnia Policy*, Washington, DC, 2000, p. 36.
[14] For an example, see Anthony Loyd, *My war gone by, I miss it so*, London, 1999.

allegedly influenced then President Clinton's thinking regarding what to do, or not to do, about the Bosnian war)[15] Maria Todorova has shown how 'as in the case of the Orient, the Balkans have served as a repository of negative characteristics against which a positive and self-congratulatory image of the "European" and the "West" has been constructed'.[16] This may precisely capture the attitude towards Bosnian society among many members of the international community who have worked there. It may also help explain why so many adventure-seekers, missionary zealots on civilizing field expeditions and careerists from comparatively dull and boring post-industrial Western societies have been drawn to exotic and tortured Bosnia in the past decade. In an important modification and extension to Todorova's thesis, Milica Bakic-Hayden has shown how 'Balkanism' (Todorova's term) has been internalized by some among the South Slav peoples themselves. The consequence has been profoundly disturbing—the rhetorical deployment of the alleged dividing line between civilized Europe/West and uncivilized/half-Oriental 'Balkans' by intellectual and political leaders of the former Yugoslav nations *against one another* in the post-Yugoslavia phase. All aim to extricate themselves from the 'Balkan' label and claim 'European' (hence civilized) status, while designating other former Yugoslavs as 'Balkan' rather than 'European', with all the pejorative connotations that implies. This has been a staple of a certain type of Slovenian and Croat discourse *vis-à-vis* the former 'southern' republics of Yugoslavia, the Serbs and Serbia in particular, and appears in a virulent form in the discourse of some Serb politicians and intellectuals *vis-à-vis* suddenly 'othered' Bosnian Muslims, as Bakic-Hayden clearly shows.[17] But interestingly enough, it also appears in a variant of Bosnian Muslim discourse directed against BiH Serbs and Croats. Thus in an interview in a BBC documentary on post-war Bosnia broadcast in October 2000, Alija Izetbegovic claimed that Bosnian Muslims never had any problems with those Serbs and Croats in Bosnia 'who thought of themselves as Europeans', only with those who did not.

Some writers on the contemporary Balkans, Bosnia included,

15 Robert Kaplan, *Balkan Ghosts: A Journey through History*, New York, 1993.
16 Maria Todorova, *Imagining the Balkans*, New York, 1997, p. 188.
17 Milica Bakic-Hayden, 'Nesting Orientalisms: The Case of Former Yugoslavia', *Slavic Review* 54: 4 (1995), pp. 917-31.

have understandably reacted to such essentialist caricatures of entire peoples and societies. They have instead chosen to highlight what they regard as the *true* essence of Bosnia as a society down the centuries, defined by such virtues as tolerance, mutual understanding, and coexistence.) These accounts regard the violent episodes of the 1940s and 1990s as historical aberrations rather than as events confirming a pattern of ingrained communal hostility and proclivity to violence. The contributions of Mahmutcehajic, and Donia and Fine, fall into this category.[18] Not coincidentally, these and other authors of similar views are strong proponents of a single, united Bosnian state, and are strongly opposed to both the perceived separatism of BiH Serbs and Croats and the perceived irredentist agendas of the Serbian and Croatian states *vis-à-vis* Bosnia & Herzegovina. In a somewhat different and more subtle vein, Misha Glenny too has emphasized the role of *external* interference and instigation in eruptions of inter-group violence in the Balkans, particularly in the nineteenth and twentieth centuries.[19]

(This perspective serves the limited purpose of being a useful corrective to the more commonly prevalent stereotypical view. However, in attempting to defend Bosnians/Balkanites against negative stereotyping, it tends to selectively exaggerate and romanticize positive aspects of Bosnian history, simplifying in particular the picture of everyday relations between people of different communities at the local level.) Writers of this camp also tend to downplay the endogenous sources of violence in Balkan, specifically southern Slav societies.[20] Its greatest failing, however, is the attempt to substitute one essence in the place of another. This translates into a failure to adequately come to terms with the periodic incidence of severe violence in Bosnia in the modern era, from the Herzegovinian troubles in 1875–6 down to the most recent episode. In a way, western Europeans (and north Americans) cannot be faulted for being horrified at what hap-

[18] Robert Donia and John V.A. Fine, *Bosnia and Hercegovina: A Tradition Betrayed*, London, 1994; Rusmir Mahmutcehajic, *Bosnia the Good: Tolerance and Tradition*, Budapest, 2000.

[19] Misha Glenny, *The Balkans, 1804-1999: Nationalism, War and the Great Powers*, London, 1999.

[20] For a survey of these, see John Allcock, *Explaining Yugoslavia*, London, 2000, Ch. 13.

pened in Bosnia in the 1990s, for Bosnia is, to appropriate Todorova's phrase, 'geographically inextricable from Europe', and westerners thought that Europe had left that sort of past behind for good in 1945. The tacit moral expectation, not unreasonable, 'is that times should have changed by the 1990s'.[21] Bosnians (along with other former Yugoslavs, especially in Serbia-Montenegro and Croatia) will have to bear a significant share of culpability for the fact that times had, apparently, not changed in some respects as much as they could (and should?) have in the former Yugoslavia, a country that had otherwise been transformed from a predominantly rural, illiterate, agrarian society into a significantly urbanized, industrial and literate society between 1945 and 1991.

The real challenge in the tolerance-or-hatred debate is to move, decisively, beyond essences—*all* essences. Much has been made for example of the cosmopolitan mix and ethos of Sarajevo before 1992. This celebration of pre-war Sarajevo may be completely justified or somewhat exaggerated and romanticized— since I never visited the city before the war I don't really know. However, it is clearly not concocted, since it is common knowledge that urban centres in the former Yugoslavia, particularly nationally mixed Bosnian towns like Sarajevo or Mostar, were sites where a cosmopolitan ethos, including substantial inter-marriage, prevailed.

However, there are obvious limitations to this thesis as well— Radovan Karadzic, after all, was also a Sarajevan, albeit a first-generation one. More importantly, though, it is important to remember that Bosnia's five largest towns—Sarajevo, Banja Luka, Tuzla, Zenica and Mostar—accounted for barely one-quarter of its 4.4 million citizens in 1992. The other three-quarters lived in scores of smaller towns and rural municipalities, where attitudes and inter-community relations were markedly different. One of the first things to appreciate about Bosnia is that it is a country of enormous variations. Understanding this one particular type of variation may help us move beyond essentialized representations of complex Bosnian realities.

In Prijedor, a middle-sized (by Bosnian standards) town in

---

[21] Susan Woodward, 'Genocide or Partition: Two Faces of the Same Coin?', *Slavic Review* 55: 4 (1996), p. 756.

northwestern Bosnia with a notorious reputation from the war, I stayed with the Trifunovic family, Serbs displaced since September 1995 from another nearby middle-sized town called Sanski Most (Sanski Most was under Serb control for almost the whole duration of the war, but fell to Bosnian Muslim forces which advanced from the Bihac enclave towards the end of hostilities). In July 1990, Prijedor was chosen by Ante Markovic, the last federal prime minister of socialist Yugoslavia, as the venue for the launching of his alternative, supranational Yugoslavia-wide political party, the Alliance of Reform Forces of Yugoslavia (ARFY/SRSJ)— apart from a highly multiethnic population (almost equal numbers of Serbs and Muslims, plus a sprinkling of Croats), Prijedor was a typical socialist-era industrial working-class town. Sanski Most was similarly a very mixed town until 1992, the population almost evenly balanced between Serbs and Muslims, with a small smattering of Croats adding to the variety.

Mr Trifunovic was a retired factory worker in his early sixties, employed in an 'enterprise' in Sanski Most for most of his working life with a stint abroad during the 1980s in Libya. Asked to reflect on relations between Serbs and Muslims in Sanski Most before the war, he replied, thoughtfully, that relations were cordial. Muslims and Serbs worked side by side in the workplace, their children studied together in school, citizens of different communities usually greeted each other politely on the street, and the two groups shared a host of other public spaces and facilities. 'But', he added, 'at home we always referred to them [Muslims] as "Turci" [Turks].' He hastened to clarify that this did not carry any pejorative meaning, but was simply established practice. Indeed, 'under Ottoman rule the Slavic Muslim population called themselves "Turci", a term which they understood to mean "adherents to Islam". For Turks in an ethnic sense, they used the term "Turkusi" [Turkics] or "Osmanlija" [Ottoman].'[22]

So Mr Trifunovic was not necessarily wrong. But given the centrality of the figure of the 'Turk' (whatever the exact meaning of the term in a specific context) as the 'other' in Serbian national consciousness, it is unlikely that private references to the town's Muslims as 'Turci' were totally devoid of a latent meaning that

[22] Steven Burg and Paul Shoup, *The War in Bosnia-Herzegovina: Ethnic Conflict and International Intervention*, Armonk, NY, 1999, p. 19.

would become significant in 1991-2. Several years after the end of the war, Mr Trifunovic was still concerned about the "Turci" and their intentions. He was convinced that in municipal elections held under international (OSCE) supervision in April 2000, Muslims had regained control of Prijedor's town assembly and government, harking back to a situation in 1991. This struck me as highly implausible, since the Prijedor area had been emptied of Muslims in the summer of 1992 and only a few thousand had returned to districts in the town suburbs starting in mid-1999. But Mr Trifunovic was very sure. He claimed that 24 of 31 newly-elected town councillors were Muslims, and assured me that the international community had even appointed a Muslim as the town mayor. The facts were that only eight of 37 municipal councillors were Muslims, and the town did have a Muslim deputy mayor, placed in that office under internationally mandated formulas for 'equitable' sharing of executive positions in local government. But Mr Trifunovic, an average citizen in an average Bosnian town, sincerely believed what he believed.

The family of another Bosnian friend, Amela, live in Zavidovici, a smallish town of about 30,000 in the northeastern part of central Bosnia, close to two somewhat larger industrial towns in the region, Zenica and Doboj. Zavidovici was 60% Muslim in 1991, but had a Serb minority of over 20%. Amela has a strong sense of Muslim national identity, and firmly believes in the unity of the Bosnian state. She comes from a prominent local family—her maternal grandfather was the *imam* (head cleric) of the town mosque until his death in 1989. She is, however, also one-quarter Serb. Her father had one Serb and one Muslim parent—her paternal grandfather was a Muslim communist party member and Yugoslav People's Army (JNA) officer who fell in love with a Serb woman while stationed in Serbia after the Second World War. After Amela's mother married Amela's father some thirty years ago—Amela was born in the early 1970s—the Imam refused to speak to his daughter until his death in 1989. She had given mortal offence by marrying someone who was not Muslim, but rather partly Serb and partly Muslim.[23]

[23] Some researchers have questioned the belief that exogamous (i.e., intercommunal) marriage was widespread during the second Yugoslavia, or that it steadily increased through the socialist period, either in BiH or in Yugoslavia as a whole. Nikolai Botev, who has analyzed marriage registration data over four

It is possible that places like Sanski Most and Zavidovici are more representative of the character of life and society in pre-war Bosnia than the intellectual circles of Sarajevo. That character is such a compound of different and even contradictory elements that it is difficult to describe in mere words. But Tone Bringa has it about right when she notes that while the residents of the mixed Muslim-Croat village in central Bosnia she studied had a well-developed sense of sharing a locality and a history with members of the other group, they had an equally developed sense of the boundaries of their own community and their differences with the other group.[24] That community-based identity and perception of difference remained innocuous while the Yugoslav framework was stable, but became the basis of political mobilization as that framework crumbled. In BiH, those competing mobilizations eventually escalated to a point where entire towns and villages were torn apart by communal violence. But it is clear that the tolerance-or-hatred dichotomy is a false one, and that 'too much weight should not be placed on what Bosnia-Herzegovina was "really" like... there were several Bosnia-Herzegovinas, which coexisted and were in tension with one another'.[25] Bosnia was, and remains, a plural, complex society not just in the national

periods (1962-4, 1970-2, 1980-2, 1987-9), contends that 'mixed' marriages in Yugoslavia stayed put at a level of 12-13% of total marriages over three decades. Of Yugoslavia's republics and autonomous provinces, only Vojvodina had a rate of inter-marriage much higher than the country-wide average. The figure for Bosnia-Herzegovina was close to the Yugoslavia-wide average—it varied between 10-12% of marriages between 1962 and 1989. Given that BiH was by far the most heterogeneous Yugoslav republic, this means that the overwhelming majority of Bosnian marriages were 'in-group' unions. Botev finds that the Serbs and the Croats of BiH are significantly more endogamous than in their respective home republics, Serbia and Croatia. Bosnian Muslims are relatively more exogamous; nonetheless, 'levels of endogamy among the Muslims in BiH are still relatively high'. His conclusion is that all 'three communities remained very much closed (endogamous) during the period under study' (1962-89), although 'there are indications that in the large urban centres, especially Sarajevo, inter-marriage was more prevalent'. See Nikolai Botev, 'Seeing Past the Barricades: Ethnic Inter-Marriage in Former Yugoslavia, 1962-89', in J. Halpern and D. Kideckel (eds), *Neighbours at War: Anthropological Perspectives on Yugoslav Ethnicity, Culture and History*, University Park, PA, 2000, pp. 219-33.

[24] Tone Bringa, *Being Muslim the Bosnian Way: Identity and Community in a Central Bosnian Village*, Princeton, NJ, 1995.

[25] Burg and Shoup, *The War in Bosnia-Herzegovina*, p. 60.

sense but in many other senses as well. As Bougarel puts it, this is a society where 'the words tolerance, hate, coexistence and fear are all equally applicable'.[26] It is not surprising that a 'tragic cycle of conflict and coexistence'[27] has defined modern Bosnia.

Civil war or aggression? The latest Bosnian conflict, in 1992–5, aroused perhaps even greater passions outside Bosnia and the former Yugoslavia than within the region. Academic and popular literature on the war is deeply divided on a basic issue: was it primarily a case of internecine bloodletting *among* Bosnians, or was it an avoidable war caused primarily by the 'aggression' of Serbia-Montenegro—and secondarily, Croatia—*against* Bosnia[28] and the failure of the 'West' to confront the aggressors in good time?[29] Not surprisingly, believers in the 'essentially tolerant Bosnia' thesis subscribe strongly to the latter view,[30] while those with a more nuanced understanding of Bosnian and Yugoslav history tend to be noticeably more careful and circumspect in their engagement with this debate.[31] Moreover, supporters of the 'external aggression' thesis are strong proponents of preserving and developing BiH as a single, united state, while those who believe the 1992–5 conflict was primarily a 'civil war' have a range of attitudes towards the post-1992 state, from cautiously neutral to actively hostile.

With regard to post-war Bosnia, the former group tend to vocally advocate concerted action by the 'international community' to 'integrate' Bosnia & Herzegovina, while those in the latter category are normally more sceptical about the capacity and merits of international intervention—some openly argue for a *de jure*

[26] Xavier Bougarel, 'Bosnia-Hercegovina: State and Communitarianism' in D. Dyker and I. Vejvoda (eds), *Yugoslavia and After*, London, 1996, p. 87.
[27] Gordon Bardos, 'The Bosnian Cold War: Politics, Society and International Engagement after Dayton', *Harriman Review* 11: 3 (April 1999), p. 26.
[28] A level-headed survey of some of this literature can be found in Gale Stokes, John Lampe, Dennison Rusinow and Julie Mostov, 'Instant History: Understanding the Wars of Yugoslav Succession', *Slavic Review* 55: 1 (1996), pp. 136–60.
[29] David Rieff, *Slaughterhouse: Bosnia and the Failure of the West*, New York, 1995; James Gow, *Triumph of the Lack of Will: International Diplomacy and the Yugoslav Wars*, New York, 1996.
[30] Donia and Fine, *Bosnia and Hercegovina: A Tradition Betrayed;* Rabia Ali and Lawrence Lifschultz (eds), *Why Bosnia?*, Stony Creek, NY, 1993.
[31] Burg and Shoup, *The War in Bosnia-Herzegovina;* Susan Woodward, *Balkan Tragedy: Chaos and Dissolution after the Cold War*, Washington, DC, 1995.

three-way partition of BiH as a logical finale to the process of nationalization of sovereignty and statehood in the former Yugoslav area. The civil war-or-aggression debate thus intersects in significant ways with other debates on the past, present and future of Bosnia & Herzegovina. The divide among scholars, practitioners and analysts in the Western world is mirrored in disagreement within Bosnia & Herzegovina. Within BiH, the vast majority of Serbs and Croats I know think the 1992-5 conflict was a 'civil war', while the vast majority of Bosniacs I have spoken with prefer the 'external aggression' thesis. Both points of view, within the region as well as outside of it, would acknowledge (with few exceptions) that it is not possible to understand Bosnia except within the context of the former Yugoslavia. However, agreement ends at this point and disagreements begin.

The opposed positions of the parties to this debate are rooted in the fact that their mental frame of reference consists of distinctly different territorial units. For example, when Bosnian Muslims assert (as they usually do) that the war was a case of external aggression, their implicit frame of reference is Bosnia & Herzegovina, *separate* from the rest of former Yugoslavia. In that case, any involvement of governmental, government-backed or even entirely non-governmental agents from Serbia and Croatia in the Bosnian war becomes, *by definition*, external aggression. When Bosnian Serbs, by contrast, advance the opposite viewpoint, their implicit frame of territorial reference is normally the whole of what was Yugoslavia, including Serbia (and Montenegro). When that is the implicit political geography, a conflict between Serbs, Muslims and Croats inside BiH—with involvement of forces who are from outside BiH but nonetheless from inside the territory of former Yugoslavia—becomes, also by definition, a civil war.

The civil war-or-aggression argument is therefore, actually, simply a reflection of a more fundamental debate—the debate over the legitimacy of the sovereignty and borders of the state recognized as the 'Republic of Bosnia & Herzegovina' in April 1992 and reaffirmed as 'Bosnia & Herzegovina' by the Dayton Peace Agreement at the end of 1995. That question of legitimacy is discussed in the next chapter, where I suggest that an unequivocal resolution to this debate is not possible.

In several senses, it is difficult to deny that the armed conflict in Bosnia between 1992 and 1995 was in fact a 'civil war'. This was, after all, a conflict among people who were until as late as 1991 all 'Yugoslavs'—citizens of a common state called Yugoslavia—that flared, not unpredictably, on the territory of the most multinational unit (republic) of that state. Moreover, even if one accepts the problematic and contested proposition that BiH, rather than former Yugoslavia as a whole, became the legitimate unit for interpreting this war from 1992 onwards, that still does not necessarily make the fighting on BiH territory any less a 'civil war'. Most civil (intra-state) wars throughout the world in recent times have had some sort of external, 'foreign' involvement—usually of neighbouring states—often on a very extensive scale. So long as domestic belligerents are the ones who are overwhelmingly doing the fighting, such conflicts are still very much 'civil wars'.

This seems to have been the case in Bosnia & Herzegovina. A study conducted in BiH on behalf of the International Committee of the Red Cross (ICRC) in late 1998 and early 1999 found that 87% of Serb Bosnians, 72% of Muslim Bosnians, and 70% of Croat Bosnians identify strongly with their respective 'sides' in the Bosnian war. Massive military mobilization occurred among all groups—38% of all Serbs, 30% of all Croats and 26% of all Muslims fought as combatants, including the vast majority of able-bodied men in all three communities.[32] This simply flies in the face of assertions that 'participation in the [1992-5] war was relatively low compared to the Second World War.'[33] As Bougarel has argued, 'Bosnia is a land where, with extraordinary regularity, other people's wars have nourished and been nourished by the internal conflicts of Bosnian society'.[34] This is only to be expected. History and geography have fated Bosnia to be a frontier society in which contending forces intersect and clash—empires in the pre-modern era, nationalisms in modern times. Chuck Sudetic has crafted a masterful reconstruction of the local history since the mid-nineteenth century of one mixed Serb-Muslim

---

[32] See the ICRC/Greenberg Research report, *People on War: The Consultation in Bosnia and Herzegovina*, Sarajevo, October 1999.
[33] Vesna Bojicic and Mary Kaldor, 'The 'Abnormal' Economy of Bosnia-Herzegovina', in C. Schierup (ed), *Scramble for the Balkans*, London, 1999, p. 97.
[34] Bougarel, 'Bosnia-Herzegovina: State and Communitarianism', p. 87.

community in the Drina Valley of eastern Bosnia, in the hinterland of the town of Visegrad.[35] His narrative brings out the complexity of Serb-Muslim relations in this area over 150 years of conflict and coexistence, and shows that the exogenous and endogenous sources of outbreaks of severe violence in the Drina Valley during the First and Second World Wars and the 1990s are so organically intertwined that they are practically inseparable. While all episodes of severe violence have been sparked by 'external' events and forces, local society too has been deeply implicated in that violence.

For all these reasons, it makes relatively more sense to regard the 1992-5 conflict in Bosnia as a 'civil war'—albeit obviously with a vital dimension that is territorially external to Bosnia. It is important to make elementary distinctions as the one between 'Bosnian' (any person from Bosnia, whether Serb, Croat, Muslim or other) and 'Bosniac' (a Bosnian of Muslim nationality)—a distinction some influential commentators on wartime and post-war Bosnia conspicuously fail to make.[36] The competing explanation, external aggression 'against' BiH, is far too simplistic and politically loaded, and incoherent in the perspective of both distant and recent history. Defining the Bosnian war as a 'civil war' in this nuanced, clarified sense is very different from the self-serving standpoints of Serb and Croat nationalists (and their apologists) on this question. It does not seek to downplay the role of the Milosevic and Tudjman regimes in the horrors of the Bosnian war, nor does it necessarily impute equal moral culpability to the warring *Bosnian* parties, either in starting the war or in committing violence against civilians. It is eminently possible that some of the parties to the Bosnian 'civil war'—as I define it—are much more guilty than others in these respects. My perspective does, however, flow from the belief that there were belligerents and victims among all three communities in the Bosnian war, depending on location—the Bosnian war can plausibly be regarded as a sum

[35] Chuck Sudetic, *Blood and Vengeance: One Family's Story of the War in Bosnia*, New York, 1998.
[36] For example, Holbrooke, *To End a War*, who conflates the term 'Bosnian' with Bosnian Muslims, to the exclusion of the two other, equally Bosnian communities. The same mis-characterization is evident in Gary Jonathan Bass, *Stay the Hand of Vengeance: The Politics of War-Crimes Tribunals*, Princeton, NJ, 2000.

total of conflagrations in numerous distinct locales[37]—and suggests that it is improper to assign the label of 'aggressor' or 'victim'
in a blanket sense on a national-collective basis. It also implies an
approach to the debate over post-Dayton Bosnia and its future
that does not pre-judge the core issues in the debate.

Integration or partition? Bosnia would not exist today as a state but
for international support. International recognition of its sovereignty and borders in 1992 was confirmed in end-1995 by the
settlement at Dayton. Since that accord, a multitude of international agencies and western governments have been expending
enormous human and financial resources (including the largest
per capita reconstruction plan in history, $5.1 billion between
1996 and 2000) in an effort to breathe some life into this comatose state, given a ground reality that in many ways resembles *de
facto* nationalist partition rather than a single, sovereign state.

Bosnian sovereignty within the borders of the former Socialist
Republic of BiH, one of six units that constituted the Yugoslav
federation, has come at a high price. It was bound to. The international engineers of post-war Bosnia are trying to construct a
viable joint state of Muslims, Serbs and Croats in a regional context which has witnessed over the past decade the violent demise
of the common Yugoslav state and the total marginalization of the
'Yugoslav idea'—which is, roughly, a concept of coexistence and
solidarity among the South Slavic peoples dating to the mid-nineteenth century. In other words, they are trying to re-build a
microcosmic model of the former Yugoslavia—which is what
Bosnia was prior to 1992—amid the ruins of the Yugoslav state
and the Yugoslav idea. From 1992 until today, the decisions and
policy orientations of the government of the United States, more
than any other external actor, have played a critical role in deciding the fate of Bosnia and its peoples.

International recognition in 1992—strongly encouraged by
the United States—represented the climactic moment in the
countdown to a three-cornered civil war and the partition of BiH
into three national(ist) statelets. The Dayton settlement, also a
result of forceful intervention by the United States in the Bosnian
war, had to come to terms with the radically changed circum-

[37] The localized character of the Bosnian war is underlined in both Woodward,
Balkan Tragedy, and Burg and Shoup, *The War in Bosnia-Herzegovina*.

stances of Bosnia after 43 months of fighting and 'ethnic cleansing'. Thus, even while guaranteeing the right of all refugees and displaced persons to return to their homes, the DPA invented a political framework that makes Bosnia & Herzegovina perhaps the most decentralized state in the world. Even then, the BiH Serbs (and to a less obvious degree at the time, the BiH Croats) had to be corralled into this settlement. The presidents of Serbia and Croatia, rather than their own representatives, signed for them, a fact that can itself be interpreted as a blatant infringement of BiH's sovereignty.

The Dayton compromise meant the recognition of Republika Srpska, a radically autonomous political unit (formally described as an 'Entity') across almost half of Bosnia's territory. With some modifications, most significantly in the area of Greater Sarajevo, the military confrontation line became the Inter-Entity Boundary Line (IEBL) between the RS and the rest of the country, meandering 1,100 km across BiH in a zig-zag pattern. The Dayton peace virtually made the RS a 'state within a state', a status the overwhelming bulk of Bosnian Serbs are determined to preserve. The other constitutive Entity of the state, the so-called Federation of Bosnia & Herzegovina (FBiH), is the troubled product of a shotgun alliance of warring Bosniacs and Croats engineered by and in Washington, DC in 1994, with the purpose of turning the military balance in the post-Yugoslav wars against the BiH Serbs and Serbs in Croatia who had declared a rebel statelet—the Republic of Serbian Krajina (RSK)—on the 27% of Croatia held by the rebels since the Croatian civil war in the second half of 1991. In order for the FBiH to exist at all, it too had to be radically decentralized. The Federation was therefore divided into ten cantons, and this cantonal level was designated as the decisive level of governance and administration, enjoying a huge range of devolved powers. Five of the ten cantons—centred on the towns of Sarajevo, Tuzla, Zenica, Bihac and Gorazde—have large Bosniac majorities. Three others, in western Herzegovina, western Bosnia and a small slice of the Posavina (northeastern Bosnia) that escaped Serb conquest, have heavily Croat populations. Political control was therefore not a major issue in these largely mononational cantons. However, the other two cantons, located in the central Bosnian heartland and in the Neretva valley of

Herzegovina (centred on the city of Mostar, itself partitioned into Croat and Bosniac enclaves) have heavily mixed populations and witnessed severe armed conflict between Muslims and Croats in 1993-4. The bitter divide between Croats and Muslims that endures as political reality in these two multi-national cantons is illustrative of the precarious character of the Bosniac-Croat Federation. It would not be inaccurate to say that the FBiH is itself divided on an approximate 60:40 basis between Bosniac and Croat zones. At the time of formation of the Federation, a Bosniac politician remarked that it was like a house without a proper foundation and lacking walls, supported only by a roof full of gaping holes. Relatively little has changed in the years since Dayton.

The jurisdiction and competencies of the central institutions of BiH are of a threadbare character. They are so limited that the common Bosnian state has been described as 'essentially a customs union with a foreign ministry' attached. [38] The minimal purview of the central government in even the most loosely organized federation includes, in addition to foreign affairs, defence as well as currency and communications. In BiH, where mutual security fears continue to dominate the groups' perceptions of one another, defence is in the Entity domain, which means that the RS is entitled to maintain its own army while Croat and Muslim units exist more or less separately within a nominally integrated Federation military. Bosnia & Herzegovina has had a common currency (the Bosnian convertible mark, or KM) since mid-1998, but this had to be imposed by the international presence through the Central Bank and initially faced strong hostility in many Serb and Croat areas (which preferred the Yugoslav dinar and Croatian kuna, respectively). Three separate telecommunications systems continue to exist in the country, despite an internationally sponsored renovation of the infrastructure. One writer, a former United States air force general and deputy commander of US forces in Europe with extensive experience of Bosnian affairs during the war, argued in early 1998 that one reason 'a formal partition is unwise [in Bosnia] is that it is unnecessary. Partition is what exists in Bosnia today'. [39] Robert Hayden, a forthright critic of

---

[38] Robert Hayden, *Blueprints for a House Divided: The Constitutional Logic of the Yugoslav Conflicts*, Ann Arbor, Michigan, 1999, p. 126.
[39] Charles G. Boyd, 'Making Bosnia Work', *Foreign Affairs* 77: 1 (1998), p. 46.

Western policy towards the wars in Croatia and Bosnia as well as of the post-war state-building intervention in Bosnia, plausibly observes that the post-war state is 'a legal fiction', and that the internationally validated sovereignty of BiH is largely a 'negative sovereignty... it holds to the point where neither the Herzegovinian Croats nor the Bosnian Serbs can accede officially to Croatia or Serbia'[40] (nor, one might add, can the RS declare fully independent status, an idea popular in the western region of the RS around Banja Luka). But enthusiastic supporters of drastic international action in Bosnia equally agree that Dayton Bosnia is more or less dysfunctional as a state. One such author, who advocates a 'non-nationalist settlement' for Bosnia superseding Dayton, including 'erasure' of the self-governing Republika Srpska, argues, also plausibly, that the 'unworkable series of interlocking local, cantonal, federal and (few) state-wide institutions... is unaffordable in the long-term and dysfunctional in the short-term.'[41]

In fact, Bosnia's situation is not without parallel. It is easy to scorn (Hayden) or lament (Borden) the embarrassing gulf between the Bosnian state's *de jure* juridical sovereignty and the three *de facto* empirical sovereignties that operate on the ground. However, sovereignty in the juridical sense, which is gained by international recognition of a country's independence and borders, is vitally important. It is a status to which numerous national self-determination movements—would-be states—throughout the world aspire, usually without success or even any realistic hope of success. Jackson and Rosberg have argued that many states on the African continent once thought unviable have nonetheless survived over time as sovereign units, because juridical recognition has assured them a permanent position and status in the international state system and its institutions.[42] Some Europe-conscious Bosnians and Bosnia advocates in the Euro-Atlantic world might be offended by comparisons to Africa. But in addition to being a

---

[40] Hayden, *Blueprints for a House Divided*, pp. 152-3.

[41] Anthony Borden, 'Time to Rewrite Dayton?', a debate with Daniel Serwer in *Balkan Crisis Reports* 203, December 12, 2000. Borden is director of the Institute for War and Peace Reporting, a London-based think-tank that regularly urges more forceful intervention by Western governments and agencies in the Balkans.

[42] Robert Jackson and Carl Rosberg, 'Why Africa's Weak States Persist: The Juridical and Empirical in Statehood', *World Politics* (October 1982), pp. 1-24.

'quasi-state'—meaning a juridical construct[43]—Bosnia resembles some states in Africa in another compelling attribute. Some such states in Africa are chronically beset by factional conflicts and warlordism and the corrupt, even predatory activities warlordism engenders. A weak 'quasi-state' provides ideal terrain for the emergence of predatory elite networks which routinely exploit what should be public resources for personal enrichment.[44] The three statelets that divide BiH between them are all products of warlordism—they are, in Carl Bildt's phrase, 'warrior states'[45]—and all suffer from predatory oligarchical networks characteristic of such states. It is not surprising that Bosnia is a place where privatization of firms is often just a cover for 'crony capitalism', scandals involving defalcation or illicit diversion of funds by officials are routine, trans-border smuggling of cars, cigarettes, drugs and humans is practically the only growth industry, and Mafia kingpins travel in the latest luxury models from Audi or BMW while the majority of the population struggle to survive.

By the time of the DPA's fifth anniversary, two distinct forms of Dayton revisionism had developed in Bosnia. One is an *integrationist* form of revisionism, while the other is a *partitionist* revisionism.

The chief spokesman of integrationist revisionism is prominent Bosniac politician Haris Silajdzic. Silajdzic, a SDA member since before the war and a top official in the SDA-dominated Sarajevo government during the war, left the SDA and formed his own party, the Party of Bosnia & Herzegovina (SBiH) after the war. In January 2000 Silajdzic, then co-chair of the BiH council of ministers (a common-state institution) published a memorandum in which he pointed to a 'disequilibrium between [Bosnia's] integrity from the perspective of international law and its partition from the perspective of internal law'. Bosnia, he noted, 'is now too strong to die, but too weak to function as a self-supporting state'. Further noting that 'the state institutions of Bosnia & Herzegovina function more like international conferences than organs of state', he called for 'some reconstruction' of the DPA. While 'preserving and strengthening all its relevant positive elements', he argued that it was also 'essential to urgently and radi-

43 Robert Jackson, *Quasi-States*, Cambridge, 1990.
44 William Reno, *Warlord Politics and African States*, Boulder, CO, 1998.
45 See Bildt, *Peace Journey*.

cally reconstruct those elements that are non-integrative, ineffective and even partly counterproductive'. The memorandum concluded with a demand that the international community take steps to 'bring about rapid, mass returns of refugees and displaced persons' and remove elements in the institutional structure and electoral system 'that favour... nationally exclusivist political options'.[46]

Among the three communities in BiH, the Bosniacs alone associate their collective identity and interests—indeed, their very future as a people—with the development of a functional Bosnian state. Silajdzic's broadside reflects deep frustration among many Bosniacs with the divided state of BiH after five years of post-conflict reconstruction under international supervision. Hence the call for 'reconstruction' of the reconstructive project. In local-government elections held in April 2000, the SBiH polled respectably in most Bosniac areas, holding the balance between the SDP and SDA in many municipalities. During the year, it gradually became clear that the revisionist Bosniac position is strongly radical *vis-à-vis* the Dayton settlement. In elections to common-state, federation and cantonal institutions in November 2000, the SBiH campaigned on the slogan 'Bosnia without Entities!'. This clarion-call for integration struck a chord among sections of the Bosniac electorate. The SBiH polled about 15% of the vote on Federation territory, compared to 27% for each of the two larger parties with bases in the Bosniac community, the previously dominant SDA (severely discredited by corruption scandals implicating its ruling oligarchy) and the rising SDP.

Partitionist revisionism is articulated by the Croat nationalist party in Bosnia & Herzegovina, the HDZ-BiH. The HDZ-BiH has since its inception been disproportionately influenced by the extreme-nationalist outlook of a group based in western and central Herzegovina, a region with a strong tradition of far-right Croat nationalism dating to the interwar period and the Second World War. In 1992, only a minority of the then 800,000 BiH Croats lived in this region, in generally Croat-dominated areas contiguous or close to Croatia. However, in early 1992 the 'Herzegovinian Mafia' was able to take control of the HDZ-BiH

---

[46] Haris Silajdzic, 'Memorandum on Change: The Dayton Peace Accord—a Treaty that is not being Implemented', Sarajevo, January 25, 2000.

with the blessings of the Tudjman regime in Zagreb, where Herzegovinian Croats enjoyed almost unlimited access and influence until Tudjman's death in end-1999. It then embarked on a policy of territorial acquisition designed to carve out an all-Croat statelet (called 'Herceg-Bosna') on as much of BiH territory as possible, with Mostar as the capital. By 1993, this attempt led to a crisis and breakdown in Muslim-Croat relations, and precipitated heavy fighting not just for control of Mostar but also in mixed areas of central Bosnia, where the Croat side, despite being better-equipped, was ultimately at a numerical and strategic disadvantage. The 'Herceg-Bosna' project was apparently thwarted by the Federation agreement of March 1994, which was subsequently incorporated into the Dayton deal. But HDZ-BiH hardliners have remained fundamentally unreconciled. Since the DPA, the IC has been engaged in an uphill and largely ineffectual battle to uncover and eliminate a vast, well-financed network of parallel Herceg-Bosna institutions in the Croat-controlled areas that make up 20% of Bosnia & Herzegovina.

The position of extremist BiH Croats, put simply, is that Bosnia is not partitioned sufficiently to their liking. They claim that as a result, the very survival of Croats as a people is endangered in BiH. Ever since Dayton, a muted but effective campaign inside BiH Croat communities has argued that Croats are subject to an unjust situation in Dayton Bosnia. The solution, according to this view, lies in the formal establishment of a territorially defined, third Entity for Croats, giving them the same status and protections as the RS. With regard to Mostar, the argument goes that since the Muslims 'have' Sarajevo and the Serbs Banja Luka, it is only logical and fair that the Croats (who were, incidentally, only a third of pre-war Mostar's population) should be given possession of Mostar.

This argument, which depicts the Bosniac-Croat Federation as a forced marriage that violates Croat rights, has significant resonance among Croat communities in Bosnia. Ordinary Croats have long-term security concerns in places such as the Mostar region and central Bosnia, which saw bitter armed hostilities between Muslims and Croats in 1993-4, and fears regarding equality of treatment in these places and elsewhere in the Federation. To many Croats, the problem is eventually one of numbers. Bosniacs outnumber Croats by at least 4:1 in the Federation, inevitably making the Federation a lop-sided arrangement, even assuming the most benign Bosniac intentions. The Croat share in BiH's population has also declined significantly from 18% in 1992 (mostly due to emigration), further aggravating insecurities among those who remain. When the HDZ-BiH escalated its simmering confrontation with the international community in 2000, most Croats closed ranks behind their national party. The party largely maintained its overwhelming support base among Croats, despite latent dissatisfaction among the Croat electorate with the corruption and self-enrichment of the party elite, in the series of elections held during 2000. Parallel to the November 2000 elections, the party organized a referendum in Croat communities throughout BiH, asking for endorsement of its demand that the international community concede 'full political and cultural equality' for Croats in Bosnia. This was code for the 'third entity' demand, as much as the SBiH's demand for 'reconstruction' of the Dayton framework was a barely disguised call for the IC to 'integrate' Bosnia. Of 303,367 registered Bosnian Croat voters, 71% participated in this parallel referendum—condemned as illegal by international bodies such as OSCE and the Office of High Representative in Bosnia (OHR)—and turnout was substantial not just in traditionally hardline Croat areas but also among Croat minorities in Sarajevo and other Bosniac-dominated parts of the Federation.[47] 99% of those who voted endorsed the HDZ stand.

Integrationist and partitionist revisionisms both respond to real shortcomings in the Dayton framework, and both have sizeable popular following in Bosnia. Neither, I believe, represents a feasible or a desirable course. Sharp oppositions within Bosnian politics are mirrored in a debate that continues in Europe and the United States. Organizations such as the International Crisis Group (headquartered in Brussels) and the Institute for War and Peace Reporting (based in London) continuously urge forceful Western intervention to the end of integration, while pro-partition sceptics such as *New York Times* journalist Thomas Friedman and University of Chicago international relations professor John Mearsheimer, among others, advise the opposite. This book will

---

[47] More than 70 per cent of Croats support Rights declaration', AFP, Mostar, November 14, 2000. The background to this situation is analyzed in 'Special

argue that viewing Bosnia through the prism of this starkly posed debate— as if 'integration' and 'partition' are the only possibilities of the future—is misleading.)

The Western politicians and diplomats who head the extensive network of international organizations in Bosnia are typically reluctant to entertain either integrationist or partitionist revisionism. They generally tend to favour working within the broad parameters of the *status quo,* despite the frustrations and constraints that entails, since they know that any revision of Dayton *in response to pressure orchestrated by a particular faction* will not only open up a Pandora's Box of competing claims but reopen issues lying dormant since the war.

This is on the whole a sensible position. The broadly *status quo* bias of the international peace-implementation bureaucracy is fervently shared, ironically enough, by the Bosnian Serbs, conventionally viewed as the principal culprits of the Bosnian war and the prime 'anti-Dayton' element for several years afterward. (Five years after the war, BiH Serbs are broadly satisfied with the political structure of Bosnia laid down by Dayton.) Aware that post-Milosevic FRY, internationally rehabilitated, is in a position to provide much more effective political and diplomatic support to the RS's core concerns—a special-relations agreement between Belgrade and Banja Luka, expressly permitted by the DPA, was finally signed in March 2001—even parties like the SDS now swear by the Dayton system.

(But even if the international community were to be more receptive to integrationist or partitionist agendas, thus rendering them *feasible,* they would still be highly inadvisable courses of action.) Silajdzic's agenda—rightly or wrongly—represents to Bosnian Serbs (and Croats) a revived version of an allegedly 'unitary' or 'centralized' model for Bosnia & Herzegovina to resist which, in their perception, they were prepared to go to war in 1992. The SBiH call for the RS's liquidation, in particular, is intolerable to Serbs and puts the clock back significantly on any healing of relations between Serbs and Muslims. These two communities together make up almost 90% of Bosnia's population and the future prospects of the Bosnian state hinges, consequently, on their being able to find a *modus vivendi.* The RS's relatively liberal

Report on Sixth HDZ Congress in Sarajevo, July 15, 2000', an internal United Nations Mission in Bosnia-Herzegovina (UNMiBH) paper.

prime minister, Mladen Ivanic, has warned that any attempt to abolish the RS cannot be tolerated, and it is possible that the SBiH's campaign slogan in November 2000 helped the SDS's resurgence in those elections in the RS. Indeed, Silajdzic is deeply disliked by many Bosniacs, who regard his style of politics as intemperate and personalistic. It has been argued that the unitarist vision for Bosnia has more to do with 'Austrian tradition than the practices of modern multinational federations in Europe like Belgium and Switzerland', and that it was in response to Bosnian and Yugoslav realities that 'autonomy and power-sharing was the core of every international peace plan from Lisbon [March 1992] to Dayton'.[48] Indeed, a self-serving effort by the Austro-Hungarian administration of Bosnia & Herzegovina (1878-1918) to encourage a nationally neutral 'Bosnian' identity that would eliminate the appeal of national (particularly Serb) identities failed completely at the turn of the nineteenth and twentieth centuries[49]—even before all the upheavals the twentieth century brought with it. Integration, in the conventionally understood sense of the term, is simply not an option in Bosnia.

Partitionist revision of Dayton is equally not an option. Many Bosniacs do regard their 'federation' with the Croats with bitter scepticism, given the record of hardline Croat opposition to this arrangement since 1994. However, dismantling the Federation, a key element and building block of the Dayton framework, is an extreme step that the international overseers of Bosnia simply cannot contemplate, and the appearance of a third nationally defined 'Entity' on Bosnian soil is likely to be unacceptable to Bosniac opinion. Indeed, even a more limited agenda of HDZ-BiH leaders—formally partitioning the two nationally mixed cantons in the Federation (central Bosnia & Herzegovina-Neretva) to create largely mono-national Bosniac and Croat cantons out of each—is likely to elicit stiff Bosniac opposition.[50] The concerns of ordinary Croats regarding their status and future in the FBiH are exaggerated but not unfounded. However, that is not sufficient grounds to capitulate to the partitionist agenda of the

---

48 Burg and Shoup, *The War in Bosnia-Herzegovina*, p. 60.
49 See Donia and Fine, *Bosnia and Herzegovina*, Ch. 6.
50 If this were to be done, the Federation would consist of seven mainly Bosniac cantons and five mainly Croat cantons—instead of five largely Bosniac cantons, three largely Croat cantons, and two mixed cantons.

Herzegovinian oligarchy in the HDZ-BiH. This parasitic oligarchy's confrontational and polarizing strategy is motivated by self-preservation above all else: maintaining its dominance of Bosnian Croat politics in the wake of the electoral defeat of the patron party and regime in Croatia. Its espousal of Croat rights serves as a cover for the range of shadowy activities that have made the 'Herceg-Bosna' oligarchs wealthy. They are possibly the most retrograde example of entrenched Bosnian cliques who for purely selfish reasons 'want no part of economic integration, transparent budgets and rule of law',[51] and exploit issues of national identity and survival to that end.

If neither integration nor (further) partition—then what? That is a difficult question to answer. It is difficult because the economic and political situation of the ex-Yugoslav region as a whole is still unsettled (perhaps excluding Slovenia), and the precise pattern of relationships that will develop among the fragments of the former Yugoslav state is still unclear. Bosnia, a microcosm of the South Slav lands, has in the modern era invariably refracted the overall climate of the region, so the yet indeterminate situation of a region trying to pick up the pieces of a transition interrupted for almost a decade makes it difficult to predict Bosnia's future with precision. I would hazard a guess that for the next few years, this exceptionally complex society at the vortex of an exceptionally complex region will remain a limbo state, suspended in the grey zone between integration and partition. 'Integration' in the classic sense is unlikely, but growing *cooperation* between Bosnia's fragments is likely, as it is likely between the successor-states to former Yugoslavia as a whole, including Bosnia. The beginnings of that process are already evident in the region in 2000-1. It will, in an optimistic prognosis, lead in the next ten to fifteen years to a clearer situation where the fragments of Yugoslavia—and of Bosnia—develop coherent political and economic frameworks for a *closely linked* (though not a shared or common) future characterized by mutual cooperation.

Within Bosnia, such a process will require significant reforms to the Dayton structure of the country, without which the country cannot accede even to Council of Europe membership, leave

---

[51] Daniel Serwer, 'Time to Rewrite Dayton?', in response to Anthony Borden. Serwer is making a general point in his piece; the particular illustration is mine.

alone aspire to an associative status with the EU.[52] But such reforms cannot succeed if they are seen as being imposed by external agents, or as the will of only one segment of the people of Bosnia.) It was still too early to contemplate such an agreed course of change at the fifth anniversary of the end of the war, but things may well have changed significantly—for the better—by the time the tenth anniversary comes around. The renewal of some traditional linkages between most of the post-Yugoslav states, statelets and peoples will not necessarily lead to the emergence of a strong central authority in Sarajevo. Banja Luka's traditional orientation for most purposes had been towards Zagreb, Tuzla's towards Belgrade, and Mostar's towards Split. But it is likely to lead to the borders erected between the Yugoslav peoples after 1991 becoming much softer, which will help ease—though not erase—the dividing lines within Bosnia.

Meanwhile, in the near and longer term future, Bosnia's prospects of recovering from the war and becoming a 'normal' state and society depends critically on three factors.

The first is the degree to which the effects of 'ethnic cleansing' on the ground can be reversed. Until 1992, Bosnia's map was like a patchwork mosaic of the three major national groups. Only about 20% of the pre-war republic's municipal districts were overwhelmingly populated by members of any one community.[53] The war displaced 2.3 million of BiH's 4.4 million citizens. Of these, 1.3 million became refugees outside the country (including those who sought refuge in Serbia and Croatia), while over a million others were internally displaced within the country. By the end of the war, there were almost no non-Serbs left on RS territory, where some 500,000 Bosniacs had lived until 1992. The numbers of Serbs remaining in the Federation, including in Muslim-controlled areas, had also fallen drastically, to negligible totals compared to pre-war levels. Some 70,000 more fled the Sarajevo suburbs in early 1996 as the area reverted to Muslim control after Dayton.[54] Within the 'Federation', few Bosniacs and Croats remained in zones controlled militarily by the other group.

52 United States Institute of Peace, *Bosnia's Next Five Years: Dayton and Beyond*, Washington, DC, November 2000.
53 See Xavier Bougarel, *Bosnie. Anatomie d'un conflit*, Paris, 1996, p. 144.
54 See Louis Sell, 'The Serb Flight from Sarajevo: Dayton's First Failure', *East European Politics and Societies* 14: 1 (2000), pp. 179-202.

Starting from this very low base, a total of about 231,000 'minority returns' took place in BiH in the five and a half years until July 31, 2001. These are returns by members of a national group to their original homes in an area where their group is now a minority of the population—although it may well have been a pre-war local majority, plurality or very substantial minority—i.e., where the population majority as well as political control now rests with another group. This type of return alone has the effect of partially restoring the pre-war population mix.

This level of minority return is clearly a trickle rather than the flood that would be required to reconstruct multinational Bosnia at the grassroots. The overwhelming majority of Bosnians, well over 90%, now live in areas that are largely homogeneous in the national sense. However, there is some cause for limited optimism on this front. International organizations had set 100,000 as the target for minority returns in 1998 and 120,000 in 1999—in both years, minority returns hovered around the 40,000-mark. However, in 2000 the figure climbed sharply to over 67,000. During the year, almost 19,000 Serbs returned to the Federation (including 7,500 to Sarajevo and its environs), while over 25,000 Bosniacs, for the first time a really substantial number, returned to the RS. The majority of these 25,000 people returned to four RS municipalities: Prijedor in the northwest, Doboj in the centre, and Bijeljina and Zvornik in the east. All have an odious wartime reputation, indicating that at the local level, relations between Serbs and Muslims may be slowly recovering in some places. Another 4,800 Bosniacs returned, amid some tension, to the formerly Serb part of the municipality of Brcko, which straddles the land corridor connecting the eastern and western parts of the RS and has been internationally administered since March 1999 as a neutral District of Bosnia & Herzegovina. In the divided central Bosnia canton, more than 5,000 Bosniacs returned to Croat-controlled municipalities like Vitez and Kiseljak, while over 4,000 Croats returned to Bosniac-controlled municipalities like Bugojno, consolidating a relatively strong record of reciprocal minority returns in this canton. These are considerable figures for a small country like Bosnia & Herzegovina.[55] During the first seven months of

[55] Registered Minority Returns from January 1, 2000 to December 31, 2000 in BiH', UNHCR Statistics Package, Sarajevo, February 2001.

2001, minority returns across BiH totalled over 43,000. Of these 19,500 were Serb returnees to the Federation, of whom over half—almost 10,000—were returnees to the city of Sarajevo and its outskirts. During the same period, more than 14,000 Bosniacs returned to the RS, including 1,800 to Banja Luka, 1,600 to Bijeljina, 1,700 to Doboj, 1,642 to Prijedor, and 994 to Teslic.[56] By the end of 2001 it is probable that the total number of minority returns across BiH since the end of the war will have reached 250,000.

The surge in minority return has been facilitated by the improved security situation in most parts of BiH, apart from a few chronic trouble-spots like Stolac, a stronghold of Croat extremists in south-central Herzegovina. It is important not to under-estimate this factor. On travels on buses throughout Bosnia in 2000, I noticed the enhanced freedom of movement compared to 1998 across unpoliced, and in some cases unmarked Entity lines: Serbs travelling from Banja Luka to Sarajevo, Muslims in the opposite direction, and so on. The phenomenon of increasingly porous borders applies beyond Bosnia. Bosniacs are once again holidaying on Croatia's Adriatic coast in substantial numbers, and some are even travelling to the less expensive resorts on the Montenegrin coastline. The increase in minority returns has also been greatly facilitated in urban locales by the international high representative's imposition of legislation in October 1999 requiring occupants of others' properties to move out if the original owners or occupants wish to return, and in rural areas by prospective returnees' realization that donor aid for reconstruction of damaged properties will dry up almost completely after 2002.[57]

However, these returns still amount to a few drops in the pond. A large proportion of returnees consist of elderly persons and couples. Relatively few families with children, and even fewer young individuals, tend to return, raising questions of how 'sus-

---

[56] 'Registered Minority Returns from January 1, 2001 to July 31, 2001 in BiH', UNHCR Statistics Package, Sarajevo, September 2001.

[57] For a generally favourable assessment of the effectiveness of the Reconstruction and Return Task Force (RRTF), a specialist group of officers established by the OHR and UNHCR in January 1997 to work on returns, see the European Stability Initiative's study, 'Interim Evaluation of the RRTF', Sarajevo, September 1999.

tainable' these returns will prove to be in the longer run.[58] Bosnia's demographic map has probably changed forever. Even if substantial minority returns occur during 2001 and 2002, what will emerge are *minority enclaves* within areas otherwise solidly dominated by the majority, rather than a restoration of the pre-war leopard-spot mix. This is exemplified in the area of Prijedor, where Bosniac returns, almost 5,000 between January 2000 and July 2001, are concentrated in two town suburbs—Kozarac to the east, where a large Muslim settlement was practically erased by Bosnian Serb forces in the summer of 1992, and Hambarine to the west of the town. All said and done, however, the restoration of some semblance of a mixed society is better than an untrammelled victory for the logic of 'ethnic cleansing'. The international military and civilian presence in Bosnia can justly claim credit for modest progress in this direction.

The international community has, however, proved unable to check the other form of demographic change that is crucial to Bosnia's future—post-war emigration. States, and societies, have no future without populations, particularly certain kinds of population like educated younger people, highly trained professionals, and specialists in various fields. By 1998, 500,000 of the 1.3 million war refugees abroad had found 'durable solutions' outside Bosnia. In other words, they had migrated permanently, to return to Bosnia only periodically to visit elderly relatives and homesteads, usually during the summer months. These half-million emigrants include much of pre-war Bosnia's intelligentsia and middle class. Since the war, BiH has been haemorrhaging more of the kind of people necessary to sustain a modern society. Responding to a situation where the majority of citizens are unemployed and those in work are usually paid a pittance (except those lucky to be employed by international agencies, where even drivers and interpreters earn respectably by local standards), at least another 100,000 Bosnians, including many highly qualified ones, have left the country in the post-war period.[59] Meanwhile, 225,000 Bosnians, overwhelmingly Serbs, continue to be refugees

---

[58] Author's interview with Harry Leefe, acting deputy chief of mission of UNHCR in BiH, Sarajevo, August 2000.
[59] 'Some 100,000 Bosnians Left Country Since War', Reuters, Sarajevo, November 10, 2000.

in the FRY as of end-2000; another 85,000, mostly Croats, are in Croatia. 850,000 people were still internally displaced within the country five years after the war ended. Internal dislocations and the 'brain drain' combine to produce a situation where the resident population is increasingly older, of rural or small-town origins, and less educated. In one UNDP opinion survey conducted in 2000, 62% of young Bosnians, frustrated by sub-standard higher education facilities and the prospect of joblessness after graduating, expressed the desire to leave the country if they could.[60] More than the deep political divisions made salient and intractable by the end of Yugoslavia, Bosnia's future is rendered tenuous by this factor. To cite just a couple of examples: the turnover in 1999 of Sarajevo's massive pre-war engineering firm, Energoinvest, was 5% of what it was in 1991,[61] and according to some estimates, 90% of the RS's population live in poverty.[62]

The third factor threatening post-war 'normalization' in Bosnia is the alarming spread of organized crime in the country. As can be expected in a broken post-war society facing severe economic hardship, corruption is rife at all levels of Bosnia's political structures, administration, and police services. Taking advantage of this semi-anarchic climate and the porous nature of Bosnia's external and internal borders, trans-national criminal networks have turned the country into a haven as well as major east-west transit point for trafficking in smuggled cigarettes, stolen cars, contraband narcotics and desperate human beings from Iran, China and Turkey, among other places. In the summer of 2000, the United Nations in Bosnia inaugurated a professional, multiethnic State Border Service (SBS) to control Bosnia's borders. Four posts were established in the first instance, at Sarajevo airport, in Metkovic (southern Herzegovina, bordering Croatia), in the Bihac region (northwestern Bosnia, also bordering Croatia) and Zvornik (eastern Bosnia, bordering Serbia). The eventual strength of this force is projected at 3,000. By late 2000, 1,000 potential

---

[60] Cited by high representative Wolfgang Petritsch in his bi-annual report to the UN Security Council. See 'Address by HR to the UN Security Council', OHR, Sarajevo, October 26, 2000.
[61] 'Bosnia Energoinvest to Start Privatization in March 2001', Reuters, Sarajevo, January 6, 2001.
[62] 'Over 90% of Bosnian Serbs Live in Poverty', AFP, Banja Luka, February 17, 2001.

recruits had been identified and 350 trained in Switzerland, Austria and Hungary.[63] A major expansion in the number of SBS posts is planned for 2001,[64] but it remains to be seen how effective this will eventually turn out to be in a country beset with predators from within and without.[65]

Epilogue and prologue: a Bosnian story

Bosnia has produced some remarkable storytellers in the twentieth century, including Ivo Andric and Mesa Selimovic.[66] I am unable to resist telling a story of my own as epilogue to this introductory chapter and as prologue to what is still to come.

During 2000, I visited Bosnian friends who now live in Florida, in the United States, part of a growing Bosnian émigré community there. We reflected together on the war and its aftermath. One friend, 'Dado' (a dimiunitive form of his name), just turned forty, was born and raised in Mostar. Like many Bosnians of post-Second World War generations, he is of 'mixed' parentage—father Muslim, mother Croat. He was working in an engineering firm in Sarajevo when the war erupted. For the first year of the war, until April 1993, he was a soldier on the Sarajevo frontlines. He served in the western suburban district of Ilidza, which was mostly held by Serb forces and one of the most volatile sectors of the frontline around Sarajevo. The commander of opposing Serb forces in the Ilidza sector was his best friend since childhood, Savo, whose men would periodically rain mortar shells and grenades on Dado's unit from their positions on higher ground.

After a year, Dado decided he had had enough. He planned to

[63]   Author's interview with Kishore Mandhyan, deputy head of UNMiBH civil affairs, Sarajevo, July 2000.
[64]   'UN Appeals for Funds To Fight Illegal Migration Through Bosnia', AFP, Sarajevo, February 6, 2001.
[65]   In July-August 2001, UN-IPTF investigations revealed that the Bosnian airline, Air Bosna, had been directly involved for some time in trafficking people from Turkey on flights from Istanbul to Sarajevo and Tuzla, mainly for onward transit to EU countries. See Antonio Prlenda, 'Bosnian Smuggling Ring Smashed: UN Exposes Major People-Smuggling Ring Implicating Leading Bosnian Airline', *Balkan Crisis Reports* 278, London, September 7, 2001. Air Bosna was set up after the end of the Bosnian war by highly-connected supporters of the Muslim Party of Democratic Action (SDA).
[66]   Ivo Andric, *The Bridge on the Drina*, London, 1959; Mesa Selimovic, *The Fortress*, Evanston, IL, 1999 (original publication by Svjetlost, Sarajevo, 1970).

leave Sarajevo and travel south, through Mostar and on to the Croatian coast, then seek refugee status in a Western country. However, he made it only as far as a small town called Jablanica, about 80 kilometres south of Sarajevo and 45 kilometres north of Mostar. In April–May 1993 Croat-Muslim skirmishing escalated into a full-scale war in some parts of BiH. The Mostar region was in flames. Jablanica was the last town on secure Armija BiH territory. For the next six months, Dado worked in a munitions factory in Jablanica, producing ammunition and grenades to supply beleaguered Muslim forces facing a ferocious Croat offensive in Mostar. These munitions would be loaded on horses in a village close to Jablanica under cover of darkness and transported overnight on mountain tracks to Armija units in and around Mostar. Dado also participated in local Armija offensives to rid the mountains overlooking Jablanica of Croat units who were shelling the town from those positions.

Towards the end of 1993 Dado made another attempt to get out of Bosnia. This time he got as far as Ljubuski, a small town in western Herzegovina, an overwhelmingly Croat slice of BiH adjacent to Croatia. Here he was questioned, then detained, at a Croat military checkpoint. Before he was consigned to a detention centre in the town, he managed to make one telephone call to a relative on his mother's side who happened to be an officer serving in the Croatian Army (HV). This relative promised to come immediately to Ljubuski to get him released, but he would only arrive the following morning after travelling all night from his base in a fairly distant part of Croatia.

'I knew he was coming', Dado said, 'and that he would be there first thing in the morning.. [...]But during that night, I thought he would arrive only to find my dead body. Around eight o'clock in the evening, they started torturing me, and they didn't stop till four in the morning.'

'Nobody can explain what happened in the war', Dado told me, 'what happened to people.'

Sometime in early 2000 Dado received a telephone call from Canada. It was from Savo, who had also migrated from Bosnia. Savo wanted to re-establish contact, even to come down to Florida to visit Dado and his family. Dado refused to speak to him, and asked his wife to tell Savo that a visit was not possible.

Dado is probably right that nobody can really explain what happened in the war, above all what 'happened to people'. In his powerful reflections on the war, Bosnian writer Semezdin Mehmedinovic has sketched a fascinating portrait of someone he knew quite well in pre-war Sarajevo's intellectual milieu. This man wrote poetry for children, much appreciated by Mehmedinovic's young son, and 'gave the impression of being a peace-loving and good-natured fellow'. 'In all our meetings he seemed to present very reasonable suggestions', writes Mehmedinovic. 'He seldom spoke when we hung out in a group in cafés, he just listened. When he did join a conversation, his words were calm and reassuring, perhaps because of his years as a psychiatrist... After the fall of socialism, he founded the Green party [in Sarajevo]. That seemed quite in character.'[67] 'He' is Radovan Karadzic.

Karadzic's was not an isolated case of apparent metamorphosis. Mehmedinovic has an equally gripping vignette about Miroslav Toholj, another writer and 'my friend at the time'. After giving a reading in Sarajevo, Toholj stayed overnight in Mehmedinovic's home: 'At my house early the next morning, my mother was making us breakfast when my son, still drowsy, appeared at the door in his pajamas. Toholj slipped a pencil and notebook into his hand... And while my son was busy drawing potato-head people, the owner of the notebook brushed his fingers through my son's hair. There was real warmth in Miroslav Toholj's gesture', writes Mehmedinovic. 'Not long after that visit' Toholj became information minister of the Bosnian Serb wartime statelet, a Karadzic associate with a reputation of being a 'hardliner'.[68]

So Dado is probably right. But whether he and Savo will speak to each other again will determine the shape of Bosnia and the region in the coming years.

[67] Semezdin Mehmedinovic, *Sarajevo Blues* (trans. Ammiel Alcalay), San Francisco, 1998, pp. 14-23.
[68] Ibid., pp. 31-32.

2

A STATE BY INTERNATIONAL DESIGN? LIBERAL INTERNATIONALISM AND 'THE BALKANS'

'In multiethnic Bosnia, where the Dayton accords have forced Bosnian Serbs, Bosnian Croats and Bosnian Muslims to live together in an artificial state, pluralism and democracy are going backward... Five years and $5bn. in aid have done little to produce a self-sustaining, multiethnic democracy... In a region like the Balkans, where ethnic identity and hatreds run so deep, it is easier to produce a self-sustaining democracy in ethnically homogenous countries, like Serbia and Croatia, than in diverse ones like Bosnia... America's democratic pluralism is built on individuals from different religious backgrounds who have voluntarily chosen to live together. That is not where Bosnia starts. Here you have religious groups living together against their will, under NATO, after a terrible war... We can continue using NATO to force Bosnian Serbs, Croats and Muslims to live together in an artificial Bosnian state, as the Dayton accords mandated. Or the NATO allies can abandon Dayton and instead push for a soft partition of Bosnia, letting the Serbian sector fall under Serbia and the Croatian sector under Croatia, and leaving the rump Muslim sector as an independent mini-state. Serbia and Croatia, the two big powers in the region, would then be responsible for stabilizing the area, and NATO could operate a small protectorate around the Sarajevo Muslim mini-state... So the real question for the Bush team is not how many troops to keep in Bosnia but what is Bosnia to be about: Dayton or democracy? It can't be both.'—*Thomas Friedman, American journalist, January 2001*[1]

'There are those who argue that a reconstituted Bosnia would in some sense be an artificial creation, and that if the gravitational pull of the region is towards separation then however noble the ideal it is futile to try to hold it together... My own view is that there is nothing artificial about Bosnia as an integrated entity. Nothing in its geography, shape, the way it functions economically, argues for partition. The regions of Bosnia complement and need each other. When the country is performing nor-

---

[1] Thomas Friedman, 'Democracy Isn't Happening in Bosnia', *New York Times*, January 24, 2001.

mally and not straitjacketed by artificial distinctions of nationality, the gravitational pull is absolutely towards integration... In 1992, when you asked a Sarajevan how many students in his final-year high school class were Serb, how many Muslim and so on, they could not answer the question. It seems to me that it is these distinctions that are artificial. I am convinced that the peoples of Bosnia will want to live together again, in a state that is decentralized... The alternative is to create three small dependencies, hamstrung by artificial borders.'—*Allan Little, British journalist, in November 2000*[2]

A question of legitimacy

Liberal internationalism, the hegemonic ideology of the post-Cold War global (dis)order, faces a real dilemma in the form of post-Dayton Bosnia. The response is usually to fall back on one or the other variant of the 'artificiality' paradigm. In Thomas Friedman's construction, which predictably sparked furious denunciations from advocates of a united Bosnia in Sarajevo and the West,[3] it is the artificial nature of the Bosnian state that is the source of the problem. In Allan Little's opinion, it is the national identities that divide Bosnians psychologically and territorially that are the artificial constructions.

There are two distinct elements in Friedman's argument. The first is a *general* suggestion that sustainable democratization within a common political framework is next to impossible in societies that are deeply divided along ethnic or communal faultlines. This was the conventional view among academic political scientists some thirty years ago. In 1972, two such scholars argued that 'the plural society does not provide fertile soil for democratic values or stability', because of 'incompatible, intense ethnic feelings held by members of communal groups'.[4] Within the 1970s another group of political scientists challenged this blanket pessimism about prospects of democracy in divided societies. Arend Lijphart and his supporters claimed that while the traditional *majoritarian* version of democracy might be next to impossible (indeed inappro-

---

[2] Transcript of BBC Radio 4 broadcast, November 20, 2000.

[3] For one such rejoinder see Janez Kovac and Tanya Domi, 'Friedman Triggers Bosnian Controversy', *Balkan Crisis Reports* 214, February 1, 2001.

[4] Alvin Rabushka and Kenneth Shepsle, *Politics in Plural Societies: a Theory of Democratic Instability*, Columbus, OH, 1972, pp. 92, 186.

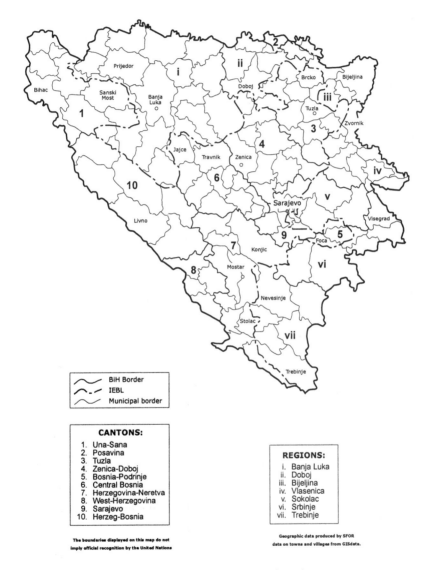

Prijedor

i

ii

Brcko

Bijeljina

Bihac

Sanski
Most

Banja
Luka
○

Doboj

iii

Tuzla
○

Zvornik

1

3

Jajce

Travnik

Zenica
○

4

iv

10

6

Sarajevo

v

Livno

Visegrad

9

Foca

5

7

Konjic

8

Mostar

vi

Nevesinje

Stolac

vii

Trebinje

	BiH Border
	IEBL
	Municipal border

CANTONS:
1. Una-Sana
2. Posavina
3. Tuzla
4. Zenica-Doboj
5. Bosnia-Podrinje
6. Central Bosnia
7. Herzegovina-Neretva
8. West-Herzegovina
9. Sarajevo
10. Herzeg-Bosnia

REGIONS:
i. Banja Luka
ii. Doboj
iii. Bijeljina
iv. Vlasenica
v. Sokolac
vi. Srbinje
vii. Trebinje

Map 3: Bosnia & Herzegovina after Dayton: Cantons and Regions

priate) to institutionalize in such societies, an alternative form of democracy—'consociational' democracy, based on equality and power-sharing between the segments via their representative elites—was both more possible and more appropriate as an institutional model. For over 25 years the claims of the consociationalists have been the subject of spirited debate among academics and practitioners. The Dayton settlement in Bosnia is a clearly consociational settlement, and I evaluate in detail the merits, demerits and prospects of that consociational formula in Chapter 5. The major contribution of consociational theory was to suggest that innovative ways exist to build and stabilize democratic structures even in divided societies, and that there is no basis for blanket pessimism in this regard. Its critics have contended that the consociational formula works only in *moderately* divided societies, not deeply divided ones, a debate which I evaluate with reference to post-Dayton Bosnia in Chapter 5.

During the 1980s scholars of nationalism and national identity moved away from the previously dominant conception that such identities were of a 'primordial' nature—i.e. fixed, immutable and given. The consociational school had not challenged the primordial conception of group identities *per se*—they had simply advanced a model that they claimed would make such identities compatible with democracy in a multiethnic framework. For the last twenty years, however, most studies of nationalism as a contemporary phenomenon have emphasized the 'constructed', 'contingent' character of such identities, and have pointed out that even in an age of nationalism, most individuals who belong to communities called 'nations' still have multiple identities—the 'national' identity is not the only claim on their allegiance and loyalty, though it may be a salient focus of identification in certain contexts. According to scholars, 'it is the possibility of such multiple identities'—involving concurrent loyalties to nation, state and other foci of collective identity—'that makes a multinational democracy possible'.[5] The first element in Friedman's argument is too deterministic. It does not take sufficient account of either the possibility of the emergence of simultaneous, mutually reinforcing

---

5 Juan Linz, Alfred Stepan and Richard Gunther, 'Democratic Transition and Consolidation in Southern Europe, with reflections on Latin America and Eastern Europe' in P.N. Diamandouros and H. Puhle (eds), *The Politics of Democratic Consolidation*, Baltimore, MD, 1995, p. 122.

multi-layered identities (for example, Serb national and Bosnian citizen), or the longer-term potential of non-standard, creative models of democracy as a response to the specific circumstances of societies with ethno-national cleavages.

The second strand of Friedman's argument is even more problematic. This is the representation of 'the Balkans' as a realm of 'ethnic hatreds' and of Bosnia as a society divided into antagonistic 'religious groups'. The first is a typical example, to paraphrase Todorova once again, of the representation of the region and its peoples as a repository of negative characteristics against which a positive and self-congratulatory image of the American and the United States can be juxtaposed. The second reveals an extremely superficial understanding, indeed a fundamental misunderstanding, of the causes of the 1992-5 Bosnian conflict. Although this conflict did pit people of three faiths (Orthodox, Muslim and Catholic) against one another, religious differentiation *per se* was incidental to the conflict, which occurred after several decades of state-sponsored 'modernization' and 'secularization', compared to pre-modern or early modern Balkan conflicts. If Balkan and Bosnian society is not as fundamentally, essentially different from the liberal-democratic societies of the 'West' and the United States as Friedman believes, it may be premature to write a definitive obituary of the liberal-internationalist project in Dayton Bosnia.

Allan Little's views on Bosnia perhaps deserve to be taken more seriously than Friedman's tendentious, overdrawn statements, since he has far more direct experience of Bosnia and 'the Balkans' and has even co-authored a fine study of the break-up of Yugoslavia.[6] In his haste to defend the standard liberal-internationalist perspective of what Bosnia should be, however, Little resorts to invoking the same unconvincing paradigm of 'artificiality' as Friedman. His argument that the different national identities which divide Bosnians psychologically and territorially in the post-Yugoslavia context are 'artificial' is not only unpersuasive but borders on the absurd. In the modern period, collective consciousness among Bosnians and other southern Slavs developed largely along the lines of the 'national' community. This was so true of Bosnia in the late nineteenth and early twentieth centuries that (the first political parties to emerge in Bosnia, under the

[6] Laura Silber and Allan Little, *The Death of Yugoslavia*, London, 1997.

watchful tutelage of the Austro-Hungarian administration, were entirely 'national' parties of (Orthodox) Serbs, (Catholic) Croats and (Muslim) 'Bosniacs'. In post-Second World War Yugoslavia the national-communitarian origins of collective identity were further reinforced by a system of rights and representation which took those identities as a basic building block of the multinational socialist state. Historical and institutional precedent combine to make national distinctions an overwhelming reality—and problem—in Bosnia after Yugoslavia. Wishing them away will just not do. Little's invocation of the (purportedly) group-blind society of Sarajevo prior to 1992 is simply unconvincing. As was argued in Chapter 1, it is a mistake to equate the specific context of Sarajevo with Bosnia & Herzegovina as a whole, as so many scholars and journalists have done. Even if one accepts the contention that pre-war Sarajevo in fact represented a unique haven of multiculturalism and tolerance—itself a debatable proposition—this was one particular social context that cannot be readily extrapolated to Bosnia as a whole. If anything, Bosnia as a society was (and is) is defined by the numerous small to middle-sized towns that dot its landscape, where the majority of the population lived in 1992 and continue to live, albeit largely now in nationally homogenized environments. In these towns, and their surrounding clusters of villages, the ethos of inter-community relations exhibited a complexity in the pre-war era that is clearly beyond the straitjacketed constructs of both Friedman and Little. Since 1992, the attitudes of many Bosnians towards members of other groups, as well as in some instances towards those groups collectively, have hardened, radicalized by the traumatic experience of civil war. This factor too does not seem to find a place in Little's wishful prognosis.

Indeed, an excursion outside Sarajevo appears to have benefited Friedman's understanding of Bosnia. In the second instalment of his two-part article, datelined Zvornik (a grimy eastern Bosnian town on the Drina river border with Serbia), the superficial but sharp-eyed American writes evocatively about the 'ambiguous reality' of post-war Bosnia. He visits a market in the town centre where the razed mosque once stood, but when he looks up into the hills above the town he discerns that 'thousands of Zvornik's ["cleansed"] Muslims have returned, with international aid and protection, and rebuilt their homes.' Indeed, over

3,200 Muslims returned to the Zvornik municipal area in course of 2000, although—following a more general pattern of minority returns—mostly to settlements in the hinterland of the town than to the town proper, where many former Muslim apartments are occupied by 'Serbian refugees from Sarajevo'. On his trip to an average Bosnian town, Friedman seems to realize what the real problems of Bosnia, faced by Muslims, Serbs and Croats alike throughout the divided country, are about: economic depression, unemployment, narcotics and human trafficking across porous borders. This journey of discovery prompts him to stop calling Bosnia an 'artificial' country and instead invent an alternative, more subtle label—a 'sort of' country—'sort of united, sort of divided, sort of peaceful, sort of corrupt, sort of coming back, sort of not coming back, a place where NATO armies feel sort of good about what they've done to stabilize the country but NATO diplomats feel sort of bad that Bosnia's Serbs, Muslims and Croats still have not come together enough for the state to function on its own'.

Friedman goes on to observe, accurately, that 'civil wars' like the one in Bosnia 'end in one of three ways': with a military victory for one side, as in 'the US Civil War'; in a 'soft partition' with 'a lot of mixing' between territories and peoples, guaranteed and watched over by a powerful external party, such as Syria in Lebanon; or in a 'hard partition' with little or no mixing, as in Cyprus after 1974. The Bosnian civil war was eventually inconclusive in military terms, precluding the first possible outcome. The international community 'will not allow a hard partition', effectively ruling out another solution. So post-war Bosnia is a case of 'soft partition, with a weak [central] government and ideally, more mixing of people each year'.[7] This is a considerably more nuanced depiction of the ongoing evolution of post-war Bosnia than the 'artificial state' construct. The distinction between 'hard' and 'soft' partitions is useful, and it is a point to which we return in Chapter 4, where the experience of post-1995 Bosnia is situated in the context of the comparative history of partition. But above all, it suggests that the legitimacy, or otherwise, of the Bosnian state is still not a foregone conclusion in either direction. It is also a much stronger and sophisticated perspective on the

---

[7] Thomas Friedman, 'Bosnia, Sort Of', *New York Times*, January 27, 2001.

issue than Little's, who appears to argue that the state is legitimate while the national identities of Bosnian citizens (implicitly, Serb and Croat Bosnians) are 'artificial' and hence illegitimate. Framing the Bosnian state's legitimacy problem in such either-or, zero-sum terms and then validating the 'state' above the 'nation(s)' is a way of avoiding the problem, not a solution to it. The legality of BiH's statehood was recognized in April 1992 and reaffirmed in December 1995. Legality and legitimacy are two entirely different things, however. In the wake of the end of the Tudjman era in Croatia and the Milosevic era in Serbia, it has become abundantly clear that the Bosnian state's legitimacy problem is not solely, or perhaps even primarily, the result of evil machinations and hostile behaviour from 'Zagreb' and 'Belgrade' respectively. The RS Serbs are as intent as ever on consolidating their semi-sovereign status, and are poised to take advantage of the FRY's international rehabilitation to formalize and develop a variety of linkages with Belgrade, rather than Sarajevo. The Bosnian Serbs regard themselves, to borrow McGarry's phrase, as 'orphans of secession'[8]—a community left orphaned by the Bosnian Muslims' and Bosnian Croats' decision to quit the disintegrating Yugoslav federation in late 1991-early 1992. To them the Bosnian Muslims are the real 'separatists'—in colluding with the Croats to wreck a multinational, federal state, Yugoslavia, that was beginning a transition to political pluralism—and they are merely paying the Muslims back in their own coin within BiH. The RS's bunker mentality has proven impressively resilient in the post-war years. The fall of the HDZ in Croatia following the death of Tudjman had the counter-intuitive effects of radicalizing the behaviour of the HDZ-BiH and magnifying the insecurity of most ordinary Croats in BiH. The HDZ-BiH leadership escalated its confrontation with Bosnia's international overseers in early 2001 emboldened by the fact that the party and its allies received 93% of the Croat votes polled in the November 2000 elections. In short, the Bosnian state's chronic legitimacy crisis, while rooted in the failure of the Titoist formula of Yugoslav coexistence throughout its regional neighbourhood, is perpetuated by the fact that in the post-Yugoslav era, Bosnia's three communities have very different

8 John McGarry, 'Orphans of Secession: National Pluralism in Secessionist Regions and Post-Secession States' in M. Moore (ed.), *National Self-Determination and Secession*, Oxford and New York, 1998, pp. 215-32.

preferences on fundamental issues of allegiance and identity. This is ultimately a problem that is internal or endogenous to Bosnia & Herzegovina, which no amount of accusatory finger-pointing towards neighbouring states and their capitals will eradicate or resolve.

Neither political philosophy nor international law seems to be capable of conclusively resolving the legitimacy question one way or the other. Frederick Whelan, a political theorist, has noted that 'controversies over boundaries [are] among the most intractable and bitter types of political conflict'. The question of what constitutes the appropriate boundaries of the political community—in the dual sense of territory and citizenry—is 'logically prior' to the operation of democratic institutions and decisionmaking processes. When different segments of a polity have radically different notions of 'the appropriate boundaries, or the extent and composition of the political community', the legitimacy of the sovereign unit itself becomes the crux of the dispute. This type of dispute is, according to Whelan, 'insoluble within the framework of democratic theory'.[9] Robert Dahl, another eminent political thinker, agrees that 'we cannot solve the problem of the proper scope and domain of the unit [of citizenship and governance] from within democratic theory', since any democratic process presupposes the 'rightfulness of the unit', which is precisely the crux of the conflict in such situations.[10] Dahl notes that 'a crisp, unimpeachable solution' to the boundary/legitimacy problem of internally fractured states 'would be a marvellous achievement of democratic theory and practice... [but] alas, no altogether satisfactory solution seems to exist'.[11] In other words, the views of the three Bosnian communities on the sovereignty and statehood of Bosnia & Herzegovina are all more or less equally legitimate, and there is no way of definitively resolving their disagreements on the matter.

The international community's decision to recognize Yugoslavia's successor-states, including a multinational, contested territory like BiH, on the basis of the principle of *uti possidetis*

---

[9] Frederick Whelan, 'Democratic Theory and the Boundary Problem' in J.R. Pencock and J. Chapman (eds), *Liberal Democracy: NOMOS XXV*, New York, 1983, pp. 13-47.

[10] Robert Dahl, *Democracy and its Critics*, New Haven, CT, 1989, p. 207.

[11] Robert Dahl, 'Democracy, Majority Rule and Gorbachev's Referendum', *Dissent*, fall 1991, p. 493.

juris—meaning, in effect, the conversion of the federation's internal, inter-republic borders into international boundaries between sovereign states—has been a topic of fierce debate and a target of considerable criticism. In a frequently cited and controversial passage of his memoirs, David Owen, the EU's co-mediator in the Bosnian and Croatian wars between 1992 and 1995, has held that 'to have stuck unyieldingly to the internal boundaries of the six republics in the former Yugoslavia... as the boundaries of independent states was a folly far greater than premature recognition itself' (of Croatia in January 1992 and Bosnia in April). According to Owen, 'the refusal to make these borders negotiable greatly hampered the EC's attempts at crisis management in July–August 1991 and put all peacemaking from September 1991 onwards in a straitjacket... It is true that there could not have been a total accommodation of Serb demands, but to rule out any discussion or opportunity for compromise in order to head off war was an extraordinary decision'.[12] This decision, especially some of the judgments issued in the critical months of late 1991 and early 1992 by the Badinter Arbitration Commission of the EC which served as legal justifications for the *uti possidetis juris* policy, have also been severely criticized by some scholars as misguided and counter-productive to prospects of a non-violent resolution to Yugoslavia's terminal crisis.[13]

Uti possidetis juris was adopted as a doctrinal rule in the spate of African decolonizations that occurred from the mid-20th century onwards because of one consideration only. It was judged by the departing imperialists and most African anti-colonialists that while the conversion of (mostly arbitrary) colonial administrative boundaries into the borders of sovereign states was problematic, such a rule was essential to prospects of an orderly transition. The alternative was to risk opening up a veritable Pandora's Box of competing claims and counter-claims on territory) In the African context, the expectation that *uti possidetis juris* would enable an orderly transition from colonialism to independence was substan-

---

[12] David Owen, *Balkan Odyssey*, London, 1996, p. 34.

[13] Robert Hayden, *Blueprints for a House Divided*, Ch. 5; Peter Radan, 'The Badinter Arbitration Commission and the Partition of Yugoslavia', *Nationalities Papers* 25 (1997), pp. 537-57; and Peter Radan, 'Yugoslavia's Internal Borders as International Borders: A Question of Appropriateness', *East European Quarterly* 33: 2 (June 1999), pp. 137-55.

tially fulfilled. In the former Yugoslavia, on the other hand, the strict application of the principle arguably had the opposite effect. It made it rather likely that those who felt their rights were denied by the application of this principle—notably, the Krajina and Slavonian Serbs of Croatia and the Serbs in Bosnia—would resort to violence in a desperate attempt to change, on the ground, borders that had been declared inviolable. The international community's decision to recognize BiH as a sovereign state within those borders on the basis of the results of a polarizing referendum organized on February 29 and March 1, 1992—which was massively boycotted by the Serbs and produced an illusory Croat-Muslim majority coalition in favour of independence which was to disintegrate within a year—merely pushed the Serbs over the edge.[14] Steven Ratner, a specialist in public international law, calls *uti possidetis juris* an 'idiot rule'. He admits that the rote extension of *uti possidetis* to cases like Yugoslavia 'leads to genuine injustices and instability by leaving significant populations both unsatisfied with their status in new states and unsure of [rights of] political participation there', and warns that the insistence that 'post-independence borders must coincide with pre-independence lines has meant expulsions, refugee crises, 'ethnic cleansing', even genocide'. Applying *uti possidetis* as a default rule 'rewards the leaders of secessionist movements by more readily granting them a new territory, but offers uncertain prospects for the human rights and political participation of inhabitants and for public order in the region'.[15]

These criticisms are all well taken. However, they still beg the vital question of whether a superior, less disruptive strategy could have been feasibly devised to cope with the incompatible claims to self-determination unleashed by the unravelling of Yugoslavia, above all on the territory of Bosnia & Herzegovina. It seems probable that a feasible formula for 'drawing a better line', as Ratner puts it, may have been difficult to find and impossible to implement in the conditions of 1991-2. Ratner has made a spirited attempt to outline the basic principles of such an alternative

---

[14] The turnout rate in this referendum was 63%, and 98% of those who voted supported independence for BiH.

[15] Steven Ratner, 'Drawing a Better Line: *Uti Possidetis* and the Borders of New States', *American Journal of International Law* 90 (1996), pp. 590-624, on pp. 591, 616-17, 624.

strategy. In his thinking, *uti possidetis* would be provisionally applied, and the use of force by any of the parties to the conflict to alter this provisional *status quo* would be prohibited. Capitalizing on this breathing space, 'international diplomats, conciliators and arbitrators' would go to work on assessing the internal boundaries to determine 'their suitability as international frontiers'. In their assessment exercise, they would use such criteria as 'the age of the line', 'the process by which the line was drawn' and 'the viability of the entities that would emerge from secessions or break-ups along existing lines'. Finally, 'some form of consultation with the populace of a disputed territory on its future' would be required. Ratner recommends 'a renewed look at... the internationally supervised plebiscite', although he concedes that 'plebiscites contain the seeds of their own frustration'.[16]

This theoretically appealing model would not have been a feasible option for former Yugoslavia or Bosnia in the circumstances of 1991-2. It would probably not have been possible to provisionally stabilize the existing internal borders and prevent the use of force in a context of inflamed sentiments, spiralling tensions, and escalating military-style mobilizations at the local level. Even if that were possible, the strategy would surely have foundered on the next step. The criteria used to decide the 'suitability' (or not) of republic boundaries as interstate frontiers would be susceptible to various arguments and multiple subjective interpretations in conflict with one another, and it would almost certainly be impossible to find a *modus vivendi* between such contradictory standpoints. Finally, the popular referendum or plebiscite, at least in its conventional majoritarian variant, is an inappropriate, perhaps even dangerous mechanism for settling disputes of this nature. It has been pointed out that plebiscites 'cannot measure intensities of belief' and preclude 'working things out through discussion'.[17] By framing deeply volatile conflicts over territory, sovereignty and citizenship as a zero-sum game, referendums run the risk of inflaming and polarizing such conflicts and heralding a short countdown to civil war. As a device, the plebiscite resembles a blunt instrument when the complexity and volatility of the con-

---

[16] Ibid., pp. 617-23.
[17] David Butler and Austin Ranney, *Referendums: A Comparative Study of Practice and Theory*, Washington, DC, 1978, p. 36.

flict calls for tools of surgical precision.[18] It is doubtful that a form of plebiscite can be devised, leave alone implemented, in divided societies that would avoid all these dangerous pitfalls.

In conclusion, neither normative theory nor international legal theory has any convincing solutions, one way or the other, to the Bosnian state's 'legitimacy question'. In this situation, it is not unusual that the DPA fashioned a hybrid model for post-war Bosnia's political framework, which could be described as a model of layered sovereignty. The operation of this framework, reminiscent in some ways of the constitutional settlement that effectively confederalized socialist Yugoslavia in 1974, does manifest some dysfunctional characteristics, primarily because of the deep distrust among Bosnia's constituent peoples that is the legacy of the war. Predictably, it also frustrates both Bosnian integrationists and Bosnian partitionists, and provokes strong revisionist demands from both sectors. With some significant reforms, however, this apparently dysfunctional, neither-here-nor-there structure could in the medium term provide a workable basis not just for effective association and cooperation among Bosnia's peoples, but, optimistically, also provide a model for renewed cooperation throughout the region of which Bosnia was and still is a microcosm. That, if realized, would not be an insubstantial achievement for a messy constitutional compromise 'to end a war' whose origins are dubious to say the least.

A levelling of the cleansing field? Foundations of the Dayton peace

Richard Holbrooke, the principal American official involved in the negotiations leading to the Dayton accords, has written that 'on paper, Dayton was a good agreement; it ended the war and established a single, multiethnic country'. He has added, however, that 'the results of the international effort to implement Dayton

---

[18] For very similar reasons, I reject any kind of plebiscitary approach to the conflict between India and Pakistan over the disputed territory of Jammu and Kashmir, whose population is divided into pro-independence, pro-India and pro-Pakistan segments. See Sumantra Bose, *The Challenge in Kashmir: Democracy, Self-Determination and a Just Peace,* New Delhi, Thousand Oaks and London, 1997, pp. 125-27, 180; and Sumantra Bose, 'Kashmir: Sources of Conflict, Dimensions of Peace', *Survival: IISS Quarterly* 41:3 (autumn 1999), pp. 154-5.

would determine its true place in history'.[19] Holbrooke has made the same distinction between the agreement and the implementation process to ward off criticism from those who think the DPA is insufficiently integrative. Responding to one such author, he says: 'She misstates the goals of Dayton and confuses the Dayton agreement with the way it has been implemented'.[20]

Sceptics might say that this is a clever way for Holbrooke to take credit for his role in brokering the DPA, while evading any responsibility for the woes of post-Dayton Bosnia, attributed to the flaws of an implementation process that is separate from the basically 'good' agreement. I argue that the distinction made by Holbrooke is untenable, as is the argument derived from that distinction. The cold, sinister, yet thoroughly compelling logic of 'ethnic cleansing' provided the essential framework for the General Framework Agreement on Peace in Bosnia & Herzegovina. The DPA was made possible by a conscious strategic compromise with the two individuals most directly responsible for former Yugoslavia's descent into war and the Bosnian tragedy—Slobodan Milosevic and Franjo Tudjman. With that strategic compromise—and the imprint of the masterminds of 'ethnic cleansing'—deeply embedded in the edifice of Dayton, it is not surprising that the struggle to build a 'single multiethnic country' in any meaningful sense has proved to be an uphill battle in the years since Dayton. In fact, despite the many criticisms that can be directed against the 'implementation process', that process has had at least a few remarkably able individuals at the helm, such as the prescient and thoughtful Carl Bildt from Sweden, head of civilian implementation for the first 18 months after Dayton.

In Holbrooke's own detailed account, as well as other accounts of the American-led negotiations that culminated in the DPA,[21] Slobodan Milosevic stands out as the key figure among the gaggle of nationalist-authoritarian potentates from Croatia, Serbia and Bosnia involved in the talks. The American would-be brokers of peace clearly regarded him as the key to a breakthrough accord. This was perhaps unavoidable, given Milosevic's position as over-

---

[19] Holbrooke, *To End a War*, p. 335.
[20] Ibid., p. 385. He is responding to Radha Kumar, *Divide and Fall? Bosnia in the Annals of Partition*, London, 1997.
[21] See for example Silber and Little, *The Death of Yugoslavia*, Chs. 28, 29 and 30.

lord of Serbia (and Montenegro, at the time), and the incorrigible behaviour of the brutal, corrupt and faction-ridden group of gangsters who comprised the Bosnian Serb 'leadership'. Nonetheless, it is important to remember that apart from perhaps Holbrooke himself, Milosevic was the man most instrumental in the making of the Dayton peace. Milosevic, a man of substantially greater personal charm than either Tudjman or Izetbegovic, had for his part every incentive to appear moderate, reasonable and cooperative towards the Americans. The 'all Serbs in one state' slogan, which he encouraged to consolidate his own power in the late 1980s and early 1990s but which then took off on him like a magic carpet, was by the early autumn of 1995 in danger of unravelling completely. In two lightning strikes in May and August, the Croatian army recaptured three of the four enclaves that made up the 'Republic of Serbian Krajina' in Croatia, driving some 200,000 Krajina and western Slavonian Serbs[22] into Serb-controlled Bosnia and Serbia. In a stunning reversal of the military situation in Bosnia, the Bosnian Serb forces were by September suffering serious defeats and losing sizeable chunks of territory in western and northwestern Bosnia, mainly to joint offensives of the regular Croatian army (HV) and the BiH Croat militia (HVO), but also to the Muslims' Armija BiH. The 'diaspora' Serbs beyond

[22] I have a particular affinity with western Slavonia, an area in central Croatia just north of the natural Sava river border with northwestern Bosnia, an hour's drive north of Banja Luka, where I spent the summers of 1994 and 1995. Until 1991 it had had a mixed population of Serbs and Croats (one of its two main towns, Daruvar, had 10,483 Croats and 10,074 Serbs; the other, Pakrac, 12,813 Serbs and 9,896 Croats). In 1994, the area, thoroughly devastated from the fighting in the second half of 1991, was one of four enclaves in Croatia designated as United Nations Protected Area–Sector West (UNPA-W), one of four such UN zones in Croatia. The line of confrontation ran through the UNPA, with the Croats controlling the northern two-thirds and the Serbs the remaining third, which was the smallest of four Serb-held enclaves in Croatia constituting the rebel statelet styled the 'Republic of Serbian Krajina' (RSK). It bisected the town of Pakrac into Serb and Croat pockets, my first experience of a Yugoslav town partitioned by civil war.

When I returned in the summer of 1995, the Serb zone had just been over-run by the Croat military in an offensive codenamed 'Operation Flash' (May 1-2, 1995), which was to be a prelude to 'Operation Storm' launched against two much larger RSK areas exactly three months later. By the time I arrived in early June, 85% of the Serb zone's 15,000 residents had fled across the Sava into Serb-held northwestern Bosnia, and more left in UN-organized evacuations that sum-

the Drina and the Danube had since 1991 increasingly become a problem and their 'leaders' an international embarrassment; now their cause was clearly a losing proposition. There was obviously little if any rationale remaining for the FRY to continue to suffocate under economic sanctions and endure diplomatic pariah status for the sake of the Bosnian Serbs, most of whose 'leaders' seemed incapable of strategic thinking and calculated compromise. It was high time, in Milosevic's perception, for a deal to end the war in Bosnia & Herzegovina. If his role sealed such a deal it would potentially help rehabilitate his regime in rump 'Yugoslavia' in the international arena.

One factor, however, remained an obstacle to a deal to end the war. Even with Milosevic on board, it would not be possible for Holbrooke and his team to launch a final diplomatic offensive to sew up a deal unless and until the right configuration of maps emerged on the ground to buttress such a settlement. Holbrooke's senior colleague, Robert Frasure, who was killed in an accident on the Mount Igman road above Sarajevo in August 1995, was given to describing the political leaders of Croatia, Serbia and Bosnia as the 'junkyard dogs and skunks of the Balkans'.[23] By the first week of August, the Croatian regime of Franjo Tudjman had all but solved its Serbian problem through military means, emerging with a vengeance from several years of humiliation and uncertainty as both the West and the Milosevic regime looked on. In the count-

---

mer. One of my most vivid memories of that second summer is of several hours spent drinking and chatting—about the music of Ravi Shankar and Bob Dylan, among other topics—with soldiers of an openly neo-fascist unit of the Croatian army in a bar in a small western Slavonian town called Jasenovac, just recaptured from rebel Serbs. Jasenovac, perched on the Croatian bank of the Sava, was the site of Axis-occupied Yugoslavia's most infamous death camp during the Second World War, when tens of thousands of Serbs from the surrounding region, along with thousands of Croat anti-fascists, Jews and Gypsies were murdered there by the Ustashe, Nazi-backed Croatian fascists.

The military bar was the only functioning establishment in a damaged ghosttown—its Serb residents had all fled across the Sava. I smoked, drank and conversed there overlooked by a stern-looking portrait of Ante Pavelic, the extreme Croatian nationalist who was the *Poglavnik* (supreme leader) of the Nazi-sponsored Independent State of Croatia (NDH) during the Second World War. The irony was not lost on me. Exactly fifty years after the NDH was crushed by the multinational communist-led Partisan resistance movement, Ante Pavelic's spirit had returned to haunt Jasenovac.

[23] Holbrooke, *To End a War*, p. 8.

down to Dayton, the Americans turned to their favourite 'junk-yard dog' in the Balkan mess to clean up the Bosnian map as the essential precursor to a negotiated agreement.

When I lived in Mostar in the summer of 1998, the grim, sallow visage of one man stared at me from shopfronts, hotel arcades, and inside cafés, restaurants and even private homes in west Mostar, the Croat sector of the partitioned town. I was informed that he was Gojko Susak, Tudjman's minister of defence, who had overseen the successful offensives of 1995. He had just died of cancer in May 1998. Like many in Tudjman's inner circle, Susak was a native of Herzegovina. He had been born in Siroki Brijeg, an all-Croat town a half-hour drive west of Mostar with a history of extreme Croat nationalism—the Croat-populated areas of western and central Herzegovina were a notorious stronghold of the Nazi-sponsored Ustasha regime that nominally ruled the Independent State of Croatia (NDH), covering much of Croatia (excluding Dalmatia) and practically all of BiH during the Second World War. Like many other Herzegovinian Croats, Susak emigrated from his climatically and otherwise arid land in his youth (in 1967) and eventually became the owner of a successful pizza business in Canada. And like many other diaspora Croats with hardline political views, he returned to Yugoslavia as the country entered the twilight of its existence, as a major financier and official of Tudjman's HDZ in Croatia. In 1990-1, he played a direct role in stoking growing Serb-Croat tensions in some regions of Croatia, which erupted into full-scale war after mid-1991 and destroyed Yugoslavia:

> Radical HDZ activists did what they could to provoke conflict. In mid-April 1991, a group of highly placed HDZ members led by Gojko Susak, an extreme nationalist who was one of Tudjman's closest advisers… called on the regional police chief [in eastern Slavonia, bordering northern Serbia], Josip Reichl-Kir. Kir [a Croatian of German-Slovene descent]… was a moderate who had worked tirelessly, on both sides of rapidly forming frontlines [in the area] to remove barricades and restore mutual trust. Now Susak asked Kir to lead him… to the outskirts of Borovo Selo, a Serb-populated village near the town of Vukovar on the Danube. Kir was against the excursion. He knew it would inflame the local Serbs. But under intimidation he agreed. From outside the village,

Susak and his companions fired three shoulder-launched Ambrust missiles into the village. 'They're crazy', Kir later confided in disgust and disbelief to a colleague. One rocket hit a house, another landed in a potato field and failed to explode. It was later exhibited on Belgrade television as evidence of Croat aggression—Susak's jaunt had lit a slow fuse.[24]

Indeed, within weeks Josip Reichl-Kir was dead, assassinated – by a gunman allegedly acting at the behest of local HDZ leader Branimir Glavas, who had been among Susak's raiding party that night. Within months, the contested districts of Croatia including eastern Slavonia, Baranja, Srem, western Slavonia, Banija, Kordun, Lika and the interior areas of northern Dalmatia were in ruins, devastated by brutal fighting that held grim portents for Bosnia. And within a year, Gojko Susak had been appointed defence minister of Croatia. In that capacity, he played a crucial leadership role, along with Tudjman and another Herzegovinian Croat, HDZ-BiH chief Mate Boban, in the Croats' land-grab and 'cleansing' campaign in Herzegovina and central Bosnia in 1993-4. In Mostar that summer, I met a young Muslim who had been picked off a street in west Mostar in the summer of 1993 by armed men speaking, he said, in a Dalmatian accent (he subsequently learned they were Croatian Army regulars from the port city of Split). He was taken to a detention centre in a village called Dretelj, south of Mostar, from where he was released after a few days upon the intervention of a childhood friend who had become a HVO officer. He was exceptionally fortunate—hundreds of local Muslims and Serbs did not survive that camp. 'I hold that bastard Susak personally responsible for what was done in places like Dretelj and the heliodrom camp in Mostar [another notorious detention centre]', he told me. 'He and Boban were the masterminds of the Croat offensive strategy in BiH, the people behind the bombing and starving of east Mostar and the massacres in the Lasva valley [in central Bosnia].'

In his memoirs, Richard Holbrooke says that he 'simply hated' Radovan Karadzic and Ratko Mladic 'for what they had done'. On September 13, 1995, Holbrooke was closeted with Milosevic in a villa outside Belgrade when the Serbian leader announced that Karadzic and Mladic, both indicted war criminals by that

[24] Silber and Little, *The Death of Yugoslavia*, pp. 140-1.

time, were waiting to join the discussions in another villa minutes away. Holbrooke recalls that he 'felt a jolt go through my body' when he heard this. His moral dilemma in sitting across the table from those two men was acute. Although he reluctantly agreed in the larger interest of ending the Bosnian war, he 'did not shake hands, although both Karadzic and Mladic tried to'.[25] The next day, September 14, Holbrooke visited Mostar via Split (for a meeting with Alija Izetbegovic and Haris Silajdzic) where he was 'appalled' by the 'rubble and tension... along the line dividing the two halves of Mostar'.[26]

On September 17, shuttling frantically between the region's capitals in the quest for peace, Holbrooke found himself in the presidential palace in Zagreb, accompanied by the American ambassador to Croatia, Peter Galbraith. While the senior members of Holbrooke's entourage 'met with Susak', Holbrooke and Galbraith met with Tudjman. By this date, NATO aerial attacks, which had begun at the end of August, had thrown the Bosnian Serb forces' command-and-control systems into disarray. Taking advantage of this situation, Croat armies, fresh from their Krajina triumph, were sweeping across a wide swathe of western Bosnia and into parts of central Bosnia, taking one Serb-held town after another—Drvar, Mrkonjic Grad, Jajce. In Holbrooke's words, 'at least 100,000 Serb refugees were pouring into Banja Luka or heading further east to escape the advance'. Holbrooke recalls that he told Tudjman: 'Mr. President, I urge you to go as far as you can, but not to take Banja Luka [the biggest city in northwestern Bosnia]'. Specifically, he 'urged Tudjman to take Sanski Most, Prijedor and Bosanski Novi, all important towns [in northwestern Bosnia] that had become worldwide symbols of ethnic cleansing' by Serbs. Holbrooke writes that 'even while encouraging the offensive, Galbraith and I expressed great concern over the many refugees... We told Tudjman that there was no excuse for the brutal treatment of Serbs that followed most Croatian military successes. The abuse of Serb civilians, most of whom had lived in the area for generations, was wrong. Using a provocative phrase normally applied only to the Serbs, I told Tudjman that the current Croatian behaviour might be viewed as a milder form of ethnic cleansing. Tudjman reacted strongly but did not quite deny it; if

[25] Holbrooke, *To End a War*, pp. 148-9.
[26] Ibid., p. 154.

our information was correct, he said, he would put an immediate stop to it.'[27] (Ten months after this meeting, on July 22, 1996, the Croatian weekly *Feral Tribune* reported that '942 elderly civilians of Serbian nationality who had stayed in their homes in the Krajina were killed since September 1995, i.e. since all military actions in the Krajina were stopped.'[28]

Two days later, on September 19, 1995, at the end of a meeting between Izetbegovic and Tudjman organized by the Americans in Zagreb, during which the Croatian president created a scene by shouting insults at the Muslim leader, Holbrooke 'pulled Defence Minister Susak aside'. Holbrooke, who days earlier had refused to shake hands with Karadzic and Mladic, appears to have been on first-name terms with Susak. 'Gojko, I want to be absolutely clear, I said. Nothing we said today should be construed to mean that we want you to stop the rest of the offensive, other than Banja Luka. Speed is important. We can't say so publicly, but please take Sanski Most, Prijedor and Bosanski Novi. And do it quickly, before the Serbs regroup!'[29]

Why not Banja Luka, 'a city we knew Susak wanted to go for... as quickly as possible'?[30] Holbrooke says: 'Humanitarian concerns decided the case for me... I did not think that the United States should contribute to the creation of new refugees and more human suffering in order to take a city *that would have to be returned later*' (my emphasis) for, as Holbrooke had told Tudjman in Zagreb two days earlier, 'the city was unquestionably within the Serb portion of Bosnia' and even if taken would have to be returned to the Serbs 'in any peace negotiation'.[31] Banja Luka's fall that autumn would have generated at least another 200,000 homeless and destitute refugees, in addition to the 200,000 from the Krajina districts and western Slavonia and the 100,000-plus from the areas of western and northwestern Bosnia overrun by Croat and Muslim forces. But Holbrooke's 'humanitarian concern' sounds half-hearted at best and hypocritical at worst. What seems to have been the deciding factor in the case for

---

[27] Ibid., pp. 154, 160-2.
[28] Gordana Uzelac, 'Franjo Tudjman's Nationalist Ideology', *East European Quarterly* 31: 4 (1998), p. 465.
[29] Holbrooke, *To End a War*, p. 166.
[30] Ibid., p. 160.
[31] Ibid., pp. 160, 166.

him is the consideration that the capture of Banja Luka was certainly unnecessary and probably counterproductive to his own strategy and goals.

Sanski Most did fall to the Armija BiH's legendary fighting force, General Atif Dudakovic's Bihac-based V Corps, at the end of September, while the Serbs were able to hold on to Novi, Prijedor, and Banja Luka. The foundations of the Dayton peace were cemented during those fateful weeks in September 1995. As Holbrooke explained in a handwritten fax to his superiors in Washington on September 20: '[The] basic truth is perhaps not something we can say publicly right now... In fact, the map negotiation, which always seemed to me to be our most daunting challenge, is taking place right now on the battlefield, and so far, in a manner beneficial... In only a few weeks, the famous 70-30 division of the country has gone to around 50-50, obviously making our task easier....'[32]

Holbrooke is owed a debt by students of Bosnia for penning such candid memoirs. The settlement reached at Dayton two months later was founded, above all, on the levelling of the cleansing field achieved by September 1995. Perhaps there was no alternative but this brutal form of *realpolitik*. But it is vital to remember that the remaking of the map 'in a manner beneficial', leading directly to the forging of the Dayton Peace Agreement, was accomplished not only in close consultation with Slobodan Milosevic (who further tidied the map at Dayton by voluntarily relinquishing Greater Sarajevo to exclusive Muslim control), but also with the likes of Franjo Tudjman—and Gojko Susak. Bosnia's travails since Dayton become quite intelligible in light of a clear understanding of the foundations of the Dayton peace.

Structure of the Dayton state

Bosnia is a state by international design and of international design. Its post-war institutional design reflects the circumstances of the state's birth in March-April 1992, its effective demise immediately afterwards, and the painful, tentative rebirth engineered at Dayton. The following section surveys the multi-layered architecture of the Dayton state, as provided for in the three con-

[32] Ibid., p. 168.

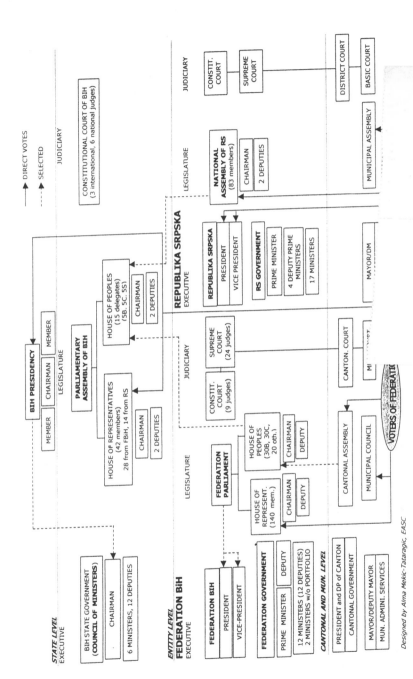

Political Structure of Bosnia & Herzegovina und

Designed by Alma Mekic-Tataragic, EASC

Legend:
→ DIRECT VOTES
- - → SELECTED

STATE LEVEL

EXECUTIVE

BIH STATE GOVERNMENT (COUNCIL OF MINISTERS)
- CHAIRMAN
- 6 MINISTERS, 12 DEPUTIES

LEGISLATURE

BIH PRESIDENCY
- MEMBER | CHAIRMAN | MEMBER

PARLIAMENTARY ASSEMBLY OF BIH
- HOUSE OF REPRESENTATIVES (42 members) 28 from FBIH, 14 from RS
  - CHAIRMAN
  - 2 DEPUTIES
- HOUSE OF PEOPLES (15 delegates) (5B. 5C. 5S)
  - CHAIRMAN
  - 2 DEPUTIES

JUDICIARY

CONSTITUTIONAL COURT OF BIH (3 international, 6 national judges)

ENTITY LEVEL

FEDERATION BiH

EXECUTIVE

FEDERATION BIH
- PRESIDENT
- VICE-PRESIDENT

FEDERATION GOVERNMENT
- PRIME MINISTER | DEPUTY
- 12 MINISTERS (12 DEPUTIES)
- 2 MINISTERS w/o PORTFOLIO

LEGISLATURE

FEDERATION PARLIAMENT
- HOUSE OF REPRESENT. (140 mem.)
  - CHAIRMAN
  - DEPUTY
- HOUSE OF PEOPLES (30B, 30C, 20 oth.)
  - CHAIRMAN
  - DEPUTY

JUDICIARY

- CONSTIT. COURT (9 judges)
- SUPREME COURT (24 judges)
- CANTON. COURT
- MI...

CANTONAL AND MUN. LEVEL

- PRESIDENT and DP of CANTON
- CANTONAL GOVERNMENT
- MAYOR/DEPUTY MAYOR
- MUN. ADMINI. SERVICES

- CANTONAL ASSEMBLY
- MUNICIPAL COUNCIL

VOTERS OF FEDERATI...

REPUBLIKA SRPSKA

EXECUTIVE

REPUBLIKA SRPSKA
- PRESIDENT
- VICE PRESIDENT

RS GOVERNMENT
- PRIME MINISTER
- 4 DEPUTY PRIME MINISTERS
- 17 MINISTERS

- MAYOR/DM

LEGISLATURE

NATIONAL ASSEMBLY OF RS (83 members)
- CHAIRMAN
- 2 DEPUTIES

- MUNICIPAL ASSEMBLY

JUDICIARY

- CONSTIT. COURT
- SUPREME COURT
- DISTRICT COURT
- BASIC COURT

stitutions that operate on its territory: the constitution of the common state of Bosnia & Herzegovina, and the constitutions of its Entities, the Republika Srpska (RS) and the Bosniac-Croat Federation (FBiH).)

Bosnia & Herzegovina. The constitution of BiH (Annex 4 of the DPA) is primarily the work of lawyers from the United States' Department of State. It establishes a fairly skeletal framework of common-state institutions based on equality and parity represen-tation of Bosniacs, Serbs and Croats as collectively defined com-munities, and limits those institutions to a narrow band of com-petencies.[33]

The preamble affirms 'the sovereignty, territorial integrity and political independence of Bosnia & Herzegovina in accordance with international law', and the status of Bosniacs, Serbs and Croats 'as constituent peoples (along with Others)' of the state. Article 1.4 guarantees 'freedom of movement... of persons, goods, services and capital throughout Bosnia & Herzegovina'. Article 2.5 grants 'all refugees and displaced persons... the right freely to return to their homes of origin', the right to have pre-war prop-erty restored to them and to be compensated for property that cannot be restored. These rights are elaborated in Annex 7 of the DPA, which deals specifically with the right of return. Article 2 also promises all citizens 'the highest level of internationally rec-ognized human rights and fundamental freedoms'.

Article 1.7 stipulates that 'there shall be a citizenship of Bosnia & Herzegovina... and a citizenship of each Entity', and a sub-clause permits BiH citizens to concurrently be a citizen of anoth-er country, so long as a bilateral agreement, approved by the BiH parliament, exists between the two countries. Article 3.2 says that 'the Entities shall have the right to establish special parallel rela-tionships with neighbouring states, consistent with the sovereign-ty and territorial integrity of Bosnia & Herzegovina'. The FBiH signed such a framework agreement with the Republic of Croatia in 1998, and the RS with the Federal Republic of Yugoslavia in 2001. While both relationships are yet to acquire real substance, the RS-FRY agreement, although delayed, is likely to do so soon-er because the FBiH is a house divided along the national(ist)

[33] The full text of the constitution is reproduced in Cazim Sadikovic, *Human Rights Without Protection*, Sarajevo, 1999, on pp. 129-44.

faultline. Article 3.1 sets out the subjects which are the jurisdiction of the common state and its institutions—foreign policy, foreign trade policy, customs policy, monetary policy (in conjunction with an internationally supervised Central Bank of BiH), immigration, refugee and asylum policy and regulation, international and inter-Entity criminal law enforcement, establishment and operation of common and international communications facilities, regulation of inter-Entity transportation, and air traffic control. According to Article 3.3, all other 'governmental functions and powers' (including, notably, defence) 'shall be those of the Entities'. The constitutional model here is clearly based on a conception of diffuse, layered sovereignty and citizenship. Multiple forms and levels of citizenship are expressly allowed (state, entity, other countries). Sovereignty is devolved downwards and outwards simultaneously—the Entities are the repository of all residual powers and functions, and they are empowered to establish and develop special parallel relationships with neighbouring states, which can only be Croatia and Serbia-Montenegro.

The legislative organ of the Bosnian state, as elaborated in Article 4, consists of a bicameral Parliamentary Assembly. The first chamber, the House of Peoples, has 15 Delegates—five Croats and five Bosniacs from the FBiH and five Serbs from the RS. The five Serb delegates are nominated by the RS's legislature, the National Assembly, while the Bosniac and Croat delegates are selected by the Bosniac and Croat delegations, respectively, to the House of the Peoples of the (also bicameral) Federation parliament. The presence of nine out of 15 delegates constitutes a quorum, with the proviso that at least three Serbs, three Bosniacs and three Croats must be present. The other chamber, the House of Representatives, consists of 42 directly elected Members, 28 from the Federation and 14 from the RS. A simple majority of these 42 members constitutes a quorum in this house. It is noteworthy that the composition of this chamber is not strictly based on the principle of equal representation on a national-collective basis, beyond the 2:1 distribution assigned to the FBiH and the RS on a territorial basis. In the House of Representatives elected in November 2000, a majority of seats, 22 in all, were won by three parties whose vote base is either solely (SDA, SBiH) or overwhelmingly (SDP) in the Bosniac community, while smaller Bosniac-based parties won a further two seats. The HDZ, which has massive support among BiH Croats, secured only five seats in this chamber, while another tiny Croat party obtained another. RS-based Serb parties collectively secured a total of only eleven seats.

Both the House of Peoples and the House of Representatives select three members each—one Serb, one Bosniac and one Croat—to act as chair and deputy chairs, with the chair rotating among the three. Decisions are taken in both chambers by a majority of those present and voting, with one vital *caveat*—a decision thus taken 'may be declared to be destructive of a vital interest of the Bosniac, Croat or Serb people by a majority of, as appropriate, the Bosniac, Croat or Serb Delegates' to the House of Peoples. This institutionalizes a veto right for the representatives to the BiH state parliament of each of the three national segments. Decisions thus blocked are referred in the first instance to a three-member commission convened by the chair of the House of Peoples, which must include one Serb, one Bosniac and one Croat delegate. If this commission fails to resolve the issue within five days, the matter is referred to the Constitutional Court of BiH for its binding opinion. The responsibilities constitutionally mandated to the Parliamentary Assembly as a whole are limited but not necessarily insignificant—enacting legislation to implement decisions made by the BiH state presidency, approving a state budget, deciding whether or not to consent to the ratification of international treaties. In practice, the BiH state parliament has been largely a talking-shop since 1996, often immobilized by disagreements and sheer incompetence.

Two of the four classic features of a 'consociational' or group-based power-sharing system are evident in the legislature of the Bosnian state: allocation of seats in a way that takes account of group membership, including a strict parity formula in the House of Peoples, and veto rights for representatives of national segments. The Bosnian state's principal executive organ, the Presidency, includes these two features as well as a third defining element of consociation:[34] central decisionmaking by grand coalition between representatives of the segments. In a replication of

---

[34] The consociational paradigm of government is most commonly associated with the work of its principal proponent, Arend Lijphart. See Lijphart, *Democracy in Plural Societies: A Comparative Exploration*, New Haven, 1977, and *Democracies:*

the socialist Yugoslav model, (the executive is a *collective state presidency* that consists of three members or co-presidents—'one Bosniac and one Croat, directly elected from the territory of the Federation, and one Serb directly elected from the territory of Republika Srpska' (Article 5). The co-presidents serve a four-year term, the chair rotates among them every eight months, and they are supposed to 'endeavour to adopt all Presidency Decisions by consensus' (Art. 5.2). Decisions may be adopted by two presidency members, but in that eventuality the dissenting member has the right to declare such a decision destructive to the vital interest of the Entity he has been elected from. Such a disputed decision would then be referred to the National Assembly of the RS, or to the Bosniac or the Croat delegations to the House of Peoples of the FBiH, depending on whether it was the Serb, Bosniac or Croat co-president who exercised his veto power. If the dissenting declaration is confirmed by a two-thirds vote in either the RSNA or among the Bosniac or Croat members of the Federation House of Peoples, as appropriate, the decision stands nullified.)

The joint presidency's major constitutional mandate is 'conducting the foreign policy of Bosnia & Herzegovina' (Art. 5.3), including appointing ambassadors and other diplomatic representatives abroad, 'no more than two-thirds of whom may be selected from the territory of the Federation',[35] and 'representing Bosnia & Herzegovina in international and European organizations'. Not unpredictably, the collective presidency has mostly served as a photo-opportunity for its members, in Sarajevo, at UN headquarters in New York and other transnational forums. The presidency's other tasks include nominating the chair of a council of ministers (CoM), whose appointment is subject to approval by the Parliamentary Assembly's House of Representatives. That chair, in turn, is supposed to nominate ministers and deputy ministers of foreign affairs, foreign trade, civil affairs and communica-

---

Patterns of Majoritarian and Consensus Government in 21 Countries, New Haven, 1984. The fourth defining element of the consociational paradigm, characteristic of the Dayton state, is segmental autonomy (a principle which can take several institutional expressions).

[35] In practice, ambassadorships and lesser diplomatic appointments are also shared out on a national-quota basis. Top posts in countries like Russia and China tend to go to Serbs, while Bosniacs (and to a lesser degree, Croats) predominate in missions in Western capitals.

tions, human rights and refugees, and European integration, the latter three ministries having been added to the original two in the years since Dayton. It is stipulated that no more than two-thirds of these ministers may be from Federation territory, and further that each minister and his deputy minister must belong to different nationalities. In practice, the CoM has remained more or less a cipher, both because of the deeply disunited reality of the country in almost every sense and because some of the functions apparently assigned to it overlap with Entity and sub-Entity institutions (the RS, for example, has its own Minister of Foreign Economic Relations, a Muslim appointed to Prime Minister Mladen Ivanic's cabinet at the end of 2000). The presidency members also jointly possess 'civilian command authority over armed forces' (Art. 5.5) of BiH in yet another replication of the former Yugoslav model. This cannot be more than a purely nominal jurisdiction, since the 'armed forces' of BiH consist one purely Serb element (VRS, Army of the Republika Srpska) and Croat and Muslim elements which exist more or less separately within a formally integrated Federation force; moreover, defence is a subject entirely in the Entity domain in constitutional terms. The Dayton constitution did task the collective presidency to 'select a Standing Committee on Military Matters to coordinate the activities of armed forces in Bosnia & Herzegovina'. This coordinating body was not established until 1999, and it was only in 2001 that the first joint exercises between the RS and FBiH militaries were held.)

Ironically, the most robust of Bosnia's central institutions is the one on which non-Bosnians play a direct role. This is the country's supreme judicial organ, the Constitutional Court of BiH. The court has nine judges, of whom four are selected by the FBiH's House of Representatives, and two by the National Assembly of Republika Srpska. In effect, this has meant two Bosniacs, two Croats and two Serbs. The other three judges are appointed by the president of the European Court of Human Rights, after consultation with the tripartite BiH presidency. They cannot be citizens of BiH or of any neighboring state (Article 6.1). A majority of the nine judges is sufficient to constitute a quorum, and the court issues rulings by majority decision as well.

The jurisdiction of the constitutional court is wide-ranging. It is the ultimate guarantor of the BiH state constitution. The court has 'exclusive jurisdiction to decide any dispute that arises... between the Entities, between Bosnia & Herzegovina and an Entity or Entities, or between institutions of Bosnia & Herzegovina'. Among other matters, the constitutional court is empowered to rule on 'whether an Entity's decision to establish a special parallel relationship with a neighbouring state is consistent with this [state] constitution, including provisions concerning the sovereignty and territorial integrity of Bosnia & Herzegovina', and on 'whether any provision of an Entity's constitution or law is consistent with this constitution' (Art. 6.3). The court also has appellate jurisdiction over constitutional issues arising out of judgments delivered by any other court in BiH, and jurisdiction over constitutional matters referred to it by any other court.

These significant powers, together with the fact that the court operates by majority vote rather than consensus—thus rendering it much less prone to deadlock and paralysis—makes the Constitutional Court of BiH a potential tool in the hands of international state-builders and democratizers. In mid-2000, that potential appeared to be actualized when the court delivered a landmark verdict on a matter referred to its attention by Alija Izetbegovic, Bosniac member of the joint presidency, some two years earlier. The court ruled that the constitutions of both BiH Entities were in contravention of the BiH common state's constitutional requirement that all three constituent peoples be fully equal throughout the territory of the country. Article 1 of the RS constitution defines the Republika Srpska as 'the State of Serb people and of all its citizens' while Article 1 of the FBiH constitution declares only 'Bosniacs and Croats as constituent peoples' of the Federation, 'along with Others'. The judgment essentially enjoins upon the Federation that Serbs be explicitly made a constituent people, with rights and obligations thereof, and on the RS that Muslims and Croats as groups be accorded the same collective constitutional status as Serbs. The decision was hailed by international operatives in BiH and by Bosnian liberals as a major advance for the cause of constitutional reform and equal, non-discriminatory citizenship rights. There are at least three 'ifs' involved however. First, the advance was secured only by further confirming and entrenching the (collective) principle of constituent nations in Bosnia's multi-layered constitutional framework. Second, the issue once again highlighted the deep divisions within the country—five judges voted for the decision (the three international members and the two Bosniacs) while four (the Serbs and Croats) opposed it) Third, ordinary Bosnians expressed scepticism about whether the judgment, even if implemented by the Federation and RS authorities (itself a big question-mark) would make any real difference to most Bosnians' lives. A visibly sceptical Bosnian official of the constitutional court told me in Sarajevo shortly after the ruling became public knowledge that her elderly mother-in-law's response to the news had been— 'Does this mean I will receive my pension on time from now on?' The answer—of course not.[36]

Nonetheless, the ruling does qualify as one of the more notable events in Bosnia's post-Dayton history. It may help encourage minority returns throughout the country, especially of non-Serbs to RS but also of Serbs to Federation towns. The fact that the Constitutional Court was able to deliver such a 'controversial' judgment—albeit by a 5-4 split vote—makes it a rare example of a common-state institution that functions. It shares that distinction with the Central Bank of BiH, which is 'the sole authority for issuing currency and for monetary policy throughout' the country (Article 7). This institution introduced the common Bosnian currency, the convertible mark (KM) in mid-1998, pegged 1:1 to the German mark (DM), as the sole tender for official transactions throughout the country at all levels of government from the municipality upwards. After an initial period of opposition and obstruction in many Serb and Croat-dominated areas, the KM achieved wide circulation across the country. As with the constitutional court, non-Bosnians play a pivotal role in the central bank, which occupies an imposing Habsburg-era building in the heart of central Sarajevo. It is run by 'a Governor appointed by the International Monetary Fund... who shall not be a citizen of Bosnia & Herzegovina or any neighbouring state'. He heads a governing board which includes three Bosnians, 'two from the Federation (one Bosniac, one Croat, who shall share one vote) and one from Republika Srpska'. The foreign Governor is entitled to 'cast tie-breaking votes on the Board', meaning, in

[36] Author interview with Biljana Potparic, secretary-general of Constitutional Court of BiH, Sarajevo, August 2000.

effect, that he has the decisive say in a procedure that operates on a tacit majoritarian principle.⟩

Republika Srpska. The institutional frameworks of Bosnia & Herzegovina and the Bosniac-Croat Federation borrow heavily from the confederal, consociational model of the last two decades of Titoist Yugoslavia. However, these constitutions are written in a crisp, direct style unmistakably of Western provenance. The imprint of American architects is obvious. The Republika Srpska's constitution[37] is fundamentally different. Here the style is pedantic and repetitive, full of didactic statements and vacuous clauses, the trademark signature of intellectuals socialized by and under state-socialist regimes.

The main goal of the framers of the RS constitution is to convey that the RS closely approximates a sovereign state. The 'Basic Provisions' of the constitution declare that 'Republika Srpska shall be the State of Serb people and of all its citizens' (Article 1), and that 'the territory of the Republic shall be unique, indivisible and unalienable' (Article 2). Further, 'all State functions and powers shall belong to the Republic, with the exception of those which were by the Constitution of Bosnia & Herzegovina explicitly transferred to its institutions' (Article 3) and, leaving nothing at all to chance, 'the Republic may, according to the Constitution of Bosnia & Herzegovina, establish special parallel relationships with the Federal Republic of Yugoslavia and its member republics' (Article 4). Beginning on this note, the constitution concludes with 'Final Provisions' which state that 'when enactments of the institutions of Bosnia & Herzegovina or enactments of the Federation of Bosnia & Herzegovina, in contravention of the Constitution of Republika Srpska and the Constitution of Bosnia & Herzegovina, violate the equality of Republika Srpska, or when its rights and lawful interests are otherwise endangered without any protection being provided, agencies of the Republic shall temporarily, pending a decision of the Constitutional Court of Bosnia & Herzegovina, and in cases where irredeemable detrimental consequences might occur, pass enactments and undertake measures for protection of rights and interests of the Republic' (Article 138). The siege mentality of Republika Srpska's architects

[37] *Constitution of Republika Srpska*, mimeo. In translation, with amendments, 2000. Obtained by the author from the OHR's legal department, Sarajevo.

is also evident in Articles 81, 85 and 137, which are devoted to laying out extraordinary provisions to apply 'during a state of war or imminent threat of war' (A warrior statelet born of implosion and civil war, the RS has since Dayton been defined by a bunker mentality characteristic of a garrison surrounded by enemies. The constitutional provisions relating to 'Defence' say that 'the defence and protection of the territory and constitutional order of Republika Srpska is the right and duty of all citizens' (Article 104). This is the amended version; the original form enjoined upon citizens the duty to defend the 'sovereignty' and 'independence' of Republika Srpska. And of course, 'Republika Srpska shall have its own Army, consisting of standing units and reserve units' (Article 105). This aspect of the Dayton treaty may have been unavoidable, given the mutual security fears of the three Bosnian communities. But it also means that the Bosnian state does not have jurisdiction over defence, a competency assigned to the central authority in even loosely organized variants of federations.

Several commentators on post-war Bosnia have sneered at the extremely ambitious human rights clauses incorporated into the common-state and FBiH constitutions.[38] The RS constitution is even more generous in this regard. The single largest section, consisting of 40 articles, is dedicated to enumerating the 'human rights and freedoms' of RS citizens which, if substantively true, would make the RS not just an exemplary liberal democracy but also a full-fledged welfare state. This is prefaced by Article 5 of the basic provisions, which states that the constitutional order of the Republic is based on 'human freedoms and rights in accordance with international standards', 'assurance of national equality' of citizens, and 'protection of the rights of... minorities'. Article 28 stipulates that 'religious communities shall be equal before the law and shall be free to perform religious affairs and services', going on to assert that 'the State shall materially support the Orthodox church and shall cooperate with it in all fields'. Article 7 declares 'the Serbian language' the official language and Cyrillic the official script, although allowance is made for use of the 'Latin alphabet' and 'other languages'. According to Article 34, 'citizens shall be guaranteed freedom of profession of national affiliation' and 'no

---

[38] For example, Robert Hayden, *Blueprints for a House Divided*, p. 133; David Chandler, *Bosnia: Faking Democracy after Dayton*, London, 1999, pp. 91-2.

one shall be obliged to declare national affiliation', while Article 31 says that 'inciting national, religious or racial hatred and intolerance shall be prohibited'. Indeed, 'foreign citizens and stateless persons may be granted asylum in Republika Srpska if prosecuted for participation in movements of social and national emancipation, for supporting democracy, human rights and fundamental freedoms or for freedom of scientific and artistic creativity' (Article 44). Many, perhaps most eastern European and Balkan states (along with many other countries in the world, including the Euro-Atlantic democracies) can be charged with a credibility gap between rights proclaimed under the constitution and what is really practised or observed.[39] However in the case of the RS—a statelet founded on expulsions of hundreds of thousands of Muslims and tens of thousands of Croats, where the first of hundreds of mosques (including some priceless historical monuments) razed during the war was rebuilt only in 2000—the credibility gap is particularly breathtaking. The origins of Republika Srpska do peep through at several points however, for example in Article 6 of the basic provisions, which states that 'the citizen of the Republic... may not be extradited', and Article 46, which proclaims that all citizens are 'bound... to take part in elimination of general danger'.

The RS's social-welfare provisions are no less impressive. It is laid down that 'children, pregnant women and elderly persons shall be entitled to health care financed out of public funds' (Art. 37), that 'everyone shall have the right to work and to freedom of work' (Art. 39), that 'employed persons shall be entitled to limited working hours, daily and weekly rest and annual holiday and

---

[39] See Julie Mostov's compelling article, 'Democracy and the Politics of National Identity', *Studies in East European Thought* 46: 1, 2 (1994), in which she examines the hiatus between constitutional principles regarding universal citizen rights and actual practices and realities in post-1990 Croatia, post-1989 Romania and post-1991 Macedonia. Indeed, practically all the successor states and statelets of former Yugoslavia are 'ethnic democracies' in Smooha and Hanf's sense of the term, systematically biased in practice in favour of one collective identity group (almost invariably the 'majority' nation) and against other, minority communities. See Sammy Smooha and Theodor Hanf, 'The Diverse Modes of Conflict Regulation in Deeply Divided Societies', *International Journal of Comparative Sociology* 33: 1, 2 (1992), and Yoav Peled, 'Ethnic Democracy and the Legal Construction of Citizenship: Arab Citizens of the Jewish State', *American Political Science Review* 86: 2 (1992).

leave with pay' (Art. 40), and that 'the Republic shall guarantee to citizens a minimum of social security and shall provide for functioning of public services' (Art. 61). These optimistic clauses are directly inherited from the elaborate welfare system of the socialist era.[40] The social reality of the RS is that unemployment is usually estimated at 60% and as much as 90% of the population is said to live in poverty while the 'State' which promises to provide such extensive benefits is literally bankrupt. In early 2001, the incoming government of Mladen Ivanic claimed that the previous administration headed by Milorad Dodik had left the equivalent of 1.5 million DM in the state exchequer, while the backlog of salaries and pensions due to various categories of state employees and the elderly amounted to 300 million DM. Those familiar with the mean streets of RS town-centres, where derelict, boarded-up façades overlook scores of pauperized citizens trying to sell everything from smuggled cigarettes to family heirlooms, will not find this hard to believe.

In keeping with one important aspect of Serbian political tradition, the RS's governmental structure is built on a model of parliamentary supremacy. The 'State government in the Republic' is 'organized according to the principle of separation of powers'(Article 69), in which 'the constitutional and legislative powers shall be exercised by the National Assembly'. The NA has 83 directly elected members, with provision being made to ensure that all the RS's municipalities are represented. The parliament is elected for a four-year term, although in the first five years after Dayton no parliament lasted that long because of instability caused by factionalism in RS party politics. The NA operates by majority vote, and has a president (speaker) as well as two vice-presidents (deputy speakers). The RS's legislature is unicameral for practical purposes; however, in addition to the directly elected National Assembly there is an upper house-type 'advisory body', the Senate, composed of 55 'distinguished persons from public, scientific and cultural life' appointed by the RS president(Art. 89).

The executive power is vested in the Government', which consists of a prime minister, deputy prime minister and about eighteen other ministers assigned various portfolios. The members of the Government may, but need not be, legislators elected to the

---

[40] For an overview of that system, see Woodward, *Balkan Tragedy*, pp. 41-5.

NA (in practice, most are not). Both the prime minister and his cabinet need to be confirmed by majority vote in the NA, and they are 'responsible to the National Assembly' (Art. 94). The Government can be unseated by a majority vote of no-confidence in the NA, and such a no-confidence motion can be tabled in the house by a minimum of twenty deputies. Proposals for amendments to the RS constitution may be moved by the president of the RS, by the Government collectively, or on the initiative of at least thirty NA legislators. Such proposals need a majority in the NA in order to be passed (Article 132).

(The role of the president of the RS in this scheme of parliamentary supremacy and cabinet government is mostly, though not wholly, of a symbolic and titular nature. According to the constitution, 'the Republic is represented and its national unity symbolized by the President of the Republic'. Candidates for president and vice-president run together for election on the same ticket (for major contenders, usually a party ticket), much on the lines of the United States, and are elected simultaneously by popular vote for a five-year term. No individual may serve as president or vice-president for more than two consecutive terms. The president, assisted in his duties by his vice-president, is obliged to 'promulgate laws by decree within seven days of their adoption by the National Assembly' (Article 80). He may within that time-frame request the legislature to reconsider its decision, but if the law in question is passed again by the NA, he has no option but to promulgate it. However, the president has certain responsibilities which, although they may appear routine at first glance, can assume political significance. For example, he is supposed to 'propose to the National Assembly a candidate for Prime Minister' (Article 80), which can only then vote on the matter. The man narrowly elected as RS president in the autumn of 1998, Nikola Poplasen, a leader of the ultra-nationalist Serbian Radical Party (banned from running in elections and holding public office by the international high representative's decree in October 1999), refused to thus nominate the international community's favoured candidate, Milorad Dodik, for the post of prime minister. He paid for his obduracy when the high representative summarily dismissed him for 'obstructionism' after several tense months, in March 1999. The president also has certain powers that may be exercised in exceptional circumstances. For instance, 'if he assesses that there has been a crisis in the work of the Government, the President of the Republic may, at the initiative of at least twenty Assembly representatives and after obtaining the opinion of the President of the National Assembly and the Prime Minister, demand that the Prime Minister resign. Should the Prime Minister refuse to resign, the President of the Republic may then dismiss him' (Article 94). The president is also responsible for proposing to the NA names of persons to be considered for judgeships on the RS's own constitutional court, including the post of president of that court. Finally, the president is vested with command authority over the Republika Srpska's military forces under Art. 106.

As for judicial powers, the RS has its very own constitutional court, comprising seven judges who serve a non-renewable eight-year term. This court is empowered to decide 'conflicts of jurisdiction between bodies of legislative, executive and judicial branch', as well as 'conflicts of jurisdiction between agencies of the Republic, city and municipality' (Article 115). The RS's own network of ordinary courts has at its apex 'the Supreme Court of the Republic' (Art. 123), whose judges enjoy life tenure (Art. 127). There is also a 'public prosecutor's office', designated as 'an independent State body' (Art. 128), whose head also holds life tenure.

Is the Republika Srpska a centralized or decentralized state? Unlike the Bosniac-Croat Federation, the other 'Entity' of BiH, the RS is not cantonized. There is thus no intermediate layer of decisionmaking and administration between the panoply of 'State' institutions and the governments of the sixty-plus RS municipalities. The municipality is supposed to 'take care of construction, maintenance and use of local infrastructure and other public facilities', and also 'take care of meeting specific needs of citizens in the areas of culture, education, health and social welfare, public information, handicrafts, tourist trade and catering services, and environment protection' (Article 102). According to Article 103, 'the city and municipality shall be entitled to revenues as established by law, and resources for administering the tasks entrusted to them'. The municipality is not an unimportant level of government in Republika Srpska. Indeed, it plays an important role in such crucial areas as minority return, since it is in charge of *administering* a host of services, including the issuance of identity documents to minority returnees. However, the municipality's role is largely limited to *implementation* and *administration*. It is by and large not a centre of autonomous *decisionmaking*, and just two of the RS constitution's 140 articles are devoted to the city and municipal levels of government. Fundamentally, the RS seems to be an heir to the tradition of centralized governance of the pre-1914 Serbian state and the interwar (1918-41) Yugoslav state. Centralization breeds great discontent on the 'peripheries'. For example, in Trebinje, a RS town in eastern Herzegovina located in the hinterland of the Croatian coastal town of Dubrovnik and less than an hour's drive from the BiH border with Montenegro, local officials chafe at the apathy and neglect they claim their town and its region are shown by 'Banja Luka', the seat of parliament and government located hundreds of kilometres away in the Bosnian Krajina.[41] According to a United Nations Mission in Bosnia & Herzegovina (UNMiBH) report in 2000 on prospects of policing reform in the Trebinje police district (which includes six stations in eastern Herzegovina—Ljubinje, Trebinje, Bileca, Gacko, Nevesinje and Berkovici), a major obstacle to such reform in the region is that 'the RS Ministry of Interior [based in Banja Luka]... is so centralized as to make the [Trebinje district] police chief unaccountable for any action... and implementation of law enforcement.'[42]

For all its bloated posturing, the RS does qualify as a 'state within a state' in Bosnia & Herzegovina. It has its own radio and television broadcasting network (RTRS), as well as a 'National Bank' (Art. 98) whose precise role is unclear given the precarious financial situation of the RS. Ultimately, the RS's future—it contains perhaps 1.25 million people in all—is contingent on the systematic construction of formal ties with the FRY (be that Serbia-Montenegro or just Serbia), especially in the trade/economy and military/security domains. That may explain the rapturous welcome given to FRY president Vojislav Kostunica by thousands of Banja Luka citizens when he arrived in the city from Belgrade to

[41] Author's personal observations, August 1998.

[42] 'Six-Month Strategy Paper on Police Reform in the Mostar Region', UNMiBH, Mostar, August 2000, p. 37. UNMiBH and its subsidiary, the International Police Task Force (IPTF) are responsible for training, certifying, monitoring and reforming police forces in post-war Bosnia.

sign the framework agreement on special relations between the RS and the FRY in March 2001. The RS's proto-state, semi-sovereign status is sufficient to make BiH the world's most decentralized state, even without the multilayered, byzantine structure of the state's other unit—the Bosniac-Croat Federation—to which I now turn.

The Bosniac-Croat Federation. In accordance with the Dayton formula, the FBiH and the RS divide the land area of Bosnia & Herzegovina on an approximate 51:49 basis (although after the designation of the Posavina town of Brcko as a separate, neutral District since 1999, that proportion may be closer to 52:48). However, the RS has a disproportionate share of the more rural, less populous districts of the country, especially in eastern Herzegovina and eastern Bosnia. In 1992, 63% of BiH's people— 2.8 million out of 4.4 million—lived in areas that correspond to the territory of the Bosniac-Croat Federation.[*] The Federation has four of Bosnia's five largest towns—Sarajevo, Tuzla and Zenica, which are predominantly Muslim, and Mostar, which is partitioned into Muslim-controlled and Croat-controlled zones in a surreal microcosm of the reality of the 'Federation', and of the state of BiH as a whole. The Bosniac-Croat Federation was midwifed by the United States government in Washington, DC in March 1994, in order to end bitter Muslim-Croat hostilities and lay the foundation for a working military collaboration that could turn the tide of the war against the Serbs. It was reconfirmed in course of the Dayton negotiations on November 10, 1995, following intense pressure on the government of Croatia and Bosnian Muslim SDA leaders by American and German intermediaries.[44]

The constitution of the FBiH[45] was formally adopted in June 1994, a mere three months after American intervention stopped heavy fighting between Croats and Muslims in the Mostar region

---

[43] Cited in Bozo Ljubic, Boris Hrabac and Zoran Rebac, 'Reform of Health Insurance in the Federation of Bosnia & Herzegovina', *Croatian Medical Journal* 40: 2 (1999), p. 160.

[44] Silber and Little, *The Death of Yugoslavia*, p. 370.

[45] 'Constitution of the Federation of Bosnia and Herzegovina', mimeo, 2000. Consolidated translation with amendments indicated, obtained by the author from OHR legal department, Sarajevo.

and central Bosnia. It was subsequently amended in June 1996 and May 1997. 'Wishing to contribute to peace promotion', it begins with the usual pious platitudes about 'full national equality, democratic relations and the highest standards of human rights and freedoms' (preamble). It notes that the FBiH is 'a constitutive part of the sovereign state of Bosnia & Herzegovina', and 'one of two entities composing' that state, thus enjoying 'all power, competence and responsibilities' not specifically assigned to the common-state institutions of BiH. 'Bosniacs and Croats' alone have the status of 'constituent peoples' of the Federation, although unspecified 'Others' who are citizens are also mentioned (preamble, Article 1 of the section on 'Establishment of the Federation'). 'The Bosniac [?] language and the Croatian language' are designated as 'official languages of the Federation', and the Latin alphabet is the official script (Article 6, Establishment of the Federation). The Federation has its own flag and other symbols. The constitution's elaborate provisions on rights guarantee a range of fundamental freedoms, including the right of return for victims of 'ethnic cleansing' (Article 4 of the section on 'Human Rights'), a term that does not appear in the BiH state constitution. The constitution provides for 'three Ombudsmen, one Bosniac, one Croat and one Other... appointed by the Federation Legislature' with wide powers of oversight to 'protect human dignity, rights and liberties' of Federation citizens, and a 'human rights court' is also built into the Federation's judicial system, with three judges, one Bosniac, one Croat and one other. Article 5 of the section on Human Rights and Fundamental Freedoms states that 'all citizens of the Federation of Bosnia & Herzegovina, according to the Constitution of Bosnia & Herzegovina are citizens of Bosnia & Herzegovina and, according to the citizenship conditions prescribed by the Constitution of Bosnia & Herzegovina have the right to hold citizenship of another state'. This clause is transparently intended to reassure Croats in the FBiH that they are entitled to hold dual citizenship with the Republic of Croatia.

The fact that the Federation is granted all residual powers not expressly assigned to BiH state institutions suggests that at the theoretical level, the FBiH is a genuinely autonomous Entity of Bosnia & Herzegovina. However, the internal structure of the Federation is itself radically decentralized. This internal devolution was essential to secure even grudging Croat acquiescence to the Federation idea. The FBiH is therefore 'composed of federal units with equal rights and responsibilities', and these federating units are the 'Cantons'—ten in all, five predominantly Bosniac, three predominantly Croat, and two with mixed populations—that make up its territory (Articles 1 and 2, Establishment of the Federation). It is stipulated that 'the Cantons shall be named solely after the cities which are the seats of the respective Cantonal governments or after regional geographic features'. This is an obvious prohibition on names with national and nationalist connotations to either Bosniacs or Croats. This particular stricture is reminiscent of a dictatorial constitution of interwar Yugoslavia (promulgated in 1931), which divided the unitary interwar state into nine *banovine* (administrative regions, literally 'governorates') named after rivers and other geographical features in an effort to banish names of Serbian or Croatian national(ist) connotation.[46] FBiH cantons thus have neutral names such as 'Una-Sana', 'Zenica-Doboj' and 'Herzegovina-Neretva'.

How are powers divided between the federal and cantonal levels of government? The Federation is given exclusive responsibility for defence, specifically the formation of 'a joint command of all military forces' on its territory; making economic policy (whatever that means) at the federal level; regulating finances and fiscal policy at federal level; combating terrorism, inter-cantonal crimes, drug trafficking and other forms of organized crime; making energy policy; allocating electronic frequencies for radio and television broadcasting outlets; and financing the above activities through 'taxation, borrowing or other means' (Article 1 of the section on 'Division of Responsibilities Between the Federation Government and the Cantons'). This arguably adds up to an even more limited central government for the Bosniac-Croat Federation than that provided by the BiH constitution for the state as a whole, excepting for the clause relating to common defence. Six years after the end of the war in BiH and seven and a half years after the end of the Muslim-Croat armed conflict, the Federation's armed forces are formally integrated, with a standard uniform for personnel and insignia reflecting the national symbols of both Croats and Bosniacs. In practice, however, erstwhile HVO

[46] See Joseph Rothschild, *East-Central Europe between the Two World Wars*, Seattle, WA, 1974, pp. 201-81 on interwar Yugoslavia.

and Armija BiH units exist more or less separately within this nominally unified force, and despite the appearance of a 'joint command', there is little scope for illusions.

The FBiH constitution elaborates a fairly extensive *concurrent list* of powers for the federal and cantonal tiers of governance. The spheres of *shared responsibility* include: human rights, public health, environmental policy, communications and transport infrastructure, tourism, and social welfare policy. It is stated that these responsibilities 'may be exercised jointly or separately, or by the Cantons as coordinated by the Federation Government... Accordingly, the Cantons and the Federation Government shall consult one another on an ongoing basis with regard to these responsibilities'. In this process the 'the Federation shall act with respect for Cantonal prerogatives, the diverse situations of the Cantons and the need for flexibility', while 'the Cantons shall act with respect for inter-Cantonal comity [and] for coordinated approaches to inter-Cantonal matters' (Articles 2 and 3, Division of Responsibilities section). This complicated injunction could be a recipe for confusion, but in practice the cantons exercise most of the powers included on the concurrent list. In the sphere of health care, for example, 'it has been adopted after lengthy discussions that health care will be organized in the cantons but coordinated by the federal government. This intermediary option corresponds to the actual situation in the Federation and provides prospects for establishing a decentralized health care system'.[47] The references to the 'actual situation' that prevails as well as to 'lengthy discussions' on the matter are telling—in the Croat-controlled 40% of the Federation, it is normally difficult, often impossible, to bring resources and facilities under the control of central Federation institutions, which is what Bosniacs usually prefer and push for.

All residual powers are vested, in this framework of cascading federalism, in the cantonal regimes and their institutions. The cantons have responsibility for 'establishing and controlling police forces, which shall have identical Federation uniforms with Cantonal insignia'; making education policy, including decisions concerning the regulation and provision of education; making and

---

[47] Ljubic, Hrabac and Rebac, 'Reform of Health Insurance in the Federation of Bosnia and Herzegovina', p. 160.

conducting cultural policy; making housing policy, including decisions concerning the regulation and provision of housing; making policy concerning the regulation and provision of public services; regulating local land use; regulating and promoting local business and charities; regulating and ensuring availability of local energy production facilities; making policy concerning radio and television facilities, including decisions concerning regulation and provision thereof; implementing social welfare policy and providing social welfare services; developing tourism resources; and financing all of the above through 'taxation, borrowing or other means' (Article 4, Division of Responsibilities). The canton is clearly the decisive layer in this multi-tiered framework of government. It not only has exclusive jurisdiction and competence—making of decisions as well as implementation/administration of policy—in such important fields as policing, education, public housing, 'culture', information and broadcasting, land use, regulation of business and so on. Authorities at the cantonal level also *effectively* control, for the most part, matters falling under the concurrent list such as social welfare, health and tourism, and indeed, even subjects where policy formulation is supposedly the prerogative of the federal level, as in the field of energy resources (this is important because Bosnia and the FBiH have significant hydroelectric power resources).

The primacy of the canton means that the third level of government, the municipality, has a relatively restricted and weak role in the FBiH. The municipality—there are over eighty, of widely varying populations, on Federation territory[48]—is, rather vaguely, supposed to 'exercise self-rule on local matters'. Each municipality has a Statute which 'shall be consistent with this [Federation] constitution, the constitution of its Canton, and conform to any relevant Cantonal legislation'. There is a municipal governing council, elected directly for a two-year term, on which each party is 'allocated a number of seats proportional to its percentage of the total valid votes'. The council in turn elects the municipal execu-

---

[48] Until 1992, BiH had only about 110 municipal districts. In the post-war phase, the number has risen to about 145 (over 60 in RS and more than 80 in the Federation), mainly because many pre-war municipalities are now divided into separate parts by the IEBL. In addition, within the Federation, six municipalities have now been carved out of the pre-war Municipality of Mostar, and so on.

tive. The council's powers include the right 'to levy taxes and otherwise secure necessary financing' for its activities, but only 'insofar as not provided by the Canton or the Federation Government'. The municipality has its own judicial organs, but 'municipal courts [are] established and funded by the Cantonal government', and 'judges of municipal courts [are] appointed by the President of the highest Cantonal court after consultation with the Municipal Executive'. Generally speaking, the role and powers of the municipal tier of government are overshadowed by the looming presence of the cantonal tier (Articles 1-7 of the section on 'Municipality Governments')—with two exceptions.

The first exception occurs when a number of municipalities are consolidated to form an overarching 'City Authority', as in the case of Sarajevo and Mostar. The City then has its own statute, council (with equal number of councillors drawn from each of the constituent municipalities) and executive (a mayor) which operate parallel to the municipality and canton regimes. The City is then responsible for maintaining joint infrastructure (of the constituent municipalities), for urban planning and public transport. Even then, however, the City remains subordinate to the canton. Its 'finances and tax policy' have to be 'in accordance with Federal and Cantonal legislation', and in the specific case of the City of Sarajevo 'the Constitution of Sarajevo Canton shall regulate which municipalities shall fall within the City of Sarajevo' (sections on 'City Authorities' and 'Organization of Sarajevo').

The second and much more important exception occurs when the national composition of the population of a municipality is at variance with that of its canton. According to Article 2 of the general provisions on the structure of the cantonal governments, 'each Canton may delegate functions concerning education, culture, tourism, local business and charitable activities, and radio and television to a municipality or city on its territory, *and is obliged to do so if the majority of the population in the municipality or city is other than that of the canton as a whole*' (emphasis in original). This constitutional requirement extends the Federation's model of cascading devolution one step further. It is designed to cope with the specific circumstances of the Federation's only two substantially 'mixed' cantons, central Bosnia & Herzegovina-Neretva, both deeply divided along the national(ist) faultline. In central Bosnia, an overall Bosniac-majority canton, a number of municipalities exist which have predominantly Croat populations and Croats constitute between 35-40% of the canton's total population. In Herzegovina-Neretva canton, a large area surrounding the partitioned city of Mostar, Croats are in a slight majority overall and dominate the southern parts of the canton, but a number of municipalities north of Mostar have overwhelmingly Bosniac populations and Bosniacs constitute around 45% of the canton's total population. Indeed, these two cantons are given special status and regimes under the FBiH constitution in recognition of the reality of division, on which more below.

A variety of consociational mechanisms are built into the governmental structure at the federal level. The federation legislature is bicameral. The lower chamber, the House of Representatives, consists of 140 members elected for four years 'in a direct, Federation-wide election', in which 'each voter [is] eligible to cast a single, secret ballot for any registered party'. All parties that cross a threshold of 5% of total votes polled are then allocated seats in this chamber proportional to the percentage of the total vote they received.[49]

The upper chamber, the House of Peoples, is based on parity representation of Bosniacs and Croats. It has 30 Bosniac and 30 Croat members (officially called Delegates), plus a number (usually 20) of 'Other' delegates. The term is four years. The delegates are all elected from among members of canton legislatures, thus institutionalizing cantonal representation in decisionmaking at the federal centre in accordance with the classic federal formula of 'self-rule' for the federating units plus 'shared rule' at the centre,[50] the latter usually achieved via a second legislative chamber constituted by representatives of the regions.[51] The precise formula for election to the House of Peoples is complicated. It is mandated that the number of delegates a canton will send to the house will

[49] In BiH-wide local elections held in April 2000, the OSCE—which organizes, supervises and monitors elections in Bosnia—introduced an 'open list' system whereby voters could indicate preferences for individual candidates in addition to choosing a party list. No minimum threshold requirement was set for parties in these elections. The open-list system was subsequently also employed in November 2000 elections to state, entity and canton bodies.

[50] This is the definition of federation given by Daniel Elazar. See Elazar, *Exploring Federalism*, Tuscaloosa, AL, 1987.

[51] See Lijphart, *Democracies*, pp. 25-6.

depend on the population of the canton relative to other cantons (the cantons' population size vary considerably). 'Within that number, the percentage of Bosniac, Croat and Other Delegates of a Canton shall be as close as possible to the percentage of Bosniac, Croat and Other legislators in the Canton. However, there shall be at least one Bosniac, one Croat and one Other Delegate from each Canton that has at least one such member in its Legislature' (Article 8 of the sub-section on 'The Federation Legislature' of the section titled 'Structure of the Federation Government'). Moreover, it is provided that 'Bosniac, Croat and Other Delegates from each Canton' shall be elected by the cantonal legislators belonging to the *respective groups.* Just before the November 2000 elections in Bosnia, a change in electoral rules sponsored by the OSCE and OHR sought to replace this intra-ethnic selection process of delegates with a cross-ethnic process. In practical terms, this would mean that with Bosniac cantonal legislators playing a part in selecting Croat delegates to the House of Peoples, the number of Croat delegates owing allegiance to the nationalist HDZ would decline, to the likely benefit of the liberally inclined SDP, which has the support of a small minority of BiH Croats. The HDZ claimed that such a change was unconstitutional and illegal, as well as unfair, since the party has demonstrated over-whelming support among the BiH Croat electorate,[52] and made the issue its pretext for withdrawing entirely from the Federation in March 2001.

Each chamber of this bicameral parliament elects a chairman (speaker) and deputy chairman (deputy speaker) from among its members; in both houses, if the chair is a Bosniac the deputy must be Croat, and vice versa. (Legislation normally requires the approval of a simple majority in *both* chambers. However, 'decisions that concern the vital interest of [either of] the constituent peoples shall require', in addition to an overall majority in the

[52] In elections to state, entity and canton institutions held in November 2000, the HDZ polled absolute majorities of the popular vote in two cantons: western Herzegovina (71%) and western Bosnia (55%). It fell marginally short of winning an outright majority in the ethnically polarized Herzegovina-Neretva canton (49%), and emerged as the single largest party in central Bosnia canton (31%), followed by the Muslim SDA with 26%. In tiny Posavina canton, it polled 47%, followed by the NHI, a minor breakaway group of the HDZ, which got 17%. In local elections conducted in April 2000, the HDZ won outright control of more than 25 predominantly Croat municipalities.

House of Peoples, 'a majority of the Bosniac delegates and a majority of the Croat delegates'. No substantive criteria for determining when a national-collective 'vital interest' might be at stake are specified, although at various other points in the constitution it is mentioned that concurrent majorities among the Bosniac and Croat caucuses in the House of Peoples are required in order to pass amendments to the FBiH constitution (in addition to a two-thirds majority in the House of Representatives), in order to elect the president and vice-president of the Federation, in order to approve shared Federation symbols, and in order to approve appointments to the joint command of the Federation military forces. In procedural terms, it is specified that 'this [concurrent majority] provision may be invoked by a majority vote of the Bosniac or Croat delegates' to the House of Peoples (Article 18, The Federation Legislature). This is suggestive of why it is considered important by the HDZ to retain a solid majority of the Croat caucus in the House of Peoples. This *concurrent majority* requirement effectively gives the HDZ a *veto right* over any federal-level legislation it does not like, so long as the party can muster a majority among the Croat delegates to the House of Peoples. If the invocation of the 'vital interest' clause by a majority of either the Bosniac or the Croat delegates is opposed by a majority of the remaining delegates, the disputed legislation is referred in the first instance to a joint commission of Bosniac and Croat delegates, and after a week, to the constitutional court of the FBiH, which is to resolve the matter 'in an expedited procedure'. However, since this court has, under the FBiH constitution, an equal number of Bosniac and Croat judges on its bench, its capacity to expeditiously resolve legislative deadlocks is far from certain.

The House of Peoples also plays a defining role in electing the president and vice-president of the Federation. Its Bosniac and Croat segments each nominate one candidate. The two separately nominated candidates are then subject to approval as a joint slate by majority vote in the House of Representatives and by majority vote in the House of Peoples, including concurrent majorities among its Bosniac and Croat delegations. Once approved, the duo rotate one-year terms as president and vice-president of the Federation over a four-year period. In addition to being the titular commander-in-chief of the Federation armed forces, the president is responsible for formally nominating the Federation government, which comprises a prime minister, a deputy prime minister and various ministers, each with a deputy minister attached. It is mandated that if the prime minister is from one constituent people (e.g. Bosniac), the deputy prime minister must be a member of the other constituent people (i.e. Croat), and vice versa. The same rule applies to all ministers and their deputy ministers. It is further guaranteed that at least one-third of the ministers will be Croats. Any 'decisions of the cabinet that concern the vital interest of [either of] the constituent peoples shall require consensus' (my emphasis), and the vital interest provision may be invoked by one-third of the ministers. When the prime minister determines that such a required consensus cannot be reached, he is to refer the dispute to either the president or vice-president—depending on which one is not from the same nationality as he is—for, very optimistically, 'a decision without delay' (Article 6 of 'The Federation Executive' subsection of the 'Structure of the Federation Government').

There is a blanket rule that all judicial organs of the Federation must have 'an equal number of Bosniac and Croat judges', while Others should 'also be appropriately represented' (Article 6 of 'The Judiciary' sub-section of the 'Structure of the Federation Government'). This rule applies to both the Constitutional Court and the Supreme Court (the highest court of appeals in the Federation, including appeals derived from canton court decisions), each of which has nine judges. The constitutional court is charged with issuing 'final and binding' decisions on inter-cantonal disputes, as well as those between a canton and the Federation government, between any city and its canton or the Federation government, between any municipality and its city, between any municipality and its canton or the Federation government, and between or within any institutions of the Federation government. The court also has the authority to decide whether any law or regulation proposed or adopted at municipal, city, cantonal or federal level is consistent with the FBiH constitution.

Each canton has its own constitution, popularly elected legislature, a cantonal 'governor' elected by the legislators, and an executive government headed by the canton's 'prime minister'. The canton legislature is unicameral, elected every four years. The number of legislators varies between twenty and thirty-five depending on the population size of the canton. The legislature is directly elected by voters who cast a single ballot for a party; all parties that cross a minimum 3% threshold are then allocated seats according to the usual proportional representation formula. An assembly chairman is then selected from among the members.

The canton Governor is elected by majority vote in the legislature, to serve a two-year term, and can be removed by a two-thirds vote in the legislature. The governor nominates the canton government, which is then confirmed by majority vote in the legislature. It is provided that the allocation of ministerships in the government 'shall reflect the [national] composition of the population [of the canton]...but provide for representation of each constituent people'. It is also mandatory that the national composition of the canton police force reflect that of the canton's population; however, it is also required that the composition of the police of each Municipality reflect the composition of the municipality's population (Articles 8 and 10 of 'The Cantonal Executive' sub-section of 'The Cantonal Governments' section). Canton courts have appellate jurisdiction over municipal courts and original jurisdiction over matters not within the competence of those courts. Judges are nominated by the governor and confirmed by majority vote in the legislature, and it is required that the composition of the bench reflect the national make-up of the canton's population. Each canton judiciary also has its own president (Article 11 of 'The Cantonal Judiciary' sub-section of 'The Cantonal Governments' section).

Special constitutional regimes are in place in the only two cantons that have substantially mixed—and deeply divided—populations (Article 12, 'The Cantonal Governments'). In central Bosnia & Herzegovina-Neretva, it is mandatory that the cantonal institutions *devolve* their powers in the fields of education, culture, radio and television, local business and tourism to the municipal governments. Decisions of the canton legislature that affect the 'vital interest' of either constituent people require *concurrent majorities* among Croat and Bosniac delegates to pass. As in the Federation parliament, this provision may be invoked by a majority vote of either the Croat or the Bosniac caucus. If a majority of the remaining delegates oppose the invocation, the dispute is referred to a joint commission of Croat and Bosniac delegates, and after a week, to the highest canton court for its opinion, which can be appealed in the constitutional court of the FBiH. The two mixed/divided cantons have a deputy governor in addition to the governor's post. As with the Federation presidency and vice-presidency, candidates for these positions are separately nominated by the Bosniac and Croat delegations in the canton legislature, then subjected to confirmation as a joint slate by majority vote in the legislature, *including* concurrent majorities among the Croat and Bosniac caucuses. The persons thus elected then alternate as Governor and Deputy Governor of the canton over a two-year period. Several additional safeguards and power-sharing mechanisms are built into the political frameworks of these two cantons. The Government (list of ministers) is nominated by the Governor, with the concurrence of his deputy, and its confirmation requires a two-thirds majority of all legislators, rather than just a simple majority as in the more homogeneous cantons. Finally, ministerships are to be equally divided between Croats and Bosniacs, with 'appropriate' representation for 'Others', and ministers and their deputy ministers should belong to different constituent peoples.

How has it all worked? In August 2000 the Mostar region's UNMiBH prepared a detailed report on progress in unifying the cantonal police, which over the summer had been 'physically' integrated to a substantial degree—i.e. 42 Bosniac officers and administrative staff had been allowed into the formerly all-Croat police building in west Mostar while 109 Croat officers and administrative staff would work in the Bosniac police headquarters in the Muslim sector of the divided city. In its assessment of prospects of a real, 'functional' unification of the divided police service, the report made the following observations on the 'political context for the integration of the Ministry of Interior' (which controls the police) in Herzegovina-Neretva canton:

> It cannot be ignored that UNMiBH is attempting to integrate the Ministry of Interior in a broad political context where the rest of the Cantonal Government remains completely divided. This state of affairs is best symbolized by the fact that when last year [1999] UNMiBH at the weekly IC Mostar press confer-

ence was condemning the lack of progress on integration of the Ministry of Interior, the same day the Cantonal Government commended the Ministry of Interior for having made huge progress in integration compared to any other unit of the Cantonal Government. With the rest of the Cantonal Government lagging far behind the Ministry of Interior and joint cantonal institutions—except now the multi-ethnic Cantonal Court and the privatization agency—more or less unfunctional, it remains to be seen how substantive or meaningful Ministry of Interior unification can be given the political environment. Many IC observers are of the opinion that in the final analysis the unification of the Ministry of Interior can only be achieved when the parallel, para-state Herceg-Bosna structures which drive the divisions are eliminated... It has been pointed out that while the Serbs have their own Entity its institutions don't function very efficiently. While the Croats do not [in the legal and constitutional sense] have their own Entity they have fully functioning entity-type institutions. In such an environment... an integrated Ministry of Interior presents a unique challenge and some feel this is necessarily an impossible goal. There is another view which claims that the Croat side of the Ministry of Interior is such an integral part of the Herceg-Bosna para-state that its integration would be *the first brick out of the wall* that divides this Canton on ethnic lines (my emphasis).[53]

The report goes on to note that 'there is hardly any relationship or cooperation between the Federation Ministry of Interior and the Canton Ministries of Interior, certainly [those] in Croat-majority areas'.[54]

The Bosniac-Croat Federation is unmistakably of the power-sharing, consensual type, as distinguished from the more common variant—majoritarian-democratic federations. From its wartime inception as a construct of elements in the United States administration, the Federation's existence has been dogged by a gap in the ways in which most Croats and most Muslims perceive their framework of enforced cohabitation. That gap in perceptions was

---

[53] 'Six-Month Strategy Paper on Police Reform in the Mostar Region', p. 23.
[54] Ibid., p. 37.

well-expressed in September 1996 by Jadranko Prlic, foreign minister of BiH from end-1996 until early 2001 and a leading HDZ
moderate who left the party in the second half of 2000: 'It is well-
known that the Croatian and Bosniac sides do not perceive the
role of the Federation identically. For us Croats the Federation is
the ultimate goal and an acceptable form of association. The
Bosniac side, however, attaches only a temporary position to the
Federation on the way towards a centralized state with their own
domination.'[55] Whether this characterization is fair to Bosniac
intentions, it captures neatly the typical Croat view of the
Federation. In the negotiations at Dayton (mediated primarily by
Michael Steiner of Germany, later deputy international high representative in Bosnia in 1996-7) which confirmed the Federation
agreement struck under American auspices in Washington in
March 1994, 'in more than a week of embittered bilateral meetings, the Bosnian government [i.e., Sarajevo-based SDA Muslim]
delegation proved hopelessly divided among itself. The Muslims
wanted the division of power to be based on... the population
[proportions], while the Croats wanted equal representation.'[56]

The Croats clearly got their way; otherwise there would have
been no federation at all, even on paper. But this uneasy compromise has meant that any attempts or proposals to rationalize the
Federation to make it more workable are interpreted by most
Croat opinion as a step toward a majoritarian federation and
Bosniac domination. This situation is readily exploitable by the
entrenched 'Herceg-Bosna' interests that run the vast, shadowy
network of parallel structures which make official Federation
institutions redundant in most of Croat-controlled Bosnia, and
which are well-financed even after reductions in Zagreb's funding
following the death of Tudjman and the fall of the HDZ in the
mother-country. Under the Dayton scheme, Bosnia is constructed as a confederation of two semi-sovereign Entities linked in a
loose union. The HDZ-BiH contends that one of those two
Entities is a marriage between two incompatible partners who are
unable to find a mutually agreeable formula for staying together,
and that it is both fair and sensible for BiH to be constituted as a

[55] Jadranko Prlic, *The Imperfect Peace*, Mostar, 1998, p. 71. His comment is from a
longer article originally published in a Croatian publication called *Hrvatski Glas*
(Croatian Voice), issued in Mostar in September 1996.
[56] Silber and Little, *The Death of Yugoslavia*, p. 370.

confederal union of three equals. The vast majority of BiH Croats clearly agree or sympathize with this view, despite the venality of many of the politicians who are its most vocal proponents. Most Serbs understand the Croats' position, as do many Muslims who are increasingly convinced that the Bosniac-Croat Federation is fated to remain a phantom rather than develop into a living reality, given the determination and mass base of Croat intransigence. The question is—where does the 'international community' stand on the matter and more importantly on the deeper dilemmas of the international state-making and democracy-building project in Bosnia that are exposed by the crisis of the Federation?

Conclusion: dilemmas of liberal internationalism

Liberal internationalism, a compound of two separate terms, is the hegemonic global ideology of the post-bipolar world. This worldview promotes the international diffusion of the 'liberal' economic and political order of the United States and other Euro-Atlantic democracies.[57] As Roland Paris has argued, it provides the framework for practically all peace-building operations conducted under international aegis in societies emerging from violent, divisive conflict in the post-Cold War era. The basic premise of liberal-internationalist interventions is that the way to a lasting peace is 'to transform war-shattered states into stable societies that resemble the industrialized market democracies of the West as closely as possible'. In the process, the wards of liberal-internationalist projects are not only 'expected to become democracies and market economies in the space of a few years—effectively completing a transformation that took several centuries in the oldest European states—further, this monumental task must take place in the fragile political circumstances of states that are just in the process of emerging from civil war.'[58] This is clearly not a feasible agenda. Moreover, as Paris points out, both democracy and capitalism involve inherently conflictual, even adversarial processes, and their implantation by international design can further

---

[57] For a review of the chequered career of the American conception of liberal internationalism in the twentieth century, especially after 1945, see Stanley Hoffmann, 'The Crisis of Liberal Internationalism', *Foreign Policy* 98 (1995).

[58] Roland Paris, 'Peace-Building and the Limits of Liberal Internationalism', *International Security* 22: 2 (1997), pp. 54-89, on pp. 63, 78.

destabilize the weak, unstable and damaged social and political frameworks of war-torn societies.

Does this mean that the liberal internationalist paradigm for stabilization is infeasible? perhaps counter-productive to the goal of fostering stability? In any event, not worth the enormous effort and expense, as in places like Bosnia? While acknowledging the problems intrinsic to liberal internationalism as a paradigm guiding action in such cases, Paris concludes, I think correctly, that it still provides a better basis for international engagement with conflict-torn societies than the alternatives—giving up on the challenge of building democracy and effectively condemning these societies to authoritarianism(s), and giving up on the challenge of building co-existence between groups and effectively sponsoring partition.[59] Rather than throw out the baby with the bathwater, Paris wants to retain the liberal-internationalist model of peace-building while seeking to minimize the disruptive, even counter-productive effects of its practical applications. In his words, 'peace-building agencies should preserve the principal goal of liberal internationalism... but rethink the way in which they pursue this goal'. 'Accepting the broad objective of liberal internationalism', he asserts, 'does not preclude criticism of the *methods* that peace-builders have employed in pursuit of that objective' (emphases mine).[60] His critique thus boils down to a set of general prescriptions about how to go about *implementation strategies*, which he calls a 'blueprint' for 'strategic liberalization'.[61]

Two of the prescriptions regarding political aspects of peace-building are noteworthy for practitioners. The first is advice to significantly delay the first post-war competitive elections, which might otherwise reinforce divisions and hardline politics produced by war. In Bosnia, the international community, stampeded by the United States, committed precisely this 'electoralist fallacy'. The second piece of constructive counsel, to design electoral systems in ways that encourage moderation within groups and alliance-building across groups, can still be usefully undertaken in Bosnia, albeit in a limited way; I discuss this topic among others in Chapter 5. The other broad recommendations have all been prac-

---

[59] Ibid., pp. 79-81.
[60] Ibid., pp. 58, 81.
[61] Ibid., pp. 58-9, 82-8.

ticed by the international intervention in Bosnia to varying, sometimes quite considerable degrees—promoting citizen groups and civil society associations (by the OSCE democratization branch), excluding 'extremists' from political participation (by HR decree), cracking down on inflammatory ethnic media (by SFOR in collaboration with civilian agencies), achieving better inter-agency coordination and strategic vision (through the OHR; the Peace Implementation Council (PIC) consisting of major Western countries and donors involved in the Bosnia intervention, which meets twice a year in a European capital to review progress; and until early 2001 the US State Department's own Dayton imple-mentation office, reporting directly to the secretary of state). Paris' final suggestion, that international organizations extend the time-frame of peace-building missions to an average of 7-9 years and plan operations according to that more flexible timetable is already a *fait accompli* in Bosnia; yet there is no end in sight.

In fact, the dilemma of liberal internationalism in Bosnia goes far deeper than the relatively superficial debate over implementa-tion strategy suggests.[62] The underlying dilemma is this: exactly what kind of state is international intervention trying to construct in post-war Bosnia? The Dayton accord, in the manner of all com-promises achieved by grand diplomacy, is permissive of quite dif-ferent interpretations of this basic question.

The post-Dayton intervention is clearly trying to build a decentralized, federal state in BiH. However, as Brendan O'Leary has argued, there are two very distinct types of federalist philoso-phies.[63] The first is a 'national[izing] or mono-national' variant of federalism, of which O'Leary cites 'the USA... as the paradigmat-ic case'. 'National federalism', he says quoting Samuel Beer,[64] 'was part and parcel of American nation-building'. Other historical

---

[62] Some participants in this occasionally interesting but fundamentally limited debate are activist think-tanks given to compiling extensive wish-lists of what the international community should do in Bosnia 'to get it right, now'; see for example the publications of the International Crisis Group. The language quot-ed is from the ICG report 'Bosnia's November Elections: Dayton Stumbles', Sarajevo, December 18, 2000, p. 22.

[63] Brendan O'Leary, 'An Iron Law of Nationalism and Federation?', text of the fifth Ernest Gellner Memorial Lecture delivered at the London School of Economics, May 24, 2000, pp. 10-11.

[64] Samuel Beer, *To Make a Nation: The Rediscovery of American Federalism*, Cambridge, MA, 1993.

examples of nationalizing or mono-national federalism include
the Netherlands, the German-speaking Swiss lands, and what
became the second German Reich. In all instances, the aim was
'to make the sovereign polity congruent with one national culture'. National federalists have frequently viewed 'federation as a
stepping stone towards a more centralized, unitary state'.

Multi-ethnic or multi-national federalism is based on a very
different conception of the meaning and goal of the federal idea.
This version of federalism 'seeks to express, institutionalize and
protect at least two national or ethnic cultures, often on a permanent basis. Any greater union or homogenization, if envisaged at
all, is postponed for the future. It explicitly rejects the strongly
integrationist and/or assimilationist objectives of national federalism. It believes that dual or multiple national loyalties are possible,
and indeed desirable'. In various forms and incarnations, the concept of multinational federalism has played a part in the making of
post-colonial federations in Canada, the Caribbean, Nigeria,
South Africa, India, and Malaysia, and of post-communist federations in the Russian Federation, Ethiopia and rump Yugoslavia.
'The recent democratic reconstructions of Spain and Belgium' are
also influenced by the notion of multinational federalism, and an
even more contemporary, ongoing example of the prospective
development of a multinational federation is the confederation
called the European Union.

These very different conceptions of federalism have become
the crux of the major divide in post-Dayton Bosnia. Generalizing
somewhat, Bosniacs typically favour the first model of federative
association, Serbs and Croats the second. Where does the 'international community' stand? The best answer probably is that ambiguity and confusion prevails, especially since 'Dayton' can be read,
and interpreted, in very different ways. Some recent statements of
Bosnia's international supervisors seem to lean towards the first
conception, however. On November 29, 1999, the high representative and the head of the OSCE mission in Bosnia (an Austrian
and an American, respectively) issued a joint statement justifying
the high representative's decision to dismiss 22 popularly elected
Bosnian public officials—nine Serbs, seven Muslims and six
Croats—from their posts as city mayors, municipal mayors, and
cantonal officials. The statements accused the errant officials—

many with an unambiguous record of corrupt and/or sectarian behaviour—of 'consistently refusing to take ownership of the laws of their *own nation*' and justified their removal on the ground that 'serious and persistent obstruction of the Dayton/Paris peace accords has no place in the politics of *this nation*' (emphases added).[65] The crucial questions here are: *which nation, whose,* and *on what terms?* Judging by their choice of terminology, Bosnia's top international officials seem either oblivious or insensitive to these very important and basic questions (aside from the consideration that the Bosnian multinational state's 'laws' are mostly crafted and/or imposed by foreigners). Speaking at the inauguration of a postgraduate course in European studies at the University of Banja Luka in April 2000, the high representative justifiably decried 'three parallel education systems, with parallel curricula and parallel sets of textbooks' that operate in BiH. He then went on to express outrage about some Bosnian schoolchildren 'not [being] taught about BiH, its history, geography, literature etc., but about neighbouring countries instead!'[66]

Both models of federalism described above are compatible with liberal-internationalist principles. However, in a longer-term perspective, the second conception is more suitable for Bosnia. There are three reasons why.

First, the explicitly multinational variant of federalism is more in tune with the realities of a country and region where historical context and institutional precedent combine to make national-collective identities an inescapable feature of the political landscape. Bosnia (and former Yugoslavia as a whole) are different and specific in this regard and will remain so. This is a fact that Western liberal internationalism, premised on notions of individual autonomy and rights, is fundamentally uncomfortable with. But it is a reality that will over time need to be creatively coped with by Euro-Atlantic structures; it cannot be wished away.

Second, a *supra-state regional perspective* is vital when pondering the dilemmas of international intervention in Bosnia after Dayton. The ultimate aim of liberal-internationalist engagement

---

[65] 'Statement on the November 29 Decisions by the High Representative and the OSCE Head of Mission', Sarajevo, November 29, 1999.
[66] 'Address by High Representative Wolfgang Petritsch at the University of Banja Luka on April 19, 2000', accessed from OHR website, *http://www.ohr.int.*

with the post-Yugoslav region is (or at least, should be) the nurturing of links not just between Sarajevo, Banja Luka, and (west) Mostar, but between Sarajevo, Banja Luka, (west) Mostar, Zagreb and Belgrade. Indeed, it may be inescapable that the road between Sarajevo and Banja Luka will pass through Belgrade, while that between Sarajevo and west Mostar will pass through Zagreb. There is nothing wrong at all with some (indeed, preferably all) Bosnian schoolchildren being taught about 'neighbouring countries', *so long as they are also taught* to respect fellow-Bosnians of other faiths and nationalities.

Finally, in Robert Dahl's words, the only possible institutional framework for any state with a serious internal legitimacy problem 'may well be a complex system with several layers of democratic government, each operating with a somewhat different agenda'.[67] If so, the emphasis of the liberal-internationalist project in Bosnia should squarely be on promoting *constructive cooperation* between Bosnia's fragments—steering a skilful course between the temptations of coercive integration and sectarian-chauvinist partition—as a subset of a broader policy of promoting constructive cooperation and renewed links among the fragments of the former Yugoslavia as a whole, including Bosnia. *Good neighbourly relations* between the national groups within Bosnia and throughout former Yugoslavia is both feasible and desirable, and should be the ultimate objective of all international policy vis-à-vis the region. That may in the end leave the *least divisive* and *most usable* legacy for Bosnians themselves, in collaboration with other former Yugoslavs, to build on for the future.

---

[67] Robert Dahl, *Democracy, Liberty and Equality*, Oslo, 1986, pp. 124-5.

3

MOSTAR, 1994-2001

NATIONALIST PARTITION AND INTERNATIONAL INTERVENTION IN A BOSNIAN TOWN

'Bosnia is a wonderful country, fascinating, with nothing ordinary in the habitat or people... Undoubtedly are Bosnians rich in hidden moral values, rarely found... But, you see, there is one thing the people of Bosnia must realize and never lose sight of—Bosnia is a country of hatred and fear... Yes, Bosnia is a country of hatred. That is Bosnia. And by a strange contrast, which in fact isn't so strange, it can also be said that there are few countries with such elevated strength of character, so much tenderness and loving passion, such depth of feeling, loyalty and unshakeable devotion, or with such a thirst for justice... Perhaps your greatest misfortune is precisely that you do not suspect just how much hatred there is in your loves and passions, traditions and pieties... You Bosnians have, for the most part, got used to keeping all the strength of your hatred for that which is closest to you. Your holy of holies is, as a rule, three hundred rivers and mountains away, but the objects of your revulsion and hatred are right beside you—in the same town, often on the other side of your courtyard wall. And you love your homeland, you passionately love it, but in three... different ways which are mutually exclusive, which often come to blows, and hate each other to death.'—*Ivo Andric*[1]

Emina Catic was twenty-five, and a survivor of the war in Mostar, the historic centre of Herzegovina. She was an orphan. Her father died in 1992, one of many citizens killed in April and May of that year by a merciless artillery and tank bombardment of Mostar conducted by all-Serb units of the Yugoslav People's Army (JNA) positioned on heights overlooking the town. JNA units in the area were operating in conjunction with a section of local Serbs, who had erected barricades on some roads leading into and out of the town as part of a makeshift insurrection against BiH's departure

1 From 'A Letter from 1920', a short story by Andric. The story is included in Ivo Andric, *The Damned Yard and Other Stories* (ed. and trans. Celia Hawkesworth), Belgrade, 2000, on pp. 107-119.

from federal Yugoslavia. The shelling heavily damaged the town. But Emina and her mother survived the carnage, and the Serbs were driven from their commanding heights by a joint Croat-Muslim counter-offensive in June, 1992.

A year later Mostar was at war again. This time it was a vicious struggle for control of the town between the erstwhile allies. The Croatian Defence Council (HVO), heavily reinforced by soldiers and heavy weaponry originating in Croatia, had the upper hand in this battle against the rag-tag and under-equipped Muslims fighting in the Army of Bosnia-Herzegovina (Armija BiH). The HVO used its heavier guns to mercilessly pound the Muslim-held sector on the east bank of the Neretva, where thousands of trapped civilians had holed up along with Muslim fighters (Mostar is built on both banks of this emerald-green river which flows through central and southern BiH into the Adriatic). The HVO and its patrons did not succeed in their intention of driving out this historic Ottoman town's Muslim population and making Mostar the all-Croat capital of an all-Croat statelet ('Herceg-Bosna') in BiH. The Muslims clung on tenaciously in the rubble of east Mostar and a slice of the west bank which constituted the frontline with the Croats, where the Armija's men successfully defended their positions amidst shattered buildings in neat streets turned into free-fire zones. But in the single most notorious act of vandalism of the post-Yugoslav wars, the HVO targeted and destroyed, in November 1993, the symbol of Mostar, the graceful arched footbridge across the Neretva constructed in 1566 by an architect called Hajrudin on the orders of Ottoman emperor Suleiman the Magnificent. And around the same time HVO fire killed—along with numerous other civilians trapped in the inferno of east Mostar—Emina Catic's widowed mother.

However tragic, this is a fairly typical Bosnian (in this case, strictly speaking Herzegovinian) story. Survivors have to do their best to rebuild their lives from the ruins and move on, and that is what Emina was trying to do. On a sultry Saturday evening in July 1998, she was sitting in an outdoor café on a packed street on the east bank, enjoying the weather and the evening ritual of strolling, people-watching and socializing like hundreds of other Mostarians. Suddenly, the other Mostar—the large Croat zone on the west bank—erupted in a cacophony of honking horns, slo-

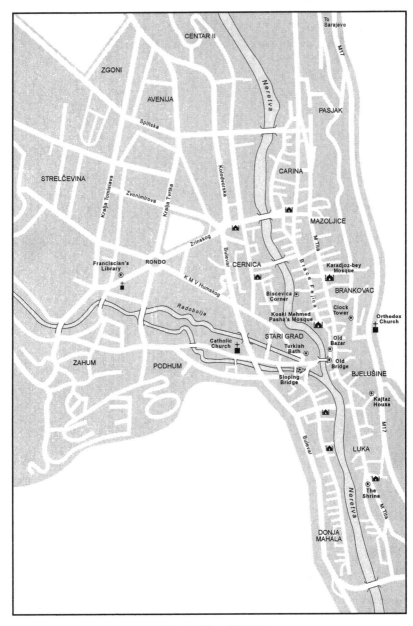

Map 4: City of Mostar

gan-shouting, and celebratory gunfire. The football World Cup was in progress, and Croatia, playing in the quarter-finals that evening against Germany, had just won the game 3-0 against all expectations. Several thousand rounds were fired on the streets of west Mostar that evening. One of them hit Emina Catic in the neck. She toppled over and died instantly. Three other east Mostar civilians were hurt that evening by the gunfire, whether by design or accident. One of the injured, an elderly man, was hit in the head and lapsed into coma.

Despite the shocking circumstances, Emina's death did not cause more than a minor stir in Mostar. The next day a grenade was hurled, in apparent retaliation, from a car at a west Mostar bar known to be frequented by Croat extremists, but failed to explode. The funeral did not turn into a demonstration that would ratchet up tension in a divided town, as some international officials based in Mostar feared in the immediate aftermath of the incident. It passed off quietly, attended by only a few dozen relatives, neighbours and friends. Emina's grave is just another among hundreds—mostly of young people—in Mostar's cemeteries. The only unusual feature on her tombstone is the date—1998 rather than 1992 or 1993.

Emina Catic's life ended on that summer night. But for those who continued to live, life in post-war Mostar is almost without exception a cruel experience, all the more disconcerting because of its contrast with an almost idyllic pre-war period, when Mostar was a town renowned for culture and cosmopolitanism throughout Yugoslavia and the Balkans. In March 1998, Aida V., a stunningly attractive doctor in her mid-thirties, returned to Mostar from a prosperous wartime exile in South Africa, only to find the apartheid system whose dismantling she had just witnessed enjoying a robust lease of life, in a Balkan variant, in her hometown. Born into one of Mostar's most prominent old families, Aida had lived until the war in the family home, a handsome mansion-type residence right in the centre of town on a tree-lined residential street. On a refreshingly cool, breezy evening after an almost unbearably hot summer day, she took me to see the house where she had grown up. We picked through weeds in what had once obviously been a large garden, and then I was looking at a ghostly, gutted shell of a house. Aida's house was located on a street just

off the Boulevard, Mostar's main north–south artery running parallel to the Neretva on the western bank, very close to one of the
town's landmark Austro-Hungarian-era buildings, the elite high
school (gymnasium) which has educated generations of
Mostarians in the twentieth century. The Boulevard became the
frontline in 1993. The house fell on the Croat side of that frontline. On the first night of the Muslim–Croat war in Mostar in May
1993, the house was looted, then burned. After her return, Aida
lived with her family in a cramped apartment complex pock-
marked with bullet holes overlooking the Boulevard from the
other (Bosniac) side, a few hundred feet from the remains of her
real home. She earned a meagre salary working in the emergency
department of a public health centre built with international
donor aid on the east bank (the main city hospital is a sparkling
facility on the Croat side of the Boulevard). In July 1999 she left
Bosnia to live and work in the United States.

   Until 1992 Mostar was a charming microcosm of Bosnia and
the former Yugoslavia—a captivating blend of south Slavic,
Ottoman Turkish and Mediterranean cultural traditions with one
of the most multinational population structures of any Bosnian or
Yugoslav town. Its fate during the war, and since, has symbolized
the destruction of that hybrid heritage. The post-war division of
the town into rival enclaves refracts the fate of Bosnia as a whole,
and the failure of international intervention to achieve any significant degree of 'reunification' and 'reconciliation' is symptomatic
of the difficult challenges encountered by international state-
builders and democratizers in post-war Bosnia. In the first half of
2001, (west) Mostar was once again in the eye of the storm, as the
epicentre of the most serious challenge yet to the Dayton state—
the rebellion led by the Croatian Democratic Union (HDZ-BiH)
and its allies against the Muslim-Croat federation and the international authorities supervising the peace implementation
process. The basic state-building dilemmas revealed by that revolt
are discussed in Chapter 2. All in all, Mostar is a dramatic and illuminating example of the interplay of local and international forces
shaping Bosnia's post-war transition in a context of deep division
and chronic systemic crises. Its story is told in this chapter.

The city that was

Until 1991 Mostar was by all accounts a glittering town, the jewel of the Neretva valley. Nestled in a striking natural setting amidst the stark beauty of Herzegovina's rugged mountain ranges, it was better known for beautiful women and fine cuisine than as a potential cauldron of sectarian conflict. The town has a notable literary and intellectual tradition—one of the most devastated streets in the town centre (partly reconstructed since 1999) is named after one such figure, the Serbian writer Aleksa Santic. Mostar also enjoys the distinction of being the cradle of the Serb and Muslim communitarian movements that emerged during the period of Austro-Hungarian rule in the late nineteenth and early twentieth centuries. Initially focused on issues of religious, cultural and educational rights, these movements gave rise to Bosnia's first organized political parties by the first decade of the twentieth century.[2] Mostar was one of very few places where young, educated Bosnian Muslims joined the clandestine communist movement during the interwar period.[3] During the Second World War, the town, taken over by the Ustashe, was an important centre of underground resistance activity. To this day, a square in east Mostar contains a sculptured bust of one such Partisan hero, Rifaat Frenjo, captured and executed in 1942. During that war, the Herzegovinian countryside turned into a killing field as Ustasha cadres murdered Serbs on a mass scale and Serbian Chetniks attacked Muslims in eastern Herzegovina. But 'the Serb, Croat and Muslim population of Mostar was famous for resisting the temptation of mutual loathing that gripped the rest of western and eastern Herzegovina and the Neretva valley. Mostar Croats saved Serbs, Serbs protected Muslims, and communal life revived faster in Mostar than almost anywhere else in BiH after the war.'[4]

For the next four and a half decades, Mostar was a showpiece of the Titoist ideology of 'brotherhood and unity'. The town's cosmopolitan ethos and legacy of cross-community understanding and cooperation had a natural partner in the multinational population mix. In 1991, there were 76,000 citizens of whom 34 per

---

[2] See Donia and Fine, *Bosnia and Hercegovina*, esp. pp. 101-109.
[3] Burg and Shoup, *The War in Bosnia-Herzegovina*, p. 37.
[4] Glenny, *The Fall of Yugoslavia*, p. 160.

cent were Muslim, 29 per cent Croat and 19 per cent Serb. The remaining 18 per cent chose the supranational identification of 'Yugoslav', an unusually high local proportion compared to the BiH-wide proportion of 5.5 per cent and the countrywide average of 3 per cent in that year. The whole of the Mostar municipal area, including the town's surrounding cluster of villages, had 126,000 people—35 per cent Muslim, 34 per cent Croat, 20 per cent Serb and 11 per cent Yugoslavs. The possibility of a Croat west Mostar and Muslim east Mostar was simply an unimaginable prospect. About 6,000 Croats lived among the east bank's nearly 30,000 residents. At least 15,000 Bosniacs were among the 45,000-plus on the west bank. Large minorities of Serbs were spread across both sides of the city. Indeed, every individual Mostarian was a minority in a sense, since none of the four identity categories had anywhere close to a majority, with Muslims constituting only a slender overall plurality in the town and its environs.

War and partition

By 1994 this vibrant, cosmopolitan city had become history. Mostar's fate has been determined above all by its geographical location. The town itself may have had an ethos of tolerance and coexistence. But it is at the vortex of a region where community traditions and the historical legacy are markedly different. To the east and south-east lies the arid, mountainous terrain of eastern Herzegovina, historically a redoubt of rurally based Serb traditionalism. The town closest to Mostar in this zone is Nevesinje, and it was in the Nevesinje district that an Orthodox peasant revolt against Muslim landlords originated in 1875,[5] rapidly escalating within a year into full-fledged warfare throughout eastern Herzegovina between peasant guerrillas supported by Serbia and Montenegro on the one hand and Ottoman and local Muslim forces on the other. The crisis heralded the countdown to the end of Ottoman control over Bosnia-Herzegovina. Although eastern Herzegovina as a whole is a Serb-dominated region, most of its municipal districts, including Nevesinje, Ljubinje, Gacko, Bileca and Trebinje had sizeable Muslim minority populations until

[5] Glenny, *The Balkans*, 1804-1999, pp. 103-105.

1992. By 1993 these Muslims had almost all been expelled, the mosques of the region systematically razed, and many sought shelter in Mostar, itself about to be consumed by the Croat-Muslim war. Only a trickle had returned to the eastern Herzegovina districts until 2001.

To the west, south-west and south of Mostar lies an area even less given to inter-group compromise and coexistence. The closest town immediately to the west is Siroki Brijeg, which was already 99 per cent Croat in 1992 and counts Gojko Susak, Tudjman's defence minister whose antecedents and exploits have been recounted in Chapter 2, among its most illustrious sons. Siroki Brijeg is typical of a swathe of overwhelmingly Croat-populated districts in western Herzegovina, including Citluk, Medjugorje, Ljubuski, Grude and Posusje, contiguous or close to the border with Croatia, which collectively form an arc of uncompromisingly hardline Croat nationalism. This belt extends northwards to such municipalities as Duvno (renamed Tomislavgrad in honour of a medieval Croat monarch), Livno and Prozor, with some dilution of the overwhelming extent of the Croat majority. It was this band of territory which, together with the rural, impoverished region of Lika in Croatia proper, supplied the highest concentration of recruits to the Ustasha movement and regime in the 1930s and 1940s.

To the south of Mostar, along or just off the M-17 motorway leading to another border with Croatia and the southern Dalmatian coastline, are two areas where Croat demographic predominance was not as pronounced. The municipality of Capljina had only a bare Croat majority of 54 per cent in 1991, while 28 per cent were Muslim, 14 per cent Serb and 4 per cent Yugoslav. Stolac, on the cusp of central and eastern Herzegovina, was only one-third Croat; Bosniacs comprised 45 per cent and Serbs 22 per cent. The Serbs were driven out of the towns of Stolac and Capljina in 1992, usually to seek refuge in the homes of Bosniacs being evicted from eastern Herzegovina. Within a year, the Bosniacs of Stolac and Capljina met the same fate. Proximity to Croatia, reinforced by the Tudjman regime's resolute military support for the Herceg-Bosna enterprise, gave the Croats an insuperable strategic advantage in the war for control of these areas. A small, historic town called Pocitelj, just north of Capljina on the

M-17, has sported a huge Catholic cross on top of its Ottoman-era fortress since that time, an unmistakable signal of who dominates the area where a sizeable population of Muslims once lived. Returns of displaced Serbs to the village of Tasovcici, also in the Capljina municipality, represent little more than a drop in the bucket. In Aladinici, a settlement in the Stolac municipality, one Muslim returnee has been subjected to multiple mortar attacks on his property between 1998 and 2000. In the town of Stolac, once classified as a UNESCO heritage site along with Dubrovnik, Muslim returnee families are confined to a ghetto existence on a couple of more or less derelict streets, a far cry from a proud Muslim presence in Stolac dating to the Ottoman era. Today, Stolac has the worst record of violence against returnees of any place in BiH. It is controlled by hardline Croats with a symbiotic nexus to transnational organized-crime rackets. The town sits astride a notorious smuggling route leading from Montenegro through the Serb and Croat-controlled areas of Herzegovina to Croatia and beyond.

In 1992-3 this hinterland came to Mostar. In retrospect, the writing may have been on the wall as early as December 1990, when multiparty elections were held to constitute the Mostar municipal assembly and administration. Of the 100 seats in the assembly, national(ist) parties won 64—the HDZ obtained 30, the SDS 15, and the SDA 19 mandates. The two major non-sectional parties, the reform-communist SDP and Ante Markovic's multi-national party, secured 16 and 12 seats respectively, a total of twenty-eight. Smaller liberal and ecological parties won another eight mandates. However, the strength of the non-nationalist groups was largely concentrated in the town of Mostar. The less urban areas around the town, included in the jurisdiction of the municipality of Mostar, overwhelmingly returned candidates of the national(ist) parties. Moreover, of the three national communities, only the Muslims voted in substantial numbers for supra-nationalist alternative formations, revealed by the fact that the SDA received only 19 per cent of seats in a system of proportional representation, whereas Muslims made up at least 40 per cent (counting in a likely Muslim component among declared 'Yugoslavs') in the Mostar municipal area.

In early 1992 Mate Boban, a onetime local communist party

apparatchik from Grude, a western Herzegovina town synonymous with Croat paramilitary and organized-crime networks, assumed leadership of the HDZ-BiH with Tudjman's blessings. In early May 1992 Boban met with his compatriot, SDS leader Radovan Karadzic, in the Austrian town of Graz to negotiate the terms of BiH's carve-up. They apparently failed to agree the terms of Mostar's partition. Karadzic, who was concerned that the borders of his statelet should coincide with the 'natural' boundaries demarcated by rivers—Sava in the north, Drina in the east, Neretva in the south, etc.—demanded that the entire eastern bank of Mostar should be given over to the Serbs. Boban advanced an alternative proposal under which the boundary between Croat and Serb control would be Marshal Tito Street, the main north-south arterial road in east Mostar, just parallel to the M-17 running down to the Adriatic coast. This would bring almost the whole of Mostar's urban limits, including the charming Ottoman-era Old Town, under Croat control.[6] In June, the disagreement became moot as the JNA withdrew from the immediate area of Mostar, abandoning considerable assets including a barracks and a military airport, and the Serbs ceased to be a factor in the struggle for control of the town and its outskirts. With the Serb threat neutralized, Boban and his associates could concentrate all their energy and resources on seizing exclusive control of Mostar, already designated as the future capital of the purified BiH Croat statelet of 'Herceg-Bosna'.

The Muslim-Croat war for Mostar erupted one night in the early summer of 1993, climaxing months of rapidly escalating tensions. According to a Bosniac soldier, the atmosphere in the city resembled a tinderbox in those last days of 'peace', and gunmen from both sides had already taken up positions on either side of the Boulevard in anticipation of an imminent outbreak of fighting. His position on the side of the Boulevard closer to the Neretva faced Croat positions on the other side of the wide street. That night, according to his account, Croat militiamen holed up in the gymnasium building just across the Boulevard from his position brought a 17 year-old Bosniac schoolgirl abducted from west Mostar to the school. They then apparently gang-raped her before throwing her out of a top-floor window. Several years later

[6] Silber and Little, *The Death of Yugoslavia*, p. 308.

the former Bosniac fighter recalled to me his most vivid memory of that night: the absolute stillness and silence for a few minutes after the girl's screaming ended. Then heavy firing broke out from both sides of the Boulevard.

When the firing ended ten months later with the Washington Agreement (March 1994) establishing the Muslim-Croat Federation in BiH, Mostar was unrecognizable. The frontline had cut through the town centre, with Croat and Bosniac positions usually no more than twenty to thirty feet apart, often on two sides of the same street. The buildings in the centre of town had either collapsed or been totally gutted, the streets leading off the centre pitted with the distinctive 'flower' imprints of hundreds of mortar impacts. This bleak landscape, still largely ruined years after hostilities ended, stands as a silent, eerie monument to the ferocity of the battle that raged here. According to war-crimes indictments of two Croat commanders/criminals active in the Mostar fighting, Vinko Martinovic ('Stela') and Mladen Naletilic ('Tuta'), both currently on trial at the Hague tribunal, at least a dozen detained Bosniacs were killed in the autumn of 1993 while being used as human shields by Croat units in the town-centre turned into no-man's land, along and just off the Boulevard.[7]

The Bosniacs had managed to fend off the onslaught. They controlled the east bank of town and a slice of the west bank—roughly 2.5 km. long and 1 km. deep—encompassing the west-bank neighbourhoods of Donja Mahala, Stari Grad (the Old Town, which spills over on to the eastern bank) and Cernica. But the entire Bosniac sector consisted of buildings either destroyed or heavily damaged by superior Croat firepower. Its shell-shocked citizens emerged from basements and bunkers hungry for the morsels of food provided by aid agencies and UN soldiers, with no access to water and electricity supplies. Even while recalling those months of horror and hardship, however, east Mostarians express pride that they managed to survive their ordeal, which for many included spells in Croat detention camps such as the notorious heliodrom facility near Mostar. The Muslim forces in Mostar had been practically besieged, with only one tenuous supply line running across mountain tracks to the nearest Armija base in

[7] Vjera Bogati, 'Mostar: Dressed to be Killed', *IWPR Tribunal Update* 232, July-August 2001

Jablanica, located 45 km. north in the direction of Sarajevo (the Mostar-Jablanica stretch of the M-17 road that snakes alongside the Neretva was unusable for supply purposes during the fighting because it was directly exposed to Croat guns from the mountains to one side, and less directly also to Serb artillery located some distance to the east). They had nonetheless managed to withstand an devastatingall-out assault by an enemy with an overwhelming superiority in heavier weapons and numerous unimpeded supply routes, liberally aided by units and equipment of the army of Croatia (HV).

But the Croats still retained control of most of the sprawling west bank, including the bulk of the city's residential housing stock, civic facilities and public utilities. Today, every major street in western Mostar bears an emphatically Croat name, ranging from a variety of medieval kings and dukes to more modern personalities like Ante Starcevic, Stjepan Radic and Cardinal Stepinac; some are also named after Croatian cities like Zagreb, Split and Dubrovnik.

Beyond this devastation, and the destruction of the Stari Most (Old Bridge) spanning the Neretva, other more profound changes had occurred in Mostar, altering the character of the city beyond recognition. By 1994 only a few dozen Croats remained in what had become the Bosniac-controlled zone, down from approximately 6,000 before the violence. A sizeable Croat enclave just north of town in the area of Potoci and Bijelo Polje, on the eastern bank, had been completely decimated by Bosniacs, and its inhabitants had fled to west Mostar. About 85 per cent of the 15,000-plus Bosniacs who had lived in what had become the HVO-controlled zone had either fled or been expelled, and further forced evictions occurred as late as 1996 and 1997. The hundreds of apartments vacated as a result became sources of easy profit for many HVO and HDZ officials, either rented out or sold in return for hard cash—sometimes to Croats who had lost their homes, but often to persons who simply wanted to have an apartment in Mostar. Fewer than a thousand Serbs remained in the divided city, of an urban Serb population of perhaps 20,000 in 1991-2. The remnants were either elderly persons or persons of 'mixed' birth discreet about the Serb element of their identity. The historic Orthodox church on the eastern bank, said to be the most beautiful in Bosnia-Herzegovina, had been reduced to a pile of rubble.

Apart from the expulsion of the Serbs and the reciprocal population transfers between the 'Croat' and 'Muslim' sectors of Mostar, something else had happened to Mostar's social and demographic character. The bulk of Mostar's intelligentsia and middle-class professionals fled the destroyed, divided city—and usually, destroyed, divided Bosnia—for any country that would offer them asylum and hopefully, employment. This haemorrhaging of educated, qualified people has continued in the post-war years. They have been replaced by several major wartime influxes of internal refugees (DPs). These include Muslims expelled from Serb-controlled eastern Herzegovina and Croat-controlled western, central and southern Herzegovina who flooded into the Bosniac sector of the city. Croats fleeing Muslim-controlled areas of central Bosnia, and upper Neretva valley municipalities like Jablanica and Konjic (which lie north of Mostar, towards Sarajevo) similarly arrived in west Mostar. As these seismic population movements took place, Mostar, caught in the vortex of a much wider conflict, was fundamentally, permanently transformed as a place. Today, the dominant element in east Mostar (and to a lesser degree in the western part) consists of dispossessed people, less educated and trained, typically of rural or small-town origins. This is the other fundamental sense in which Bosnia & Herzegovina came to Mostar, turning its pre-war social fabric upside down and inside out in the process.

A tenuous bridge: international intervention in partitioned Mostar, 1994-2001

Since 1994 Mostar's reunification has been regarded by the international community as a litmus-test of the viability of the Muslim-Croat Federation, and since the DPA, it has also been viewed as a measure of the development of the common state of BiH as a whole. Shortly after the US-brokered truce in March, 1994, a special, interim European Union Administration of Mostar (EUAM) was instituted to supervise the reconstruction of the battered city and the reintegration of its communities within a shared framework of government. The EUAM lasted from July

1994 to January 1997. For most of that period (until March 1996) it was headed by Hans Koschnick of Germany, formerly the social-democrat mayor of Bremen. After the end of the EUAM's mandate, its responsibilities were collectively entrusted to the regional offices of the consortium of international organizations that entered Bosnia after the Dayton peace—the UN/IPTF (police monitoring, training and reform/restructuring), the OSCE (conduct and management of elections), UNHCR and RRTF (refugee returns), SFOR (security) and OHR-South, based in Mostar, responsible for overall strategy and coordination of the civilian agencies.

The EUAM started off in Mostar literally with a big bang. During the night of September 11-12, 1994, Koschnick was having a late-night drink in the lobby-level bar area of the Hotel Ero, where the EUAM had established its headquarters. The Ero, located on the western bank of the Neretva just across the impressive Carinski Most bridge with the Bosniac east (destroyed in the war but rebuilt since), was a frontline position for Croats during the fighting and is owned and operated by hardline Croat interests. The following morning, Koschnick was to preside over the ceremonial reopening of the first foot-bridge connecting the western and eastern banks. That late-night drink saved his life, for while he was unwinding downstairs, his personal apartment on an upper floor was completely destroyed by a bazooka (anti-tank) rocket fired by unidentified persons.

During its two and a half years in Mostar, the EUAM poured 300 million DM of donor money into the reconstruction of the city. The more damaged and poorer Bosniac sector received two-thirds of that assistance, although it is smaller and less populous than the Croat zone. Since the population of Mostar in the first two years of recovery had declined to around 60,000, this aid amounted to an average of 5,000 DM per citizen. More reconstruction aid—from governments ranging from the United States to Islamic countries, and from a variety of international agencies—has come into Mostar in the years since. The results are obvious and superficially impressive. Utilities such as water, electricity, gas and telephones were restored fairly quickly, although with separate systems for the two zones. Schools and hospitals also reopened in due course, once again on a segregated basis. Most of the city's damaged houses and buildings, concentrated largely in the Bosniac zone and along the former frontline, have been or are being repaired. Every summer a conference of conservation specialists convenes for a week in Mostar's Stari Grad quarter, bringing together local and international expertise on preservation of the city's Ottoman and Austro-Hungarian architectural heritage. Café-bars, restaurants, nightclubs and chic designer stores selling clothing and jewellery proliferate across the divided city—in keeping with Mostar's pre-war reputation for fashion and style— along with the ubiquitous hairdressing salons. A well-equipped exhibition and performance centre co-sponsored by and named after Luciano Pavarotti opened in December 1997 in the heart of east Mostar, and the Bosniac slice of the west bank has an equally well-equipped computer training and Internet centre.

This reconstruction of war-damaged buildings and utilities, and the revival of a portion of the service sector however masks the painful reality that the local economy remains largely a gutted wreck, characterized by massive unemployment as in Bosnia & Herzegovina as a whole. In other words, economic reconstruction has been superficial rather than structural, and in no way provides the basis for a real recovery and a sustainable economy. Moreover, various forms of criminality and corruption permeate much of the economic and business activity that does exist, and organized-crime rackets are deeply entrenched on both sides of the divide, invariably in collusion with local political power-brokers. Indeed, the tentacles of corrupt practice extend further than one would imagine. In early 2001 Pavarotti, along with a host of other celebrity patrons, publicly denounced the British charitable NGO that had been instrumental in building the Pavarotti Centre in Mostar after it emerged that representatives of the group had accepted a large bribe from the firm that received the contract for constructing the complex in 1996. Various other financial irregularities in the operation of the UK-based NGO were also discovered; in Mostar and Bosnia, however, such practices are the norm rather than a scandalous exception.[8]

Koschnick's farewell from Mostar was almost as memorable as his welcome. During the rest of 1994 and throughout 1995, he

[8] 'Pavarotti Quits Charity in Bosnia Bribe Scandal', AFP, London, January 10, 2001

had concentrated his energies on negotiating with the principal local power-brokers—notably Safet Orucevic, the shady SDA leader of the Muslim zone and Mijo Brajkovic, the hardline HDZ strongman on the Croat side—in search of a mutually agreed formula for an Interim Statute for the City of Mostar, which the EUAM was charged with devising. By early 1996 it had been decided that the territory of the former municipality of Mostar, inclusive of the town and its outlying hinterland, would be split up into as many as six municipal districts. Three would in the Croat-controlled areas—Mostar South-West, Mostar West and Mostar South—and three in the Bosniac-controlled pockets (Stari Grad, Mostar South-East and Mostar North). The capstone of this structure of local government would be a neutral central zone in the middle of the town, to be administered by a multinational city-wide authority. This would give a joint Croat-Muslim city administration direct control of a chunk of territory in the town-centre, in a way that would balance the division of the rest of the town and the outskirts into zones of control. By early 1996, talks centred on the size and extent of this central district. The Bosniacs wanted it to be as large as possible, while the Croats, opposed to the idea itself, wanted it to be as small and token as possible. Koschnick, although aware that the final resolution would have to be a compromise between the two positions, pushed for a central zone that could provide a territorial basis for a jointly run city authority and, in time, act as a focal point for the rejuvenation of the multinational character of Mostar. On February 7 the EU supervisor issued an order delineating the structure of Mostar, including a substantial central zone. This provoked a riot by several hundred Croat protestors who attacked Koschnick's car outside the Ero and laid siege to the EUAM offices in the hotel. The German was trapped inside his car, surrounded by a hostile mob, for almost a hour and shots were fired in the fracas, until IFOR troops dispersed the rioters. Following this debacle, a EU emergency meeting called in Rome on February 18 made concessions to Croat demands, diluting the reach of the central zone.

This modified structure was incorporated in the Interim Statute document published on February 20, 1996. Koschnick understandably felt let down. In a bitter interview to an Austrian newspaper, he accused the German government's delegation at the Rome meeting of showing gross partiality towards the Mostar Croat hardliners and their patron, Tudjman's Zagreb. Indeed, 'this was the first time that a German official involved in the former Yugoslavia had been prepared to accuse his government of favouring the Croats, not just over the Serbs but over the Muslims as well'.[9] Koschnick resigned his post a month later, and the EUAM's credibility was fatally damaged by an apparent climbdown in the face of confrontational tactics of local bullies. In fact, however, the size and extent of the central zone is not insubstantial even in the modified version. It still covers a fair chunk of land in the bombed-out town-centre, on the western bank close to the Neretva, and contains a number of buildings which, if repaired and renovated, could serve as the kind of focal point Koschnick obviously envisaged. This potential has not been realized. Reconstruction of damaged buildings has proceeded piecemeal, often initiated unilaterally by one side (usually the Croats) without the concurrence of the other, or has remained stalled due to the absence of agreement. That the central zone has been more frequently a focus of contention than of cooperation between the Croat and Bosniac leaderships is a sign of the depth and intensity of the divide in Mostar. Indeed, a sizeable section of the Mostar HDZ and the Croat population remain unreconciled even to the formal reorganization of their fief, for administrative purposes, into three separate municipal districts. These elements have since 1996 advanced a notion called the 'Union of Croat Municipalities', which has no legal status yet remains in circulation. Even in 2000 I noticed various public events of a 'cultural' nature being advertised in west Mostar under the banner of the Union of Croat Municipalities.

Koschnick was eventually replaced by Sir Martin Garrod, a suave and competent Briton who found Mostar an equally frustrating proposition. His travails included being declared 'persona non grata' in Mostar by the city's HDZ Deputy Mayor Ivan Prskalo in mid-1998. Shortly before his (unconnected) departure from Mostar in autumn 1998, Garrod, supremely understated, described the situation in Mostar during an informal conversation over dinner as 'rather fragile'. Nonetheless, it was during the closing months of his term that the international community started

---

[9] Glenny, *The Fall of Yugoslavia*, p. 292.

implementing two important measures throughout BiH, which in time had a softening effect on the hard line of division running through Mostar.)

The first was the introduction of common license-plates for all BiH cars, replacing license plates carrying distinctive national(ist) symbols that instantly flagged the identity of the owners. When this was made mandatory in mid-1998, Mostar was a tense city, with few citizens crossing the former line of confrontation. For men who had fought in the war, in particular, the 'other' side was positively a no-go area. Mostar is a large small-town, and people tend to know each other, including who (allegedly) did what in the war. When the license plates were introduced, sceptics pointed out that cars could still be identified by whether they display labels of Croatian or BiH insurance companies. Yet the new license plate system played a role in significantly increasing freedom of movement between the two zones, although it took some months for the effect to become discernible. That summer, I met a young Croat whose home was in west Mostar but who had stayed in the Bosniac sector during the war because his Muslim girlfriend lived there. He had been mobilized into east Mostar forces during the fighting. As a result he was persona non grata on the Croat side and had not ventured into west Mostar even once between 1994 and 1998 for fear of being killed. Shortly after he received the new set of license plates for his car, he felt sufficiently emboldened to undertake a very quick drive through some of west Mostar's streets close to the central zone. By 2000 freedom of movement with motor vehicles was close to total in Mostar, although it remains (self-)limited for pedestrians. This may have happened in any case with the passage of time, but the license plates did serve as a catalytic factor. (The main intent, which was successful, was to increase vehicular traffic across the IEBL between the Federation and Republika Srpska, but it also helped soften *de facto* intra-Entity boundaries in the FBiH, including in Mostar.) Two automobile bridges (Carinski and Hasan Brkic) between the western and eastern banks have been functioning for several years now, and a third, the Tito bridge, is scheduled to be opened in 2001. In addition, there are several footbridges, including a pontoon structure at the point where the Stari Most once stood.

(The second step was the introduction around the same time of
the common Bosnian currency, the convertible mark (KM),
pegged 1:1 to the German mark, by the internationally run BiH
Central Bank as the sole legal tender throughout the country.)
Until 1998 three currencies were in circulation in Bosnia, including the Yugoslav dinar in the RS and the Croatian kuna in Croat-
controlled areas. In the first weeks and months after the arrival of
the common currency, I tried to pay with the new money in gro-
ceries, butchers shops, retail stores, café-bars, restaurants and hotels
in west Mostar. In some establishments this medium of payment
was refused outright, while in others people frowned, accepted
the KM and invariably returned the change in kune. That has
changed. The KM now circulates freely in west Mostar and is used
to carry out most everyday transactions. The kuna, although still
in evidence occasionally, has largely been squeezed out. A similar,
gradual process has unfolded in RS towns, where in middle to late
1998 I could not persuade even desperate vendors, hawking cigarettes on the street to survive, to accept the Bosnian mark instead
of the dinar. By 1999, that visceral hostility had begun to yield to
resigned acceptance, and by 2000 the process was all but complete.

(A large degree of freedom of movement, the creation of a single monetary space and substantial reconstruction of war-damaged infrastructure, utilities and buildings have all been enabled by
international intervention in Mostar. Unfortunately, this is where
the story of achievement ends and that of frustration and failure
begins.) After seven years of international presence and activity,
Mostar's politics remains highly polarized, and its educational system and cultural life remain segregated into two separate spheres.
An employment-providing economy by and large does not exist,
but the few plants and factories in operation 'belong' to one side
or the other (mostly to the Croats). The city continues to have
duplicate sets of almost every kind of institution and facility. These
include two different telecommunications networks, making it
necessary to carry two sets of phonecards—issued by the PTT
companies of BiH and Croatia (PTT-BiH and HPT) respectively—in order to make calls from public telephones in the two sectors. There are two public health systems as well. There is a proposal to turn the largest hospital located just off the Boulevard on
the Croat side into a shared facility with mixed staff, but as a

Bosnian Croat employee of the Federation health ministry in Sarajevo pragmatically observed to me in mid-2000, 'this will take time'. A World Bank loan worth twelve million dollars to support the construction of a modern water supply and sanitation system for the whole city was salvaged in May 2000 only after intense international effort, in the face of stiff opposition from the controlling interests in the west Mostar water company led by HDZ hardliner Mile Puljic, a pioneer of the 'Union of Croat Municipalities' concept. The first meeting of the management board of the future common enterprise, which will have joint management supervised by the anaemic city-wide administration but will still retain 'two branch units', was held after great difficulty in May 2000.[10] The superficial integration of Mostar's policing structure during 2000, after years of international effort, was dealt a severe setback by the fall-out of the HDZ-led revolt against the FBiH framework in 2001 (on that, more later). Some of the more irrational aspects of the division of Mostar have dissipated over the years. For example, 2000 is different from 1998 in that *karlovacko*, a Croatian beer, is now available along with *sarajevsko* and *lasko*, a Slovenian brand, in café-bars on the Stari Grad's cobblestoned streets (although *sarajevsko* normally cannot be found in the equally numerous café-bars on west Mostar's more modern-looking, tree-lined streets and avenues). But in most substantive senses, Mostar's society and polity remains partitioned into distinct enclaves.

(A basic factor underlying this situation is Mostar's poor record of returns by refugees and displaced persons to their homes.) Until the end of 1999 Bosniac returnees to the Croat-controlled areas numbered only in the hundreds, and even this was at least partly offset by more Bosniacs leaving or being evicted from their homes in west Mostar after the fighting stopped. Returns by displaced Croats to Bosniac-controlled areas have been even more negligible, attributable in part to pressure from HDZ extremists intent on sealing a permanent partition. In comparison, there has been a steady trickle of returns by Serbs to both parts of Mostar in the

[10] 'Decision of the Office of the Mayor of the City of Mostar on Implementation of World Bank Project of Water Supply and Sanitation for the City of Mostar', mimeo, April 11, 2000 (obtained by the author from the OHR-South, Mostar); 'The Session of the Management Board of Mostar Vodovod', OHR-S press release, Mostar, May 5, 2000.

post-war years, starting with a brave return by about 60 elderly persons to their destroyed village in Ortijes, a Croat-controlled Mostar suburb close to the city airport (reopened under international auspices in July 1998 and served by Austrian Airlines among other carriers) in the summer of 1998. Serbs are a more or less marginalized group in the Mostar area's power equations, and limited Serb returns do not threaten the agendas and interests of either of the two major players in local politics. Indeed, both Bosniac and Croat power-brokers (more frequently the Bosniac leader Orucevic) have a habit of courting remnant and returning Serbs in order to reinforce their own position and isolate the rival side.

There was a surge of minority returns in Bosnia & Herzegovina in the year 2000, a development discussed in Chapter 1. In 2000 minority returns throughout BiH jumped to 67,000 from the level of around 40,000 achieved in each of the preceding two years. The rise was hardly felt in Mostar, where returns continued to languish at an abysmal level. In course of the year, just 90 Bosniacs returned to Mostar West and 37 Croats to Mostar East. Serb returns were slightly better: 127 to Mostar East and 103 to Mostar West.[11] The problem extends beyond Mostar. The city is situated in the middle of the most polarized and divided canton in Bosnia & Herzegovina. This canton, Herzegovina-Neretva, is split into areas of Bosniac and Croat demographic and political predominance. Jablanica and Konjic, located north and north-east of Mostar in the direction of Sarajevo, are Bosniac-dominated, in addition to Mostar East (for example, Konjic, 55 per cent Bosniac in 1992, is over 90 per cent Bosniac today). The southern part of the canton, including the municipalities of Capljina, Stolac and Ravno, is overwhelmingly Croat, as is Prozor, located in the northwestern corner of the canton on the border with central Bosnia. As discussed in passing in Chapter 2, the government structures of this canton, designed to encourage power-sharing and cooperation between Croats and Bosniacs, have remained dysfunctional, and the Croat zones of the canton are effectively run by an elaborate set of HDZ-HVO parallel institutions.

[11]'Registered Minority Returns from January 1, 2000 to December 31, 2000 in BiH', UNHCR Statistics Unit, Sarajevo, February 2001.

In 2001, however, a significant increase occurred in the rate of Bosniac returns to west Mostar. Between January 1 and September 30, 1,477 Bosniacs returned to their homes in west Mostar, a huge increase on returns in the entire preceding year. This is all the more striking given the enhanced turmoil and friction in Mostar resulting from the crisis of the Federation, which escalated during precisely those months. A decisive factor has been the emphasis on vigorous implementation of property legislation, entailing eviction of illegal occupants and repossession by the original occupants, during the tenure of high representative Petritsch. Towards the end of 1999, Petritsch used his decree powers to dismiss as many as 23 corrupt and chauvinist Bosniac, Serb and Croat local officials, among them Stipe Maric, the unsavoury mayor of the Mostar South-West municipality, along with the head of the housing department in the same municipality. Mostar South-West is easily the most urban and populous of the six city municipalities and contains the highest density of the city's publicly owned apartments.[12] Maric and his accomplices, particularly an individual called Karlo Dzeba, who commanded the wartime heliodrom detention centre and served as chief of the notoriously brutal Mostar South-West police for several years after the war, had long been active in blocking returns to this area, the core of urban Mostar. An increased number of Serbs, 962, also returned to west Mostar during these nine months (plus another 311 to east Mostar), although the number of Croat returnees to east Mostar registered during the same period totalled just 231, a modest figure by any standards.[13]

Has the increasingly healthy climate for minority returns in many parts of BiH finally arrived in Mostar? Some signs are encouraging. In May 2001, 416 Mostar Serb families living in Nevesinje since 1992 announced their intention to hold a mass sit-in in the central zone on June 1, in a dramatic demonstration of their desire to return and repossess their properties. At the time of writing (autumn 2001) it is too early to say whether returns

[12] 'Implementation of the Property Laws, Statistics', UNHCR/OHR/OSCEBiH/UNMiBH joint publication, Sarajevo, February 28, 2001; 'Statistics: Implementation of the Property Laws in BiH', UNHCR/OHR/OSCEBiH/UNMiBH/CRPC joint publication, Sarajevo, July 31, 2001.

[13] 'Registered Minority Returns from January 1, 2001 to September 30, 2001 in BiH', UNHCR Statistics Unit, Sarajevo, Novemner 2001.

will continue at an accelerated pace sufficient to make a decisive difference to the way Mostar's future evolves over the next few years. Even in an optimistic prognosis, however, the formidable legacy of distrust and division that permeates all aspects of life in a deeply damaged city will be difficult to overcome.

Politics: the persistence of polarization

Mostar's first post-war elections were organized under EUAM/NATO (IFOR) supervision in end-June, 1996. This local election was the first-ever held under the Dayton regime, preceding elections to constitute Bosnia's joint-state, entity and cantonal institutions in September 1996. The Mostar poll, as well as the bigger elections that followed, took place in the shadow of a divisive debate in international community circles over the necessity and efficacy of competitive elections so soon after the end of a devastating, polarizing civil war. The pro-election lobby, spearheaded by influential elements of the Clinton administration, eventually asserted its will against sceptics who argued that early elections in a traumatized, polarized society would simply deepen divisions and entrench hardliners in power. Mostar, which had been at 'peace' for over two years by mid-1996, would be a test-case for this debate.

The sceptics were proved right by the election results in Mostar and subsequent developments. The OHR proclaimed the Mostar election 'without doubt a success for Mostaris and the EU administration of the city. The astonishingly high turn-out of almost 60 per cent provided substantial proof that people want elections, sending a strong positive signal for the general elections in September. The atmosphere was peaceful, sometimes even festive... Voters travelled freely between east and west Mostar while local and international police, supported by IFOR, worked well together and provided the necessary level of security'.[14] The participation rate was in fact only about 55 per cent (58,301 of 106,568 eligible) including almost 7,500 refugee ballots cast in overseas polling centres. The electorate confirmed the transformation of Mostar by simply collapsing along the national(ist) fault-line. A SDA-led list won 49 per cent of the vote and the HDZ got

---

[14]OHR press release cited in Chandler, *Bosnia*, p. 81.

46 per cent (28,505 and 26,680 respectively). A non-nationalist
list, organized by Josip Jole Musa, a anti-sectarian Mostar busi-
nessman of Croat background, also ran. This slate included the
SDP, Liberals and the Croatian Peasants' Party (HSS) among other
groups. It polled 1,937 votes, around 3.5 per cent of the total.
Under election rules, the city council was comprised of 37 seats
allocated on a national-quota basis—16 for Bosniacs, 16 for
Croats, and five for others. The results gave the SDA coalition 21
members (including five Serbs) and the HDZ sixteen. This city
council and the six municipal councils elected at the same time
proved utterly still-born. It was only after several months of protracted negotiations and direct pressure on the Tudjman regime in
Zagreb by Western governments that the Mostar HDZ even
agreed to token participation in the city council, on condition
that the first Mayor would be Croat (and his deputy, Bosniac).
Government formation in the three Croat-dominated districts
was blocked by the HDZ until the middle of 1997. During this
period of transparent deadlock in late 1996 and early 1997, forced
evictions of remnant Bosniacs in west Mostar picked up significantly, and a particularly ugly confrontation took place just inside
the Croat side of the 'border' between the two zones in February
1997 (on this incident, more later). The mess in Mostar notwithstanding, general elections went ahead as scheduled throughout
Bosnia in September 1996, and the outcomes yielded further
ammunition to critics of American 'electoralism'. Local elections
to municipal bodies throughout Bosnia were, however, postponed
to September 1997.

A keystone of international community strategy in Mostar has
been to encourage power-sharing (consociation) and consensual
decisionmaking and action between representatives of the two
major groups at the levels of city and municipal government.
Until 2000, the unified city government remained notional, practically paralytic, held hostage to Croat-Muslim hostility both at
the lower (municipalities) and higher (canton) levels of politics
and administration. During 2000 limited progress in invigorating
the joint city authorities was achieved with strong international
backing, and more seemed possible, but even so the city government remains weak and ineffectual. What of power-sharing and
joint governance at the level of the municipal governments?

OSCE-supervised city and municipal elections held in September 1997 substantially replicated the results of the previous year. The only 'change' was that this time the SDA's Orucevic and HDZ's Prskalo switched positions, the former becoming Mayor and the latter Deputy Mayor. In addition, six municipal assemblies were elected as mandated (25 members each), and six municipal governments came into existence. Each of these six municipal regimes had power-sharing mechanisms built into their functioning, under internationally sponsored regulations. Specifically, in the three-Croat controlled districts, Muslims were guaranteed a certain share of the executive offices of local government, and vice versa. It was stipulated for example that in a Croat-controlled municipality the mayor would be Croat but the deputy mayor, who would be responsible for routine administration and also have charge over refugee and DP returns, would have to be a Muslim—and vice versa for a Bosniac-controlled municipality.

The intent behind this scheme is clear and unimpeachable. But the realities on the ground in Mostar (indeed, in Bosnia as a whole) tend to be at variance with neat formulas and formal arrangements. In July 1998 I found that Marko Rozic, Croat deputy mayor of the Stari Grad district, had not attended office once in ten months since he assumed his post, for the simple reason that the office is in the *de facto* Bosniac pocket of the west bank. In June 1998 Mustafa Skoro, Muslim deputy mayor of Mostar South-West since the previous autumn, decided to start repairs to his damaged house, located in that municipality, in anticipation of permanently returning there. The first night after he began the repairs, an empty Bosniac home next-door to his was firebombed, in an obvious warning to him not to take his responsibilities—or his rights—at face value. Attempts by international regulators to promote a multiethnic police force in Mostar and the surrounding region via guaranteed minority representation and power-sharing formulas have produced a similar, unsettling discrepancy between form and reality, as is discussed below. A more general analysis of why consociational structures have largely failed to work in substantive practice at various levels of the Dayton system can be found in Chapter 5.

Mostar's international supervisors have also attempted to engineer a multinational democratic framework in the city and its municipalities through another technique: the design of the electoral system and its laws and regulations. As in elections to legislative bodies at all levels of the Dayton state, a system of proportional representation (PR) is employed in elections to Mostar's city council and the six municipal councils. The number of seats won by each party list, coalition list or independent candidates' list is calculated according to a formula known as the Sainte-Lague distribution method. This involves dividing the total valid votes received by each list by 1, 3, 5, 7 and so on. The resulting quotients are then ordered from highest to lowest. Each list is then awarded the number of seats corresponding to its quotient in the range of one (1) to the number of available seats. The Sainte-Lague formula is commonly used in countries with PR-based electoral systems, to ensure the closest possible match between the proportion of votes polled by a party or coalition of parties and the proportion of seats it receives. In the Bosnian local elections of April 2000, the supervising agency, OSCE, introduced an 'open list' system for the first time, meaning that voters could now vote for specific candidates on a list in addition to indicating a preference for the list as a whole. Once the total number of seats obtained by a party or coalition list is determined by the Sainte-Lague method, the seats are then distributed among individual candidates on that list in rank-order, starting with the candidate who has received the highest number of individual votes among those on the list. Proceeding in this fashion, the seats won by the list are allocated in descending order to individuals on that list. If the party or coalition still has a surplus of individual mandates to be filled after all candidates who have won at least 5 per cent of the list's total vote have been elected, then the allotment of the remaining seats won by the party is done according to the order of candidates on party's slate.[15]

This electoral system is used in Mostar elections as well, but with one very important qualification: the number of available seats on the city council and the municipal councils are divided up in advance by nationality, with fixed numbers assigned to Croats, Bosniacs and Others, respectively. Thus the 30 members elected to the city council must include 10 Croats, 10 Bosniacs

15 Organization for Security and Cooperation in Europe, 'The Mandate Allocation Process in BiH', Sarajevo, 2000.

and 10 Others. Eighteen of these members are elected from the
six municipalities constituting the city, three from each. The
remaining twelve are elected from city-wide lists. Each of the
municipal districts elects a council of 25 members, with the composition by nationality stipulated by Article 56 of Mostar's Interim
Statute:

Municipality	Croats	Bosniacs	Others
Mostar North	4	11	10
Mostar-Stari Grad	4	12	9
Mostar South-East	3	19	3
Mostar South	12	6	7
Mostar South-West	12	6	7
Mostar West	10	6	9

The great majority of Mostar citizens thus vote on three ballots—one for their municipal council, one for the three members
of the city council elected from their municipal district, and one
for the twelve members of the city council elected from city-wide
lists. The only voters exempt are the few thousand who live in the
central zone. They vote only for the twelve city council members
chosen from city-wide lists.

The obvious intention of this complicated electoral framework
is to ensure that all three groups who made Mostar a multinational
mosaic until 1992 are represented in its institutions (the 'Others'
are, in practice, Serbs). There is a further purpose to this framework, however, that may not be immediately apparent. Thus in the
municipal councils, the seats are allocated to parties in the first
instance according to the Sainte-Lague method. However, once
the stipulated quota of any of the three national groups is filled,
the next candidate on the same list belonging to one of the two
other groups is elected. If there is no such candidate on that party's

list, the seat is automatically given to the party list with the next quotient which does have such a candidate. If no such candidate(s) can be found, the seat(s) remain vacant. The same procedure is used in filling the twelve city council places from the city-wide lists, which is done after the eighteen seats elected from the municipalities have been distributed. Those 18 seats are filled by a step-by-step process. In the first step seat 1 for each district is allocated, then seat 2, and so on. If, during any step one national community is poised to get more than its total allocation of 10 seats on the city council, the seat passes to the next candidate on the same list from one of the two groups whose quota is not yet filled. If that party or coalition does not have such a candidate on its list, the seat goes to the party or coalition with the next quotient that does have such a candidate on its list. Seats cannot be filled even after repeated applications of this method remain vacant.[16]

This electoral system amounts to an invitation to cross-national politics cutting across communal boundaries. In only one of the six municipalities—the relatively sparsely populated outlying Mostar South-East district—does one nationality have a majority of seats pre-assigned in its favour (in this case Bosniacs, who are entitled to 19 of the 25 seats). In all others, no national group has a majority share of seats assigned to it. In Stari Grad and Mostar North, Bosniacs are entitled to 12 and 11 seats respectively. Croats are entitled to receive 12 seats each in Mostar South-West and Mostar South, and just 10 seats in Mostar West. Similarly, all three communities are supposed to be equally represented—one-third each—on the city council. This electoral system is designed to favour parties and coalitions with 'mixed' candidate lists (it also tends to favour small parties within each of the three blocs). As such, it provides a built-in incentive to the major players in local politics to put forward multinational slates.

The electoral system has not given rise to the substantively multinational political environment it is intended to foster, for a complex of reasons. The first reason is the nationally segmented character of the party system, and the predominance of national(ist) parties in that system. In the April 2000 local elections, for example, a SDA/SBiH coalition on the one hand, and the HDZ on the other, together polled four out of five votes cast in the race

16 Organization for Security and Cooperation in Europe, *Provisional Electoral Law—Annex 1: Elections for City of Mostar*, Sarajevo, 2000.

for the twelve city-wide seats on the city council (42 per cent and 37 per cent respectively). The SDP, the leading party of multinational orientation—though not multinational base, since its support is overwhelmingly among liberal and leftist Bosniacs—was far behind with less than 13 per cent. This domination of sectional and (to varying degrees) sectarian parties, the weakness of parties of cross-national orientation, and the virtual absence of parties with a cross-national vote base means that the substantive multinationalizing potential inherent in the electoral system cannot be realized. What has happened is that the SDA and HDZ have figured out the logic behind the design of the electoral system and have refined their tactics in response. Thus, in the key Mostar South-West district, where Croats are entitled to only 12 seats, the HDZ retained majority control in the 2000 local elections by winning 15 seats. Several Serbs included on the HDZ list were elected to the municipal council here, including well-known professor Milan Bodiroga. In Mostar West, Croats are supposed to fill only 10 seats but the HDZ won 15 seats here as well, again including a number of Serb candidates. In Mostar South, where Croats are entitled to a maximum of 12 seats, the HDZ performed spectacularly, winning 19 of the 25 seats, including at least three Muslims in addition to several Serbs. This surely does not mean that the HDZ in the Mostar region can be trusted to represent Serb and Bosniac interests. It does show that the HDZ has engaged in strategic selection of candidates, in order to protect its own interests and beat the electoral system at its own game. Similarly in each of the three Muslim-dominated districts, the SDA/SBiH list gained the majority of seats, although the SDP did well in Stari Grad, winning most of the seats reserved for non-Bosniacs. Only 18 and 21 seats could be filled in Mostar North and Mostar South-East, respectively, because of a lack of non-Bosniac candidates on the party lists.

In the contest to fill the thirty seats on the city council, the SDA-SBiH list secured 16 seats, the HDZ 11, and the SDP three. Of the twelve seats decided in the city-wide ballot, the HDZ and SDA won five each and the SDP two. The SDA came out on top in the race for the eighteen seats on the city council elected from the municipalities. It won eight of the nine seats from the Bosniac-controlled districts (the SDP got the other), where there are almost no resident Croats and where few displaced Croats bother to cast their votes. It also bagged three of the nine seats elected from the three Croat-controlled districts, thanks to the votes of remnant Bosniac residents in Mostar West and South-West and 'out-of-municipality' ballots cast by Bosniacs displaced from all three Croat-dominated districts, particularly Mostar South. The HDZ won only six of the nine city council seats elected from 'its' municipalities.[17]

What the electoral system does do is give the most marginal of the three groups—the Serbs—a certain representation on the city council that would otherwise not be the case. The SDA coalition's city councillors elected in the city-wide race include prominent local Serbs, Milan Jovicic and Ratko Pejanovic (also the Croat Jole Musa, who died in December 2000), and Jovicic subsequently became the deputy speaker of the council. It also gives remnant and returnee Serbs a foothold and leverage in some of the municipal districts. Beyond that, however, the experience of Mostar illustrates the limits of electoral engineering designed to encourage cross-national politics.[18] Apart from the dominance of national(ist) parties in local politics and the ability of such parties to tactically adapt to electoral rules, there are additional factors. Mostar is far from the kind of 'normal' political environment in which a creatively designed electoral framework can have maximum effect. The city council (and government) remains a marginal body, disliked by hardline Croats and periodically exploited by Bosniac politicians for their own, sectarian purposes. As in Bosnia as a whole, local power is primarily exercised through informal channels. Real power in eastern Mostar thus rests with the manipulative Bosniac strongman Safet Orucevic, hardly the model of a democratic politician who can be trusted across community lines. In western Mostar, power rests with a more collective cast of unsavoury characters who have some core shared characteristics—they tend to be from a HVO paramilitary background and/or linked with *Hercegovacka Banka* (Bank of Herzegovina), the finan-

[17] The source of these figures are the detailed results of the April 2000 Bosnian local elections posted on the OSCE-BiH website, *www.oscebih.org*.

[18] Chapter 5 evaluates institutional constraints and possibilities in contemporary Bosnia in light of debates about federalism and federation, power-sharing and consociation, the structure and configuration of competitive party systems, and the uses and limits of electoral system design.

cial nerve-centre of Croat hardliners targeted by the international community in April 2001.

Finally, the international project of a unified city is undermined not just from below but from above as well. Given the primacy of the cantonal layer of government in the crisis-ridden Federation's framework (see Chapter 2), the *de facto* territorial division of Herzegovina-Neretva canton into Bosniac and Croat zones and the *de facto* existence of separate, parallel Bosniac and Croat administrative and financial structures throughout the canton's government makes the task of Mostar's would-be unifiers doubly difficult. The endurance of polarization in Mostar is reinforced not only by the city's own fragmentation into two enclaves but by the polarization evident in the larger canton. In general elections in September 1998 the HDZ-BiH won 49.5 per cent of the total vote in the canton; in November 2000 the party polled 48.2 per cent. This makes the HDZ easily the single largest party in the canton, and along with minor allied groups it commands a slight majority of the electorate. In autumn 1998 the major Bosniac parties together polled around 43 per cent, with four-fifths of that vote going to the SDA-SBiH coalition. At the end of 2000 the Bosniac parties again polled around the same percentage, this time split more evenly between the SDA, the SDP and the SBiH, in that order.[19]

The international community's intensive efforts to promote a single, multinational police force in Mostar have of necessity been conducted in a canton-wide context, since policing is under cantonal jurisdiction in the FBiH. The canton's Interior Ministry (MUP), which has a Croat minister and Bosniac deputy minister as per the standard parity and power-sharing formula, is essentially the police ministry. After years of effort, a breakthrough of sorts was achieved in May–June 2000, with the 'physical' (as distinguished from 'functional') integration of the Interior Ministry. Until this time, there had been duplicate interior ministries in the literal, physical sense, with an all-Croat ministry located in a west Mostar building and a Bosniac counterpart in a building a small distance away in the Muslim zone of the town. In the future, there is supposed to be a single, unified Interior Ministry based in the central zone. But in 2000, the land for this future building had not

[19] Source: The canton-wise results of the 1998 and 2000 general elections posted on the OSCEBiH website, *www.oscebih.org.*

yet been identified, and the amount of money set aside for future construction (5 million marks) was clearly not sufficient. So 'physical integration' for the time being meant that the crime-investigation department and, legal, personnel and administrative sections of the ministry would operate from the Stone building (on the west side) and the ministers' office, uniformed police department and the finance section from the UPFM building in the Bosniac sector. This involved a reciprocal move by 42 Bosniac police and other ministry employees into the Stone building and 109 Croats into the UPFM premises, and happened in the early summer of 2000. At the same time the BiH Croat intelligence service was constrained to move out of the Stone building by international pressure.

This development, a major breakthrough by Mostar standards, amounted to only one step towards the creation of a genuinely unified, multiethnic police service in the city and its region. Numerous obstacles and problems remained on the long road towards 'functional'—i.e. substantively meaningful, operational integration. The first barrier, as an internal UNMiBH assessment noted in the aftermath of the long-overdue physical integration, is that 'the structure as it exists in the Ministry is completely untenable. The Bosniac side reports to the Bosniac deputy minister of interior and the Croat side to the Croat minister... All sections in the ministry have the position of deputy filled by [a member of] the other ethnic group. This creates parallel chains of command....'. This observation is absolutely accurate, but the problem is that the entire structure of the cantons (especially the two bi-national ones, Herzegovina-Neretva and central Bosnia) are built on this principle of parity and reciprocity, as is the edifice of the Muslim-Croat federation as a whole. These principles cannot be abandoned without bringing the whole, fragile edifice down, and undoing the entire post-war settlement in the process. Yet in the meantime, mutual distrust and hostility, still strong in the wartime zones of armed conflict, means that a key institution like the police force and administration is effectively splintered along the national divide. The frustration with this state of affairs in the Mostar canton, as expressed in this report, is emblematic of a basic, general IC dilemma in Bosnia & Herzegovina. But as this report points out, duplicate budgets continued to exist in the interior ministry—in 2000, 18 million marks for the wealthier Croat side versus 8 million for the poorer Bosniacs—making a Croat patrol officer posted to the police station in Bosniac-dominated Jablanica better-paid than the Bosniac station chief. During 2000 the Bosniac and Croat payment systems in the canton were nominally 'merged' under international mediation, but in a typically peculiar, counter-intuitive Bosnian twist nonetheless continued to maintain their separate existences. One high-ranking UN official explained this apparent discrepancy to me in the following terms during an interview in Sarajevo: 'Earlier, they were like accounts in two different banks. Now they are like two different accounts in the same bank'.

The Herzegovina-Neretva canton's interior ministry has 13 police stations under its jurisdiction. Of these six are in Mostar—three on each side of the divided city, corresponding to the municipal districts. Of the remainder, some like Capljina, Stolac and Prozor are on Croat turf, while others like Jablanica and Konjic are on Bosniac-dominated territory. In every police station the position of deputy chief is occupied by a member of the 'minority' group, as per international regulations. Audits conducted during 1999-2000 by international officials in some of these police stations found that 'in all police administrations the deputy is almost always bypassed, does not attend high command meetings within the administration and does not issue subordinates with instructions and directives'. The extent of marginalization varies between stations in Bosniac and Croat-majority areas. Bosniac deputy chiefs tend to be a more or less token presence in the Croat-dominated stations, while Croat deputy chiefs in stations in Bosniac-majority municipalities fare slightly better, generally shown routine forms of respect by Bosniac subordinates and allowed to sign official correspondence. In one station located in a particularly hardline Croat area with a reputation for being a centre and transit point for organized-crime activity, 'communication between Bosniacs and Croats at all levels was non-existent or superficial. Information and orders passed through two separate chains of command. There were no joint senior staff meetings. A network of formal and informal institutions and individuals exercised inappropriate influences [on police work]... Senior Bosniac officers were not given any significant management responsibilities. No investigations were assigned to Bosniac [detective] officers. The Bosniac uniformed officers were under-utilized and marginalized'. This police station had, in mid-2000, 11 Bosniac officers attached to it, one-third of the target of thirty-four. However, in all police stations surveyed, whether Croat or Bosniac-controlled, 'the minority police officers are not working as their job descriptions envisage... In some Bosniac-controlled stations the Croat deputies do not spend the required time at work and seem to have no real intention to work as effective deputies'. Indeed, police officers of different nationalities working in the same police station receive their supplies from the different wings of the nominally integrated but effectively segmented interior ministry, and personnel matters (administration, disciplinary action etc) are based on separate filing systems for Bosniac and Croat employees in each station. In all stations, the vast majority of 'minority' officers live in their 'own' areas and commute to work—Bosniacs to Stolac, Capljina, Neum, Prozor and the west Mostar stations, Croats to the east Mostar stations, Jablanica and Konjic. As for Serb representation in the police, Herzegovina-Neretva is supposed to have a total of 170 Serb officers deployed in its 13 stations, but as of late 2000 it had been possible to deploy fewer than fifteen.

In Mostar, according to UNMiBH sources interviewed during the second half of 2000, 'no communication' and 'no cooperation' exists between the three police stations in west Mostar and the three in eastern Mostar. Many Croat police in the city are members of HVIDRA, the HVO war veterans' association which acts as an ultranationalist pressure-group in local politics. The six stations had developed a single radio frequency for receiving emergency calls after intense international pressure, but still maintained separate frequencies for all other calls. The east Mostar police stations customarily have their autopsies, analysis of blood and DNA samples etc done in Sarajevo, and the west Mostar stations in Split, the nearest large Croatian city on the Dalmatian coast. Separate prisons exist in western and eastern Mostar, with the Croats in control of the pre-war city's single facility. In some stations in western Mostar and even more so in the smaller Croat-controlled towns of the region, it is commonplace to find 'the *Sahovnica* [the red-and-white checkerboard that is the Croatian state emblem and Croat national symbol], Herceg-Bosna insignia, and HDZ propaganda', in addition to statues and pictures of the Virgin Mary, crucifixes, portraits of Franjo Tudjman, and occasionally, maps of 'Greater Croatia'. This is in contravention of OHR directives that all public buildings including police stations should only display Federation symbols and insignia of 'a neutral or inoffensive nature'. During late 1999 and 2000 a piquant situation arose when the OHR ordered the divided interior ministry to implement this directive forthwith, including but not limited to uniform badges, patches and belt buckles, flags and coats-of-arms, and official seals and stamps. The Croat wing of the interior ministry reacted with an imaginative and novel form of non-compliance. Months after the 'physical integration' of the interior ministry in Mostar, Croat police officers in the city and throughout the canton were wearing the checkerboard on their belt buckles and tie pins, and no symbols at all on their caps and shoulder patches. Their Bosniac colleagues, on the other hand, were dutifully wearing Federation insignia on their caps and shoulders. This meant that in every 'joint' patrol, every station and every crime scene it was possible to instantly identify which officer was Croat and which Bosniac, making a mockery of the idea of a unified, neutral police force.

By 2000 the international community had to some degree succeeded in producing the formal framework of a nationally mixed police service in Mostar and its canton, based on a Bosniac-Croat ratio of 48:52 agreed with representatives of the two groups (this ratio applies since 1997 to police officers and since early 2000 also to several hundred administrative support staff employed in the interior ministry offices and the police stations combined). But much like a skeleton devoid of flesh and blood, the structure lacks substance, and the form remains at variance with operational realities on the ground. Even this record of superficial progress compared to the early post-war period (1995-7) when all police stations were mono-national, has been marred by the fall-out of the confrontation over Croat rights between the HDZ-led Croat National Congress (HNS) and the international community during 2001. On April 3 Dragan Mandic, interior minister of Herzegovina-Neretva canton and nineteen other senior ministry officials of Croat nationality published a statement which declared support for the HNS—whose precise aims are unclear beyond

rhetoric about 'rights' and 'equality' for BiH Croats as a people—
and condemned the Federation government as illegal and illegitimate (the Federation government, heavily backed by Bosnia's
international supervisors, does not include the HDZ and its allies,
which won 93 per cent of Croat votes polled in the November
2000 general elections, but does include Croats belonging to the
SDP and tiny HDZ breakaway groups).)On April 4, in what was
obviously a carefully synchronized move, 897 out of 923 Croat
employees of the interior ministry (police officers and support
staff) backed their leaders' statement. On April 26, Mandic was
fired from his position and three of his senior colleagues suspended by top overseer Petritsch's decree (the other sixteen had already
been suspended by UNMiBH). 'It is an honour to be sacked by
the high representative and join other dismissed Croat officials
[like HDZ-BiH leader Ante Jelavic]', Mandic told a press conference in Mostar.[20]

UN and OHR personnel have also directed sustained efforts
towards building a professional, cross-national judicial system in
Mostar and its region. Until July 1999, when the OHR handed
down a decision requiring the establishment of such a judiciary,
cantonal institutions had been had ensnared in an impasse
between Croats and Bosniacs on the issue. Two mono-national
'high courts' functioned in Mostar, one on each side of the divided city, and the composition of judges in the 'basic' (municipal)
courts were also mono-national. It took a number of months for
the new system to be set up at various levels, both because of normal delays in recruiting judges, public prosecutors and other necessary personnel and because of chronic disputes over procedural
matters between Bosniacs and Croats involved in the process.
However, by mid-2000, the new-look multinational cantonal
court had started operations and a public prosecutor's office had
been established in the Mostar central zone with the usual sharing of positions—cantonal court president a Croat, public prosecutor positions equally shared between Croats and Bosniacs, president of the cantonal minor offence court a Bosniac, the cantonal public attorney a Croat with two Bosniac deputies, and so on.

[20] 'Bosnian Croat Police Support Self-Rule', Reuters, Sarajevo, April 3, 2001;
'Nine Hundred Bosnian Croat Policemen Join Nationalist Drive for Self-Rule',
AFP, Mostar, April 5, 2001; 'Bosnian Croat Police Chief is Sacked, Says He
Doesn't Care', AFP, Mostar, April 27, 2001.

A Serb element was also included among the judges of the canton judiciary, in addition to Croats and Bosniacs. Some 59 Bosniac, Croat and Serb judges have in addition been appointed by the cantonal legislature to nine multinational municipal courts, and a smaller number of prosecutors drawn from all three groups to the corresponding municipal public prosecutor's offices. Curiously, however, the canton's Ministry of Justice (which has a Bosniac minister and Croat deputy) remained segmented, physically as well as in practice.

The canton court hit the headlines soon after its formation. In late 2000 and early 2001, in two separate cases, it tried three Croat and six Bosniac ex-soldiers accused of committing war-crimes against combatants and civilians of the other side during the battle for Mostar. It had received clearance from the International Criminal Tribunal for the Former Yugoslavia (ICTY) in The Hague to go ahead and try these 'low-level' indictees. Five Croats and as many as 23 Muslims had in fact been charged by the canton prosecutor's office, but only some surrendered to the court. The two trials—the Croats' trial began in late 2000 and the Bosniacs' in early 2001—rapidly unravelled, as key prosecution witnesses withdrew, a detained Croat had to be released for lack of evidence while a detained Muslim was freed on grounds of mistaken identity, etc. Eventually both trials ended in acquittals. A newly formed judiciary in a deeply divided town, in a deeply divided region in a deeply divided country, was clearly not the appropriate site for a pilot experiment in locally conducted war-crimes trials. Far from fostering the cause of truth and reconciliation, the trials exposed the deeply opposed perceptions in the town regarding what happened in Mostar, and who was responsible. A Croat resident of western Mostar remarked that it was 'about time someone has been put on trial for committing crimes against Croats'. A citizen of the east bank approved of the concept of retributive justice, but expressed resentment that only 'minor criminals' had been indicted. 'Will anyone ever be held accountable for shelling us, killing, persecuting and starving us for months?', she asks.[21] The episode clearly reveals that the persistence of duplicate, parallel regimes in Mostar and its region cannot

---

[21] Mirsad Behram, 'Mostar Divided Over Trials', *Balkan Crisis Reports* 220, February 21, 2001.

be attributed to the manipulations of sectarian, oligarchic leaderships alone. It reflects deep divisions in society.[22]

Other dimensions of partition: economy, education, culture, symbols

Mostar does not really have a viable local economy, but rather fragments of an economy. Massive unemployment (perhaps 70 per cent) is a serious barrier to 'normalization' of the city and its environs, and life is hard for most ordinary citizens, even in the relatively better-off Croat-dominated areas. The few plants and factories that do operate reflect, and reinforce, the city's social, political and territorial divide.

Mostar's most successful enterprise by a wide margin is its aluminium plant, *Aluminij Mostar.* It produces primary aluminium, alloys and anodes, and has business links with firms in Croatia (TLM Sibenik), Germany (a division of Daimler-Chrysler), Switzerland (Glencore International AG) and the United States (Venco-Venture Coke Company in Houston, Texas). Before the war, Aluminij employed over 5,000 Mostarians. It now employs a fraction of that number (1,000-plus) but is still a rare example of a BiH company that is viable and makes profits. Indeed, the *Financial Times* has described Aluminij Mostar as an example of 'what the Bosnian economy could be—efficient, profitable and

---

[22] In late February 2001 Dario Kordic, a top wartime HDZ-BiH leader and Tudjman favourite, and Mario Cerkez, a wartime HVO commander in central Bosnia, were sentenced to 25 and 15 years respectively by the Hague tribunal for their role in massacres and other atrocities committed against Muslims in central Bosnia's Lasva valley in 1993. Local Croats and Muslims reacted to the news in diametrically opposite ways. In Busovaca, Kordic's hometown in central Bosnia, over 2,000 Croats turned out in a noisy protest to abuse the tribunal's judgment and hail 'heroes' Dario and Mario. In Ahmici, a village close to Travnik where over a hundred Muslims died in one of the worst HVO massacres, Muslim returnees to the largely rebuilt village bitterly criticized the sentences as far too lenient. 'Bosnian Croats Protest UN War Crimes Sentences', AFP, Busovaca, March 1, 2001; 'Bosnian Death Villagers Regret 'Light' War Crimes Sentence', AFP, Ahmici, February 27, 2001. Exactly a year earlier, in late February 2000, HVO general Tihomir Blaskic had received a sentence of 45 years at the Hague, which led to outrage among Croats and a similar polarization of opinion in Mostar and other volatile towns like Kiseljak; see Mirsad Behram, 'Mostar: Balkan Berlin Remains Divided', *Balkan Crisis Reports* 123, March 10, 2000.

exporting to some of the world's top companies'.[23]
Aluminij Mostar was taken over after 1992 by hardline Croats.
It has been controlled ever since by Mijo Brajkovic, a local strongman who has been HDZ mayor of west Mostar and HDZ president of the cantonal government. It was revived after the fighting ended by generous infusions of capital from sources in Croatia whose identity is not clear. According to the Muslim leader Safet Orucevic, 'Tudjman and Susak invested in that company. It is the principal means to fight for the division of the Federation'. Brajkovic retorts that what matters is that the company provides jobs and fosters contacts with international business. Both are right after a fashion, and it is only by combining their accounts that we can get a full picture of the economic basis of Mostar's partition. Aluminij is indeed an employment-providing, profitable firm with an international profile. It is also an 'ethnically cleansed' enterprise with all-Croat management and an exclusively west Mostar workforce that, together with a bunch of similar firms such as the Stolac-based Renner Company provides an important part of the economic foundations of the separate and resilient 'Herceg-Bosna' regime.

Mostar's other major pre-war industry was a public enterprise called SOKOL ('Falcon'). Capitalizing on the former Yugoslavia's (especially Bosnia's) tradition of excellence in engineering and the presence of sizeable JNA facilities in the region, SOKOL produced military helicopters among other things (though its production line had a civilian side as well), and exported to countries in the Middle East. It is now a shadow of its former self with an estimated 200-300 workers, and helps assemble buses for a partner based in Split. Since the war period, the remnants of SOKOL have been in the hands of Croat hardliners. Dragan Covic, a locally prominent HDZ politician, has been the company's director in the post-war years. In November 2000, the SOKOL factory hosted a concert by the group Boney M., whose popularity elsewhere in the world peaked in the late 1970s. The all-Croat audience (diluted only by a few foreigners working for the IC in Mostar) included a large contingent of skinheads who were observed shooting heroin in the toilets in between songs.

---

[23] 'Survey of Bosnia-Herzegovina', *Financial Times*, December 14, 1999, pp. 35-38, on p. 36.

East Mostar's only sizeable enterprise is a state-owned tobacco factory, *Fabrika Duhana Mostar*, which produces the inexpensive, popular Drina and Mond cigarettes. The firm has an assured market since chain-smoking is the norm in local society, but it is just not enough to sustain the poor Bosniac sector of the city. The pretty Stari Grad and its bridge were tourist magnets in the prewar years for people throughout Yugoslavia as well as foreigners, but that is in the past and will not be revived in any significant form in the immediate future. The United States Agency for International Development (USAID) operates a credit scheme (15,000 marks each) designed to stimulate small-scale entrepreneurship in the city, with special emphasis on the citizens of eastern Mostar. There is a pattern of recipients using the money to buy a new car or open up yet another café-bar in a town already chock-full of such establishments. Eastern Mostar has a number of good restaurants (indeed, so does the west) located close to the beautiful natural setting of the Neretva bank, but a large proportion of patrons consists of international civilian and military personnel based in or close to the town and it is not clear what the prospects of some of these establishments will be once this customer-base dries up. The only other visible sign of entrepreneurial commerce is the appearance of a large Chinese-run variety goods store in the centre of the east bank. In early 2001 Japan Tobacco Inc. expressed a preliminary interest in buying a stake in Fabrika Duhana Mostar, but developed cold feet about investment risk after riots erupted in west Mostar in April, provoked by a SFOR-backed international raid on the premises of Hercegovacka Banka. [24] On both sides of the city a major source of employment continues to be the organs of cantonal and municipal government, controlled by the respective political parties and their power-brokers. In addition, jobless youth on both sides are constantly tempted by the lure of criminal networks engaged in a range of smuggling and racketeering activities, almost always in connivance with political power-brokers.

The Mostar area has a valuable natural resource, hydro-electric power, thanks to its location in the Neretva valley. There are three hydelpower-based public utilities in the vicinity of the town—HE Salakovac, HE Grabovica and HE Mostar. According to the

[24] 'Bosnia Instability Scares Investors', Reuters, Sarajevo, May 22, 2001.

Interim Statute their premises and facilities are part of the central zone and belong to the city as a whole, but in practice they are controlled by rival power-broking oligarchies. The Salakovac and Grabovica plants, which are on Bosniac territory and supply electricity to eastern Mostar are operated by Elektroprivreda BiH, the central power-utility concern headquartered in Sarajevo. It was control of this concern that provided the power-base of Edhem Bicakcic, top SDA leader and prime minister of the Muslim-Croat federation until late 2000, since disgraced on a variety of embezzlement, slush-fund and related fraud charges. In 1996 an EU offer of 12 million DM of assistance to reconstruct the three plants as part of a single system was rejected by the Sarajevo-based SDA leadership, for reasons that were murky then but patently obvious several years later. HE Mostar, which feeds into the west Mostar grid, is managed by the central power-utility company of the 'Croat Community of Herceg-Bosna' (Elektroprivreda HZHB, it retains the name of the BiH Croat statelet of the war and immediate post-war period), and attracted substantial investment from Spain as early as 1997. In February 2001 representatives of the US energy giant Enron disclosed that Enron was in negotiations with Elektroprivreda HZHB and the Sokol company to construct two new hydroelectric plants and one thermal power plant in Croat-controlled BiH.[25] The cases of Aluminij, Elektroprivreda BiH and others illustrate the symbiotic nexus between economic and political vested interests that drive the dynamic of partition in post-war Bosnia.

The greatest long-term threat to those aspects of Mostar's heritage which derive from values of inter-group respect and coexistence lies in the segregated character of the post-war schooling system. This, once again, is a problem across Bosnia as a whole, where children are taught according to three different curricula in three separate and highly politicized educational systems. In May 2000 the OHR mediated an 'education agreement' signed by the FBiH's education minister and deputy education minister (a Bosniac and a Croat, respectively) as well as the RS's education minister. This agreement seeks to build bridges across the three systems. Point 3 of the agreement says that 'while each constituent

[25] 'Enron Puts Bosnia Projects on Hold Amid Government Crisis', Reuters, Sarajevo, February 8, 2001.

people of Bosnia & Herzegovina is entitled to preserve and develop its own cultural and linguistic heritage, common and shared elements which facilitate inter-cultural understanding and communication should be stressed and reflected in all curricula and relevant textbooks. Measures to be taken throughout the country include the teaching of both Cyrillic and Latin alphabets, the teaching of the shared literary and cultural heritage of the three communities, and teaching about all major religions practised in BiH'. In a follow-up meeting to this agreement in July, progress was made on the issues of expunging 'offensive material' from all three sets of textbooks[26] and appending 'supplementary annexes' to textbooks published in Zagreb and Belgrade which are used in Serb and Croat schools. However, the OHR noted that 'disappointingly, no common position could be reached on the teaching of the second, cyrillic or latinic alphabet and the curricular modules for language, literature, culture and religion which are in effect confidence, mutual understanding and knowledge-building measures for pupils of the three constituent peoples and especially returnee children'.[27]

Mostar's tradition of educational excellence—and its fate—is symbolized by the bombed-out shell of the elegant Austro-Hungarian-era building, located on the so-called Spanish square, in the middle of the central zone just off the Boulevard, which housed the city's *Gimnazija* (elite high school). During 1993-4, the building where generations of Mostar's best and brightest have received their secondary-level education was caught on the frontline bisecting the city (on the 'Croat' side of the Boulevard) and extensively damaged. In 1999 the Croat-controlled Mostar South-West municipality unilaterally started repairs to the building, and in 2000 classes commenced for west-side children in the repaired section under the banner of 'Fra. Dominik Mandic Grammar School'. In June 2000 the OHR's regional office in Mostar responded to Bosniac objections to this development by mediating an agreement between the two sides on 'future joint use' of

[26] For an illuminating essay on the political obstacles to textbook reform in the canton of Sarajevo, see Robert Donia, 'The Search for Tolerance in Sarajevo's Textbooks', *Human Rights Review* 1: 2 (2000), pp. 38-55.

[27] 'OHR disappointed with lack of agreement on implementation of May 10th education agreement', OHR press release, Sarajevo, July 21, 2000; 'School Subject 'Culture of Religions'', OHR press release, Sarajevo, December 1, 2000.

the gymnasium premises. Under the terms of the agreement,[28] 'Grammar School 'Fra. Dominik Mandic' shall provide the conditions for the [Bosniac-run] Grammar School 'Aleksa Santic' to be accommodated at the same premises. The building shall be used when [its] reconstruction is complete'. This bitter pill for west Mostar's hardliners was sweetened with a couple of ancillary provisions requiring the Bosniac side to accommodate a secondary school from Mostar South-West on the present premises of a Bosniac-run elementary school located in the Bosniac enclave of the west bank, and to ensure conditions for the accommodation of a school for Croat returnee children on the premises of the elementary school located in the east-bank suburb of Bijelo Polje 'to the extent required' (Bijelo Polje's substantial Croat population was expelled or fled to west Mostar during the war, and only limited returns have occurred). The agreement noted the existence of an Organization of Petroleum Exporting Countries (OPEC) proposal for funding the reconstruction of the gymnasium building and other Mostar schools, and urged the Federation BiH parliament to approve this as soon as possible.

The gymnasium issue starkly highlights the travails of international engagement in post-war Bosnia. Given the realities of the post-war context, restoration of integrated schooling and an identical curriculum are practically impossible. On the other hand, it is vitally important to build bridges across the three systems if the agenda of the most retrograde segregationist and partitionist forces is to be thwarted. Encouraging schools teaching different curricula to operate from the same premises, and introducing 'shared and common' elements into those curricula, are incremental, realistic steps in the right direction. This strategy will be more likely to find acceptance among Serbs and Croats if international offi-

---

[28] 'Gimnazija Mostar, Central Zone: Terms of Agreement', signed at the OHR offices in the Hotel Ero on June 28, 2000 (document obtained by author from OHR-South, Mostar). The signatories are Judge Finn Lynghjem (then deputy high representative in Mostar), Rade Bosnjak (Croat governor of Herzegovina-Neretva canton), Hamo Maslesa (Bosniac deputy governor), Safet Orucevic (Bosniac city mayor), Neven Tomic (Croat deputy mayor), Mirjana Dujmovic (canton minister of education, science, culture and sports, Croat) and Nijaz Slipicevic (deputy minister, Bosniac). The Croat head of Mostar South-West municipality and the Bosniac heads of the Mostar North and Stari Grad districts are also signatories.

cialdom in Bosnia emphasizes that the 'shared and common' heritage pertains not just to all Bosnians cutting across distinctions of denomination, nationality and entity, but to the peoples and successor-states of former Yugoslavia as a whole. In a truly striking manner the issue of the educational framework encapsulates the dilemmas of reconstructing Bosnia's divided society. In education and all other areas of policy, the realistic and fair option for the IC, providing the best basis for further progress by Bosnians themselves in the future, lies in resisting both coerced integration and chauvinist partition and promoting a necessarily 'grey' third way that steers clear of both extremes.

In the course of 2000 international intervention resulted in the allotment of four classrooms and one staff-room to accommodate a school for some 80 children of Bosniac returnees in the primary school building of the notoriously hardline Croat-controlled municipality of Stolac, south of Mostar. This is very obviously unsatisfactory by conventional standards in most other parts of the world. But Bosnia is not a conventional context. In a society recovering from a catastrophic civil war which left numerous local communities destroyed and divided, even this represents progress. The Mostar region's OHR noted that that this 'interim compromise solution resulted from long-lasting negotiations' with Croat cantonal and municipal authorities led by a senior deputy high representative, and that before the agreement 'Bosniac returnees' children had been taught in two private houses 'under very poor conditions'.[29]

Mostar's university system remains divided into two separate institutions—a Croat-controlled 'University of Mostar' and a Bosniac-dominated 'University Dzemal Bijedic'. The latter was the name of the pre-war university, named in honour of Dzemal Bijedic, a top Bosnian communist leader from Mostar who joined the clandestine communist movement while studying at the University of Belgrade in 1939 and ended his career, tragically cut short by a plane crash, as Prime Minister of socialist Yugoslavia in 1971-7. In October 2000 High Representative Petritsch held a round-table discussion with students from both institutions. Following the meeting—coincidentally held during the heated

---

[29] 'Opening of Premises for Bosniac Returnees' Children in the Stolac School Building', OHR press release, Mostar, May 2, 2000.

run-up to the crucial November 2000 elections—HDZ-controlled media in west Mostar kicked up a furore, claiming that he had questioned the right of Croats 'to study in their own language and about their own culture'. Petritsch clarified in response that he had simply 'stressed... that resources for higher education in Mostar should be pooled', and 'expressed the hope that cooperation between the two existing universities becomes the norm'.[30] These words are well-chosen, and reflect a sound approach to the complicated problem of post-war Bosnia. Systematic encouragement of cooperation across the dividing lines, not 'integration', represents the most effective way forward for this fractured society. It is, in the circumstances, the best legacy that international intervention can leave to Bosnians to build on in the future.

The constraints to international action are evident in the continuing segmentation of Mostar's cultural life into distinct spaces. In a society known for appreciation of good theatre, two theatre companies lead separate existences—one in a repaired and renovated east-bank building run by Mrs Hadjibajramovic, a colourful local personality, the other based in the *Hrvatski Dom* (Croatian House) located on the 'Rondo', a circular junction of six tree-lined streets in west Mostar (apparently pending the completion of a grand 'Croat National Theatre' in the central zone, a plan for which was announced by the HDZ in 1997). The Hrvatski Dom regularly hosts performers and troupes from Zagreb and Split, but dialogue between cultural personalities and institutions across the Neretva remains limited in spite of efforts by the regional OSCE. International efforts to restart the city's puppet theatre for children, located in an east-bank building which was once Mostar's Jewish synagogue, with participation from both sides, have also faltered. It is not that people from different sides uniformly do not want to work together again, although plenty of distrust, even hatred, does exist in both parts of the city. In 1998 I attended the first post-war meeting of the two pre-war directors of the puppet theatre—Hamica Nametak, a Bosniac, and Petar Surkalovic, a Croat—arranged in the Hotel Ero through the good offices of the regional OSCE. The two were clearly pleased to see each other and cordial—it transpired that Nametak was from west Mostar

---

[30] 'OHR clarifies its statement on Mostar's universities', OHR press release, Sarajevo, October 23, 2000.

and Surkalovic from east Mostar, but neither had visited what had become the 'other' side since the war. Yet a proposal to stage a jointly organized performance to which all of Mostar's children would be invited failed to materialize in practice. Fashion shows and beauty pageants also come in duplicate versions. Bosniac beauties strut their stuff in the Hotel Bristol, perched in a scenic setting on the bank of the Neretva in the slice of west-bank land that is part of the Bosniac sector of the city. The Bristol was semi-destroyed by the fighting but has been repaired, renovated and reopened. Croat lovelies meanwhile parade in venues literally a stone's throw away in west Mostar. Nightspots are booming on both sides of the city, but young people normally keep to 'their' side of the turf. The Bosnian Cultural Centre, opened shortly after the war in a building renovated and equipped with EU funding, is located in the Bosniac enclave of the west bank, very close to commercial and residential streets across the divide in the Croat zone. Its director, Jelka Kebo, is a Croat married to a Muslim. The Centre organizes a range of cultural events including photography exhibitions and musical performances—its clientele, however, consists almost entirely of residents of the city's Bosniac sector and foreigners employed by international organizations present in the city. During 2000 Mostar's new Deputy Mayor, the genuinely liberal Croat Neven Tomic, breached a psychological barrier when he started attending, along with his wife, concerts held on the plush premises of the Pavarotti Music Centre, located in the heart of the eastern bank. But in August 2000 a scheduled performance by popular Bosnian singer Dino Merlin in the Bijeli Brijeg stadium, located on the western fringes of the town, had to be cancelled at the last minute after a rash of threats (Merlin is a Muslim from Sarajevo's Stari Grad quarter and has long been identified with the SDA). A week later, Merlin did perform in Mostar, but on the premises of east Mostar's bus and railway terminuses (buses to and from Croatia do not use this facility but park in a west-side street), across from the Carinski Most bridge with the west bank.

In contrast to the early post-war years, newspapers and magazines are now freely available throughout Mostar regardless of political tilt or content. But west Mostar readership is dominated by *Jutarnji List* and *Slobodna Dalmacija*, large-circulation Croatian dailies published from Dalmatia. The latter, which is based in Split and publishes a special section for its readers in Herzegovina, was taken over by the HDZ in the early years of the Tudjman era and has propagated a nasty nationalist line ever since. Eastern Mostar, on the other hand, is dominated by *Dnevni Avaz*, published from Sarajevo and considered a pro-SDA paper until a bitter falling-out with that party's leadership in early 2000. However, instead of emerging as a truly independent paper, *Dnevni Avaz* appears to have shifted its allegiance in the direction of the SDP. As for local radio and TV stations in the Mostar area, the Helsinki Committee for Human Rights notes in its report for the period January-June 2001 that 'a real media war is raging in Mostar between the media from the east (Bosniac) and west (Croatian) side. According to the report of our monitor, each of the sides claims that whatever the other side does is bad.'[31]

'Civil society' groups, in the conventional Western sense of the term, do exist in the divided city but are isolated and marginalized. The largely destroyed Aleksa Santic Street, situated on the former frontline of the west bank beside the Neretva, where Muslim and Croat positions were in talking distance of each other, houses one such organization, the Association of Citizens for Human Rights Protection. The office is situated in what is now the central zone, but the group is led by Amra Kazic, a middle-aged Bosnian Muslim woman who has continued to live in west Mostar throughout the war and post-war years. For Mrs Kazic, a lawyer, and her small multiethnic team who specialize in providing legal assistance to prospective returnees regardless of nationality, the struggle is difficult but it goes on.[32] The prospects of civic activism in Mostar have been seriously weakened by the continuous exodus of educated professionals and bright young people, now remaking their lives and careers in many distant lands, during the war and post-war years. However, distinctly uncivil influences thrive in Mostar. One example is a flourishing

---

[31] Helsinki Committee for Human Rights in BiH, *Analysis of the State of Human Rights in Bosnia and Herzegovina, January-June 2001*, Sarajevo, July 2001, p. 15.

[32] See Association of Citizens for Human Rights Protection, 'Civil Initiative Contributions to Integration Process and Confidence-Building in the City of Mostar,' in N. Dimitrijevic (ed.), *Managing Multiethnic Local Communities in the Countries of Former Yugoslavia*, Budapest, 2000, pp. 271-80.

trade in hard drugs. To compound the tragedy of Mostar, substantial numbers of teenagers and other young people have become addicts in the last few years. The situation is especially bad in western Mostar, which is part of a Split-Mostar trafficking axis. In early 2001 Ivan Andabak, a former HVO commander, went on trial in Croatia, charged with being a key member of a transnational narcotics-trafficking ring. During the war, Andabak was deputy commander of the HVO's 'convicts' battalion', led by another hard-core criminal, Mladen Naletilic (popularly known by his nickname, Tuta), which wreaked terror in the Mostar region. Andabak is the prime suspect in the car-bomb assassination of HDZ-BiH leader Jozo Leutar, the FBiH's deputy interior minister murdered in Sarajevo in March 1999. Tuta is currently on trial in The Hague, but the legacy lives on in Mostar.[33]

The most striking aspect of Mostar's partition consists of visual symbols used to mark zones and boundaries of territorial control. The periphery of Muslim territory on the west bank, on the eastern edges of the Boulevard, is marked by a long line of slender minarets belonging to *dzamije* (mosques) erected since the war. Just across the Boulevard, the beginning of Croat turf is signalled by an enormous Catholic cathedral, under construction at an expense of 25 million marks, its spire rising into the sky. The concept of *shared space*, belonging equally to all communities, which has been the key to coexistence in Bosnia for centuries, has been grievously damaged by the violent demise of Yugoslavia as a state, the eclipse of the Yugoslav idea and the Bosnian war. On Liska Street, a quiet tree-lined street on the Croat side of town just off the former Muslim-Croat frontline, there is a cemetery where some 80 per cent of the graves are Muslim and the remainder Catholic. All belong to Mostarians who were killed in 1992 during the confrontation with the JNA and area Serbs, hence the side-by-side burial in a common graveyard. In February 1997, a group of about a hundred Bosniacs crossed the Boulevard and entered Liska Street to visit some of the Muslim graves on the occasion of Bajram, the festive day that comes at the end of the annual month of fasting. They were immediately confronted by a crowd of Croats, which included civilians as well as uniformed

[33] 'Bosnian Croat Militia Chief on Trial for Drug Trafficking', AFP, Zagreb, February 12, 2001.

and plainclothes police. In the ensuing melee, shots were fired in the air by uniformed officers, then by two plainclothes officers (including the then deputy chief of police in west Mostar) directly into the Bosniac crowd. They fled back across the Boulevard, but one Bosniac suffered a fatal gunshot wound and almost twenty others were injured. They had transgressed the new borders defining Mostar and suffered the consequences. Shortly thereafter, some west Mostar politicians suggested that the Muslim graves in the Liska Street cemetery be exhumed and transported across the river for reburial in the 'Muslim' part of town, just in order to prevent recurrence of such incidents in the future. In June 2000 the HDZ and HVO installed an enormous cross—symbolizing Christianity and specifically Catholicism—on Mount Hum, overlooking the entire town but particularly the Bosniac parts, and inaugurated it in an elaborate ceremony. 'Muslim' Mostar was very tense on that day. In the keynote speech of the ceremony, former HVO general Stanko Sopta described Mostar as 'the capital of the Croat nation' in BiH. The topic of wartime destruction and postwar denial of the concept of a shared, inter-communal space is treated in Chapter 4, which discusses the Bosnian case in the context of partition as a modern phenomenon.

Conclusion: lessons of Mostar

The change of regime in Croatia in early 2000, following the death of Franjo Tudjman, raised international expectations about an imminent breakthrough in Mostar. The HDZ-BiH held its own in Croat-dominated areas in municipal elections in April 2000, including Mostar. However following the elections, which saw a low turn-out of voters in many traditional HDZ-BiH strongholds, Neven Tomic, a moderate Mostar Croat with a 'clean' wartime reputation, was appointed interim head of the Mostar city HDZ board—hitherto a preserve of hardliners—by HDZ party leader Ante Jelavic. Tomic also assumed the post of Mostar's Deputy Mayor with Jelavic's support. In end-May, the Herzegovina-Neretva canton's legislature adopted, after a delay of over two years, two laws on local self-government and distribution of public revenues in Mostar. Under these laws the joint city government, which has lacked a financial base, is supposed to receive 30 per cent of all revenues collected in the six municipalities. The laws had been stalled at the canton level by HDZ obstruction. At the same time the winds of change blowing through Croatia began to affect Herzegovina. The rows of hundreds of partially constructed houses by the M-17 motorway leading from Mostar to the coast, meant to consolidate the Croat presence in the area by settling HVO war veterans and displaced Croats from elsewhere in BiH, hinted at a severe erosion of financial support from Croatia. Ivan Bender, hardline HDZ-BiH mayor of Neum, the southern Herzegovina municipality that is BiH's only outlet to the Adriatic Sea, was relieved of control over BiH Croat pension funds for war invalids and the elderly—financed for years by the Tudjman regime—amidst allegations of serious irregularities and misappropriations. It appeared that the tide was finally turning in Mostar and its hinterlands. In June, a bus service commenced between the western and eastern banks of the town.

The HDZ-BiH's sixth party congress was held in Sarajevo in mid-July in these circumstances of uncertainty and change. Confusing signals emanated from this gathering, a sign of the genuine disorientation of the party in the post-Tudjman context, and of pulls and pressures in different directions from various factions, interest-groups, and modes of thinking. On the one hand, Jelavic delivered a presidential address in which he said: 'This is the year 2000. We have to understand that five years ago we could go by the rhetoric of national romanticism of the 19th century. But now we have to face concrete problems'. Presenting a pragmatic, even reformist face, he asserted that the HDZ-BiH would evolve into a modern European political party of the centre-right, and claimed that there was no contradiction between protecting Bosnian Croat national interests and helping build the common state of BiH. The hymn of BiH was played at the convention alongside the patriotic crowd's sentimental favourite, the national anthem of Croatia. On the other hand, the conference featured a ranting diatribe by the principal guest speaker, Croatian Army general and onetime HVO chief of staff Slobodan Praljak, who takes pride in claiming that he ordered the demolition of the Stari Most in Mostar. Jadranko Prlic, the HDZ-BiH's best-known moderate face and a favourite of international officialdom, narrowly failed to win election as party vice-president after warning the gathering against 'traitors who motivate the autistic national consciousness in which the fruits will be enjoyed only by the oligarchy, while the population is led to believe that their everyday difficulties are a natural condition for the preservation of the national identity' (Prlic left the party later in the year). While some of the most notorious hardliners like Brajkovic, Bender and Dragan Meter (power-broker and dismissed mayor of Prozor) were not accommodated in the reconstituted party presidency and vice-presidency, the other liberal, Tomic, 'did not even submit his name for election for the post of head of the Mostar HDZ Board', according to a private assessment of the conference and its implications prepared by one international agency, 'because he knew he would lose'. The whole exercise seemed to be geared to the consolidation of Jelavic's personal control over the party through implantation of loyalists in key positions.

By this time the initial euphoria in IC circles was beginning to dissipate. The same international assessment of problems and prospects pointed out that 'Tomic finds himself in a somewhat impossible situation' in Mostar. 'As Tomic makes promises to unify utilities and wrest control of public services from the three Croat-majority municipalities', the report noted, 'he will have to fight those who control these structures and wish to keep Mostar and the canton divided. It is far from clear that he will succeed because they [still] have more funds than he does'. Local opinion surveys claimed that 78 per cent of west Mostarians opposed his moderate orientation. In end-July 2000 Croatian prime minister Ivica Racan visited Mostar. He walked around the Old Town and announced a Croatian government donation towards the reconstruction of the Old Bridge. He attended a dinner jointly hosted by Safet Orucevic and Neven Tomic, with local Serb Civic Council leaders, including a returned Orthodox prelate, in attendance. But the Croatian PM's Mostar itinerary also included a visit to the Aluminij plant and a meeting with Mijo Brajkovic.

In the November 2000 BiH general elections, the HDZ-BiH polled over 80 per cent of ballots cast by Croats (93 per cent counting its satellite parties in the Croat National Congress), campaigning on its tried and tested platform of Croat national rights, complete with inflammatory anti-Muslim television advertising and posters advising the Croat electorate that the choice was 'self-determination or extinction') The IC's major hope in this election in Croat-dominated areas was a list sponsored by a group of formerly pro-HDZ businessmen that ran against the official HDZ slate in the Croat stronghold of western Herzegovina. Like another internationally supported breakaway HDZ faction before it, Kresimir Zubak's New Croatian Initiative (NHI), this alternative list only marginally dented the HDZ's vote bank. Despite the local popularity of its chief backers, brothers Mladen and Jerko Ivankovic who run the successful Siroki Brijeg-based meat-processing plant, *Lijanovici*, the list mustered eight per cent of the vote in western Herzegovina canton, against 71 per cent for the HDZ.

Following these elections the festering contradictions of the Muslim-Croat Federation escalated into full-blown crisis in 2001. A major confrontation between the IC and the premier party of BiH Croats has been brewing for some time. In October 1999, SFOR troops raided three Croat police/intelligence buildings in west Mostar; in February 2000 the peacekeepers closed down Erotel, a hardline Croat TV station broadcasting from the Mostar area. As a result, graffiti proclaiming SFOR an occupation force and calling for a Croat uprising were already a common sight in west Mostar by 2000. 2001 saw further dramatic developments, including a riot on west Mostar's Kneza Domagoja Street after a SFOR-backed raid on the main office of Hercegovacka Banka, the evacuation of international staff from the once-again besieged Hotel Ero, a walkout from the Federation army by most officers and soldiers of the army's Croat formations stationed in Herzegovina, central Bosnia and Posavina, and a declaration of solidarity with the Croat National Congress by the Croat police in Mostar canton. The root causes and escalation of this crisis have been touched upon in Chapters 1 and 2, and its underlying issues are discussed further in the rest of this book, especially when I dissect the question of 'post-Yugoslav futures', as it pertains to Bosnia, in Chapter 6.

The events of 2000-01 expose the limitations of the conventional notion that Bosnia's problems are largely, perhaps even solely, the result of malign interference from and by Serbia-Montenegro and Croatia. To be sure, the most extremist elements among the Croats of Bosnia & Herzegovina have been sustained by the disproportionate influence of right-wing Herzegovinian

Croats at the centre of the Tudjman regime throughout the 1990s, and by Zagreb's financial support of parallel BiH Croat institutions. Nonetheless, deeply troubled relations between the peoples of Bosnia & Herzegovina, and their conflicting aspirations, have provided an *endogenous* motor of conflict throughout the 1990s and beyond, the legitimacy of the Bosnian state among BiH Serbs and Croats remains fragile at best, and it can be plausibly argued that Serb and Croat citizens of BiH have a fundamental, normal democratic right to build and nurture links with the two other successor-states of Yugoslavia in which most of their co-nationals live.

The endgame of the Bosnian drama, rather than reaching its climax at Dayton, is possibly unfolding only now. In tackling the 'Croat question', one of many unresolved contradictions of the Dayton peace, Bosnia's international supervisors and Western governments, NATO and the EU have to contend with the reality that the HDZ-BiH, for all its brutal and venal antecedents, has the sympathy of the overwhelming majority of BiH Croats in the showdown with the 'foreigners' and their relative handful of Croat supporters mobilized in the hotch-potch 'Alliance for Change' that runs that Federation and common-state governments. The 'known devil' is still regarded as a necessary guarantee of their future by most ordinary BiH Croats, and the RS, despite the horrific circumstances of its birth, is regarded in much the same way by most BiH Serbs. At the same time, even the most nationalist BiH Croats know in their heart of hearts that the Greater Croatia project, in the form conceived by the Tudjman-Susak-Boban triumvirate, has been thwarted and is not going to be realized. In fact, 'the leadership of the HDZ [BiH] has neither the [financial] resources nor the political support [from Croatia] for such a policy. The pre-conditions of "Herceg-Bosna" no longer exist.'[34]

Mostar refracts in a concentrated microcosm practically all the problems Bosnia & Herzegovina faces in the aftermath of the apocalypse of 1992-5. Seven years of international presence and engagement have certainly not undone or substantially reversed the partition of Mostar. But even here, in what is perhaps the single most difficult local site for the international state-building and

---

[34] European Stability Initiative, *Reshaping International Priorities in Bosnia—Part III: The End of the Nationalist Regimes and the Future of the Bosnian State*, Sarajevo, March 22, 2001, p. 10.

democratization project in post-war Bosnia, international intervention has had, over time, a *softening* effect on that partition. It is easy to criticize the IC's record in Mostar. But the case of Sarajevo stands as a warning against shotgun reunifications of divided cities. The precipitate handover of Greater Sarajevo to Muslim control within three months of the DPA led to a mass exodus of Serbs from the area. The damage done then is only slowly, partially being redressed by sizeable Serb returns to Sarajevo in 2000 and 2001 (over 20,000 returnees between January 2000 and September 2001, mostly to the Novi Grad, Novo Sarajevo and Ilidza districts). Mostar's 'reunification' on the Sarajevo model would have satisfied Bosniacs but been intolerable to Croats. A gradual, incremental approach may eventually yield better dividends in the longer term even if unsatisfying in the short run.

The transition to a post-Yugoslav future is very much open and ongoing in Mostar, as in Bosnia as a whole. To the dismay of both integrationists and partitionists, that transition seems to be leading not to a *singular, unambiguous* future but to a future that is a compound of hybrid elements and competing influences.

When the international community arrived in Mostar in 1994, its soldiers constructed a pontoon footbridge across the Neretva at the point that used to be spanned by the old Ottoman bridge. In late 1999 that footbridge was washed away by flash floods that caused a sudden rise in the river's water-level, perhaps underlining, in the metaphoric sense, the tenuous character of the internationally sponsored bridge across the Neretva. By late 2000 the temporary footbridge had been rebuilt by Hungarian peacekeepers. Meanwhile, a World Bank-UNESCO project to reconstruct the real bridge is underway, with financial help from the governments of Italy, the Netherlands and Turkey. The bankers for the project are *Hrvatska Banka* (Croatian Bank), a Mostar-based bank linked to the some of the leaders of the moderate minority faction in the HDZ-BiH. Many of the original slabs of limestone have been recovered for this purpose from the river-bed, and more will come from the quarry close to the town that supplied Mimar Hajrudin and his colleagues with their raw materials 436 years ago. On June 7, 2001, the reconstruction process formally began with a ceremony at the site, in the Old Town. It is scheduled for completion in 2003. Emir Balic, a Stari Grad resident aged sixty-seven, holds the record for the maximum number of dives, over a thousand, by any individual into the Neretva from the Stari Most (the traditional diving festival, held every August, has long been a highlight of Mostar's calendar). 'My biggest wish is to jump from the new Old Bridge, health permitting', he says.[35]

[35] 'Reconstruction of Bosnia's Famous Bridge Begins', Reuters, Mostar, June 8, 2001.

4

BOSNIA AND THE PARTITION DEBATE

AN INTERVENTION

'If we start by partitioning one country, where would we draw the line? Wouldn't partition embolden those who advocate ethnic separation and are prepared to commit terrible crimes to achieve their goals?'—*A commentary in 'Balkan Crisis Reports', February 2001*[1]

'Whether Bosnia will disintegrate completely or whether it becomes stronger depends, above all, on economic laws and future circumstances. But that is not something [to determine] for the current generation or for [older] citizens who are alive today... What our children and grandchildren choose to do is up to them.'—*Momcilo Krajisnik, senior Bosnian Serb leader, in November 1997*[2]

In 1947 Britain's Indian empire was partitioned into two independent 'dominions'—Hindu-majority India and a Muslim state called Pakistan. It was a time of tragedy for the subcontinent, unprecedented then and unparalleled since. When the dust finally settled on the partition of India, between 500,000 and one million people of all religious communities—Hindu, Muslim and Sikh—had died in massive communal violence that engulfed not only the partitioned province of Punjab, but areas in Pakistan like Sind, (including the capital city, Karachi) and the North-West Frontier Province; regions in India such as the post-independence provinces of Bihar, Uttar Pradesh and the national capital, Delhi; the other partitioned province of Bengal; as well as the Jammu

---

[1] Kovac and Domi, 'Friedman Triggers Bosnian Controversy', *BCR* 214, February 1, 2001.

[2] Interviewed in *NIN*, Belgrade, November 6, 1997, pp. 20-2. Krajisnik was speaker of the BiH parliament in 1991, and a key member of the Bosnian Serb political high command during the war. From September 1996 to September 1998 he was the elected Serb/RS member of the tripartite BiH state presidency. In April 2000 Krajisnik was arrested from his home near Sarajevo by SFOR troops and transported to The Hague. At the time of writing, he is being tried by the ICTY.

area of the region of Jammu and Kashmir, disputed then and ever
since between the two successor-states to British India. The near-
total breakdown of civil order in the affected areas generated not
just mass murder but mass rapes and abductions of women
belonging to the community (or communities) that suddenly
became the vulnerable 'minority' in a particular local or regional
context. We can and will never know how many women suffered
this fate, but 75,000-100,000 is an estimate that appears in the literature on India's partition.[3] (Between 15 and 20 million people
were permanently uprooted from their homes and hearths.)
Western Pakistan (the entire territory of post-1971 Pakistan) was
almost emptied of Hindus and Sikhs, and large numbers of
Hindus also moved from eastern Pakistan (eastern Bengal, contemporary Bangladesh) to inhabit squalid squatter settlements in
and around Calcutta, the city that after August 1947 became the
capital of the rump Indian province of 'West Bengal'. Eastern
Punjab, in India, was almost emptied of its Muslim population.
During and after partition, millions of Muslims also left their
ancestral homes in various other parts of the new Indian state and
migrated to Pakistan.

This episode of mass murder, mass rape and mass expulsion (or
'transfer', in sanitized terminology) had the side-effect of spawn-
ing a rich literary tradition on both sides of the new borders.[4] The
most remarkable exponent of that tradition is a man called Saadat
Hasan Manto, who was born an Indian in 1912, became—
ineluctably—a Pakistani in 1947, and died of health problems
caused by chronic alcoholism in 1955. The partition of India had
the unintended and unforeseen consequence of unleashing
Manto's creative genius. He wrote in Urdu, an Indic language
written in the Arabic script and born of the fusion of Sanskrit (the
ancient, classical language of pre-Islamic India) with Persian, the
court language of India's Muslim dynasties. Fortunately for the

---

[3] For an essay on the Indian state's attitude and policy towards non-Muslim
women abducted by Muslims in course of partition violence, see Ritu Menon,
'Reproducing the Legitimate Community: Secularity, Sexuality and the State in
Post-Partition India' in P. Jeffery and A. Basu (eds), *Appropriating Gender: Women's
Activism and Politicized Religion in South Asia*, New York and London, 1998, pp.
15-32.
[4] For a collection see Alok Bhalla (ed.), *Stories about the Partition of India*, Delhi,
1994.

wider world, some of his writings have been published in English translation in recent years.

Manto wrote extensively on the theme of partition. His acknowledged masterpiece, however, is a short story of fewer than 3,000 words titled 'Toba Tek Singh'. The story begins like this:

> A couple of years after the Partition of the country, it occurred to the respective governments of India and Pakistan that inmates of lunatic asylums, like prisoners, should also be exchanged. Muslim lunatics in India should be transferred to Pakistan and Hindu and Sikh lunatics in Pakistani asylums should be sent to India.
>
> Whether this was a reasonable or unreasonable idea is difficult to say. One thing, however, is clear. It took many conferences of important officials from the two sides to come to this decision. Final details, like the date of actual exchange, were carefully worked out. Muslim lunatics whose families were still residing in India were to be left undisturbed, the rest moved to the border for exchange. The situation in Pakistan was slightly different, since almost the entire population of Hindus and Sikhs had already migrated to India. The question of keeping non-Muslim lunatics in Pakistan did not, therefore, arise.

News of the impending transfer of mentally ill populations to the countries where they belong sets off great excitement as well as confusion in the asylum located in the Pakistani city of Lahore, close to the Indian border. A Muslim inmate and Pakistan supporter, asked by his fellows where exactly Pakistan is, announces after deep thought that Pakistan is 'the name of a place in India where cut-throat razors are manufactured'. A Hindu inmate, a young lawyer who had lost his mind after an unhappy love affair, has been in deep depression ever since he heard that Amritsar, the Punjab town where his beloved lives, in now on the Indian side of the border. The prospect of imminent transfer to India, the country of his sweetheart, nonetheless fails to cheer him up, since he believes that his legal practice is better off in his hometown, Lahore, than in Amritsar. Generally, the inmates are simply confused by the turn of events, 'unable to decide whether they are in India or Pakistan. If they are in India, where on earth is Pakistan?

And if they are in Pakistan, then how come that until only the other day it was India?' One inmate, upset by the whole controversy, climbs up a tree in the asylum compound and perches on a branch. When the guards try to persuade him to come down, he declares forthrightly: 'I wish to live neither in India nor in Pakistan. I wish to live in this tree.'

The central character in Manto's tale is a Sikh who has been confined in the asylum for fifteen years. The man's real name is Bishan Singh, but he is known as Toba Tek Singh, the name of the village he comes from. Apparently he was a fairly prosperous landlord in this village until suddenly and inexplicably he became insane. Bishan Singh (Toba Tek Singh) speaks a strange gibberish language that nobody can understand. His other special characteristic is that he never sits or lies down. He has been standing on his legs for fifteen years, occasionally leaning against the asylum walls for relief. As a result, his legs are bloated and swollen. But such eccentricities aside, the old man is considered 'a harmless fellow' by the staff and other inmates. The only thing that bothers him is that ever since Partition, he hasn't had a single visit from his family members, including a teenage daughter who used to visit him every month. 'He missed his family, the gifts they used to bring and the concern with which they would speak to him.' Moreover, 'he was sure that they would have told him whether Toba Tek Singh was in India or Pakistan.'

A few days before the exchange of mental patients is due to take place, the old man suddenly has a visitor. It is Fazal Din, a Muslim friend from his native village, who tells him that he has been 'meaning to come for some time to bring you news. All your family are well and have gone to India safely. I did what I could to help. Your daughter Roop Kaur—he hesitated—she is safe too... in India.' As Bishan Singh keeps completely quiet, Fazal Din informs him that 'soon you will be moving to India. What can I say, except that you should remember me to Bhai [Brother] Balbir Singh, Bhai Vadhawa Singh and Bahain [Sister] Amrit Kaur [all Sikh names]. Tell Bhai Balbir Singh that Fazal Din is well by the grace of God. The two brown buffaloes he left behind are well too. Both gave birth to calves but unfortunately one of those died after six days. Say I think of them often and to write me if there is anything I can do.' He then takes his leave after presenting the old Sikh with a farewell gift—a bag of Rice Crispies.

A few days later, on a bitterly cold winter evening, the Hindu and Sikh inmates are crammed into buses and transported to the India-Pakistan border. The exchange gets under way, supervised by a huge posse of armed police and senior officials from both sides. However, to the chagrin of the supervisors, 'most of the inmates appear to be dead set against the entire operation. They simply cannot understand why they are being forcibly removed, thrown into buses and driven to this strange place'. Pandemonium breaks out. Some just refuse to disembark from the buses. Others do so but then start running pell-mell in every direction. Some lunatics tear off their clothes and prance around stark naked in protest. Others start weeping hysterically. The women being exchanged 'are even noisier'. There are competing slogans of 'Long Live Pakistan' and 'Death to Pakistan', followed by fights.

In the midst of this bedlam Bishan Singh asks an official who is recording his name in a register whether Toba Tek Singh now lies in India or Pakistan. On being informed that the place is now in Pakistan, he attempts to run away but is overpowered by guards who try to push him across the frontier into India. The old man resists fiercely, and in the end the guards give up. So, as the night wears on and the exchange continues around him, he 'stands in no man's land' between the countries, 'on his swollen legs, like a colossus'. 'Just before sunrise, Bishan Singh, the man who had stood on his legs for fifteen years, screamed. As officials from the two sides rushed towards him, he collapsed to the ground. There, behind barbed wire on one side lay India and behind more barbed wire, on the other side, lay Pakistan. In between, on a bit of earth that had no name, lay Toba Tek Singh.'[5]

Manto's hatred of the principle and the consequences of Partition is startling both in its clarity and its ferocity. He regards the principle as obscene and its consequences as criminal. The writer's use of lunacy as a metaphor for partition and its population exchanges is simply a literary master-stroke. As a character in *Ran*, the Japanese director Akira Kurosawa's cinematic rendition of

[5] Saadat Hasan Manto, 'Toba Tek Singh' (trans. Khalid Hasan) in M. Hasan (ed.), *India's Partition: Process, Strategy and Mobilization*, Delhi, 1994, pp. 396-402. A translated version can also be found in Salman Rushdie and Elizabeth West (eds), *The Vintage Book of Indian Writing, 1947-1997*, London, 1997, pp. 24-31.

Shakespeare's *King Lear*, says in the most memorable line in the film -- 'In a mad world, only the mad are sane'. Saadat Hasan Manto's uncompromisingly savage, searing satire of India's partition and those who masterminded it is emblematic of the strong passions the topic of partition arouses among proponents and opponents alike. Indeed, emotions run equally strong among its supporters.

The last *Blue Guide* to Yugoslavia, published in 1989, devotes one paragraph to Banja Luka, 'the main industrial and cultural centre of the Bosanska Krajina, the northern region of Bosnia traversed by the Vrbas river, on which the town is situated'. The 'most noteworthy' of the town's Ottoman-era monuments, the *Guide* notes, 'is the Ferhadija Dzamija, a beautiful large mosque built in 1579. At the centre of the inner court the *shadrvan* is surrounded by the *turbe* [shrine] of the founder (1587), his standard-bearer, and a certain Safi Kuduna (early 17th century). To the right of the mosque is the *sahat kula'* (clock tower). The *Guide's* author also makes brief note of another Banja Luka mosque, the Arnaudija Dzamija, commissioned in 1587 by the Ottoman treasurer of Bosnia, Effendi Hausan. The *Guide* then moves on to describe Jajce, another Ottoman town 77 km. from Banja Luka, reached via 'the spectacular Vrbas Gorge, a wild, narrow canyon guarded by ruined castles'.[6]

The Ferhadija mosque stood for exactly 414 years. It survived, during those four centuries, numerous vicissitudes of war and peace in Bosnia & Herzegovina and the Balkans, and even a major earthquake that levelled much of Banja Luka in 1969. It was razed by extremist Bosnian Serbs one night in early May 1993. When I visited Banja Luka in June 2000 to speak at an academic conference at the city's University, all that remained of the Ferhadija was an oddly empty space near the town centre. Barely a kilometre away a similar empty space, overgrown with weeds, marks the site of the Arnaudija Dzamija. In 1992, Banja Luka had sixteen mosques. When the war ended, all had been destroyed.

On the eighth anniversary of the demolition of the Ferhadija, in May 2001, a ceremony was arranged to lay the foundation-stone for a new structure at the site of the destroyed mosque. The

[6] Paul Blanchard, *Blue Guide: Yugoslavia*, London and New York, 1989, p. 355.

Banja Luka city authorities had given permission for reconstruction to begin only after years of sustained pressure from international officials and organizations working in Bosnia but on May 7, the day of the ceremony, a serious riot erupted. A mob of Serb demonstrators, variously estimated to number between 2,000 and 4,000, successfully disrupted the event. Unruly crowds, gesticulating menacingly and chanting Serb nationalist slogans and anti-Muslim taunts, laid virtual siege to the site of the ceremony. International officials, foreign diplomats, Bosnian government leaders and Bosniac civilians arriving to participate in the ceremony were greeted by a hailstorm of missiles including rocks, stones, bottles and eggs. Several Bosnian and foreign dignitaries were hit and their cars damaged. After several attempts, the vanguard of the mob broke through police cordons around the site and physically attacked Bosniacs who had come to participate in the event. Several were brutally beaten. At this point, the assembled guests fled into the Islamic community centre building, located next to the ceremony site. They sheltered there for the next few hours while the rioters rampaged outside. Prayer carpets were set on fire. The green flag on the Islamic community centre building was torn down and set ablaze, and the Republika Srpska tricolour was hoisted in its place. The window panes of the centre were shattered by an avalanche of bricks and rocks. Elements of the mob then ravaged a number of buses in a nearby parking lot that had brought in Bosniac civilians from Federation towns. Five of the buses were burned, sending huge plumes of smoke spiralling across Banja Luka's skyline. The rest were stoned and damaged but their drivers managed to escape with their vehicles. The climax of the demonstration was reached in the late afternoon, when some of the protestors set a piglet loose in front of the besieged building, in a calculated affront to Muslim religious sentiment. 'The animal peacefully sniffed in front of the entrance... Then it moved on to the spot marked for the corner-stone and started to turn up the ground with its snout'.[7] The crowd, delirious with delight, responded by chanting 'Raso, Raso' (for the poet-psychiatrist Radovan Karadzic).

During this disturbance, a couple of SFOR helicopters circled

[7] Branko Peric, 'Reporter's Record: Demonstrations in Banja Luka', AIM, Banja Luka, May 8, 2001.

overhead and some thirty SFOR armoured vehicles, plus four British tanks, were parked on a street about 200 metres away. Wisely, SFOR personnel did not intervene. Any forceful intervention may well have played directly into the agenda of the rioters and escalated the situation dangerously. The problem was that the considerable numbers of Banja Luka police deployed to maintain public order for the ceremony proved manifestly unwilling and unable, barring a few courageous individual exceptions, to effectively confront the rioters and protect the participants from verbal and physical abuse. In the midst of the mayhem, the city's police chief entered the Islamic community centre building and requested that the ceremony be postponed, an admission of total failure to maintain public order. RS prime minister Mladen Ivanic also arrived, entered the building and announced to the 300 international bureaucrats, ambassadors, public officials (including two ministers in his own government, Fuad Turalic and Dusan Antelj, in addition to Bosnian foreign minister Zlatko Lagumdzija) and frightened civilians holed up inside that he would not leave until everybody else had been safely evacuated. Then RS president and vice-president Mirko Sarovic and Dragan Cavic, together with RS national assembly speaker Dragan Kalinic—all three SDS leaders—appeared on the street outside and set about pacifying the crowd. As the mob gradually dispersed, units of the RS interior ministry's special police began evacuating those trapped inside the building. Everyone was evacuated by the evening. Thirty persons had been hurt, including eighteen Muslim civilians visiting for the ceremony and three local police officers. One of the injured, Murat Badic, 61 years of age, had been beaten unconscious on his prayer-rug. He was taken to hospital in a comatose condition, and died two weeks later.[8]

The riot in Banja Luka followed a pattern set two days earlier, on May 5, 2001, during a formal ceremony to inaugurate the reconstruction of the Osman Pasha mosque in the eastern Herzegovina town of Trebinje. The Osman Pasha was one of ten Trebinje mosques razed during the 1992-5 war. The Trebinje incident, involving a few hundred rather than a few thousand demon-

---

[8] For eyewitness narratives of the riot and its aftermath, see Peric, 'Reporter's Record'; 'Rioting Bosnian Serbs Stone Officials at Mosque Site', Reuters, Banja Luka, May 8, 2001; 'Muslims Terrified After Violence in Bosnia Town', Reuters, Banja Luka, May 9, 2001.

strators, was essentially a smaller version of what happened in Banja Luka two days later. Groups of young toughs congregated from morning in bars in the neighbourhood of the ceremony site, drinking heavily. The atmosphere turned progressively ugly and eventually the ceremony had to be aborted as Muslim religious dignitaries and officers of international agencies were forced to seek refuge from a riotous mob in the town's Islamic community centre building. When the local OHR representative, a Spanish ex-army officer, attempted to prevent a gang of thugs from breaking into the building, he was viciously assaulted along with a Sarajevo journalist who tried to go to his aid. In a later interview, the official noted that local police on the scene were 'passive, unprofessional and possibly aware in advance' of the game-plan, and 'just stood there' doing nothing.[9] He said that while in his opinion Trebinje had a 'moderate majority', they were like 'sheep', intimidated by a 'small band of hooligans'. In Banja Luka, too, the mob's spearhead consisted of about one hundred hooligan fans of the local 'Borac' football club. Nonetheless, one eyewitness observer in Banja Luka noted the disturbing fact that apart from the passivity and incompetence of the police, 'thousands of Banja Luka citizens silently watched the vandalistic attack of the hooligans'.[10] In the immediate aftermath of the trouble, some Bosnian Serb officials and Banja Luka citizens expressed the view that 'maybe they [the international mission in Bosnia] should have waited a little longer' before holding the ceremony, as 'the war did not happen long enough ago for something like this to go peacefully'.[11] Others blamed diplomats and IC officials from Western countries—particularly the United States—for contributing to the causation of the incident by making strident public and media statements about the reconstruction in the days leading up to the inaugural ceremony.

These views are not entirely without basis. Yet Wolfgang Petritsch, the international community's high representative, certainly summed up the near-universal reaction to the mob violence when he expressed shock that 'Republika Srpska still appears to be a place with no rule of law, no civilized behaviour and no reli-

[9] 'Western Official Warns of Fascism in Bosnia', Reuters, Sarajevo, May 9, 2001. The intrepid official was Daniel Ruiz of Spain, head of OHR's Trebinje office.
[10] Peric, 'Reporter's Record'.
[11] 'Muslims Terrified After Violence in Bosnia Town'.

gious freedom'.[12] Indeed, the incident caused severe embarrassment to the fledgling regime of Ivanic, struggling to establish its
'moderate' and reformist credentials and steer the RS away from
its dark origins and sordid reputation. Within a week, heads
inevitably rolled as the RS's interior minister and his deputy, the
head of the RS intelligence service and the Banja Luka police
chief were all constrained to resign from their positions. In June,
the Trebinje district's newly appointed police chief was also dismissed and decertified by the UN/IPTF for failing to adequately
investigate the May 5 incident and bring the culprits to justice.
For Bosnian Muslims, the twin incidents—especially the day-long
violence in Banja Luka—reawakened some of the bitterest memories of what happened during the war to Muslim communities
and to the Islamic places of worship that constitute such an
important part of Bosnia's architectural and historical heritage.
Troublemakers on the Muslim side of the divide seized the
opportunity. Hundreds of men roamed the centre of Sarajevo on
foot and in convoys of honking cars, waving green and SDA party
flags, chanting 'Alija, Alija' (Izetbegovic), shouting 'Chetniks out!'
and threatening to make war on Serbs.[13] An explosive device was
hurled at an Orthodox church in the Muslim-controlled town of
Sanski Most in northwestern Bosnia, on the 'frontline' with RS
territory.

Six weeks later, in June 2001, the disrupted Ferhadija ceremony was held, with practically all top RS officials in attendance.
Once again, a smaller mob of 1,000-2,000 demonstrators attempted to storm the venue. This time, they were held at bay by a well-
organized and resolute police operation. Parts of downtown Banja
Luka turned into a battle-zone, as Bosnian Serb police in riot gear
fought pitched battles with other Bosnian Serbs determined to
protest, come what may, against the reconstruction of a mosque in
'their' city.

How does one interpret the Ferhadija episode? Three
groups—hard-drinking professional hooligans, an unreconstructed core of sectarian extremists intent on demonstrating their exis-

[12] 'Rioting Bosnian Serbs Stone Officials at Mosque Site'.
[13] 'Muslim Nationalists Protest in Sarajevo as Ethnic Tension Mounts', AFP,
Sarajevo, May 9, 2001; Beth Kampschror, 'Multicultural Bosnia?', *Central Europe
Review*, May 14, 2001.

tence, and aggrieved Serb refugees from Muslim-controlled areas of Bosnia—formed the bulk of the mobs in both May and June in Banja Luka. This confluence of vandals and vested interests undoubtedly helps explain the rioting. Attempts by some Muslim politicians and clerics to make political capital out of the ceremony, and the unnecessarily overheated and self-congratulatory rhetoric of some international community officials in the days and weeks leading up to it—both seen as provocative and inflammatory by Serbs—helps fill out the explanation. An *interpretation*, however, is qualitatively distinct from mere explanation. It seeks to include but also go beyond proximate and precipitating causes and uncover the underlying *meaning* of an event, the *logic* (however perverse) behind its occurrence.

From this perspective, there are some genuinely puzzling elements to the intensity *and* tenacity of the protests in Banja Luka. In the first five months of 2001, as many as 1,143 displaced Bosniacs returned to live in Banja Luka, beneficiaries of a property law implementation process reinvigorated since late 1999 by concerted international action.[14] The large majority, 899, returned during January and February 2001, but 180 returns took place during the month of May. By the end of July, 1,799 Bosniac citizens had returned to Banja Luka during 2001. All these returnees came back without any major incident. Weeks before the first Ferhadija ceremony, the three members of the BiH state presidency made their first-ever joint visit to Banja Luka, again without incident. In 2000-01 mosque reconstructions were inaugurated without incident in several other places in Republika Srpska, including Kozarac (near Prijedor), Bosanski Novi/Novi Grad, a northwestern Bosnia town which straddles the internal border with the Muslim-dominated Bihac area and the international border with Croatia, and Bosanska Gradiska, another northwestern Bosnia town perched on the Sava river border with Croatia's western Slavonia region. Nor can Banja Luka be dismissed as a backwater town in a rural and traditionally 'wild' region, as Trebinje, located in eastern Herzegovina near the border with Montenegro, can.

A full and persuasive explanation of the unrest in Banja Luka

---

[14] 'Registered Minority Returns from January 1, 2001 to May 31, 2001 in BiH', UNHCR, Sarajevo, July 2001.

in May-June 2001 requires *interpretation*, in the sense defined in the previous paragraph. Banja Luka, never anything more than a large, pleasant provincial town in former Yugoslavia, is the self-styled 'capital' and seat of government of Republika Srpska, a statelet established through war and 'ethnic cleansing'. When I visited Banja Luka several times during 2000, I noticed an ostentatiously large, new Orthodox cathedral under construction in the centre of the city's downtown area, underlining the 'Serb' character of post-war Banja Luka. 'Minority' returns by some evicted Muslim citizens (and fewer Croats, a total of 133 in the first five months of 2001) to the city may not be liked, but can be tolerated since such returns do not fundamentally undermine the role of Banja Luka as the centre of the Bosnian *Serb* statelet. However, the prospect of a reconstructed Ferhadija in the middle of Banja Luka, its dome and minarets competing with the rather newer monuments to the Orthodox faith a stone's throw away, is intolerable to some people. It signals that Bosnia's Muslim heritage has an *equal* right to exist in Banja Luka—even *after* 1992 and 1995—alongside the Serbian Orthodox tradition.

This represents a violation of and fundamental challenge to the symbolic basis of the precept of partition. It represents a negation of the principle of a space *exclusively* belonging to (or at the very least, unambiguously dominated by) one national community, and a symbolic reinstatement or re-validation in principle of the concept of an *intercommunal space* that may be shared and jointly inhabited by members of different Bosnian communities and traditions. This latter concept was destroyed by the Bosnian war and there are many—on all three sides—who would rather keep it that way. But they have a problem. Those who rioted in protest on Banja Luka's streets in mid-2001—and the rather larger number who tacitly supported or sympathized with them without actually participating—are acutely aware that while BiH may be deeply divided along national faultlines, it is *not* partitioned as fully and permanently as they would prefer. All the more reason to make a stand and demonstrate the strength of their feelings. This complicated and uncertain state of affairs is not simply because of United States and Western support for a nominally united state. It is also because Bosnia's historical legacy is such a mix of competing impulses and traditions. A short walk from where the Ferhadija

riots took place, there is a square in downtown Banja Luka, directly opposite Banski Dvor, the seat of Republika Srpska institutions.
In this square stand some twenty busts of prominent communist
heroes from the Banja Luka region. Many died because of their
beliefs (and in the case of the Serbs, their national identity) during the Second World War; others survived to participate in the
reconstruction of Bosnia and the second Yugoslavia. No doubt
deliberately, the busts are almost equally divided among persons
with discernibly Serb, Croat and Muslim names, including a
woman with a Muslim first and last name martyred in 1943 in the
cause of revolution and south Slav emancipation. The rioters of
2001 have historical as well as contemporary reasons to feel inse-
cure.

This chapter is a strategic intervention in the debate on partition, as it pertains to the particular context of post-Dayton Bosnia
& Herzegovina. The theme of partition is central to any study of
contemporary Bosnia, and as such it runs through the fabric of
this book, appearing and re-appearing frequently in various forms
in the other chapters. In this chapter, focused on the partition
debate with regard to the present and future of BiH, I argue that
the arguments of both the advocates and the dogmatic opponents
of partition miss the point. Why?

Untangling the debate

When the fervently anti-partition writers published by *Balkan
Crisis Reports* argue that 'if we start by partitioning one country,
where would we draw the line?', they have a valid, indeed unimpeachable point. They are arguing against a rival school of thought
which believes that the only guarantee for lasting peace and stability in southeastern Europe lies in completing the process of creation of national states from the debris of ex-Yugoslavia, not by
shoring up precarious multinational states such as Bosnia &
Herzegovina (and, one would logically assume, the former
Yugoslav republic of Macedonia). The problem with the argument
of the ardent Bosnia unificationist and anti-partitionist school,
such as the sample cited above, is that their vision is peculiarly
myopic. It seemingly applies only to the post-April 1992 state of
Bosnia & Herzegovina. The real power of the observation 'If we

start by partitioning one country, where would we draw the line?' becomes evident if we think of the former Yugoslavia as the country in question. All the horrors and miseries suffered by the people of wartime and post-war Bosnia can be laid at the door of that 'original sin'—the partition of Yugoslavia. Indeed, the partition of Yugoslavia unleashed a snowballing dynamic of disintegration and fragmentation which emboldened sectarian extremists and criminals across the region. The tragedy of Bosnia is the most powerful example of the consequences, suffered also by Croats, Serbs and smaller minorities in Croatia and vividly dramatized by the yet unsettled status of Macedonia, Kosovo and Montenegro. One can respond to the rhetorical question posed by the authors quoted with a counter-question—what of the saying prevalent among the Yugoslav peoples themselves that 'without Bosnia there can be no Yugoslavia, and without Yugoslavia there can be no Bosnia'?[15]

A decontextualized defence of Bosnia's unity and integrity is problematic, whether its partisans admit it or not. This view implicitly takes the borders and legitimacy of the Bosnian state for granted. I have argued in Chapter 2 that the legitimacy of those borders cannot be assumed, or established as some sort of natural truth or axiom, whether one looks at the problem from an historical, normative-philosophical or international-legal perspective. It will not do to dismiss the existence of a genuine controversy by labelling scholars such as Hayden or Radan, who expose the deeply contested nature of Bosnia's sovereignty and the contradictions of Western policy towards Bosnia and former Yugoslavia, as 'pro-Serb'. These authors are pro-Serb, but it doesn't obviously follow that their arguments are wholly without merit. Similarly, it is possible to unreservedly condemn the massive atrocities committed by some Bosnian Serbs (in the name of the entire Bosnian Serb people) against non-Serb Bosnians in the course of the war, while acknowledging at the same time that the Serbs of Bosnia had in principle a case in opposing the dissolution of Yugoslavia and the emergence of an independent Bosnia & Herzegovina against the wishes of the vast majority of their community.

The ardent unificationist, anti-partition, pro-'Bosnian' posture

---

[15] Troy McGrath, 'Dealing with Disintegration in the Balkans: Is Partition Such Sweet Sorrow?', *Harriman Review* 11: 3 (1999), p. 37.

has a troubling flaw embedded at its core. It seems to regard only *one* view—among several competing perspectives—on the legitimacy and unity of the Bosnian state as at all legitimate. Any sceptical or alternative view—even if posed in a civilized manner as a matter for democratic debate—is implicitly (indeed, sometimes explicitly) regarded as illegitimate. This is a form of moral righteousness that can assume troubling dimensions in some versions. The conversion of Yugoslavia's internal borders into international ones is a *fait accompli* today. But that doesn't mean that the debate over that conversion is a false one, or that those citizens (and groups of citizens) of former Yugoslavia who feel that real injustice was done to them by German and subsequently, American-sponsored recognition of former republics as sovereign states have no case.

One level-headed, clear-eyed analysis of the evolution of international involvement in post-Dayton Bosnia has boldly stated that 'the ultimate goal' of that involvement is 'political reconciliation between those who fought for Herceg-Bosna and Republika Srpska, and those who defended the state of Bosnia & Herzegovina' during the war.[16] If so, the recognition of only one among several Bosnian perspectives as the sole legitimate perspective, and the pre-emption of debate on the multiple ways of being Bosnian, does a singular disservice to the prospects of healing Bosnia's fractured society (the technique the Good Friday agreement on power-sharing and peace-building in Northern Ireland has used to deal with sharply divergent notions of national identity and state-allegiance among the population is to term both of them, Irish and British, as 'equally legitimate'[17]). And it is not the way to make Bosnia work as a state, something that is broadly in the shared interest of the vast majority of Bosnians notwithstanding their differences. An uncritical acceptance of the axiomatic quality of the 'Bosnia, one, united and indivisible' viewpoint can lead to admonitions such as 'Bosnia... should have been reintegrated... from the start'[18] (the start of what exactly, the war or the

---

[16] European Stability Initiative, *Reshaping International Priorities in Bosnia Part III: The End of the Nationalist Regimes and the Future of the Bosnian State*, p. 13.

[17] See the *Irish Times* website, *http://www.ireland.com/special/peace* for the full text of the Good Friday agreement of April 1998.

[18] Radha Kumar, 'The Troubled History of Partition', *Foreign Affairs* 76: 1 (1997), p. 24.

Dayton implementation process, is not quite clear). It is difficult to resist the conclusion that there is very little understanding here of the sheer complexity of the Bosnian conundrum.

Some avid proponents of a united, 'multiethnic' Bosnia see no logical or moral inconsistency in harshly criticizing Bosnian Serb and Bosnian Croat 'separatists' and their *de facto* micro-states, while enthusiastically supporting the (equally self-interested) agenda of a section of the Montenegrin political class of taking Montenegro out of the residual 'Yugoslavia',[19] an agenda pursued even after the fall of the Milosevic regime and despite the potential turmoil stemming from the vertical split in Montenegro's divided and economically depressed society on the question. One way of justifying this stance is the argument of the sanctity of the borders of the republics, which is at the very least a contestable proposition. Another, more compelling justification would be valid if the 'self-determination' of Montenegro is necessary for and co-terminous with a struggle for democracy against tyranny. This argument was used very effectively in the early 1990s 'by the new Slovene and Croatian governments, whose ex-communist leaders skilfully portrayed' themselves as 'democrats in reaction to communist dictators in Belgrade-whether federal officials or officials of the Serbian republic, the distinction was lost'—as indeed, I would add, was the distinction between the Serb-nationalist and secular Yugoslavist sections of the JNA—which helped 'to ignore or downplay the abuses of human rights and the signs of political repression by elected governments, as in Croatia'. This was a clever strategy because at the time, 'the judgment of most Western observers... was still under the influence of Cold War anticommunism'.[20] A decade later, the malevolent character of the Milosevic regime is established beyond any reasonable doubt, as is the brutal and criminal nature of Babic and Martic, ringleaders of the Krajina Serb movement in Croatia and above all, of Karadzic, Mladic, Plavsic and their associates in BiH. Yet with the benefit of retrospect, it has become almost as difficult to sustain the proposition that the likes of Tudjman and Izetbegovic ever had any mis-

---

[19] For example, the reportage and commentary carried in *Bosnia Report*, Bosnian Institute, London, issues of July-September 2000, October-December 2000, January-May 2001.

[20] Woodward, *Balkan Tragedy*, p. 152.

sion other than consolidation of personal power and the destructive pursuit of sectarian agendas. It may be equally misleading to believe that most of the leaders of the rather more benign 'self-determination' movement in Montenegro, especially in the post-Milosevic era, are in any sense motivated by commitment to democratic values and the welfare of ordinary citizens.

In an essay comparing the partition of Ireland in the early 1920s and India in mid-1940s and the British imperial role in the two cases, Nicholas Mansergh quotes Sir Penderel Moon, an actor in the Indian drama, as making the apparently paradoxical observation that the leadership of the Indian National Congress, the party leading India's independence movement, 'passionately desired to preserve the unity of India. [But] they consistently acted so as to make its partition certain'.[21] This is an overstatement. Yet it does contain a kernel of truth. During the crucial and ultimately fateful decade 1937–47, leaders of the Congress consistently refused to recognize the All-India Muslim League, the party which eventually led the successful campaign for Pakistan, as a serious political factor worthy of acknowledgement, and of engagement on respectable terms. Following elections contested by Indian parties to form provincial assemblies and administrations in 1937 (the centre in Delhi remained under iron British control) in which Congress fared extremely well generally and the Muslim League rather poorly, the Congress decided that it didn't need to take the Muslim party seriously, a decision later deemed by another British colonial official, Sir Percival Griffiths, to be 'a grave tactical blunder'. There was no need to include the sectional party in power-sharing coalition governments in the provinces, the Congress leadership concluded, for were there not Muslims participating in the Congress movement itself? As Mansergh says, 'there were, but they were noticeably thin on the ground', inflated Congress claims to the contrary notwithstanding.[22] Spurned and humiliated, the Muslim League and its leader Mohammed Ali Jinnah sulked on the margins for a while; then, in 1940, it passed the 'Pakistan Resolution' which made the radical demand that Muslim-majority areas of the subcontinent in northwestern and

[21] Sir Penderel Moon, *Divide and Quit*, London, 1961, p. 14.
[22] Nicholas Mansergh, *The Prelude to Partition: Concepts and Aims in Ireland and India*, Cambridge, 1978, pp. 15-17.

eastern India be grouped to constitute 'Independent States' which would be 'autonomous and sovereign'. There followed a complicated and contingent sequence of events which saw the Muslim League and its Pakistan movement acquire a massive base among the culturally and geographically diverse communities of Indian Muslims by the mid-1940s. In 1947 the Congress finally obtained the independence it had stood for over several decades of struggle, but it came at a terrible price: the unity of India. The Congress leaders cannot avoid their share of culpability for this sorry outcome.

There are some parallels in the twilight of Yugoslavia in Bosnia & Herzegovina in 1991-2. Robert Hayden has narrated a version of what happened at two crucial junctures in the BiH parliament, on October 14-15, 1991, and January 24-25, 1992, during debates on Bosnia's future in the ominous context of civil war in Croatia and the final unravelling of the Yugoslav federation. In both instances, in Hayden's account, there was a pattern of the SDA and the HDZ ganging up in opportunistic alliance against the SDS members, and insisting, against Serb objections, that a majority vote in the parliament—which the SDA and HDZ had between them—was enough to ratify crucial decisions on effectively declaring Bosnia a separate, independent state (the topic of the first debate) and on holding a referendum on that question (the second debate).[23] Hayden's 'pro-Serb' leanings are evident, but his argument merits critical consideration nonetheless. Did those passionately committed to Bosnia's unity act in a reckless, feckless manner that contributed to making war and *de facto* partition all but certain? Was social, political and territorial unity an unavoidable collateral casualty of Bosnia's independence? These are issues which are practically impossible to resolve definitively one way or the other, but the question of responsibility—as in India, shared rather than simply one-sided?—is worth reflecting upon with a somewhat open mind.

In a volume dedicating to demonstrating that partition is *not* a solution to problems of ethnic and communal conflict, Robert Schaeffer has identified four generic types of twentieth-century partitions. The first occurred as part of the process of *decolonization*, as in the case of British withdrawals from India, (most of)

---

[23] Hayden, *Blueprints for a House Divided*, pp. 92-7.

Ireland, and Palestine. The second type were *Cold War* partitions—
in these cases (Germany, Korea, Vietnam, China and Taiwan)
superpowers used partition as a tool to freeze disputes and demar-
cate spheres of influence. Cyprus is an example of a third, later
type of partition, in which the intervention of a neighbourhood
power, Turkey, played a decisive role. Finally, the fourth and most
recent form of partition has been a by-product of *democratization*
processes in multinational one-party states—the former Soviet
Union, the former Yugoslavia, and former Czechoslovakia are the
foremost examples.

Schaeffer comments that if the most recent trends are any indi-
cation, the character of partition may be changing. From being
'what powerful states did to weak ones', partition seems to have
become 'what weak states do to themselves'.[24] Indeed, an essential
historical feature of partition has been the presence of an *external,
third* party with a central role—a departing colonial power, a
superpower with a stake in the conflict, an aspiring regional power
intent on flexing its muscle and/or protecting a diaspora population. A particularly strong correlation (which does not necessarily
imply a causal link) exists between a history of British colonial
rule and the occurrence of partition. The British were instrumental players in the partition of Ireland, India and Palestine. Two
other countries with a British colonial past—Cyprus and Sri
Lanka—have ended up with *de facto* partitions, albeit as a result of
a failure of a power-sharing consociational system in the first case
and a Westminster-style majoritarian-democratic model in the
second. Both systems were bequests of the erstwhile British presence.

The fate of Yugoslavia, and the somewhat more complicated
fate of Bosnia, have like the earlier, 'historic' partitions also been
influenced—indeed, decisively shaped—by the decisions and
policies of powerful, external actors. The judgments of the EC's
Badinter arbitration commission, German initiative in securing
international recognition of Croatia in late 1991, and American
initiative in securing the same for Bosnia & Herzegovina a few
months later all exerted powerful, perhaps defining influence on
the behaviour and strategies of key 'domestic' players in the

---

[24] Robert Schaeffer, *Severed States: Dilemmas of Democracy in a Divided World*,
Lanham, MD, 1999, p. 7.

unfolding Yugoslav and Bosnian dramas. The Yugoslavs, and the Bosnians, clearly did not do what they did to themselves entirely on their own. Coercive diplomatic intervention by the United States was equally instrumental in ending the Bosnian war, and in superficially reversing the on-the-ground partition that had taken place during the war by reconstituting a decentralized but nominally unified single state at Dayton.

Since the early 1990s, as Bosnia has rocketed from being a more or less obscure unit of a middle-sized, federal, socialist country in southeastern Europe to global celebrity status, 'an entire school of thought and academic advocacy has emerged around the alternative of partition',[25] inspired first by the challenge of resolving the wartime crisis and subsequently in response to the frustrating, confusing ambiguity of a country which is somewhat partitioned but not quite. During the desperate summer of 1993, Muslims and Croats went to war in parts of BiH, further aggravating the apparently Hobbesian scenario prevalent on the ground since the summer of 1992. As the carnage filled television screens and newspaper columns across the Western world, two American academics published an essay immodestly titled 'The Answer', with the subheading 'A Partition Plan for Bosnia'. It was carried by a major magazine of commentary and analysis in the United States. A senior international relations professor at the University of Chicago was one of the authors, his collaborator being a professor at 'the School of Advanced Airpower Studies, Air University, Maxwell Air Force Base, Alabama'.[26]

Mearsheimer and Pape are sceptical of 'the fast-fading Vance-Owen plan' primarily because they doubt the feasibility of establishing a central government, however limited, in Sarajevo. They also point out that 'Vance-Owen would produce its own population transfers since minorities would doubtless be driven from areas designated for other groups'. This is not incorrect; in fact this was happening on the ground around that time. In areas designat-

[25] Woodward, 'Genocide or Partition: Two Faces of the Same Coin?', p. 759.
[26] John J. Mearsheimer and Robert A. Pape, 'The Answer: A Partition Plan for Bosnia', *The New Republic*, June 14, 1993, pp. 22-8. Mearsheimer has published more recent pieces urging Bosnia's formal, *de jure* partition, including a *New York Times* op-ed article co-authored with Stephen van Evera, another American political science professor.

ed by the plan as Croat-majority cantons, for example, the HVO and its patrons stepped up expulsion campaigns against Muslims in an effort to render these areas Croat-only cantons. Vance and Owen were powerless to prevent this perverse interpretation of their proposal being implemented by terror on the ground. Indeed, I consider that Vance-Owen was unworkable at that point in the war simply because it was already *too late*; too much had happened in the preceding year of fighting, mass expulsions and atrocities and BiH's political geography had changed beyond recognition, very rapidly. Vance-Owen's basic premise—BiH's population lives 'inextricably intermingled; thus there appears to be no viable way to create three territorially distinct states based on ethnic or confessional principles'—had been overtaken by events and was no longer fully valid. Mearsheimer and Pape also criticize 'the new European proposal to create UN-protected 'safe havens' for the Muslims'. They warn, quite plausibly, that the safe-haven concept is 'a potential disaster'. In any case, 'once the havens are secured, what next?'.

Their grand solution to the crisis is a detailed partition plan for Bosnia. Under this scheme, 'the Croats should get one large chunk of territory on the southwestern border' of BiH. The Croat community living in northern Bosnia, in the thin slice of the Posavina region not overrun by the Serbs, would be constrained to 'relocate to their new state'. In the event, it would probably be much simpler for them to cross the Sava river into Croatia than to relocate to a completely different area of BiH several hundred kilometres away. Oddly, there is no mention in the article of the rather larger Croat populations of central Bosnia or even Sarajevo, but it can be presumed that they too would be expected to 'relocate' to western Herzegovina and the Croat-dominated areas of western Bosnia such as Livno and Tomislavgrad.

However, 'the key territorial trade would be between the Muslims and the Serbs'. Under the plan, the Serbs would have all of northwestern Bosnia, including the Bihac-Cazin region, the northeastern extremity of Bosnia around Bijeljina, and eastern Herzegovina, with a 35 mile-wide east-west corridor connecting Serbia to Serb holdings in *Bosanska Krajina* and contiguous areas of Croatia. The Muslim statelet, 'centred on Sarajevo', would cover almost all of central Bosnia and the Drina valley in eastern Bosnia.

Its borders would connect the towns of Tuzla, Teslic, Zenica, Konjic, and extend to the western bank of the Drina near Loznica, a town on the Serbian side of the river upstream from Zvornik. If all went well, three absolutely homogeneous states would be born through organized transfers of population, and the Serbs, Muslims and Croats would control respectively 45%, 35% and 20% of the former republic's territory. A radical cure indeed. The actualization of the plan would require further seismic population movements among all three groups, on top of what had already occurred during the first year of war. This is to some degree glossed over by its authors, who merely note airily that 'the Muslims of Bihac would [have to] move to the new Bosnian Muslim state'.

However, Mearsheimer and Pape acknowledge that the plan would have to be implemented by 'the West' in the face of likely opposition from two of the three parties to the Bosnian war. They write that 'the Bosnian Muslims have shown little interest in partition and have instead argued for maintaining the multiethnic Bosnian state'. They speculate, nonetheless, that 'a multiethnic Bosnia must now [May-June 1993] have little appeal for the Muslims after their vast suffering at the neighbours' hands.' In fact, a pro-partition viewpoint did emerge and gain support in the SDA as the war progressed. However, the 'integral Bosnia' viewpoint continued to enjoy significant currency among Bosniacs. Six years after the end of the war, it is this latter viewpoint—in somewhat different versions articulated by the SDP and SDA/SBiH—that commands the greater resonance in Bosniac politics and public opinion, despite the practical difficulties of realizing such a vision. As for the Serbs, the two Americans admit that they would be 'likely to balk' if presented with their blueprint. For 'though the plan would help them realize their dream of Greater Serbia', they would also have to cede almost all of eastern Bosnia's Drina valley, plus the whole of the Sarajevo area, to the Muslim state, which 'they would likely resist'. Only 'the Croats are likely to accept partition along the lines we propose', the authors conclude; as before, the distinction between the minority of BiH Croats in western Herzegovina and southwestern Bosnia close to the Croatia border and the majority residing elsewhere in the country finds no mention.

How would the Western powers actually administer this radical cure to its Balkan subjects? The authors are convinced that Bosnian Serb obduracy would be the principal stumbling block. The Bosnian Serbs would therefore have to be compelled to accept a partition plan that is not on terms optimally favourable to their community. They would do so, the authors argue in the best realist tradition, only if their fighting forces are weakened beyond a certain threshold. The authors suggest that the Western powers (NATO, presumably) pursue this goal through a concerted strategy of 'coercive bloodletting'. This unnerving term is understood by the authors to mean that use of Western air power against the principal formations of the Bosnian Serb army would be combined with a policy of building up Bosnian Muslim ground forces to the point where they could take on Bosnian Serb troops in major battles (whence Western airpower would enter the fray against, and severely damage, Bosnian Serb troops massed to counter the Muslim ground offensives). Mearsheimer and Pape admit that 'this strategy would take time. The Muslims would require perhaps a year to halt further Serb gains... before they could move to compel Serb withdrawals', aided by Western airpower. Thus the following measures and steps would be necessary in order for the grand partition plan to be implemented:

In the first phase of military action, 'a fleet of about 100 [!] C-130s would ferry arms to the Muslims, while several hundred fighter and ground attack aircraft stand ready in Italy and on aircraft carriers in the Adriatic to destroy any large Serb offensives'. These arms would include not just a huge variety of light and medium-calibre weapons but 'also heavier weapons, including 105 mm. and 155 mm. artillery pieces'. Additionally, 'the West would deploy 200 to 400 special operations forces in Bosnia' to liaise with and train the Muslims.

In the second phase, a coercive bloodletting strategy would be launched, as outlined above, to force some Serb withdrawals and make it clear to their leadership that they have no alternative but to submit to the wishes of Mearsheimer and Pape.

Since a carrot-and-stick approach is desirable, 'the West should offer to recognize Greater Serbia if the Serbs cooperate with the Western programme. The Western powers should also promise to lift economic sanctions and perhaps even help rebuild the Serbian economy'.

Once this approach has delivered the desired results and 'a peace agreement is signed, populations would [still!] have to be moved in order to create homogeneous states'. Mearsheimer and Pape advise that 'the international community should oversee and subsidize this population exchange. Specifically, the UN should establish a Balkan Population Exchange Commission', modelled on a commission established by the interwar League of Nations which managed the transfer of more than 1.5 million people between Greece and Turkey from 1923 to 1931. This Commission, entrusted to the hapless UN, would have to 'secure safe passage for immigrants, establish a bank to help them buy and sell property', and finally, 'administer a Balkan Marshall Fund to assist the development of new housing and industry in immigrant zones'. Mearsheimer and Pape even prescribe the length and breakdown of the Commission's mandate: ten years, two for resettlement and eight for development (to my knowledge, something resembling a rudimentary 'population exchange commission' was established during the Bosnian war at the local level, the entrepreneur being a war-profiteering Serb paramilitary leader in the Bijeljina district of northeastern Bosnia).

Even this would not be sufficient to guarantee lasting peace and security in Bosnia and the Balkans, since '[Greater] Serbia would [still] be the strongest state in the region and the Bosnian Muslim state would be among the weakest' (despite Mearsheimer and Pape's best efforts to ensure a defensible Bosnian Muslim state by having its borders coincide with high ridges and rivers wherever possible, in a manner oddly reminiscent of Radovan Karadzic's obsession that the borders of his statelet coincide with natural features such as rivers as much as possible). Thus 'NATO… should issue a security guarantee' to the Bosnian Muslim state, and 'NATO should also foster a defensive alliance [against Greater Serbia, which would include the Serb territories of BiH and Croatia] between the Bosnian Muslim state, Croatia and Albania.'

After setting out all the elements of this vastly ambitious plan to end the Bosnian conflict and stabilize the region of ex-Yugoslavia, Mearsheimer and Pape acknowledge that 'this partition plan isn't perfect, and it isn't morally pure'; *but*, 'it is... realistic... It can be done.'

This last claim is ludicrous. The plan's only tenuous connection with what happened in reality in the closing months of the Bosnian war is that NATO airpower was used in tacit collusion with Croat and Muslim ground offensives to roll back the Serbs' territorial holdings, although, of course, air attacks were targeted at Bosnian Serb command-and-control facilities and military infrastructure rather than at massed formations of Serb soldiers. That aside, the plan catastrophically fails its single self-imposed standard: feasibility. Not a single major aspect or element of this plan is remotely 'realistic' given a complex of relevant factors that would have an impact on its viability: the likely extreme reluctance, at the very least, of the United States government and armed forces to commit large-scale military resources to a messy armed conflict in a strategy that would risk dramatic escalation and spread of that conflict; the extremely unlikely possibility of agreement between the United States and its NATO allies on executing such a strategy; the complex international geopolitics of the region of conflict involving Serbia (and Montenegro), Croatia, the Krajina Serbs and the Bosnian belligerents in a pattern of interaction with external powers in which Western recognition of 'Greater Serbia' was neither possible nor capable of fostering peace in either short or long term; the extremely unlikely prospect that the truly enormous financial resources needed to 'resettle' massive uprooted populations and carry out a Marshall-style reconstruction in a distant non-strategic periphery of Europe devoid of resources such as oil would actually materialize; and the altered norms of international affairs since the time the League of Nations attempted such a project would make it likely that the UN, on the eve of the 21st century, would not wish to shoulder the responsibility of running the 'Balkan Population Exchange Commission'.

Note that I have evaluated Mearsheimer and Pape's 'answer' to the Bosnian crisis not on the basis of any moral or normative criteria but by the one criterion for assessment which the authors themselves consider relevant: its realism, or feasibility. Judged by that standard alone, the radical partitionist solution to the dilemma of Bosnia is breathtaking not only for its abject poverty but its sheer, senseless absurdity. It makes one think that Saadat Hasan Manto was rather correct in equating partitionism with dementia.

Enthusiasts of partition ensconced in the academic ivory-tower are, however, not easily discouraged from indulging their pet theme. Since the mid-1990s another political scientist based in the United States, Chaim Kaufmann, has attracted attention to himself by tenaciously promoting partition as 'the best solution to many of the most intense ethnic conflicts'. He claims that this view is gaining ascendancy 'among policymakers and scholars', and that 'events in Bosnia have supported this trend'. [27] Unlike Mearsheimer, a fellow-adherent of the structural-realist tradition of studying international politics dominant in the United States, Kaufmann has advanced a general, comparative argument in support of his claim. Here I examine that argument as put forward in a recent—and compared to earlier versions, refined—article.[28] This article does not talk about the Bosnian case, but it does marshall supporting empirical data from the cases of India, Ireland, Palestine/Israel and Cyprus.

Kaufmann begins and ends his positive appraisal of 'population transfers and partition as solutions to ethnic conflict' with the standard caveats and disclaimers. Since 'noone wants to dissolve diverse societies, even deeply troubled ones, that have any hope of avoiding massive violence', 'we need to identify the threshold of inter-group violence and mutual security threats beyond which we must resort to separation and partition, and we should set the threshold conservatively'. Separation and partition 'can be justified only if they save the lives of people who would otherwise be killed in ethnic violence'.[29] This defensive posture sits somewhat uneasily with Kaufmann's faith in partition of a fairly extreme sort—i.e., not just the division of a territory into separate political and governmental units, but that preceded or accompanied by a transfer of populations as complete as possible in order to make

---

[27] Chaim D. Kaufmann, 'When All Else Fails: Evaluating Population Transfers and Partition as Solutions to Ethnic Conflict' in J. Snyder and B. Walter (eds), *Civil Wars, Insecurity and Intervention*, New York, 1999, pp. 221-60, on p. 221.
[28] See footnote 27 above. An earlier, less developed and refined statement of the same thesis can be found in Chaim Kaufmann, 'Possible and Impossible Solutions to Ethnic Civil Wars', *International Security* 20: 4 (spring 1996), pp. 136-75.
[29] Kaufmann, 'When All Else Fails', pp. 221, 248.

sure that the new units are homogeneous or near-homogeneous. The terms that recur throughout his essay are 'separation' and 'unmixing', rather than 'partition'. In his words, 'partition should never be done unless the national communities are largely [geographically] separate or will be separated at the same time. Partitions that do not unmix hostile populations actually increase violence, as in Northern Ireland, Kashmir, Palestine, and when Croatia and Bosnia seceded from Yugoslavia.'[30] In one sense this is a valid point. But it does not lead Kaufmann to reject partitions *per se* (for example, the partition of Yugoslavia, which led to the bloodbath in Bosnia & Herzegovina) as a messy, fraught, risky business, but rather to advocate a form of partition that 'separates' and 'unmixes' populations as comprehensively as possible. In short, political and territorial division in conjunction with social and demographic 'separation'.

Kaufmann's case is built on the concept of a 'security dilemma', transplanted from the structural-realist international relations paradigm of Cold War US vintage to the context of 'internal' conflicts. Quoting another American academic's language, he describes the essence of the 'security dilemma' as follows:

> Whenever ethnic communities cannot rely on a strong and impartial central state to prevent civil strife, all groups must mobilize for self-defence. However, the material and rhetorical measures that groups use to mobilize for defence also pose offensive threats to other groups, creating a security dilemma in which no group can provide for its own security without threatening the security of others. The intensity of this security dilemma is in part a function of demography: the more intermixed the patterns of settlement of the hostile populations, the greater the opportunities for offence by either side, and it becomes more difficult to design effective measures for community defence except by going on the offensive preemptively to 'cleanse' mixed areas of members of the enemy group and create ethnically reliable, defensible enclaves.[31]

This will ring a bell for anyone familiar with developments at

[30] Ibid., pp. 248-9.
[31] Ibid., pp. 222-3.

the ground level in numerous localities of Bosnia & Herzegovina during late 1991 and the first half of 1992: the competing military-style mobilizations, the escalating dynamic of mutual suspicion and tension in suddenly divided and polarized communities, climaxing in a matter of months in spasms of intense violence and mass expulsions. Much of the worst violence by Serbs against Muslims in the summer of 1992 did occur in demographically intermixed areas of northwestern and eastern Bosnia where the local Serb population had undergone a significant demographic decline vis-à-vis the Muslim population in the preceding twenty to thirty years.[32] Indeed, Kaufmann's use of the word 'cleanse' suggests that this reformulation of security-dilemma doctrine has been inspired by the experience of former Yugoslavia, and particularly BiH. In Kaufmann's frame of analysis, this kind of 'security dilemma' is not resolvable, short of 'separation' (total, preferably) of the hostile groups and the establishment of homogeneous political units (states, or at least enclaves) for each of them. The 'policy implication' is that 'the international community should endorse separation as a remedy for at least some communal conflicts', with 'protection, transport, subsistence and resettlement organized by outside powers or institutions'—in short, a comprehensive 'relocation' service. Otherwise, 'the processes of war will separate the populations anyway, at a much higher human cost', indeed 'at the mercy of their ethnic enemies and bandits'.[33]

So according to the 'security dilemma' perspective, separation/partition is inevitable—and, in fact, the least bad alternative—in certain circumstances. But what of the claim that such separation/partition dramatically increases violence in the short run? Kaufmann writes that 'the most frequently mentioned case in this debate is India. Critics of the 1947 partition blame it for causing more than 15 million refugees and hundreds of thousands of deaths'. His counter-argument is that 'this correlation... is spurious. The partition, the population transfers and the violence were *all caused* by the irresolvable security dilemmas between the Muslim and Hindu communities of India, and especially between

---

[32] For a study probing this connection, see J. Andrew Slack and Roy R. Doyon, 'Population Dynamics and Susceptibility to Ethnic Conflict: The Case of Bosnia and Herzegovina', *Journal of Peace Research* 38: 2 (2001), pp. 139-61.
[33] Kaufmann, 'When All Else Fails', pp. 223-4.

the Muslim and Sikh communities of Punjab province... generated by the removal of the imperial power that had previously guaranteed the security of all groups.'[34] Kaufmann's use of the 'security dilemma' scenario is evocative and intuitively plausible— within narrow limits. The 'security dilemma' framework does accurately *describe* local ground realities in BiH during, approximately, the last five or six months leading up to April 1992, and in the about-to-be partitioned Indian province of Punjab in the five or six months between March and August 1947. But where did the 'security dilemma' itself spring from? And how did it suddenly acquire such acute proportions? In non-scientific language, how was it possible for erstwhile neighbours, workplace colleagues, friends, even lovers belonging to 'different' communities to come to regard the other's very existence in the same locality as a mortal threat to themselves and their own community? The appearance of such an intense 'security dilemma' among Punjabi Hindus, Muslims and Sikhs in 1947, and among Bosnian Serbs, Croats and Muslims in 1992 is *itself* a puzzle, that calls for explanation. How do we account for the 'security dilemma', the *alleged* root cause of all mayhem? The 'security dilemma' fetishists are blind to the possibility, whether unintentionally or otherwise, that their crucial explanatory variable is itself a puzzle in need of an explanation.

Two large and populous provinces of British India were partitioned in 1947: Punjab and Bengal (at the time, Bengal was approximately 54% Muslim and 43% Hindu, while Punjab was about 56% Muslim, 27% Hindu and 13% Sikh). While researching in the middle to late 1970s on the partition of Bengal, its causes and its legacies, a distinguished American historian of modern Bengal 'interviewed about 70 participants in the events of the two decades before partition'. The 'two most numerous categories of interviewees' were Bengali politicians, both Muslim and Hindu, and British colonial officials who had served in Bengal. Leonard Gordon, the American scholar, asked all these people two simple questions: 'When did you think there would be a partition [of Bengal], and when did you come to believe that the British would leave India?'. The vast majority responded that they concluded at various points during the 1930s 'that the end of the British era in

[34] Ibid., p. 230. My emphasis.

India was fast approaching'. 'But', Gordon reports, 'very few said that they thought there would be a partition... before the middle 1940s. Many said that the clinching event was the Great Calcutta Killing. After that event, they said, the Hindus and Muslims [of Bengal] could not trust each other' any more. There had been communal violence in Bengal before,'but none of the earlier riots had the devastating political and psychological effect that the Great Calcutta Killing had'.[35]

What was the Great Calcutta Killing? On August 16, 1946, with 'the threat of partition hanging heavy'[36] over Bengal and the Indian subcontinent, the Muslim League called on Muslim communities throughout India to observe a 'Direct Action Day' in support of its demand for Pakistan. In the giant metropolis of Calcutta, capital of Bengal, attacks on Hindu pedestrians and Hindu-owned shops were initiated on the afternoon of August 16 by groups of persons dispersing after a Muslim League rally in central Calcutta. Within hours the city was convulsed by communal violence. A week of almost unimaginable confrontation followed. During that week Calcutta was divided into armed enclaves at war with each other, not unlike Sarajevo and Mostar four and a half decades later. Terrified Hindu families fled Muslim-dominated districts of the city, bearing harrowing accounts of atrocities. In predominantly Hindu neighbourhoods Muslim citizens were hunted down and murdered. 'Between 5,000 and 10,000 died [in under a week] and many thousands more were wounded and burnt out of their homes.'[37] For weeks afterward the city sewers were clogged with corpses. After this watershed event, a 'security dilemma' situation unfolded in Bengal. It culminated in the province's partition into regions under Indian and Pakistani sovereignty exactly one year later, in August 1947. About two-thirds of Bengal's territory became the eastern wing of Pakistan. The rest—including Calcutta—became the Indian state (province) of 'West Bengal'.

What caused the Great Calcutta Killing, and the security dilemma-type situation that ensued? (in October 1946, organized violence began against the Hindu minority population in two

[35] Leonard Gordon, 'Divided Bengal: Problems of Nationalism and Identity in the 1947 Partition' in M. Hasan (ed.), *India's Partition*, pp. 308-9.
[36] Ibid., p. 307.
[37] Ibid., p. 308.

rural, agricultural east Bengal districts, Noakhali and Tipperah, soon answered by massive reprisals against the Muslim minority in the north Indian province of Bihar, adjacent to western Bengal). Gordon provides a succint, persuasive explanation:

> Calcutta was the economic, administrative, cultural and political hub from which spokes reached out in every direction to all of eastern India. If Calcutta was to be in Pakistan, as Jinnah had promised [until the end of 1946, the Muslim League leader apparently entertained delusions that the *entire* territories of Punjab and Bengal would become part of his fantasy of Pakistan], then the Muslims wanted to show that they controlled it. If Calcutta was going to remain in India, then the Hindus wanted to demonstrate that it was their city. The Muslims were only about 20% of Calcutta's population, but they controlled the state [provincial] government [elected after the end of the Second World War on the basis of an electoral system based on compartmentalized communal representation of Hindus and Muslims, determined by the British].[38]

In other words, it was the *escalating possibility* of partition, and the tensions thus unleashed, which caused the August 1946 violence in Calcutta and the subsequent 'security dilemma' between the Hindus and Muslims of Bengal. *Contra* Kaufmann, who claims that 'the partition, the population transfers and the violence were all caused by the irresolvable security dilemmas' between India's Muslim and non-Muslim (Hindu and Sikh) communities, it seems that in reality, the so-called 'security dilemma' was caused by the looming spectre of partition.

A chillingly similar process unfolded in Bosnia in the second half of 1991 and the first months of 1992. In late June 1991 Slovenia and Croatia declared independence. Shortly thereafter, the JNA lost its one-week 'Mickey Mouse' war with well-organized, tactically competent Slovene territorial forces, and civil war gripped almost a third of Croatia. As the prospect of Yugoslavia's partition became increasingly likely, the anxieties of BiH Serbs were dramatically exacerbated (as were the aspirations, less obvi-

---

[38] Ibid., p. 308.

ous at the time, of extremist Croats in parts of BiH). It was this context of spiralling uncertainty, brought about by the prospect of imminent partition of the joint state of Yugoslavia, along the boundaries of its federal republics, that caused the acute 'security dilemma' in BiH—not the other way around. Recognition by major Euro-Atlantic powers and institutions of that partitionist claim as legitimate—contested, naturally, by outraged Croatian and Bosnian Serbs—precipitated the horror that followed. But the threat of partition, which undid the security guarantee afforded to all the groups by the complex structure of the Yugoslav state, was the real root cause of the debacle, and the so-called 'security dilemma' merely its symptom. Kaufmann's confused argument has successfully inverted cause and symptom. It is also peculiarly circular, in that it blithely conflates the root cause of the problem with its 'remedy'.

What of post-partition states? Kaufmann claims that partition generally has a 'dampening' effect on the renewed incidence of violence in the long run, although the precise extent of the dampening effect depends on how *completely* the communities are separated from each other by the lines of partition. Thus he is especially pleased with the hard partition of Cyprus, where, according to him 'the situation has remained remarkably stable since 1974… calm as well as safe for a generation', ever since '200,000 Greek refugees moved south of the line' drawn by the Turkish military intervention, while, '60,000 Turkish Cypriots moved north' of the line.[39] Cyprus may be a case where (*de facto*) partition, for all its costs and consequences, does represent an unavoidable last resort. However, the connection Kaufmann is making between the partition of Cyprus—specifically, its complete or near-complete nature in the sense of physically separating the groups—and the subsequent 'calm' and 'remarkable stability' on the island may well be a spurious correlation. The latter, credited to the partition and its completeness, could well be the result of different factors. Firstly, Greece and the Greek Cypriots, the revisionist side in this conflict, face a militarily much stronger opponent in Turkey, a deterrent in itself. Secondly and decisively, both Greece and Turkey are members of NATO, which means that the United

[39] Kaufmann, 'When All Else Fails', pp. 243-6.

States and its allies have been in a position to restrain them from restarting a war—fought either directly or more likely, via local proxies—over Cyprus.

According to Kaufmann, 'continuing or resurgent inter-group violence' in some post-partition contexts have 'resulted not from partition or separation' as such, 'but rather from the incompleteness of separation of the hostile groups' in these cases. The obvious example is Northern Ireland, where the population of the six Ulster counties retained under British sovereignty was almost one-third Catholic, a proportion that has grown to about 43% in the eighty years since the original agreement. Kaufmann argues that in this case, the 'best chance at lasting peace would have been to draw a partition line that separated the two groups as fully as possible', which would have meant 'a smaller but safer Northern Ireland'. Even then, 'since no line could [have] avoid[ed] leaving substantial minorities... the British government should have offered money [at that time] to people willing to move as well as making clear that it could not protect those who insisted on staying behind.'[40]

In fact, there was a debate in the decade preceding Ireland's partition on the size of the area that would be detached from what eventually became the Irish Free State, and later the Republic of Ireland. The historic Ulster of nine counties 'held out no assurance of a settled Protestant majority'. As early as 1912 a 'compact area of four counties', which would give the Protestants the highest possible population predominance, came up for discussion. In 1919 'the [British] cabinet reviewed all of these possibilities—the exclusion of the whole of Ulster, the six counties, or an area more narrowly defined'. In connivance with the leaders of the Protestant movement in the north, they eventually settled for the intermediate six-county formula, which gave the Protestants a solid two-thirds majority yet at the same time enabled them, in the words of one senior Ulster Unionist, 'to save as much [of Ulster] as we knew we could hold'.[41]

Kaufmann complains that while 'the partition of Ireland was unavoidable... forcing 430,000 Catholics into Northern Ireland was not.'[42] Yet, despite the manifestly incomplete nature of 'sepa-

[40] Ibid., pp. 222, 230.
[41] Mansergh, *The Prelude to Partition*, pp. 38-9.
[42] Kaufmann, 'When All Else Fails', p. 230.

ration', Northern Ireland was a rather peaceful place for almost fifty years after partition, with only minor, sporadic and quickly suppressed incidents of violence by residual IRA elements during those decades.[43] This near-absence of physical violence for a protracted period is incompatible with Kaufmann's theory of why post-partition violence does or does not occur. 'The Troubles' began only in 1969, with large-scale civil rights protests by Catholics, and escalated into serious armed violence involving a resurgent IRA, loyalist paramilitaries, the overwhelmingly Protestant Ulster police force (RUC) and the British army by the early 1970s. How does one explain this delay of almost a half-century?

The explanation is that Kaufmann has been misled by his own 'security dilemma' dogmatism. The Irish boundary settlement was unjust to northern Catholics and to the Irish Republic. However, the factor that set off the Troubles almost fifty years down the road from partition could not have been the 'security dilemma' *per se*, since that was there from the very beginning because of the number and proportion of Catholics left 'stranded' in Northern Ireland. The reason for the eruption of unrest was that the post-1922 Unionist regime in Northern Ireland, which systematically discriminated against and disadvantaged the Catholic community, was subtly undermined by a constellation of internal and external changes by the late 1960s, yet proved unwilling and unable to reform itself in time.[44] It follows that what the British government, the sovereign power in Northern Ireland, could and should have done was not to offer money to people to leave their homes and communities, but rather encourage the Protestant regime to dismantle its most repressive and discriminatory policies and undertake democratic reforms to make Northern Ireland a truly democratic and inclusive society. After more than a quarter-century of the Troubles, an agreement to that effect was finally struck between the British and Irish governments, together with moderate and hardline Irish Nationalist parties and some Unionists. That compact, premised on mutual recognition and power-sharing between the two communities of Northern Ireland is having a

---

[43] See Patrick Bishop and Eamonn Mallie, *The Provisional IRA*, London, 1987.
[44] For this history, see Brendan O'Leary and John McGarry, *The Politics of Antagonism: Understanding Northern Ireland*, London, 1993.

chequered implementation. Yet its basic attributes—promoting democratic politics and equality for all in a society which remains deeply divided on issues of sovereignty and national identity, coupled with the forging of a cooperative, almost confederal relationship betwen the two islands[45]—are entirely in tune with an era of growing regionalism and globalism. Perspectives such as Kaufmann's are manifestly not.

The sanguine, almost celebratory view of post-partition situations expectedly has trouble squaring its rosy depiction of reality with the legacy of India's partition. Since 1947, India and Pakistan have fought three full-fledged wars—in 1947-8, 1965 and 1971. Of these the first two wars were directly caused by conflict between the two countries over ownership of a territory in northwestern India called Jammu and Kashmir (J&K, or Kashmir). Both countries claimed J&K as rightfully theirs, and since the end of the first war over Kashmir in early 1949, the territory has been divided by the ceasefire line (renamed the Line of Control or LOC by bilateral agreement in 1972) into a larger and more populous area under Indian control and a smaller and less populous area under Pakistan's control. The third war, in December 1971, was also related to the troubled inheritance of partition, albeit a different one. It happened when India launched a full-scale military intervention in Pakistan's eastern wing (i.e. the eastern two-thirds of Bengal) in support of a secession bid by its overwhelmingly Bengali-speaking and largely Muslim population. The subsequent birth of a new state—Bangladesh—marked a historic reversal (in less than 25 years!) of the idea of pan-Muslim nationhood that had underpinned the subcontinent's communal partition in 1947. In addition, India and Pakistan fought a limited, localized border conflict, initiated by the Pakistanis, on one stretch of the LOC dividing Kashmir during the summer of 1999. This conflict, which happened in the backdrop of a guerrilla war against Indian rule waged since 1990 with Pakistani support in large areas of Indian-controlled Kashmir, threatened to escalate into the fourth Indo-Pak war—this time between nuclear-capable states. It blew over after two months of fierce fighting following a diplomatic

[45] For a clear and comprehensive analysis, see Brendan O'Leary, 'The Nature of the British-Irish Agreement', *New Left Review* (1999), pp. 66-96.

intervention by then US President Clinton and a reluctant Pakistani climbdown.

Kaufmann does not explicitly acknowledge the weight of this discouraging post-partition history. However, he does have a defence of his own theory. According to him, 'the problem with Indian independence was not partition but that partition did not go far enough'. Specifically, he says, 'Kashmir should have been included in the general settlement... The result would likely have been a partition [of the territory of J&K] more favourable to Pakistan than the one achieved by war and would have avoided stranding a large community [of Muslims, J&K is a Muslim-majority territory], both vulnerable and threatening, on the wrong [Indian] side of the line.'[46]

It is difficult to take Kaufmann's views on the Kashmir problem seriously firstly because his discussion of the case is littered with factual errors. He claims for instance that J&K's population was 'about two-thirds Muslim' in 1947; according to the census of 1941, the Muslim majority was in fact substantially higher, over 77%. He writes that 'in October [1947] the Maharaja [of Kashmir, a Hindu autocrat] invited in pro-Indian Sikh troops, and a few weeks later Muslim irregulars invaded from Pakistan.' This chronology has got the sequence of events that actually unfolded in October 1947 exactly upside down—the incursion by irregulars from Pakistan compelled the Maharaja to accede hastily to India and call in regular Indian Army troops, some but not all of which consisted of Sikh units. Finally, he puts the Hindu population of the Kashmir Valley at the outbreak of insurgency in 1990 at 'about 250,000'; the last available census (1981) put that number at less than half that, at 124,078.

Unfortunately, Kaufmann's ignorance does not stop at matters of detail. Lamenting the lack of a negotiated partition of Jammu and Kashmir in 1947, he claims that 'drawing a partition line through Kashmir would have been easier than in Punjab or in Bengal, because most of the Hindu population of the state resided in the southernmost division, Jammu, adjacent to India, and the boundary between Jammu and the rest of the state is largely mountainous'—making for a 'natural' border, presumably. Most of

[46] Kaufmann, 'When All Else Fails', pp. 238-9.

the Hindu population did reside in the Jammu region, but vast areas of the region were nonetheless populated primarily by Muslims and in 1947 the region had an overall Muslim majority, like the territory as a whole. Hundreds of thousands of Jammu Muslims fled to the Pakistani zone from the systematic persecution of Hindu extremists and the ex-Maharaja's forces as the majority of the territory fell to the Indian side by the end of hostilities in end-1948. Even today, three of the (Indian) Jammu region's six administrative districts have solid Muslim-majority populations, and Muslim communities make up almost one-third of the (Indian) Jammu region's population as a whole. Many areas, towns and villages still have substantially intermixed populations of Hindus and Muslims, with a good sprinkling of local Sikhs. Given the multiconfessional, multiethnic and multilingual character of the Jammu region, and the fact that Muslims were the single largest religious community in the region in 1947, 'drawing a partition line' between Jammu and the rest of the territory would have been far harder and more complicated than it appears to be in Kaufmann's breezy and incorrect account.

Academic proponents of partition like Kaufmann tend to minimize the short and long-term human costs *and*—more important from a realist point of view—the *practical difficulties and dilemmas* of drawing partition lines. Those with hands-on experience of negotiating and implementing partition tend to be much more conscious of 'economic, social and political realities': 'Was Derry to be cut off from its Donegal hinterland, the jute mills of Calcutta from the jute of East Bengal? How did you disentangle Protestant from Catholic in Northern Ireland, Muslim from Hindu in Bengal, or Muslim from Hindu and Sikh in the Punjab?'[47] The Kaufmanns, Mearsheimers, Papes and van Everas have 'the answer' to such problems, of course, but they tend to systematically understate their magnitude and complexity, and their short-run as well as long-term consequences in human, social and economic terms.

A negotiated partition of Jammu and Kashmir in 1947, which would have given the bulk of the Muslim-majority territory to Pakistan, was impossible chiefly because of another factor that Kaufmann seems to be entirely unaware of, since he fails to even

---

[47] Mansergh, *The Prelude to Partition*, p. 23.

mention it. During the 1930s and 1940s an organized popular movement for political and social emancipation from the Maharaja's oppressive regime had developed in Jammu and Kashmir. Led by a party called the Jammu and Kashmir National Conference (NC) and its charismatic leader, Sheikh Mohammad Abdullah, this movement was particularly strong in the Kashmir Valley, an overwhelmingly Muslim region (then and now) which lies north of the Jammu region. The leaders and followers of this mass movement in Kashmir were overwhelmingly Muslims. But—they did not wish to be Pakistanis (a realization that would also dawn on the Muslims of Bengal in 1971). Instead, the NC upheld a regional Kashmiri identity, derived principally from the Valley's distinct history and cultural traditions. Sheikh Abdullah and many of his lieutenants were also devout Muslims, but their political philosophy was emphatically secularist and they made efforts to broaden their base by recruiting from the Hindu and Sikh minorities. Some NC men were also inclined to various forms of socialist and even communist thought, and thus viewed the Muslim League's 'right-wing' leanings with suspicion and distaste. In the post-partition tumult in Kashmir, this movement made a strategic decision to forge an alliance with India—which promised to be a secular, democratic, federal republic—rather than sacrifice their distinct identity and agenda at the altar of pan-Muslim unity. In 1952 Abdullah justified his strategic alliance with India in ideological terms, as 'an identity of democratic and secular aspirations' held in common by Kashmiris and Indians. That alliance did not last and the Kashmir-India relationship turned more and more bitter over time, as many Kashmiris came to regard India as their new oppressor. But in 1947–8, Indian soldiers succeeded in clearing almost the entire Kashmir Valley, and most contested areas of Jammu, of Pakistani irregulars and regulars (who otherwise had certain tactical and strategic advantages vis-à-vis the Indians), thanks to the support they received from the NC organization and many ordinary Muslim citizens of Kashmir.[48]

[48] Readers interested in learning more about the Kashmir conflict can consult Sumantra Bose, *The Challenge in Kashmir: Democracy, Self-Determination and a Just Peace*, New Delhi, Thousand Oaks and London, 1997; Sumantra Bose, 'Kashmir:

Even this cursory survey of the Kashmir question exposes the crude, shallow assumptions underlying much partitionist thought. Partitionists tend to reify the (often complex) identities and (usually malleable) political leanings of their laboratory guinea-pigs. In the process, they not only inflict uncalled-for violence on empirical facts and realities, as we have just seen, but elide the *contingency* of partition as an outcome. The 'security dilemma' version of the partitionist argument, limited and static, is especially prone to the latter problem. It serves as a more or less accurate *description* of ground realities during the countdown to violent partitions, such as those in Punjab, Bengal and Bosnia. But the 'security dilemma' account still has major gaps and an inherently ahistorical, teleological bias, as I have argued earlier in this chapter. Moreover, its logic, based on reified conceptions of collective identities, has simply no space for *shifts* in identity emphases and political preferences in the *post*-partition phase.

Kaufmann tends to downplay the number and scale of communal killings and mass migrations in parts of India other than the Punjab around 1947. Punjab was the site of the most intense communal violence. But his assertions that 'Punjab accounted for most of the refugees and nearly all the deaths' (p. 231) and that '[communal] war in Punjab [between Sikhs, Muslims and Hindus] accounted for the vast majority of all the deaths in communal conflict between 1945 and 1947' (p. 236) are factually questionable and do not give due attention to the large numbers of killings and especially, mass migrations in other regions of India and Pakistan, including the United Provinces, Bihar, Delhi, Jammu, Bengal, Sindh and the North-West Frontier Province. In addition, although he claims that apart from Punjab, 'one other region of India', Bengal, 'is especially important to [the validation] of [his] analysis', all of one paragraph, riddled with factual errors, is devot-

Sources of Conflict, Dimensions of Peace', *Survival* 41: 3 (1999), pp. 149-71; Sumantra Bose, 'Kashmir at the Crossroads: Problems and Possibilities', *Security Dialogue* 32: 1 (2001), pp. 41-64; and a multimedia seminar on the Kashmir conflict, based on my interviews, lectures and photographs at *http://www.fathom.com*, an expert knowledge website run collaboratively by the London School of Economics and Political Science (LSE), Columbia University, and a host of other institutions in Britain and the United States.

ed to the case of Bengal. Although his prose is somewhat unclear, he appears to be suggesting that 'separation' of Hindus and Muslims was relatively complete as a result of the Bengal partition. In consequence, following the logic of his argument, 'very few' killings occurred in Bengal after 1947.

In reality, unmixing was quite incomplete and sizeable concentrations of minorities continued to live in both Bengals after partition. The current population of the Indian province of West Bengal is almost one-quarter Muslim and entire districts (Murshidabad, north Dinajpur) exist with majority Muslim populations. In eastern Bengal (first eastern Pakistan, then Bangladesh) some 20% of the population consisted of Hindus in the early post-partition years, *contra* Kaufmann's assertion that 'very few Hindus remained in Pakistan' after August 1947 (in fact, very few Hindus, and practically no Sikhs, remained in *west* Pakistan).[49] Robert Hayden makes the same erroneous assertion that 'Pakistan was emptied of Hindus'[50] after August 1947. Contemporary Bangladesh continues to have a Hindu minority of 10-15%. Nor did communal trouble entirely subside in Bengal after 1947. There were fresh outbreaks of violence in 1950 and again in 1964 on both sides of the border, more killing and further migrations but 'never... the virtually complete transfer of population that took place in the Punjab'.[51]

Finally, Kaufmann's claim that 'between 1947 and 1951 3.5 million people moved between India and East Pakistan in orderly, planned transfers, without loss of life' detracts from the fact that these people—mostly Hindus who came to India and west Bengal from 1947 onward— usually came as paupers, often with only the clothes they wore. West Bengal's economy and infrastructure were overwhelmed by this influx. Massive shantytowns housing impoverished, embittered *migrants sprang up overnight around Calcutta. For many of the older beneficiaries of the sanitary-sounding 'organized, planned transfers', the psychological trauma of displacement from ancestral land, home and hearth was devastating. Younger generations of new arrivals found it difficult to rise

[49] Kaufmann, 'When All Else Fails', pp. 236-7.
[50] Robert Hayden, 'Schindler's Fate: Genocide, Ethnic Cleansing and Population Transfers', *Slavic Review* 55: 4 (1996), pp. 727-48, on p. 739.
[51] Gordon, 'Divided Bengal', p. 318.

out of the squalor and hopelessness of refugee resettlement colonies. To compound their problems, locals hardly understood their dialect of Bengali—spoken by Muslims and Hindus alike in eastern Bengal and very distinct from the west Bengali version of the language.[52] Partitions and mass displacements, even when rendered inevitable by circumstances, invariably come at a terribly. high psychological, economic and human cost. Advocates of partition and 'transfer' are normally guilty of downplaying if not outrightly obscuring these costs. Perhaps they are not deliberately callous but simply unaware.

Bengal is an especially important and pertinent case because its history subsequent to August 1947 demonstrates like no other case the *contingency* of partition. As Gordon writes, 'national and ethnic identities are not fixed essences'. Thus many Bengalis, 'pushed in a time of crisis [in 1945-47] to identify with one political community having a particular national design, demanded new choices in later circumstances'. Gordon is of course referring particularly to Bengali Muslims. The majority of this community campaigned enthusiastically for Pakistan in 1946-7, demanded radical political autonomy for east Pakistan by the middle to late 1960s, and in 1971, in response to the west Pakistani military and civilian elite's continued denial of their claims, launched a movement of national liberation against the brutal repression of what they called then, and still call, 'the barbaric Pakistani occupation forces'. Yet Gordon emphasizes that

> all Bengalis, whether Hindu or Muslim, whether in Bangladesh or in India, have multiple identities. At different moments, especially 1947 and 1971, members of both communities have had to make choices about their primary identifications and their nationalities. Or stated in another way, they have had to order their multiple identity elements [during times of crisis, breakdown, systemic transition]. But these were not fixed or necessarily final choices. Many who made one choice in 1947 lived to make a different one in 1971 [an

---

[52] I have personal knowledge of Bengal, being born and raised in Calcutta of a west Bengali father and a mother whose family origins are entirely in east Bengal (she was born in Dhaka, capital city of Bangladesh).

example is Sheikh Mujibur Rahman, leader of the Bangladesh movement in 1970-1 and a young activist in the Pakistan movement in 1946-7]. The new choice, like the old one, was not inevitable until [almost] the very end, perhaps the night of 25 March 1971 [the date the Pakistani military, comprised chiefly of Punjabi Muslims, began a massive campaign of terror in east Pakistan].[53]

Note that the partition of Bengal was *not* reversed by the upheaval of 1971. During the nine-month liberation struggle (March-December 1971), West Bengal became a refuge for millions of Hindu and Muslim east Bengalis forced to leave their homes by Pakistani terror, and an important base for leaders of the Bangladeshi freedom movement and its guerrilla forces. But the paths of easterners and westerners had already diverged by 1971. There was no question of the Muslims of east Bengal coming home to India, which is what any reunification with the west would have entailed. Instead, not just a new state, Bangladesh, but a new *national identity* was born. That Bangladeshi identity 'was to be Bengali and Muslim', but differentiated from the identity of those 'other Bengalis' (the co-ethnics in Hindu-majority west Bengal) as well as the 'other Muslims' (the former fellow-citizens *and* fellow-nationals of west Pakistan). So, Bengali and Muslim but distinct from both other Bengalis and other Muslims. As Gordon writes, 'this… effort to define, however clumsily, the new nationality of the Muslims in Bengal… continues today.'[54] In the very different context of the Balkans, interesting speculations come to mind. How about a sense of Bosnian Serb identity which is, of course, Bosnian and Serb, yet differentiated and distinct from other Bosnians (of other faiths and nationalities) *and* other Serbs, notably those of Serbia proper? Many would argue that such an identity has a strong historical basis, and already exists.

Among reputed Yugoslavia specialists in the West, Robert Hayden has come closest to endorsing the partitionist line. The main target of Hayden's critique is what he sees as the folly and hypocrisy of Euro-Atlantic powers and institutions in acquiescing in if not

[53] Gordon, 'Divided Bengal', pp. 279-80, 320.
[54] Ibid., pp. 304-5.

outrightly supporting the break-up of Yugoslavia, and then proceeding to insist that Bosnia & Herzegovina *must* be kept whole.[55]
Parts of his work can also be read as a defence of Serb actions in
Bosnia and elsewhere during the wars of Yugoslav succession. He
notes that 'ethnic cleansing' has occurred repeatedly in modern
Europe, and that political not moral considerations determine
whether 'ethnic cleansing' is given the sanitized, almost normal
status of 'population transfer' (as in the case of the *Volksdeutsche*
[ethnic Germans] of central and eastern Europe after the Second
World War) or labelled 'genocide' and treated as a pathological
phenomenon. He is also concerned to distinguish 'ethnic cleansing' from 'genocide', in the Bosnian context as well as generally,
and argues for a limited, conservative definition of what constitutes genocide. Drawing parallels between the *Volksdeutsche* and
Croatian and Bosnian Serbs, he criticizes notions of 'collective
guilt' for crimes of war, and self-righteous attitudes which ignore
'real grievances' that drove people while 'listing only their
crimes'.[56] He also acknowledges, however, that in the Bosnian war
of the 1990s 'the primary victims were Muslims, at the hands first
of Serbs and then of Croats.'[57]

Hayden cites a book published in 1934 by the secretary to the
Minorities Committee of the League of Nations. On the vexed
subject of states and minorities, Macartney pointed out that in
theory, three ways exist to deal with minority questions: revision
of borders to make them congruent with ethnic population dis-
tributions, elimination of minorities through emigration or 'perhaps through exchange of populations', or a change in the basis of
the state so that it is no longer defined as a national state. He also
noted a fourth possible solution, 'physical slaughter', but added
that 'although this most effective of remedies is still in vogue in
certain countries it shall not be discussed in this humane essay.'[58]

Hayden appears to be implying that the third option, while
theoretically possible, was really a non-option in Bosnia in 1992
given the incendiary context generated by the violent demise of
federal Yugoslavia and the triumph of the principle of *national*

55 Hayden, 'Schindler's Fate', pp. 727-48.
56 Ibid., p. 745.
57 Ibid., p. 733.
58 C.A. Macartney, *National States and National Minorities*, London, 1934, quoted
in Hayden, 'Schindler's Fate', p. 735.

statehood. In this narrowed field of choice, revision of borders represented the more humane and democratic option relative to the alternatives of elimination through expulsion, or through physical slaughter. Thus, 'having ruled out the partition of Bosnia, the international community left no choice to those who rejected inclusion in a Bosnian state other than to partition it by military means, an option that both Serbs and Croats then seized'.[59]

This argument has a certain logical coherence. Hayden's conclusion is that major Western countries and institutions should have acted to ensure that Bosnia's 'partition... [was] legitimized immediately'. He claims that 'the difference between Bosnia in 1992 and Punjab in 1947 was that prior agreement on territorial division [between India, Pakistan and Britain] meant that the horror was over relatively quickly in the Punjab. In Bosnia, however, the pious insistence that partition was not possible when it clearly had to occur meant that the lines were drawn and redrawn in blood and the process took years longer.' There are clear shades of Kaufmann, Mearsheimer *et al.* here. Unlike them, however, Hayden is honest enough to frankly admit that 'this is not to say that the partition of Bosnia could ever have been accomplished without brutality, but its prolongation ensured that casualties would be higher'. He accepts that even a negotiated partition of Bosnia would have immediately produced 'mass expulsions of populations' amidst violence and brutality.[60]

There are three problems with Hayden's tight, logical argument. First, the supposition that a negotiated, internationally sponsored partition would have produced less suffering and fewer casualties is questionable. The partition of Punjab, agreed between Indians and Pakistanis and approved by the British, sparked an orgy of mass murder and mass expulsion unprecedented in the history of the subcontinent and unparalleled since. This was certainly due to a 'security dilemma', *albeit* a security dilemma aroused and unleashed in the first place, as I have argued in this chapter, by the destructive dynamic of impending partition. Around nine million Hindus, Muslims and Sikhs were 'transferred' under military and administrative supervision, or simply transferred themselves, across the new border dividing the Punjab

[59] Ibid., p. 741.
[60] Ibid., pp. 741-2.

·in a matter of a few months before and after August 14-15, 1947. It is not an unreasonable estimate that around half-a-million men, women and children did not make it. They were massacred by neighbours and friends metamorphosed into deadly enemies in their own ancestral towns and villages, or while in transit –tens of thousands were slain in grisly massacres on trains and road convoys carrying refugees to the other country on both sides of the new border in Punjab, *as well as* in other areas of the newly created states of India and Pakistan, in a macabre, unstoppable spiral of 'revenge'.[61] A negotiated, internationally supported partition may well have shortened the duration of the Bosnian war from 43 agonizing months—but there is no guarantee that it would have significantly reduced the scale of violence, the intensity of atrocities, and the depths of suffering.

Second, I have already discussed, in Chapter 2, how difficult and complicated it would have been, in the circumstances of 1991-2, to 'draw a better line' through Yugoslavia instead of simply accepting the former republics' borders—specifically in BiH and Croatia—as boundaries of sovereign states. The normative and practical problems with the latter option are real, but it is doubtful that a feasible alternative, agreed between the various ex-Yugoslav parties and their international interlocutors, could have been realized, and in time. Third and last, Hayden seriously underestimates the long-term, negative legacies of India's partition when he writes that 'since 1947, the vast majority of refugees from that period were incorporated into India and Pakistan relatively quickly and relatively completely'.[62] The reality is very different. Survivors of partition violence, whether Muslim, Sikh or Hindu, invariably coped with enormous psychological trauma, and most confronted the daunting challenge of rebuilding lives, careers and communities from scratch in new, unfamiliar, indeed 'foreign' locations and contexts in their 'own' countries (some coped with these challenges better than others). Even more important, the savagery that accompanied partition—millions of permanent displacements/expellees, hundreds of thousands of gruesome mur-

[61] For a powerful anthology of reminiscences of Muslims, Hindus and Sikhs who lived through and witnessed the violence unleashed by the partition of the Punjab, see Ahmad Salim (ed.), *Lahore, 1947*, Delhi, 2001.
[62] Hayden, 'Schindler's Fate', p. 739.

ders, tens of thousands of rapes—left a legacy of bitterness, suspicion, even hatred, that has haunted the subcontinent ever since. I have elsewhere ventured the suggestion that the conflict over Kashmir is the *chief symptom*, not the root cause, of the mutual venom embedded in India-Pakistan relations. However one may try to rationalize or even sanitize partition, the home truth is that partition and pain go together. And it is the sort of pain that refuses to go away, even after a long time.

Hayden mounts a more effective challenge to anti-partitionists when he highlights 'this external insistence that Bosnia must continue to exist despite the wishes of the elected representatives of two of its three constituent groups'.[63] The record of the war suggests that most BiH Serbs and BiH Croats rejected sovereign, united Bosnia & Herzegovina, and the first six years of the post-war settlement suggest that many are still fundamentally unreconciled, while others are at best reluctant participants. Dogmatic anti-partitionism is, both generally and in relation to the Bosnian case, uncomfortable with the reality of large-scale popular support for partition (or something approaching partition) in the *society* in question and usually, unable and unwilling to come to terms with it. In the case of Bosnia, the typical response among Bosnian integralists and their supporters in Western countries is to deny the legitimacy of the alternative view(s), and more than occasionally, to demonize those segments of the population that stand for them as misguided, evil, or both. I have argued in this chapter and throughout this book that this sort of response is neither fair nor a constructive way forward for Bosnia.

Robert Schaeffer, a thoughtful critic of partition, contends that 'partition has never, anywhere been subjected to a meaningful, indigenous electoral test.'[64] Scholars of Bosnia like Hayden, possibly Burg and Shoup, and many others would disagree with this claim. They would argue that much evidence including voting behaviour in the post-Dayton phase suggests that overwhelming numbers of BiH Serbs and BiH Croats see the common state of BiH as an imposition, and would prefer a partition of its territory. Some level of support for partition among 'realists' in the

---

63 Ibid., p. 742.
64 Schaeffer, *Severed States*, p. 253.

Bosnian Muslim camp cannot be precluded, given the difficulties of establishing a viable state in BiH, although the pattern throughout the twentieth century is that leaders of the Bosnian Muslim community generally worked hard to preserve BiH's historical borders.

Schaeffer's assertion, which exemplifies a certain 'denial syndrome' typical of opponents of partition, is questionable on historical grounds as well. On June 20, 1947, the Bengal Legislative Assembly, elected after the end of the Second World War, convened to vote on the fate of the province (elected members only, not the nominated 'European' members). The rules of procedure of His Majesty's Government specified that after a meeting of the whole assembly, the assembly would convene in two separate groups, one consisting of deputies elected from 'the Muslim-majority districts' and the other of those members elected from 'the rest of the Province'. Then, 'the two parts... sitting separately will be empowered to vote whether or not the Province should be partitioned. If a simple majority of *either* part decided in favour of partition, division will take place and arrangements will be made accordingly' (my emphasis).[65]

At the joint session 90 deputies voted for the existing constituent assembly (i.e. to stay in India), while 126 voted in favour of the new constituent assembly (i.e., to join Pakistan). The vote was almost entirely on the communal faultline—i.e. Hindu members voted *en masse* for India, and Muslims for Pakistan, with the exception of four 'low-caste' Hindu members from east Bengal who voted with the Muslims (plus a very few abstentions). The session of members elected from Hindu-majority districts then voted in favour of partition by 58 to 21, sealing Bengal's fate. In this ballot Hindu members voted virtually unanimously for partition, including two communists who had abstained from voting one way or the other in the joint sitting, while the Muslim representatives voted against. In the sitting of legislators from the Muslim-majority districts, 106 voted against partition (i.e. for a Pakistan that would include all of Bengal), while 35 others, almost all of them Hindu legislators, voted in favour of partition. As Gordon says, 'given the limited choice before them, the Hindu

---

[65] Gordon, *Divided Bengal*, p. 316.
[66] Ibid., p. 317.

Bengalis [the minority in Bengal, albeit a substantial 43%] voted to split Bengal and remain part of India.'[66]

In the weeks leading up to this ratification of partition, two progressive-minded Bengali leaders had made a last-ditch, desperate effort to stave off the axe. One was Sarat Chandra Bose, a renowned Calcutta lawyer and top Bengal Congress leader over the preceding two decades. His partner was a man called Abul Hashim, a Muslim from a Hindu-majority west Bengal district and, paradoxically enough, General Secretary of the Bengal unit of the Muslim League. Since he joined the League in 1943, it was Hashim's tireless grassroots work that had transformed the Bengal League into a well-organized, mass-based movement. Bose, for his part, was considered a giant figure of the Congress-led independence movement throughout Bengal and India. Although leaders of rival political movements, both were at one level committed Bengal patriots and ideological leftists who harboured grave misgivings about the short and long-term consequences of partitioning Bengal on communal lines, and were intent on saving the unity of the province if possible.

To circumvent the problem that Bose was basically committed to India's unity and Hashim to the Pakistan concept, the two intrepid Bengalis came up with a plan under which Bengal would remain united and be constituted as 'a Free State', with its own constituent assembly which would at an unspecified later date 'decide its relations with the rest of India'. A decision to join either India or Pakistan could be made only by a two-thirds majority of a freely elected legislature of united Bengal, the proposal specified. The Bose-Hashim plan was not simply an airy-fairy declaration of intent, but a full-fledged, detailed power-sharing pact between Bengal Hindus and Bengal Muslims. Sarat Bose and Abul Hashim signed this agreement on May 20, 1947. The agreement prescribed a complex but workable electoral system designed to ensure fair, proportional representation for all communities and groups in the future Bengal parliament. It called for the formation of an Interim Ministry (pending those elections) for undivided Bengal, comprised of an equal number of Muslims and Hindus. In this provisional government, the chief minister would be a Muslim and the home (interior) minister, who would control police and internal security, would be a Hindu. Hindus and Muslims were to have exactly 50:50 representation in the Bengal civil service, in the police, and in any military forces. A separate Bengal constituent assembly of 30 members would be formed, including 16 Muslims and 14 non-Muslims.[67] In collaboration with senior leaders of the Bengal Muslim League, Bose in particular made intensive efforts to obtain support for this proposal from Mahatma Gandhi, Jinnah, leaders of the Congress high command in Delhi, and indirectly, the British colonial government. The proposals were taken seriously enough for the viceroy of India, Lord Mountbatten, to record on May 28, two slightly different versions of the statement announcing Congress-League agreement on India's partition, to be broadcast by radio to India and the world on the evening of June 3, 1947. One version would be used if it seemed probable that Bengal would be partitioned (this, of course was the one eventually broadcast); however, the other version was kept in reserve in case it seemed likely that Bengal's partition might be averted at the last moment. This latter version, which was never broadcast, said that 'Bengal was one of the Provinces for which partition was demanded, but the newly formed Coalition Government of Bengal have asked for their case to be reconsidered'.[68]

The Bose-Hashim initiative, noble in intent and concrete in substance, features today only in the footnotes of history. It was simply too late for a salvage formula to work. Gandhi expressed sympathy but was indecisive, Jinnah was lukewarm at best, and the pro-partition Congress leaders Nehru and Patel were actively hostile. But the plan failed above all because of the communal polarization in Bengal itself. Bengal's Hindus were overwhelmingly distrustful of their Muslim brethren by this time and would not touch the United Bengal plan's framework, which promised coexistence with equality, with a barge-pole. Among Calcutta's Hindu elite, Sarat Bose's was an isolated, indeed reviled voice for tolerance and mutual respect. Some of Bengal's Muslim League leaders felt a genuine patriotic commitment to the *land* of Bengal and

---

[67]See Sisir Kumar Bose, *Remembering My Father: Sarat Chandra Bose, A Centenary Offering 1889-1989*, Calcutta, 1988, pp. 142-56.
[68]*Mountbatten Papers*, ibid., p. 149.

at an emotional level did not wish to see it subjected to a communal carve-up. But in a manner somewhat reminiscent of a dilemma of Bosnia's Muslim elite in the early 1990s, they were also committed to Muslim self-determination (and the Pakistan concept). The two cravings could not be reconciled, just as the Bosnian Muslim elite discovered in 1992 that it was impossible to have the cake and eat it too.

In a climate surcharged with communal tension, suspicion and hostility—in Bengal and the rest of India, which was going to be partitioned anyway even if Bengal wasn't—the heroic attempt to assert a secular Bengali regional/national identity, transcending the Hindu-Muslim divide, proved abortive. The parallels with Bosnia and its larger context, former Yugoslavia, some 45 years later are obvious and striking. So Bengal was divided, into Hindu-majority and Muslim-majority units under Indian and Pakistani sovereignty respectively. The key point is that this partition happened not simply because elite machinations and interests made it all but inevitable, but because at that juncture, large-scale popular support for partition as a way out of an impasse existed among both Hindus and Muslims. Gordon speaks of counter-intuitive evidence of 'support for partition among Hindus of East Bengal and for Pakistan [and therefore, indirectly but inevitably, partition] among Muslims of West Bengal',[69] both groups that would either be left as a vulnerable minority or forced to migrate if partition did come about. The vote ratifying partition in the Bengal assembly on June 20 reflected this social and political reality. From Bengal then to Bosnia now, anti-partitionist thought is yet to come to grips with partition as the people's choice, a 'democratic' expression of popular will. Of the tragic heroes of the Bengal drama, Sarat Bose never recovered emotionally from the partition of his beloved Bengal and the shattering of the freedom movement's vision of an independent, united India. His health already broken by many years of imprisonment during the long struggle for India's freedom, he died aged sixty in 1950. Abul Hashim, who was from a Muslim-minority district in western Bengal, functioned as Leader of the Opposition in the post-1947 West Bengal legislative assembly for several years before reluctantly departing for the other Bengal and Pakistan. 'He remained a Bengal unifica-

---

[69] Gordon, 'Divided Bengal', p. 321.

tionist until he died in 1974'[70] in Dhaka, capital of liberated Bangladesh, the finally sovereign but still truncated Bengali state.

Beyond the partition debate

I hope to have demonstrated why the contending positions in the polarized debate over Bosnia and partition are flawed. To be sure, Bosnia's society and polity do show strong symptoms normally associated with partitioned states. However, this is principally because Bosnia is a country whose citizens are deeply divided on the most intractable of faultlines—national identity, state allegiance, and the legitimate locus of sovereignty. It is simply silly to expect things to be otherwise in a society engaged in a protracted, tentative recovery from a recent civil war sparked by intense disagreement over these fundamental issues. Denial, and selective romanticization of the pre-war period cannot hide how much has changed in Bosnia since 1991-2. As one foreign resident of Sarajevo observes rather brutally but more or less accurately: 'In 2001, after nearly four years under siege and five and a half years of peace monitored by thousands of foreigners these constructs [of harmonious co-existence, an identical commitment to "Bosnia" cutting across group lines] are a pipe-dream. In 2001 the only things remaining of Sarajevo's so-called multiethnic character are the religious buildings of the four faiths pressed together in the city-centre.'[71] Indeed, no common 'Bosnian' symbols, only communitarian ones, are in evidence during the flag-waving celebrations that are a ritual after Bosnian weddings. The Croats flaunt their red-and-white checkerboard flag, the Serbs their national colours (the same colours, red, blue and white are patterned in different configurations for the RS and the FRY) and the Muslims display either the green flag or the *fleur-de-lys* insignia on a blue background associated with pre-Ottoman Bosnian 'statehood'.

The shrill protests of many (not all) Bosnian and foreign integrationist revisionists against the Dayton settlement are inspired, in fact, not by a value-based commitment to a multinational, civic *society* but by a desire for a less decentralized, more unitary *state* which will put the disobedient and disloyal Bosnian Serbs (and to

[70] Ibid., p. 312.
[71] Kampschror, 'Multicultural Bosnia?'.

a lesser degree, the intransigient BiH Croats) in their place. The underlying motivation is to settle accounts from the war, rather than build a forward-looking vision and strategy for the recon- struction of Bosnia & Herzegovina in the overall context of reconstruction of the Yugoslav region. Dubious motives aside, the simplistic anti-partitionist argument is also *substantively* uncon- vincing, for three reasons.

First, although Bosnia does, unavoidably, have some of the empirical symptoms of partition, it is not partitioned in the sense that it has permanent, juridical recognition as a single, sovereign state. This international guarantee of juridical status is not at all insignificant, and not only because it ensures, at the minimum, Bosnia's survival in the international arena of sovereign states. Over the first five or six years of the post-war era, its concomitant guarantee—freedom of movement and residence for all citizens across the sovereign unit and space—has visibly, discernibly soft- ened the hard internal borders that seemed so impermeable dur- ing the war and the immediate post-war period. Restoration of Bosnia's pre-war demographic mix is most unlikely, and the over- whelming majority of Bosnians live now and will live in the future in areas solidly dominated by their 'own' group. But size- able pockets of 'minority' settlements have re-emerged in many parts of the country as of late 2001, and more growth can be expected.

Second, riots in Mostar in April 2001 and in Banja Luka in May-June partly obscured the first signs of renewed regionalism across the territory of former Yugoslavia and the extremely important implications of this renewal for Bosnia. In mid-May the interior ministers of Croatia, the Federal Republic of Yugoslavia, Republika Srpska and the troubled Bosniac-Croat Federation signed an agreement to pool their resources in a joint, coordinat- ed campaign against illegal immigration and the menace of transnational organized crime rackets (the head of BiH's state bor- der service also signed the agreement).[72] Around the same time, the members of Bosnia's tripartite state presidency made their first joint visit to Belgrade, and set up an inter-state cooperation coun- cil between BiH and FRY to coordinate, in the first instance, lib-

---

[72] 'Bosnia, Croatia, Yugoslavia To Fight Crime Together', Reuters, Sarajevo, May 15, 2001.

eralization of trade, transportation and customs regimes. After meetings with Vojislav Kostunica, Zoran Djindjic and his own counterpart, FRY foreign minister Goran Svilanovic, Bosnia's foreign minister Zlatko Lagumdzija, who accompanied the co-presidents, announced a joint effort, in the shared interest, to 'restore broken links among people who used to work together'.[73] Within weeks, Lagumdzija played host in Sarajevo to a landmark visit by a high-level Serbian government delegation, led by prime minister Djindjic. In addition to further discussions on the matters mentioned in Belgrade and preliminary talks about renewed cooperation in the petrochemical, steel and food-processing sectors, the Serbian visitors' itinerary included the obligatory coffee-stop in Sarajevo's Stari Grad.[74] The day before this meeting, by coincidence, the first passenger train in a decade left Sarajevo for Zagreb, travelling for much of that distance through Republika Srpska.[75] While Lagumdzija and Djindjic walked around central Sarajevo, RS prime minister Ivanic met in Sarajevo with his Federation counterpart Alija Behmen, and the two declared a coordinated effort to determine the fate of the 20,000–30,000 Bosnian Muslims, Serbs and Croats listed as unaccounted for since the war.[76]

All of these steps were encouraged, in many cases actively facilitated, by leaders of the international presence in Bosnia and by senior officials of Western governments. This, rather than any authoritarian strategy to reform Bosnia's state structure in a centralizing direction, is precisely the correct focus and emphasis for international policy vis-à-vis Bosnia and the region as a whole. A concerted process of renewed regionalism has enormous potential to gradually soften—although not erase—the territorial and psychological dividing lines in BiH and further dilute the partition-like elements of the country's post-war condition. The pace and

---

[73] Bosnia's Presidency to Make First Common Visit to Yugoslavia', AFP, Sarajevo, May 17, 2001; 'Cooperation Council Agreed Between Yugoslavia and Bosnia', Blue News Network, Belgrade, May 29, 2001.
[74] 'Bosnia Welcomes Serbian Premier in Break with Past', Reuters, Sarajevo, June 12, 2001.
[75] 'First Train in Decade Leaves Sarajevo for Zagreb', Reuters, Sarajevo, June 11, 2001.
[76] 'Bosnia Leaders Pledge Effort to Track Missing', Reuters, Sarajevo, June 12, 2001.

extent of 'normalization' within Bosnia is contingent upon the pace and extent of normalization of ties between FRY, BiH and Croatia.

Last but not least, it is not only unfair but inaccurate to dismiss and demonize the Dayton settlement as a deal simply legitimizing partition.[77] The Dayton agreement has, unavoidably and undeniably, some elements that can be plausibly construed as 'partitionist'. However, the Dayton experiment also has elements of devolution, federalism, consociation, electoral engineering and multilingualism (the last exaggerating, even contriving, differences between 'Bosnian', 'Croatian' and 'Serbian'). In short, it incorporates an array of the available tools and technologies of managing divided societies *democratically*—and all in the aftermath since 1991 of cascading secessions, mass expulsions, *de jure* (Yugoslavia) and *de facto* (Bosnia) partitions, and, some say, genocide, committed against Bosnian Muslims as a people by some Bosnian Serbs. The debate over the institutional framework of the Dayton state is the subject of Chapter 5.

Organicist national-collectivism seemed unstoppable, indeed the only game in town, in Bosnia and across former Yugoslavia through most of the 1990s. However, with the demise of the Milosevic and Tudjman regimes and the gradual weakening of wartime structures of patronage, control and repression that formed the foundation of BiH's three post-war statelets, it has become possible to contemplate a more complicated transition and a more complex, uncertain future for Bosnia (the subject of Chapter 6)—a possibility hinted at in late 1997 by Momcilo Krajisnik. A situation has developed in which even segments of BiH's political elite notorious for recalcitrance have decided that 'it is in their strategic interest to participate in the state on the

---

[77] At the London School of Economics and Political Science (LSE), I co-teach a post-graduate course, conceived and designed by my colleague Professor Brendan O'Leary, which surveys the various methods and mechanisms of regulating ethnic and national conflict. The topics, in the order in which they are covered, are: genocide, ethnic expulsion, partition, secession, integration, assimilation, control, territorial devolution and federalism, consociation (power-sharing between groups in a single political framework), electoral system design, and multilingualism. It is remarkable, incredible even, how many of these topics apply to Bosnia and Herzegovina's post-Dayton condition.

[78] European Stability Initiative, *Reshaping International Priorities in Bosnia, Part III: The End of the Nationalist Regimes and the Future of the Bosnian State*, p. 13.

most favourable terms [that they can negotiate]'.[78] The Bosnian state has dysfunctional symptoms, *as do its parts*—but it could hardly be otherwise in a post-civil war context of deep distrust and economic collapse. It is probably true that 'it is difficult at present to determine whether shared sovereignty [which is the *de facto* and to some extent *de jure* situation in post-war Bosnia] is a durable political alternative'[79] to partition. Yet a layered-sovereignty model probably provides the only basis of bridging the gap between the reality of fracture and fragmentation, and the imperative, in the shared interest of those thus divided, of restoring some of the broken links and developing limited, strategic cooperation. The evolution of Dayton Bosnia, in the context of the evolution of the surrounding region, is likely to prove a key test-case.

[79] Schaeffer, *Severed States*, p. 253.

5

DEMOCRACY AMID DIVISION

THE INSTITUTIONAL ARCHITECTURE
OF THE DAYTON STATE

'The single most important and urgent factor in the consolidation of democracy is not civil society but political institutionalization.'—*Larry Diamond, political scientist, in 1996*[1]

'One of the most striking developments over the past year in Bosnia is that constitutions have suddenly started to matter. In the early years of the peace process, real political decisions were taken outside formal structures... As the [wartime] parallel power structures wither away, constitutions... have started to matter... Renewed interest in constitutional matters [among Bosnian parties] is therefore a sign of progress... The next phase of the peace process will be one of elaborating the Dayton system, defining the relationships between the different levels of government and among the ethnic communities... What is needed is a well-designed process for constitutional debate within Bosnia... The international community will play a vital role in setting the ground rules for such a debate.'—*European Stability Initiative (a specialist think-tank), March 2001*[2]

The post-Dayton international intervention in Bosnia is not just about building a state. It equally aims to build and stabilize a democratic institutional framework for that state, one that will be acceptable to all three national groups while paving the way for the country's eventual inclusion in institutions of trans-European cooperation.

[1] Larry Diamond, 'Towards Democratic Consolidation' in L. Diamond and M. Plattner (eds), *The Global Resurgence of Democracy*, Baltimore and London, 1996, p. 238.
[2] European Stability Initiative, *Reshaping International Priorities in Bosnia*, Part III: *The End of the Nationalist Regimes and the Future of the Bosnian State*, Berlin and Sarajevo, March 2001, pp. 1, 13-14.

The integration-partition debate concerning Bosnia's present and future has been surveyed and briefly analyzed in Chapter 1. Chapter 2 discusses the dubious foundations of the Dayton peace agreement, and provides a detailed account of the extremely complex, multi-tiered constitutional arrangement and institutional structure which resulted from that compact. Chapter 3 closely examines, through the local prism of Mostar, the difficulties encountered in realizing the state-building and power-sharing agenda of the peace implementation process. Chapter 4 places the partition debate in comparative and historical perspective. Here it is argued that for all its flaws—in making, substance and implications—it is distorted and misleading to depict the DPA as a deal legitimizing partition. This is not to deny that the DPA 'straddles the fence between partition and power-sharing, including both shared institutions and separate territorial entities with special ties to other states.'[3] But for comparative political scientists and many others, the fascinating facet of Bosnia after Dayton is the deployment of a range of institutional technologies for managing divided societies democratically, in particular an array of devices associated with federalism and consociation (mutual recognition and autonomy for, and power-sharing between, the different segments of a plural society). That this is being attempted in the aftermath of cascading secessions (since 1991) from former Yugoslavia and its fragments, forcible demographic engineering through mass expulsions within Bosnia, and even, allegedly, genocide (according to the Hague tribunal and some analysts) only heightens the novelty and the fascinating quality of the experiment.

In this penultimate chapter, the major characteristics and prospects of Bosnia & Herzegovina's political-institutional framework are evaluated in light of the existing expert knowledge about devolution and federation, consociation and other tools and techniques—specifically integration through electoral engineering (the deliberate design of a certain kind of electoral system)—in divided societies. My objective is not just to explicitly contextualize and situate the case of post-Dayton Bosnia within a sophisticated body of comparative knowledge, analysis and debate, thereby broadening the parameters of a lively but overly case-cen-

---

[3] Timothy Sisk, *Power-Sharing and International Mediation in Ethnic Conflicts*, Washington, DC, 1996, p. 94.

tred debate about the institutional architecture of the Dayton state. I equally intend to attract the attention of comparatively inclined scholars and practitioners to the particular case of post-Dayton Bosnia, and to what its specificities can illuminate about those broader, more general controversies about institutional possibilities and constraints in deeply divided societies, especially in the aftermath of violent conflict. In doing so, I restrict myself to analysis and assessment, purposely avoiding the kind of confident policy prescription that comes naturally to some outside observers of the post-Yugoslav transitions in Bosnia and its neighbouring states. The content of this chapter is, nonetheless, suggestive of 'policy' implications, especially but not only for the American and (non-'Balkan') European arbiters of Bosnia's transition.

Bosnia's party system

In March 1999, a Brussels-based advocacy concern, which urges with strident regularity a hyper-interventionist policy towards post-war Bosnia by Western countries and institutions, complained that 'for too long... has [BiH] been ruled by leaders who draw support from only one of the three main ethnic groups.'[4] The assertion is correct; the problem with the complaint is that this is all but inevitable, since post-1995 Bosnia & Herzegovina has no significant political parties which draw support across cross-'ethnic' lines, from more than one of the three 'nations' that simultaneously comprise and fracture Bosnia's society and state. The structure and configuration of Dayton Bosnia's competitive party system is a key, albeit overlooked institutional feature which conditions and overshadows the country's internationally supervised post-war political evolution. Although languishing in neglect, it is incontrovertibly the appropriate launching point for this chapter.

Why is the character of the party system so important? It is because a multi-party system is the bedrock institution of any democratic polity, and the primary mechanism for both representation of citizens and mediation of differences between citizens, and groups of citizens. Any party system thus has a dual function.

[4] International Crisis Group, 'Breaking the Mould: Electoral Reform in Bosnia and Herzegovina', Sarajevo, March 4, 1999, p. 6.

It is intended to provide an institutionalized channel for the expression of conflicts in society, through open competition, whilst also being the mechanism that ultimately contributes to the mediation of those conflicts. In a pioneering comparative study of modern party systems published in 1967, two American political scientists, Seymour Martin Lipset and Stein Rokkan, noted that party systems ultimately perform a vital 'integrative role' in society, although their functioning embodies a 'conflict-integration dialectic.'[5] The structure of the party system thus has a crucial bearing on the level of 'integration' that can be achieved in any society. It influences the nature of federal and consociational arrangements in societies which have such features in their institutional framework, and conditions the functioning of those institutions. It also influences the degree of centripetal integration that can be engineered in divided multiethnic societies via deliberate design of electoral rules and methods.

How do competitive party systems translate social cleavages into political, i.e. voting alignments? Lipset and Rokkan identified four major axes or dimensions of cleavage which influence political choices and voting behaviour in established western European democracies. These were class (specifically working-class versus middle and upper classes, typically translated into left-right voting preferences on an ideological continuum, with working-class voters preferring socialist, communist and social-democratic parties and more bourgeois electors favouring christian-democrat parties); religion, as well as religiosity (for example, Catholic and Protestant, practising and non-practising Catholics); conflicts between rural (agricultural) and urban interests; and finally, what they called 'ethnic-cultural' cleavages. Most stable party systems that can be found in the world are to at least some degree multidimensional in nature—that is, they involve the interplay in some permutation and combination of multiple dimensions of cleavage and conflict. This does not preclude one issue-dimension being more important than others in any given context. For instance, a later study by Arend Lijphart, who also happens to be the leading theorist and proponent of consociational democracy, found that in

[5] Seymour Martin Lipset and Stein Rokkan, 'Cleavage Structures, Party Systems and Voter Alignments: An Introduction' in S.M. Lipset and S. Rokkan (eds), *Party Systems and Voter Alignments: Cross-National Perspectives*, New York, 1967, pp. 4-5.

most western democracies, class identification was the single most salient factor (although Lijphart's study dates to 1984, and the salience may well have diluted in many mature democracies in the last two decades because of changing class structures and a lessening of polarization).[6]

However, the multidimensional character of party competition in most cases means that one can normally expect to find parties which have different agendas and different points of emphasis— including class, ideology, rural interests, religious issues, and 'ethnic-cultural' demands. In a multiethnic democracy, there will surely be some parties based upon and stressing the 'ethnic-cultural' dimension of cleavage. However, there will most likely also be parties which claim that other issues are at least equally if not more important, and premise their appeals on alternative identities, interests and agendas (while not necessarily denying the legitimacy of the 'ethnic-cultural' question as a basis for mobilization). An example is Quebec, where the principal competitors for popular support and power are the Parti Québecois, which is an explicitly ethno-linguistic party, and the Liberal Party, a more broadly based and oriented party which has significant support in Quebec, including among the French-speaking majority, but also elsewhere in Canada and maintains an overall Canadian and federalist political orientation. In other words, the Liberal Party has some support in both Quebec and beyond the province, and among both English-speaking and French-speaking Canadians. This cross-ethnic, cross-regional base has enabled this party to play a vital integrative role in Canada, as the 'bridge' that shores up the sometimes precarious connection between Quebec and the rest of the country. The lesson is that the existence of at least some political parties of cross-ethnic base is very important to the juridical as well as the effective unity of a multiethnic democracy. This assumes, since it normally requires, a cross-ethnic orientation, which in turn entails for practical purposes a program that appeals across ethnic lines.

The competitive party system in Bosnia clearly does not meet this standard. There are, quite simply, no significant parties of cross-national base in the country. It is probably unrealistic to

[6] Arend Lijphart, *Democracies: Patterns of Majoritarian and Consensus Government in 21 Countries*, New Haven, 1984, pp. 27, 127-49.

expect the presence or emergence of such parties within years of a polarizing civil war. But the progressive development of at least a few significant parties of cross-national orientation is essential as a driving force in the political-institutional life of the country if any substantial degree of political 'integration' is to be attained. In order to consider this second, more modest prospect, I make an explicit distinction between a party of cross-national *base* and a party of cross-national *orientation*. The latter category of party may not have a cross-national base of support, but its orientation is non-communal and non-sectarian, and it seeks to represent citizens rather than members of one national group. The litmus test that would determine whether a party whose declaratory ideology and program is not overtly group-specific actually has a cross-national orientation or not is whether that party's activists/organizers and elected public officials include representatives from the different Bosnian communities.

The SDP-BiH, reformed legatee to the communist tradition, is the only party in Bosnia that passes this test, a revealing commentary on the extent and intensity of the divisions that run through the country's society and polity. It has some urban Serbs and Croats in its leadership and cadre, and since May 2000, the mayor of Sarajevo's overwhelmingly Bosniac-populated Centar (downtown) district has been a SDP Serb, to cite one example (the same test decisively disqualifies groups such as Haris Silajdzic's 'Party for Bosnia & Herzegovina', the SBiH). But the SDP's capacity to act as an integrative force across the country (or even just within the Federation BiH) is limited by the nature of its support base. In the general elections of November 2000, the SDP received almost 100,000 votes more than it had polled two years earlier in autumn 1998. But this gain was mostly at the expense of the Muslim SDA, which lost votes especially in larger urban centres, and 90% of the total SDP vote came from the five predominantly Bosniac cantons of the Muslim-Croat federation, centred on the towns of Tuzla, Sarajevo, Zenica, Bihac and Gorazde. Since geography approximately overlaps with nationality in today's Bosnia, the conclusion is inescapable that the vast majority of SDP supporters are Bosniacs. Ironically, the geographic (and national) concentration of the SDP's support base is almost identical to that of the HDZ-BiH, an explicitly national(ist) party, which in November 2000 received 89% of its votes from the other five Federation cantons—western Herzegovina, western Bosnia, the Posavina municipalities, Herzegovina-Neretva and central Bosnia (in the case of the latter two, from the Croat-dominated areas of those cantons).[7] In short, the one party of genuinely cross-national orientation that exists in Bosnia has negligible presence and almost no support in Republika Srpska—in November 2000 its candidates for the RS presidency and vice-presidency polled 1.4% of ballots cast for this race within RS (which, of course, is overwhelmingly Serb-populated), and 41% of those cast outside RS territory by people displaced from RS (almost entirely Bosniac voters)[8]—and its support among Croats is limited to a relative handful in Sarajevo and a small minority among the Croats living in central Bosnia and Posavina cantons.

The other issue-dimensions characteristic of less exceptional party systems do feature in the party politics of contemporary Bosnia & Herzegovina. In 1997 separate studies of citizens in the FBiH and the RS reported the consistent finding that rural voters, typically with only an elementary education, tended to support the established national(ist) options, while urban electors with higher education were significantly more likely to be favourably disposed towards opposition alternatives.[9] In Bosnia the level of education can be regarded as a rough proxy for class status, and both educational level and location of residence (rural or urban setting) frequently correlate with the degree of religiosity. In other words, such variable factors as class, occupation, religiosity, location of residence and possibly, generation (age) do influence political preferences and voting choices in BiH. But they do so *not* in the context of a single, coherent country-wide electorate and party system, but rather within the confines of what are essentially three separate electorates and three distinct (sub)systems of party competition. There has been a gradual but definite liberalization and pluralization of the political space in BiH in the post-Dayton years. In the RS and in the Muslim-dominated

---

[7] European Stability Initiative, *Reshaping International Priorities in Bosnia, Part III*, p. 12.
[8] These results are posted on *http://www.oscebih.org*.
[9] See Gordon N. Bardos, 'The Bosnian Cold War: Politics, Society and International Engagement after Dayton', *Harriman Review* 11, 3 (1999), pp. 10-11.

regions of the Federation, the virtual party-statelets run by the SDS and SDA, respectively, during the war and in the early post-war period are no more. In the RS the SDS has recovered from erosion and decline in 1997-8 to re-emerge as the single largest party in local and general elections held during 2000. But in contrast to its heyday (1992-6), it now commands the allegiance of only a plurality of the RS electorate, and faces competition from a number of middle-sized and small Serb parties. In the predominantly Muslim zones of the Federation, the SDA and SDP now have roughly equal support, with the SDP stronger among urbanized, better-educated and secular-minded electorates, and the SBiH is a sizeable third party. Only the smallest of the three groups, the BiH Croats, have as yet been relatively unaffected by the phenomenon of party pluralization and the downsizing of the strength of the hegemonic wartime party.

So it is *not* the case that competitive party politics in Bosnia & Herzegovina is frozen in some sort of time-warp. There is plenty of evidence of movement and change. Along with the growth of party pluralism, and the eclipse of single-party dominance among Bosniacs and Serbs, some major parties have modified their strategies and rhetorics in a 'moderate' direction in response to changing circumstances, the prime example being the SDS. There are reasons to believe that a latent reformist tendency exists within even the HDZ-BiH, the least eroded and, in appearance at least, most unreconstructed of the ex-hegemons. The crucial point is that this pluralization and relative liberalization has not altered the basic reality of a Bosnian electorate that is more or less trifurcated along the national faultline. The challenge to traditional national(ist) politics does not come from multinational parties, since no such parties exist in Bosnia & Herzegovina (the only major party that is avowedly multinational in orientation, the SDP, has a negligible base among Croats and almost none in RS). It comes, rather, from *less* nationalist parties rooted in the same community that seek to derive political mileage from the corruption, authoritarianism and other vices of wartime elites. This does lead to increasing fluidity and competition in party politics, but within three very distinct, separate spaces and frameworks, given the absence of any major party with a cross-national base of support. The everyday issues and problems that affect the lives of ordinary Bosnians are very similar cutting across group lines, the most notable being a desperate economic situation and massive unemployment. It is a typically Bosnian paradox that virtually identical post-war predicaments have not had any substantial impact on the segmentation of Bosnia's political society.

To Arend Lijphart the test of a divided society lies in the character of 'the political parties that form under conditions of free association and competition... [specifically] whether or not its political parties are organized along segmental lines.'[10] By this criterion post-Dayton Bosnia unmistakably qualifies as a society which is deeply divided, and there is little room for surprise given what happened in Bosnia between 1992 and 1995. But the phenomenon of segmental parties dominating the political landscape is nothing new in Bosnia. In multiparty elections held at the end of 1990, the three main segmental parties won the support of almost three-quarters of Bosnian voters, which gave them 98 of 130 seats in the Bosnian parliament's chamber of citizens, 104 of 110 seats in the chamber of municipalities (thus 202 of the total 240 seats), and all seven positions on the Bosnian collective presidency.[11] Those pre-war 'election results read more like a census of national identities in the socialist period.'[12]

A note of caution is in order here. Lijphart has a tendency to go looking for what he alternately calls the 'natural', 'true' and 'real' dividing lines in multiethnic societies.[13] He claims that his test of what those allegiances and cleavages are—the nature of parties that emerge—'treats all groups, segmental and non-segmental, in a completely equal and even-handed way... [and] gives equal chances not only to all ethnic or other segments, large or small, but also to groups and individuals who explicitly reject the

---

[10] Arend Lijphart, 'Self-Determination versus Pre-Determination of Ethnic Minorities in Power-Sharing Systems' in W. Kymlicka (ed.), *The Rights of Minority Cultures*, New York, 1995, pp. 275-87.

[11] The most detailed presentation and analysis of the outcome of the November-December 1990 elections in Bosnia is in Burg and Shoup, *The War in Bosnia-Herzegovina*, pp. 46-57. See also Steven Burg, 'Bosnia-Hercegovina: A Case of Failed Democratization' in K. Dawisha and B. Parrott (eds), *Politics, Power and the Struggle for Democracy in South-East Europe*, Cambridge, 1997, pp. 122-45.

[12] Woodward, *Balkan Tragedy*, p. 122.

[13] Lijphart, *Democracies*, p. 209; 'Self-Determination versus Pre-Determination', p. 280.

idea that society should be organized on a segmental basis.'[14] It would be problematic to sustain this proposition of a neutral, level playing field if the case in question were Bosnia in late 1990. The constitutional structure of the Titoist state during its last two decades of existence was based on the institutionalization of national-collective identities and rights at all levels of the system. This inordinate privileging of national-collective identities and rights inherently pre-disposed the structure of competitive politics that emerged in the twilight of Yugoslav socialism in the same direction.[15] Moreover, the end-1990 elections in Bosnia were held in a context of Slovenia's incremental 'dissociation' from the Yugoslav federal framework, a crisis situation in Kosovo and above all, sharply rising Serb-Croat tensions in the Croatian borderlands adjoining Bosnia—all factors which influenced Bosnian voters to choose national(ist) parties. In addition, within Bosnia, the choices of large numbers of citizens of all three communities were motivated by an overriding desire to reject and eject 'communists' from power, not surprising since BiH had arguably the most rigid and conservative example of socialist Yugoslavia's mono-party regime. This too helped the national(ist) parties gain support.

Nonetheless, it remains true that even without various institutional and contingent factors that encouraged and favoured the recent political mobilizations on national(ist) lines, the very first parties to emerge in Bosnia—in the first decade of the twentieth century, during the second half of the period of Austro-Hungarian control of Bosnia (1878-1918)—formed along proto-national (confessional) lines. This happened even though the Austro-Hungarian regime had made an attempt during the immediately preceding years to promote a neutral, broadly-based 'Bosnian' identity among the subjects, largely with the (unsuccessful) intent of undermining the spread of Serb national sentiment, encouraged by the Serbian state across the Drina, among the Orthodox who made up the plurality of the Bosnian population. The Serb National Organization, the Muslim National

[14] Lijphart, 'Self-Determination versus Pre-Determination', pp. 281, 285.

[15] This argument is developed in Sumantra Bose, 'Democratization and National Self-Determination: Institutional Structure in post-Tito Yugoslavia, post-Franco Spain and post-colonial Sri Lanka', Ph.D. dissertation, Department of Political Science, Columbia University, 1998.

Organization, the Croat National Union and the Croat Catholic Association (the last a smaller group) were the parties represented in the Bosnian parliament organized under Austro-Hungarian auspices in 1910. For the first year (1910-11), the Serbs and Muslims were in uneasy alliance; in 1911 this broke down, the Serbs went into opposition and the Muslims shifted to a coalition with the Croats, which lasted until the outbreak of war in 1914 (the basis of both alliances were commitments made by Serb and Croat leaders to the Muslim landed elite that the issue of agrarian reform would not be pressed). As the Balkan wars of 1912-13 escalated into a Europe-wide conflagration in 1914, 'sessions of the Bosnian parliament… became stormy confrontations. Insults, active obstruction and walkouts became [increasingly] common… Constitutional life in Bosnia was off to a rocky start.'[16] The pattern was to endure. It repeated itself in 1991 and early 1992, with tragic consequences.

The compartmentalization of competitive party politics that emerged across Yugoslavia during 1990 along the boundaries of the federal republics (aided by the dissolution of the Yugoslav communist party, the LCY, in early 1990 and by the subsequent absence of state-wide elections), the dominance of the idiom of 'national self-determination' in virtually every republic, and the near-absence of supra-national parties cutting across republic boundaries—Ante Markovic's reformist party, which came closest to fulfilling the desperately needed 'bridge' function, had no representation in the legislatures of Slovenia and Croatia and just 50 of the 735 seats in the new parliaments of the other four republics combined—were major catalysts to the rapid disintegration of the common state in 1991-2. Not unpredictably, the end-game of Yugoslavia was enacted in its most violent and tragic form in the republic that was in ethnography a 'mini-Yugoslavia' and, to make matters worse, had a history of being contested between the rival nationalist currents in the larger region. Ironically, a decade and a civil war later, Bosnia faces essentially the same institutional problem of cohesion that precipitated the demise of the Yugoslav state. Unlike Yugoslavia, Bosnia's juridical unity is guaranteed by Western powers and European and Euro-Atlantic institutions. But its effective unity remains a big question-mark. The structure and

[16] Donia and Fine, *Bosnia and Herzegovina*, p. 109.

configuration of post-war Bosnia's party system not only makes a loose, decentralized state a *fait accompli*, but overshadows the debate over the federal and consociational structures of the Dayton state, which I discuss later in this chapter. It also plays a role in imposing strict limits on the potential efficacy of effecting integration via electoral engineering in the current Bosnian context, a topic which I now consider.

Electoral integration

'The electoral system is by far the most powerful lever of constitutional engineering for accommodation and harmony in severely divided societies.'—*Donald Horowitz, political scientist*[17]

'The electoral system is the most easily manipulated element of a political system and therefore a powerful tool for political engineering... If one wants to change the nature of a particular democracy, the electoral system is likely to be the most suitable and effective instrument for doing so.'—*Arend Lijphart, political scientist*[18]

Horowitz and Lijphart, two leading experts on comparative constitutional design, agree on some things. Both, for example, quote with approval the words of W. Arthur Lewis, an expert on problems of transition in multiethnic post-colonial societies of the developing world, that 'the surest way to kill the idea of democracy in a plural society is to adopt the Anglo-American electoral system of first-past-the-post.'[19] The majoritarian, 'winner-take-all' system has indeed been a source of degeneration into tyranny and civil war in a number of transitional democracies with multiethnic societies in the developing world.[20]

[17] Donald Horowitz, *A Democratic South Africa? Constitutional Engineering in a Divided Society*, Berkeley, 1991, p. 163. Chapter 5 of Horowitz's book is devoted to a comparative assessment of prospects and problems of electoral engineering in divided societies.
[18] Lijphart, 'Electoral Systems, Party Systems and Conflict Management in Segmented Societies' in R. Schrire (ed.), *Critical Choices for South Africa: An Agenda for the 1990s*, Cape Town, 1990, p. 2; Lijphart, 'Electoral Systems' in S.M. Lipset (ed.), *The Encyclopaedia of Democracy*, Washington, DC, 1995, pp. 412-22.
[19] W. Arthur Lewis, *Politics in West Africa*, London, 1965, p. 71.
[20] For Sri Lanka as an example, see Sumantra Bose, *States, Nations, Sovereignty: Sri Lanka, India and the Tamil Eelam Movement*, New Delhi, Thousand Oaks and London, 1994.

Beyond a shared rejection of undiluted plurality-majority systems of translating votes into seats—and political office and
power—as inappropriate and even dangerous for ethnically mixed
societies, the two scholars don't agree on very much, which is precisely why it is useful to juxtapose their views. Lijphart is a believ-
er in the merits of democracy by consociation as the appropriate
institutional choice for heterogeneous societies. The consociational model has four key principles: government by 'grand coalition'
at the centre, involving equitable and possibly equal 'distribution
of the presidency and other high offices among the different [eth-
nic or national] segments'; 'segmental autonomy', entailing 'delegation of as much decisionmaking as possible to the separate segments' and the adoption of a federal structure if the segments are
'geographically concentrated'; 'proportionality [among the
groups] as the basic standard of political representation, civil service appointments and allocation of public funds', extending in
appropriate contexts to 'parity of representation'; and rights of
'minority veto' on all policy matters and decisions that might
affect the 'vital interests' of the minority community or communities.[21]

As described in Chapter 2, the institutional framework of the
Dayton state qualifies post-war Bosnia as a classic example of
consociational settlement. Consociational rules and norms are
built into practically every aspect and every level of the Dayton
system. The state is constructed as an essentially confederal union
between two Entities, a power-sharing 'federation' based on
equality and parity for the federating national segments and a radically autonomous 'Republika Srpska'. The fairly skeletal framework of common-state institutions are supposed to operate on the
basis of either parity or at least proportional representation, with
guaranteed 'vital interest' veto rights for all three communities.
The same principles—parity, proportionality, mutual vetoes, rotating offices—are enshrined in Federation structures. In the two bi-
national cantons of the Federation (central Bosnia &
Herzegovina-Neretva), these are further complemented by special
requirements for concurrent majorities (among legislators of both
major groups) in decisionmaking, and mandatory devolution of

---

[21] These pillars of consociationalism are summarized in Lijphart, 'Self-
Determination versus Pre-Determination', pp. 277-8.

power in certain key fields to municipalities whose national majority differs from the population of the canton as a whole. At the local level, consociational techniques have been deployed as part of international strategy in such volatile, daunting places as divided Mostar (Chapter 3). Finally, Bosnia's own far-reaching, intricate consociational settlement is complemented by certain external confederal characteristics. These permit the constitutive Entities to establish and build cooperative relationships with neighbouring states and allow Bosnian citizens to conditionally hold dual citizenship with another country (implicitly also a neighbour).

Lijphart is emphatic that proportional representation (PR; 'proportional' in the sense that there should be as close a correspondence as possible between the proportion of votes gained and proportion of seats obtained by any party) based on party lists of candidates is the electoral formula that best suits the consociational system. This, broadly, is the blueprint of the electoral system that underpins Bosnia's Dayton regime. Horowitz, by contrast, is sceptical of consociation as the ultimate solution to the institutional dilemma of deeply divided societies. Critics of the consociational paradigm have isolated two basic flaws. First, consociation tends to reify ethnic/national identities and entrench cleavages and divisions based on those identities. Second, a workable consociational system depends on 'overarching cooperation at the elite level'[22] between the segments. This assumption—will and capacity on the part of segmental elites—cannot be taken for granted in all cases, particularly in deeply divided societies. Even where it may exist, does a consociational framework of governance not confer uncalled-for power and privilege on those elites? This question is especially poignant in cases such as Bosnia (and indeed former Yugoslavia as a whole), where sectarian segmental elites are considered primarily culpable for the descent into war.

I shall return to the controversy over consociationalism later in this chapter, when I evaluate Bosnia's present and (foreseeable) future in light of the consociational settlement institutionalized at, by and after Dayton. In this section, I focus on the alternative to consociationalism advanced at the scholarly level by Horowitz,

---

[22] Arend Lijphart, 'Cultural Diversity and Theories of Political Integration', *Canadian Journal of Political Science* 4, 1 (1971), p. 10.

and at a less scholarly level by others in the specific context of
post-Dayton Bosnia.

'The [alternative] approach I have advocated', says Horowitz,
'is to adopt an electoral system that will make moderation reward-
ing by making politicians reciprocally dependent on the votes of
members of groups other than their own.'[23] This is the same
approach and agenda as that of the International Crisis Group, the
hyper-interventionist think-tank, which in 1999 urged that the
post-conflict international mission in BiH work toward an electoral system for Bosnia which 'give[s] voters of all ethnic groups a
say in [determining] who are elected as leaders of each ethnic
group', adding, correctly, that 'this implies some form of multiple-
vote system.[24] Both of these prescriptions are premised on a
reluctant albeit resigned acceptance of the reality of a party system
segmented along ethnic lines—Horowitz has studied such countries as Malaysia and Sri Lanka, where ethnic, group-specific parties thoroughly dominate the political landscape.

The subject of the most appropriate electoral system for
Bosnia has been one of the most controversial issues in that country's post-war phase. It was 'in 1997 [that] the idea first began to
circulate among the international community that an electoral
system be designed which would systematically favour moderate
candidates over the nationalist parties.'[25] In December 1998 the
Peace Implementation Council (PIC) for Bosnia, convening in
Madrid, announced its intention of 'working with the people of
BiH and their representatives to develop a new electoral law
which will promote a democratic and multiethnic political
process.' A designated group of Bosnian and international experts
proffered the first draft of a permanent election law for BiH in
October 1999. In January 2000 this was rejected by the Bosnian
state parliament, which at the time was dominated by the established national(ist) parties, the SDA-SBiH coalition, HDZ and
SDS, which occupied 27 of the 42 seats in its directly elected
house of representatives (17, 6 and 4, respectively). Nonetheless,
with the support of the PIC, the OSCE-BiH incorporated select-

[23] Horowitz, *A Democratic South Africa?*, p. 196.

[24] International Crisis Group, 'Breaking the Mould', p. 7.

[25] European Stability Initiative, *Reshaping International Priorities in Bosnia, Part III*,
p. 10.

ed elements of those proposals into the rules for local/municipal and general (cantonal, federation, RS and common-state) elections conducted in April 2000 and November 2000, respectively (on this decision and its consequences, more below). In mid-2001 a revised draft was once again rejected by the BiH parliament, whose elected house had by this time a narrow majority of members belonging to constituent parties of the internationally sponsored 'Alliance for Change', a hotch-potch grouping pointedly excluding the SDA, HDZ and SDS. In August 2001, the chequered career of the draft election law finally culminated in its acceptance by the BiH parliament, by majority vote in the House of Representatives and by unanimous vote in the House of Peoples. This paved the way for BiH's membership in the Council of Europe, which requires that member-states have a permanent election law.[26]

The passage of the Election Law[27] has not conclusively put all debates and controversies about Bosnia's electoral framework to rest. It is nonetheless a milestone in that the basic, defining characteristics of Bosnia's electoral framework for the foreseeable future are now legally and constitutionally a *fait accompli*. The Election Law enshrines four major amendments to the party-list PR system established since Dayton. These are:

— an *open-list* system, whereby voters are empowered, if they so choose, to indicate preferences for *individual candidates* on a party list, rather than just for the list as a whole;

— a requirement that all parties and coalitions competing in elections at all levels have *at least one-third of their lists comprised of women candidates*, and that these women candidates be fairly distributed on each list;

— the division of both Republika Srpska and the Bosniac-Croat federation into *multi-member electoral constituencies* (MMCs) for the purpose of elections to the Republika Srpska National Assembly and to the popularly elected houses of the common-state and FBiH parliaments (the House of Representatives in both cases). This modifies and supersedes the previous system, under which the sole electoral constituencies were the respective Entity terri-

---

[26] 'Bosnia Adopts Law on Organizing Its Own Elections', AFP, Sarajevo, August 24, 2001.

[27] *Election Law of BiH*, OSCE, Sarajevo, August 24, 2001. The full document can be accessed at *http://www.oscebih.org*.

tories.The introduction of MMCs as electoral districts is complemented by a '*compensatory mandate*' (CM) mechanism, which is
based on a Entity-wide calculation of votes obtained by a particular party or coalition list. If there is any significant discrepancy
between the proportion of votes secured by a list and the proportion of seats obtained by it in the MMCs, the shortfall is *compensated* by an award of additional mandates through the CM mechanism. For this purpose, roughly 25% of the total seats in the
RSNA, the FBiH House of Representatives, and the House of
Representatives of the cross-entity Bosnian parliament are *not*
allocated though the multi-member district system, but held in
reserve for the award of compensatory mandates. This ensures
near-perfect proportionality between votes obtained and seats
secured in the above legislative institutions for all party (and coalition) lists in both Entities.

— the introduction of a *preferential voting system* in one contest—
the race for the Republika Srpska presidency (and vice-presidency, since the president and vice-president are elected in the same
race on a joint ticket, which means that every presidential con-
tender has a running mate). Under this system, all voters may
mark consecutive preferences—1, 2, 3 etc.—for as many of the
joint candidatures as they wish. A voter who does not have a
lower-order preference is free to just indicate a first (and only)
preference on the ballot and leave the polling station. However,
the tacit expectation in this form of voting is that many, hopefully most, voters will indicate at least a second choice, and possibly
lower-order preferences as well. In deciding the outcome of the
poll, the votes are first sorted, and counted, by the first preference
indicated on the ballot. If any slate wins a majority—50% plus
one—of first preferences, its candidates are declared elected. If,
however, no ticket wins a majority of first preferences cast, the
ticket that has won the lowest proportion of first preferences is
eliminated, and the second preferences of voters who selected that
eliminated list as their first choice are redistributed among the
remaining candidatures. If no majority winner emerges even then,
the slate with the next-lowest proportion of first preferences is
removed from contention and their second preferences are similarly redistributed. This is done until one slate crosses the 50%
threshold.

This is a system known in political science terminology as alternative voting (AV). It has been strongly advocated by Donald Horowitz as the optimal electoral system to produce 'fluid, shifting majorities that do not lock ascriptive minorities firmly out of power', by making 'parties...dependent, in part, on vote transfers from members of groups other than the groups they principally represent.' This is done by providing an in-built incentive for 'parties [of the ethnic majority]... [to] bid across ethnic lines for the second preferences of [minority] voters whose first choice stands no real chance of election.' Thus 'AV does not stand in the way of majoritarianism, but makes [ethnic] majorities responsive to the interests' of ascriptive minorities. In the best-case scenario, Horowitz argues, this system can act as an engine for *intra*-ethnic moderation and *inter*-ethnic accommodation. The key, in his logic, is to maximize minority influence over the electoral process and its outcome; in his words, 'lack of clarity about the trade-off between influence and office-holding is responsible for much of the confusion in thinking about electoral systems for... divided societies... with a majority threshold, achieved by reallocated second and third preferences, it is harder to win election without vote pooling [across ethnic boundaries].'[28]

The same logic lies behind the international community's decision to institute a preferential voting framework for the RS presidential elections. In the language of the OSCE-BiH, the powerful supervising agency for these and other Bosnian elections, the AV system is 'specifically designed to promote dialogue, compromise and reconciliation.' In elections to the RS presidency held before 2000, the slate that gained a plurality of (single-preference) votes won the race. 'Now', says the OSCE-BiH, 'supporters of smaller parties retain *influence* over the electoral outcome' (emphasis in the original text). Specifically, 'candidates who want to be elected will be encouraged to promote programs and policies of compromise under the new preferential voting system. Now, candidates for the RS presidency and vice-presidency will have to look beyond their narrow core of supporters and offer political platforms which appeal to a wider audience, in order to attract second, third, etc preferences of voters. Radicalism will alienate potential supporters... The preferential voting system...

[28] Horowitz, *A Democratic South Africa?*, pp. 165-6, 176-7, 191, 202.

will allow ALL citizens of RS to have a meaningful voice in the selection of their president' (capitals in original text).[29] Copybook Horowitzian in intent, this particular reform to one element of BiH's electoral system and institutional structure can also be regarded as a cautious, limited response to the shrill demands for a much more radical, far-reaching multiple-voting model for the whole country advanced by professional advocacy groups like the ICG and other proponents of Bosnia's 'integration'.

Before being incorporated into the electoral law approved and enacted by BiH legislators in the second half of 2001, all of these measures have been tested by the consortium of international peace-building organizations in BiH via dry-runs in either the local/municipal elections of April 2000 or the general (state/entity/cantonal) elections of November 2000, or both. One requirement, the mandatory allocation of positions to women candidates on party/coalition lists, dates back even further, to internationally imposed provisional regulations for general elections organized by the OSCE-BiH in the autumn of 1998. We thus have concrete, empirical evidence of how these measures have turned out in practice. Based on this evidence, I conclude that the first three reforms highlighted and outlined above are sensible as well as progressive innovations which positively serve Bosnia & Herzegovina's democratic development. However, the benefits of the fourth and last amendment, to the RS's voting system, are much less clear. My evaluation, below, of that amendment actually suggests that, contrary to some claims, the realistic prospects of 'integrating' Bosnia via creative electoral formulas are *limited*.

The 'open-list' system was first introduced at the local level of politics, in country-wide municipal elections conducted in April 2000. At these election voters could either
—mark only individual candidates on ballot papers, including those standing as part of party lists or as independents;
—mark only the party or coalition list they supported without marking any individual candidates who appeared on that list;
—mark the party/coalition list *and* individual candidates for office whose names appeared on the same list.

29 OSCE-BiH, 'Preferential Voting for the Republika Srpska Presidency', Sarajevo, 2000.

A common criticism of 'closed' party-list PR systems is that they privilege the choices of central party elites who draw up candidate lists, and allow voters no leeway to select the candidates they might actually prefer for elected positions. One way of mitigating this is to adopt an open-list scheme. The established precedent among party-list PR democracies on the European continent is Italy, where voters have long had this option and used it extensively in both the urbanized, industrial northern regions and the more rural, traditionalist south.[30] The then chief of the OSCE mission in BiH, Robert Barry, claimed before the election that open party lists invested Bosnian voters with 'the ability to select the candidates they think are best suited to represent them, rather than leaving this decision to party leaders.'[31] International authorities then launched a vigorous publicity campaign in mass media to explain the modified system to voters, and encourage them to avail of the new option. Following the elections, the OSCE-BiH stated that 'voters clearly understood and made ample use of the open list system, reflected in a low 2.5% invalid ballot rate. Many [individual] candidates received more than the necessary 5% threshold to obtain a mandate, often getting as much as 50%. In a number of cases, candidates much lower on the [party] list achieved a higher number of votes, bypassing candidates higher on the list.'[32] As is explained in Chapter 3 in the course of discussing Mostar, in counting ballots the parties (or coalitions of parties) are first allocated a total number of seats proportional to the total votes received by that list, calculated on the basis of a formula known as the Sainte-Lague method. In this stage of determining overall tallies of seats, a ballot on which one or more individual candidates have been marked by a voter counts as a vote towards that party list as a whole. Then the mandates secured by each list are allocated to individuals on that list in descending order, starting with the candidate who has received the highest number of individual preferences. If any seats are still due to that party after

[30] Richard Katz, 'Preference Voting in Italy', *Comparative Political Studies* 18, 2 (1985), pp. 229-49.

[31] 'OSCE Launches 2000 Municipal Election Campaign', OSCE-BiH, Sarajevo, February 23, 2000.

[32] 'OSCE Releases Technical Certified Results for BiH April 2000 Municipal Elections: Voters Used Open List System, Results Reflect New Plurality', OSCE-BiH, Sarajevo, April 20, 2000.

all individuals who have won more than 5% of the total vote obtained by the list have been elected, the remaining seats are filled in the order of candidate placement on the list.

The open-list formula takes care of one of the most common criticisms levelled against party-based PR systems. Local elections, in which the electoral district is the municipality and many candidates—and their reputations—are personally known to voters was clearly the most appropriate context for the pilot run of this system. Subsequently, the open-list scheme was incorporated into the provisional rules for the November 2000 elections to higher levels of government. Once again, voters widely used the option to scrutinize lists and mark individual candidates as favoured choices regardless of their position on the party list, although relatively more in Federation areas than in Republika Srpska. Open lists have now been permanently institutionalized in Bosnia's electoral framework. Article 5.14 of the Election Law stipulates that apart from the races for the three seats on the BiH joint presidency and the RS presidency, voters shall cast their ballots in all other elections in any one of the following ways:

— for an independent candidate;
— for a party, coalition or independent candidates' List;
— for one or more candidates on a party, coalition or independent list. If the voter exercises this option, the list as a whole will be considered to have received one valid vote for the purpose of allocation of seats, accomplished by the conventional proportional representation formula.

The second step taken by international decision—making it compulsory for parties to nominate a minimum proportion of women on their candidate lists—is also justifiable. Women comprise a clear majority of the population in post-war Bosnia, for the tragic reason that war casualties, largely among men, have skewed the gender balance. This is especially true among the Bosnian Muslim communities directly affected by the war, Srebrenica being an extreme example, but applies to all three groups. Many outsiders who have come into contact with Bosnian women, whether within the country or elsewhere, have been greatly impressed by their talents and capabilities. As is the case throughout eastern Europe and the Balkans, however, women tend to be thoroughly marginalized in the political arena. In 1998, the IC-run provisional election commission made it mandatory that of the top nine names on a party's list, at least three must belong to candidates of the 'minority gender'. Following this regulation, the number of women elected to the 42 seats in the BiH house of representatives rose from one (2%) in 1996 to eleven (26%) in 1998. At the local level, the proportion of female municipal councillors rose from 5% in 1997 to over 18% in 2000.

The method used in Bosnia to achieve this enhancement of women's representation in elected institutions and their participation in public decisionmaking—via parties—has numerous precedents throughout the world, in countries as geographically and culturally distant from Bosnia, and each other, as Norway and Argentina. There is a general debate, relevant to the Bosnian case, whether this formula represents a genuine, substantive empowerment of women in politics or a more or less artificial boost to their profile in the political arena, which is what happened in Yugoslavia under the socialist regime—relatively sizeable numbers of women representatives in various bodies at different levels of the system,[33] but ineffective and unsustainable without a commensurate increase in substantive gender equality. Whatever the respective merits of contending viewpoints in this debate may be, the principle, and goal, of a *more* gender-equitable democracy— one which will still be dominated by men—is hard to disagree with. On paper at least, international intervention has made Bosnia 'the leader among the states of central and eastern Europe in terms of women's participation' in politics.[34] The other international hope—that women involved in politics will be more willing and able than men to work towards bridging the national(ist) divides in the country—is debatable and remains unproven. But the requirement that parties accommodate women on their candidate lists, and the at least superficial improvement in women's representation that brings, is now a permanent feature of Bosnia's political life. The provisional regulations in force for the November 2000 elections required that at least one-third of party lists for directly elected canton, entity and state legislative bodies be comprised of women. And Article 4.19 of the Election Law stipulates:

[33] For the statistics of female representation in federal, republican and municipal assemblies in socialist Yugoslavia, see Allcock, *Explaining Yugoslavia*, p. 357.
[34] OSCE-BiH, 'Women in Politics: A Fact-Sheet', Sarajevo, 2000.

Every candidates' list shall include candidates of male and female gender. The minority gender candidates shall be distributed on the list in the following manner: At least one minority gender candidate among the first two candidates, two such candidates among the first five candidates, and three such candidates among the first eight candidates. The number of minority gender candidates on the list shall be at least equal to the total number of candidates on the list divided by three, rounded off to the closest integer.

The third major amendment to Bosnia's electoral framework seeks to address a commonly cited shortcoming of party-list PR systems operating in large constituencies. In the words of Arend Lijphart, the foremost proponent of party-list PR as the optimal electoral system for divided societies, this is the argument that 'the plurality single-member district system... stimulates close contact between the representative and the constituents of a district... every voter has a clearly designated representative to whom he can turn.'[35] A system based solely on party lists of candidates stimulates no such relationship that guarantees a degree of accountability, and the larger the magnitude of the electoral district in such systems, the greater the problem, since the 'elected' representatives remain faceless as far as most ordinary voters are concerned. Lijphart is rather cavalierly dismissive of the problem, but the criticism is serious and merits attention. In mid-2000 the OSCE-BiH, the nodal agency for the international community in Bosnia on all election-related matters, noted:

> Under the electoral system used in previous elections [1996, 1998], politicians elected to the BiH House of Representatives, the Federation House of Representatives and the Republika Srpska National Assembly were elected from one of two [electoral] constituencies, each covering one of the two Entities of BiH—the federation or RS. As politicians were not elected from a specific geographic area, they were not accountable to anyone except their political parties.

---

[35] Lijphart, 'Electoral Systems, Party Systems and Conflict Management in Segmented Societies', p. 9.

Additionally, the party apparatuses sent a disproportionate number of representatives to BiH's legislatures from Sarajevo, Mostar and Banja Luka, leaving large areas of the country under-represented.[36]

One part of the international response to this problem was to introduce the open-list system. The other has been to divide the territory of both the federation and the RS into a number of multi-member districts which elect deputies to the RSNA, the FBiH's HoR, and the state parliament's HoR. Thus, three-quarters of the RSNA's members (62 of 83) are now elected from six multi-member electoral districts on RS territory. In the FBiH's HoR, 105 of 140 seats are filled by direct election from twelve MMCs on federation territory. Of the 28 seats in the state parliament's HoR assigned to the federation, 21 are filled from six MMCs on federation territory, each electing between three and six representatives. Of the 14 seats in the same body assigned to RS, nine are elected from three MMCs on RS territory—corresponding approximately to the boundaries of the Bosanska Krajina, Posavina and Semberija, and eastern Bosnia and eastern Herzegovina, respectively—each of which elects three members. In all three legislative bodies, the residual mandates—roughly 25%—are filled through the allocation of 'compensatory' seats to various parties, based on their Entity-wide vote, as described above. This is an in-built safety mechanism to ensure proportionality between seats and votes for various lists and serves to correct any disproportionality that may be evident between the two once the allocation of mandates from the MMCs has been completed. It is necessary because reducing the magnitude of the electoral district increases the chances that such disproportionalities may occur and compromise the PR basis of the system; generally speaking, the larger the district the more proportional the correlation between votes won and seats obtained.[37]

The stated rationale for the introduction of the MMC system is that 'together with the Open List system, MMCs will enhance

---

[36] OSCE-BiH, 'Multi-Member Constituencies and Compensatory Seats: General Elections, 2000', Sarajevo, 2000.

[37] This has been demonstrated by Douglas Rae, *The Political Consequences of Electoral Laws*, New Haven, 1967, pp. 114-25.

the individual voters' potential to hold their political representatives responsible.' The system's international architects assert that their sole objective is to empower Bosnia's citizens vis-à-vis their leaders; in particular, they categorically state, the MMCs 'are not a first step towards the cantonization of Republika Srpska.' If the MMC system has in fact been 'introduced *solely* as a means of promoting the accountability of elected members of government' (emphasis in the original), since 'candidates will run in local constituencies and the voters will have a chance to know their elected representatives and their record in office',[38] it is really difficult to find fault with this measure. It potentially redresses, to some extent at least, one of the key shortcomings of party-list PR regimes—the lack of a direct relationship between the electorate and its representatives. In addition, it should help ensure that the deputies in Bosnia's legislatures come from different regions and areas of the country, thereby tackling the problem of over-representation from the major urban centres. Moreover, the use of multi-member constituencies as electoral units has a precedent in Bosnia's recent political history. In the Bosnian elections of November-December 1990, the 130-member 'chamber of citizens' of the bicameral BiH parliament was constituted on the basis of party-list PR from seven large, multi-member districts which covered the then socialist federal republic. These were: Bihac (9 seats), Banja Luka (25 seats), Doboj (14 seats), Tuzla (28 seats), Zenica (14 seats), Sarajevo (25 seats) and Mostar (15 seats).[39]

It is equally incontrovertible that the 'compensatory seats' provision helps ensure a high degree of fairness in the final allocation of seats among parties—any shortfall in vote-seat proportionality after the allocation of MMC mandates is eliminated by this process—and broadly based representation in the legislatures. Small parties with a minimum level of support across an Entity particularly stand to benefit from this mechanism, and a number of such parties have gained one or two seats in the final allocation of mandates to one or more legislatures after the November 2000

[38] OSCE-BiH, 'Multi-Member Constituencies and Compensatory Seats'.
[39] Burg and Shoup, *The War in Bosnia-Herzegovina*, p. 50. The other chamber, the 'chamber of municipalities', consisted of 110 members, elected from single-member districts corresponding to the pre-war municipalities. For this chamber, if no candidate polled an outright majority of votes in the first round, the top two contestants entered into a second-round run-off to decide the outcome.

elections, thanks to the CM system. But larger parties also stand to benefit. For example, of the 31 SDS members elected to the RSNA in November 2000, comprising the single largest contingent in that house, 24 were elected from MMCs, the remaining seven from award of compensatory mandates. In the elections to constitute the FBiH's HoR, the SDA won as many as four compensatory mandates (including a seat for controversial party official Hasan Cengic) from just one electoral district, Constituency 11, which consists of most of inner Sarajevo and parts of outer Sarajevo. Of four SBiH members elected from Federation territory to the state parliament's HoR, one is the recipient of a compensatory seat, and so on.

The CM mechanism has one significant, additional advantage. Each party or coalition is required to submit to the Election Commission of BiH (for the late 2000 elections, the competent body was still the Provisional Election Commission or PEC), in advance, a list of candidates to whom its compensatory mandates shall be awarded. These persons need to be on the party's candidate lists for one or more of the MMCs, within the same Entity and at the same electoral level. What this means in practice is that if a party strongly desires that particular individuals among its officials be elected to legislative bodies, it can place them at or near the top of its CM list, thus making almost sure that they will get elected even if they fail to make it from their particular MMC(s). Among those elected in this manner in November 2000 are outspoken SDA (Muslim) leader Sulejman Tihic to the RSNA, who subsequently became deputy speaker of that assembly; (Serb) SDP leader Dragi Stanimirovic from RS territory to the state parliament (HoR); HDZ-BiH official Ivo Andric-Luzanski and NHI leader Ivo Lozancic (both Croats) to the same chamber from FBiH territory; and Sefer Halilovic of the (Muslim) Bosnian Patriotic Party (BPS), subsequently made FBiH minister for refugees, and Stjepan Siber (Croat), standing for an even smaller party, to the FBiH's HoR. In short, prominent figures of both small and large parties gained election through this mechanism.

So far, so good. The three major electoral reforms elaborated so far can, in themselves as well as collectively and cumulatively, be expected to have salutary effects on the quality and representative character of Bosnia's fractured democracy. The fourth form of international tinkering—the system of preferential voting for the RS presidency, used for the first time in November 2000 and subsequently institutionalized in 2001 in the permanent Election Law—is a different story. It is a story worth recounting and analyzing, however, for it is most instructive.

The RS presidency/vice-presidency election in November 2000 was contested by a total of six slates, each with a presidential nominee and a running mate. Three of these belonged to RS-based Serb parties—the Serb Democratic Party (SDS), the Serb Independent Social Democrats (SNSD) led by then RS prime minister Milorad Dodik, and the Party of Democratic Progress-Republika Srpska (PDP-RS), which is led by the current RS prime minister, Mladen Ivanic. The other three slates were put up by parties whose base is primarily or entirely among Bosniacs, and predominantly or solely in the Federation. These were the SDP-BiH (which put up a Serb, Slobodan Popovic, for president and a Bosniac, Mirsad Dzapo, for vice-president); the Citizens' Democratic Party (GDS), a junior SDA ally in the Federation which nominated a Bosniac and a Croat, respectively, for the two posts; and the Bosnian Party (BOSS), another small Federation-based Bosnian Muslim party with a reputation for harmless eccentricity. The SDS ticket, comprising Mirko Sarovic for president and Dragan Cavic for vice-president, was almost elected in the first round of counting itself, on the basis of first-preference votes polled. After all first-preference votes had been counted, the SDS candidates were found to have received 313,572 first-preference ballots, 49.8% of the total and thus marginally short of the required majority threshold of 50% plus one. Then the ticket which had won the lowest percentage of first-preferences—BOSS, 12,851 or 2%—was eliminated from the contest and the second preferences cast by its voters counted and redistributed among the five remaining candidatures. As soon as this was done, the SDS topped the threshold and was declared the winner. The SDS in fact received a very small number of the second-preferences indicated by BOSS voters, but its slate was so close to victory anyway that even this was sufficient to cross the threshold.

Two very interesting and instructive trends underlie this apparently straightforward picture. According to some intelligent observers of international intervention in Bosnia, the 'changes to the electoral rules—the introduction of preferential voting—were intended to favour Dodik',[40] then RS prime minister and the presidential candidate of the SNSD in November 2000. The allegation of political bias is plausible, since international officials and agencies in Bosnia had given practically unconditional, uncritical support to Dodik's administration since he assumed the prime minister's post—with strong European and American backing, as a perceived antidote to the SDS—in January 1998. The IC had persisted with its policy of favouritism despite obvious evidence by 1999 that the 'moderate' government headed by Dodik, formerly mayor of a municipality called Laktasi, just north of the city of Banja Luka, was incompetent, deeply corrupt and almost as hostile as previous SDS regimes towards minority, particularly Bosniac returns to the RS. As Dodik's government became more and more unpopular in RS, the leaders of the international mission in Bosnia became more and more desperate to shore him up against a comeback by a resurgent SDS. Given this international record, it is possible that those who re-designed the electoral system for the RS presidency in mid-2000 calculated that while the SDS might win more first-preference votes than Dodik, Dodik might eventually scrape through with the help of a much higher number of second-preferences, especially from the voters of the Bosniac or Bosniac-led parties participating in the election.

This prospect was confounded by two factors. First, the second preferences, the key to the engineering of the desired outcome, the election of a Serb candidate 'moderate' on national issues and Bosnian state-building, were rendered almost superfluous because the SDS achieved a near-majority of first-preference ballots. This happened because the SDS candidates polled a decisive majority of first-preference votes cast *within* Republika Srpska—58.5% (307,550 of 525,325). Its overall tally of first-preferences came down to 49.8% because it received only 5.5% of first-preferences cast by absentee electors voting from outside the RS (5,692 of 103,118). Since geography more or less coincides with nationality in post-war Bosnia, voters within RS are overwhelmingly Serbs, while the absentee voters registered in RS municipalities are overwhelmingly displaced Bosniacs. The figures reveal that

[40] European Stability Initiative, *Reshaping International Priorities in Bosnia, Part III*, p. 8.

almost 60% of ethnic Serb voters in RS had cast their first-preference vote for the SDS presidential ticket. The striking fact was that this level of support was *much higher* than the proportions of 'in-RS' (i.e. overwhelmingly ethnic Serb) votes polled by the SDS in simultaneous elections to the RS's parliament, the National Assembly—just 44%—and in elections to choose the 14 RS members of the BiH state parliament's HoR (48%). In short, many more RS-based Serb voters had chosen to mark the SDS as their first choice in the RS presidential race than had voted for the SDS in simultaneous elections to RS and BiH legislative institutions. The discrepancy—almost 15 percentage points—is too significant to be ignored. One factor that could account for this discrepancy is that many RS voters had figured out the logic and purpose of the preferential voting system, and voted in higher-than-average numbers for the SDS to confound that logic and defeat that purpose. If this is correct, the deployment of an AV system actually precipitated a much higher degree of consolidation of the ethnic Serb electorate behind the SDS, an 'extremist' party in the standard international (particularly American) view,[41] than might otherwise have been the case.

In the end the gap between the total first-preferences received by the two top candidates was too huge to be bridged, leave alone overcome, by second or subsequent preferences. The SDS slate received 49.8% or 313,572 first preferences; Dodik and his running mate received 161,942 first preferences, coming in second at 25.7%. But even if this gap had been somewhat narrower, it is doubtful that second preferences would have enabled Dodik to emerge as the victor. An analysis of the second preferences that were in fact counted and distributed in order to elect a majority winner—those cast by the 2% of first-preference voters who had chosen the BOSS ticket—explains why.

[41] A week to ten days before this crucial set of elections, Richard Holbrooke, visiting Bosnia as the US ambassador to the United Nations, openly called for the SDS to be banned from BiH's political arena. He also added fuel to the simmering Croat/HDZ dispute by expressing the opinion that divided Mostar should replace Sarajevo as the capital of the Muslim-Croat federation, and referred to SDA president Alija Izetbegovic, whose party was facing a strong challenge from the SDP among the Bosniac electorate, as the 'saviour' of Bosnia-Herzegovina. See the post-election press statement of the Coordinating Board of the Coalition of NGOs in BiH, 'The International Community Helped Nationalists in Bosnian Elections', Sarajevo, November 30, 2000.

A total of 12,951 voters had marked the BOSS candidates as their first choice (the vast majority, 11,965, being ballots of displaced voters). Of these, 8,927, some 70%, had bothered to mark a '2' (second preference) on their ballots. A clear majority of these second preferences, 5,220, were marked in favour of the GDS ticket, the SDA's proxy in these elections. Almost all the rest, 3,419, were marked in favour of the SDP candidates. Just 288 of the 8,927 second preferences cast by BOSS voters—i.e. a little over 3%—indicated one or other of the three Serb candidatures. Of these 212 had marked Dodik, 41 the PDP-RS, and 35 the SDS, which emerged with 50.1% of the votes in the second round of counting as a result. In brief, almost 97% of the BOSS voters who had bothered to mark a second choice had marked the other two Bosniac (GDS) or Bosniac-led (SDP) party candidatures, despite the simple reality that these parties' tickets had no chance of getting elected either.

The key to the integrative, 'inter-ethnic accommodation' formula advocated by Horowitz is vote pooling between parties representing *different* ethnic groups, i.e. between (relatively moderate) parties *across* ethnic lines. In November 2000 just 2% of second preferences cast by BOSS voters, 212 of 8,927, were marked in favour of Milorad Dodik, the 'moderate', internationally backed candidate of the other, numerically dominant group. Had the gap between the top two candidates been narrower and the SDS not achieved the required majority after the distribution of BOSS second preferences, the second choices marked by voters of the party that polled the second-lowest proportion of first-preferences, the GDS (6%) would have been counted and distributed, followed by the third-lowest (the SDP, which got 7.8% of first preferences). Of the 37,613 first-preference votes received by the GDS, 35,157 were cast by voters not living in RS, i.e., by displaced Bosniacs residing in the Federation; the same was true of 41,893 of the 48,992 first preferences polled by the SDP slate. In other words, like the BOSS, the vast majority of voters who designated these two parties as their first choice consisted of Bosniacs displaced from RS. It is likely that their choice of second preferences, if counted, would have been identical or similar to the BOSS pattern—the vast majority for one of the two other 'in-group' parties, rather few for any Serb party, whether 'moderate' or 'extremist.' In short, the typical Bosnian voter is extremely reluctant to cross ethnic boundaries and support, even for purely tactical reasons, a party based among and run by members of a different national community. Thus we have conclusive evidence that very few supporters of BOSS, a small Bosniac-based party, could bring themselves to cast second-preference ballots for 'moderate' Serb options that had some chance at least of posing an obstacle to an SDS victory. The Serb electorate, on the other hand, consolidated behind the SDS, possibly in order to turn the preferential voting system to their own advantage. It is clear from the statistics that only about 1% of Serb first preferences in this election were cast in favour of the SDP-BiH, a 'moderate' party based predominantly among Bosniacs in the Federation, even though the SDP had nominated an ethnic Serb as its candidate for the RS presidency, unlike the BOSS or GDS, which had both nominated Bosniacs.

Two major lessons are illustrated by this episode. First, in order to be effective, 'integrative' electoral techniques require 'a [relatively] greater degree of trust among parties' representing different ethnic groups, for otherwise the 'cross-cutting ties necessary for pluralistic forces to emerge may simply be insufficiently strong.'[42] Thus 'centripetal... approaches based on AV or STV [single transferable vote] elections are likely to work best when there is a degree of fluidity to ethnic identities and lower levels of ethnic conflict', and 'systems which require a degree of bargaining and cross-ethnic voting may be less realistic in extremely divided societies.'[43]

Second, while electoral systems can be designed, there is no guarantee that the alignments and outcomes desired will necessarily be engineered. This is because while electoral arrangements are a potentially powerful tool to facilitate 'integration' in divided societies, their functioning and results are 'highly sensitive to context'. In particular, my analysis of constraints and possibilities in the Bosnian case in this chapter supports the observation that 'any electoral strategy for conflict management needs to be tailored to the realities of political geography.'[44]

Horowitz and other scholars have identified two conditions

---

[42] Sisk, *Power-Sharing and International Mediation in Ethnic Conflicts*, pp. 116-17.
[43] Ben Reilly and Andrew Reynolds, *Electoral Systems and Conflict in Divided Societies*, Washington, DC, 1999, pp. 46, 53.
[44] Ibid., pp. 1, 15.

that need to be present if AV, STV and other multiple/preferential voting models are to yield the desired, cross-cutting results:
— a reasonable degree of 'party proliferation', meaning that multiple parties should be competing for the votes of each ethnic group, especially the majority segment; and
— Electoral constituencies that are *heterogeneous* (mixed) in their ethnic make-up.

In the RS presidency election, the first condition was substantially fulfilled. The largest party, SDS, faced competition for the Serb vote from two mid-sized rivals. Three parties competed for the Bosniac vote (mostly cast by displaced people), one of which, the SDP, was demonstrably a party of moderate, cross-national orientation.

The second condition was, however, not satisfied, and this was the underlying reason for the failure of the AV system in this case. The RS population and electorate is overwhelmingly Serb. The electoral constituency for the presidential election does include non-Serbs, principally Bosniacs, who are displaced from RS areas but wish to vote in RS elections and are registered for this purpose in their pre-war municipalities of residence. Of a total of 628,443 valid ballots polled in this election, 525,325 were cast in RS polling stations (overwhelmingly by Serbs) and the remaining 103,118 were cast by absentee voters (overwhelmingly Bosniacs). Thus, by a rough estimate, only about one of every six voters in this election were non-Serbs, making for a constituency whose composition is not sufficiently heterogeneous for preferential voting formulas to 'work' in the desired manner across group boundaries.

The same problem is evident in most of the multi-member constituencies (MMCs) which now serve as the electoral districts for popularly elected entity and state legislatures: the RS National Assembly, the FBiH HoR, and the state parliament's house of representatives. The majority (three-fourths) of the RSNA's deputies are elected from six MMCs demarcated on RS territory, all of which are dominated by Serb electorates. The majority of legislators (also three-fourths) in the Federation parliament's house of representatives are elected from twelve MMCs across Federation territory. Of these, seven constituencies are overwhelmingly Bosniac, and two are overwhelmingly Croat in composition. Of the remaining three districts, two are moderately mixed, although with clear Bosniac majorities (Posavina and central Bosnia), and one is heavily mixed. The one heavily mixed MMC is, however, the FBiH's Canton 7—Herzegovina-Neretva, centred on Mostar. This is such a divided and polarized area (see Chapter 3) that it is difficult to be optimistic about prospects of vote pooling across ethnic lines. For the cross-entity Bosnian parliament's HoR, the three MMCs in RS that serve as the basis for the election of representatives from RS territory are, once again, largely homogeneous. Of the five corresponding MMCs in the Federation, only one—Constituency 4, which amalgamates Zenica-Doboj and central Bosnia cantons—can be said to have a moderately multiethnic electorate of Bosniacs and Croats. Similarly, in the vast majority of municipal and, for the Federation, cantonal districts,[45] ethnic homogeneity is the norm. The two bi-national Federation cantons that do exist are so divided along the national(ist) faultline (especially Herzegovina-Neretva) that they need special power-sharing regimes, described in Chapter 2, in order to exist at all.

The implication is that contemporary Bosnia's 'political geography' is not conducive to the effective application of multiple/preferential voting mechanisms that would encourage large-scale cross-ethnic voting, were such a system to be introduced. There is, of course, one way, in theory, of dealing with this inherent constraint: abolishing the Entity system, vesting power in central institutions and then gerrymandering constituency boundaries as much as necessary to create heterogeneous districts. In December 1998, the Madrid PIC conference which called upon the IC to develop a permanent electoral framework for Bosnia in collaboration with the people and politicians of BiH, noted that 'the Election Law must be consistent with the relevant provisions of Annexes 3, 4 and 7 of the [Dayton/Paris] Peace Agreement.' In short, it must respect the fundamentals of the constitutional structure established to end the war, while ensuring the rights of refugees and displaced persons to vote for different lev-

---

[45] The Election Law adopted in August 2001 stipulates that in future, elections to constitute municipal and cantonal assemblies will be held 'on the same day'. Until 2000, the cantonal elections were clubbed with elections to higher-tier Entity and State institutions.

els of institutions in the Entity in which they lived prior to displacement, if they so chose. Overturning the basic contours of the post-war settlement is thus a non-option. Even if it were an option, any attempt to do so would risk such renewed upheaval in Bosnia that only the truly crazy would even contemplate such a course. There is, in addition, a specific problem with the AV model of multiple/preferential voting. Its principal advocate, Horowitz, concedes that AV has an in-built majoritarian bias. It represents 'a modest reform of first-past-the-post', which mitigates the dangers an unbridled plurality system might pose to equitable group relations and to democracy itself in multiethnic societies, by making ' [ethnic] majorities responsive to the interests of others as well.' But in elections to legislatures, it is 'still more likely to produce a government with an outright majority of seats than list-system PR or STV.'[46] This raises an immediate question about the appropriateness of AV-style electoral rules in a institutional context like Dayton Bosnia's, which is built on multi-tiered structures of group autonomy and power-sharing. Horowitz's hope, of course, is the best-case scenario, in which electoral incentives to accommodation will ensure that that majority government is a pre-agreed, middle-ground coalition, based on reciprocal exchange of votes, of certain ethnic majority and certain ethnic minority parties. However, this presumes a number of conducive factors, including heterogeneous electoral districts. Where this condition is not fulfilled, 'centripetal systems like AV are likely to result in [a paradoxical reinforcement of] majoritarian mono-ethnic dominance, when applied in a situation of [demographic] group concentration.'[47] What this means is that if AV voting were to be applied in elections to the RS's legislature, the National Assembly (which is a much more powerful institution than the RS presidency, see Chapter 2), it might result in the single largest party, the SDS, winning an outright majority of seats. The present electoral system, party-list PR based on MMCs, complemented by the CM mechanism and tempered by the open-list provision, gives the SDS only a plurality. It is both fairer to all parties, large, medium and small, and the sensible choice given the particular context.

---

[46] Horowitz, *A Democratic South Africa?*, pp. 189, 201-2.
[47] Reilly and Reynolds, *Electoral Systems and Conflict in Divided Societies*, p. 50.

Given potential problems and complications, it is probably fortunate that the designers of Bosnia's Election Law eventually decided not to make the election to the tripartite BiH state presidency dependent on an AV-type multiple/preferential voting system, as was originally planned. Instead the Law retained the established system of voting, under which one Bosniac and one Croat shall be elected by voters registered to vote in the Federation of Bosnia & Herzegovina. A voter registered to vote in the Federation *may vote for either the Bosniac or Croat member of the presidency but not for both.* The Bosniac and Croat candidate that gets the highest number of votes among candidates from the same constituent people shall be elected. The member of the Presidency of Bosnia & Herzegovina that shall be directly elected from the territory of Republika Srpska—one Serb shall be elected by voters registered to vote in RS. The candidate who gets the highest number of votes shall be elected.[48]

The retention of this framework excludes a non-Serb living in RS from being elected to the RS seat on the presidency (in practical terms, a near-impossible prospect anyway even if it were constitutionally possible), and the equally academic possibility of a Serb living in the FBiH being elected to one of the Federation seats. Nonetheless, it is possibly in conflict with the 2000 BiH constitutional court ruling that Serbs, Bosniacs and Croats are constituent peoples of the state throughout the territory of BiH, cutting across the Entities. It may also be challenged as being in contravention of European human rights standards (as, possibly, will a portion of Article 20.8, which strips persons continuing to live in property legally reclaimed by the original, displaced occupant or owner of their voting rights in the current place of residence).

But despite the faults of the existing framework, there is no certainty whatsoever that any alternative formula would be free of problems and contradictions. As it is, the existing regulation contains a loophole, italicized above, which became apparent in the BiH presidential election of 1998. In that year the Croat seat was won by HDZ-BiH candidate Ante Jelavic (dismissed in March 2001 by the HR on the charge of anti-constitutional activity), who polled 189,438 votes. The IC's hope in this contest, rebel

---

[48] *Election Law of BiH,* Article 8.1.

HDZ leader and NHI candidate Kresimir Zubak, finished a poor third with only 40,880 votes. A surprisingly strong second-place finisher was SDP candidate Gradimir Gojer, a Sarajevo theatre personality, who won 113,961 votes. The vast majority of these votes came, however, not from ethnic Croats but from Bosniac SDP voters in the Federation. These voters, realizing that SDA candidate Alija Izetbegovic would easily win the Bosniac presidency seat anyway, voted instead, as they are permitted, for their preferred candidate in the race for the Croat seat. Had the ethnic Croat vote been evenly split between Jelavic and Zubak, it is possible that the SDP's man would have narrowly won the Croat presidential seat, albeit overwhelmingly on the basis of Bosniac votes via inpromptu, but legal, 'cross-ethnic' voting. Croats, of course, do not have the numbers and hence the leverage to similarly influence, leave alone determine, the contest for the Bosniac seat, and most of them would likely have regarded such an outcome as unacceptable. It is not without reason that the Croat and Serb minorities of Bosnia & Herzegovina are fearful of cross-ethnic voting formulas.

The electoral framework for Bosnia institutionalized in August 2001 will disappoint enthusiasts of 'integrative' electoral engineering among Bosnians, as well as among Westerners with an interest in Bosnia. But my analysis in this chapter suggests that the potential of radical electoral integration in Bosnia was seriously limited anyway, given mutually reinforcing constraints imposed by the post-Dayton constitutional structure, post-war 'political geography', and the three-way division of the competitive party system.

Within these constraints the international architects of Bosnia's electoral system have incorporated reforms that should help improve the representativeness and responsiveness of Bosnia's institutions and office-holders. At their most ambitious, electoral integrationists aim 'to build in accommodative incentives strongly for every office in each branch and each level of government.'[49] But the fact is that such root-and-branch electoral integration becomes increasingly difficult to implement the more a state's 'constitutional structures... diffuse and separate powers', the more 'power is devolved away from the centre', and the more 'focal

---

[49] Horowitz, *A Democratic South Africa?*, p. 185.

points of political power' exist in the system.[50] This is precisely the institutional architecture of the Dayton state. And this institutional architecture is not the result of historical accident, but the result of deep, fundamental divisions in Bosnian society, divisions expressed through violent changes in political geography during war and mirrored in a hopelessly segmented party system after it.

'It is relatively unusual in historical terms', observe Reilly and Reynolds, 'for electoral systems to be consciously and deliberately chosen… [and] if it is rare that electoral systems are deliberately chosen, it is rarer still that they are carefully designed for the particular historical and social conditions present in a given country. This is particularly the case for new democracies.'[51] If so, the careful, conscious, deliberate crafting of post-Dayton Bosnia's electoral system, with the benefit of a wide range of international expertise and under close international supervision, is clearly exceptional. Reilly and Reynolds add that 'electoral systems, once chosen, tend to remain fairly constant, as political interests quickly congeal around… the system.' If this is true, it would mean that the Dayton revisionism of both fervent integrationists and unreconciled partitionists is an unfruitful political strategy, and that both groups, especially the latter, will have to negotiate their grievances within a political system—based above all on the Entity framework—which is now clearly set to endure for the foreseeable future.

For the foreign guardians and tutors of Bosnia's fractured democracy, this represents a coming-to-terms with the limitations to the kind of state and democracy that can be built in Bosnia after Dayton. In Chapter 3, it is explained how and why international efforts to encourage cross-national politics in divided Mostar—ironically, partly through the use of such devices as reserved seats in local (city and municipal) government for the different national communities, thus almost requiring mixed candidate lists from the major national(ist) parties—have proven largely ineffective. Now, Article 14.10 of the 2001 Election Law will, it seems, have the effect of abolishing direct elections to the Mostar city council, the (nominally) joint, 'multiethnic' institution international strategists have tried for years to vitalize and invig-

---

[50] Reilly and Reynolds, *Electoral Systems and Conflict in Divided Societies*, p. 18.
[51] Ibid., p. 23.

orate, largely without success. There will still be a city council, with a mayor and a speaker, but it will be indirectly elected by the popularly elected members of the six municipal councils, three Croat and three Bosniac, that simultaneously constitute and fracture Mostar.

Federalism, federation and the Bosnian state

'Modern federalism is the institutionalization of the formal limitation of the national majority will as the legitimate ground for legislation. Any functioning federal system denies by its very processes that the national majority is the efficient expression of the sovereignty of the people. A federation replaces this majority with a more diffuse definition of sovereignty. It does this not by denying the democratic principle as such, but by advancing a more complex political expression and representation in dual, sometimes even multiple manifestations which may even be contradictory and antagonistic'—*Reginald Whitaker, scholar*[52]

A federation is defined by the statutory (constitutional) division of legislative (decisionmaking) power and fiscal authority between at least two territorial levels of government. Its hallmark is 'self-rule' for the federating units (regions/communities) plus 'shared rule'[53] for those units in the limited decisionmaking that takes place at the centre.

Beyond these essential, broad features, of course, different types of federation are possible. Toward the end of Chapter 2, I explain the categorical distinction between two very different concepts of federalism, nationalizing and multinational, and argue that the latter philosophy is unequivocally the appropriate choice for Bosnia after Dayton. This is in fact implicit in the structure of the Dayton state, which constructs Bosnia & Herzegovina as a loose, almost confederal union between a radically autonomous RS and a Federation-BiH based on equality and power-sharing between the Croat and Bosniac peoples. Nationalizing federations are typically underpinned by a usually implicit, sometimes explicit ethnic, cultural or national majority. In Bosnia, none of the three major groups constitutes a majority of the population, as far as we

[52] R. Whitaker, *A Sovereign Idea: Essays on Canada as a Democratic Community*, Montreal, 1992, p. 193.
[53] Elazar, *Exploring Federalism*.

know. But even if one community were to be a majority in the numerical sense, historical and contemporary political considerations would still make an explicitly multinational, highly decentralized, power-sharing federation with confederal links to neighbouring states—not the 'nation-building', implicitly majoritarian variant of federalism—the natural choice, indeed the only choice, for a Bosnian state.

The multi-tiered BiH (con)federation, an asymmetric union[54] between a Serb entity and a Muslim-Croat entity is, however, far from stable. During the war and for a few years afterward, Bosnian Serb nationalists were seen by the international community as the major threat to the integrity, even if nominal, of the Bosnian state. Since then, the Serbs have been superseded in that role by nationalist BiH Croats who acknowledge the nominal integrity of the Bosnian state in deference to the wishes of influential Western countries and institutions, but are unhappy with the terms of their co-habitation with Bosnian Muslims in the framework of the FBiH. The other type of Dayton revisionism critiques the postwar settlement from the opposite direction, as insufficiently integrative. This point of view, popular among a considerable section of Bosnian Muslims, essentially demands the liquidation of RS and the dismantling of the complex post-Dayton state structure. The alternative project implicit in this demand—integrative statebuilding through some form of political centralization—is actually a particularist, even sectarian agenda which would spell the death-knell for any kind of joint, tri-national Bosnian state. Recently, some sectarian BiH Croats have, for purely self-serving, tactical reasons of their own, taken up the call for the abolition of the Entity-based framework. In the words of one spokesman for the sectarian, partitionist BiH Croat agenda, which has the sympathy of some politicians in Croatia, 'with the dissolution of the Entities, the [whole] country could be administered via

[54] The asymmetry of this arrangement is being cited by some, including nationalist BiH Croats, as grounds for dissolution of the entire Dayton framework, which will kill the RS and liberate Croats from the Federation 'prison' at the same time. This argument, apart from being politically motivated, is also, in itself, unconvincing. There are many varieties of federation and multiple examples of 'asymmetric' unions. In Canada, for example, Quebec enjoys special rights and regimes in certain fields, on grounds of historical and cultural specificity, which other units of the Canadian federation do not have.

Cantons... as in Switzerland or Belgium.'[55] The tactically conver-
gent agendas of the integrationists and the partitionists are increasingly irrelevant, since six years after Dayton it is more and more
clear that the settlement that ended the war is, for all its flaws and
dysfunctionalities, in transition to becoming the permanent
framework of the Bosnian state, albeit with some reforms and
modification. Yet, since cantonalism is in fact a certain type of federalism, the question is worth considering—would a cantonized
BiH be viable?—leaving aside for the moment the more complicated question of whether the cantons would be nationally
homogeneous (which is what the BiH Croats have in mind), heterogeneous, or a mixture of both.

Simply put, ideas that talk in a loose manner about cantonization and draw parallels between Bosnia and Switzerland should be
taken with a large dose of salt. Context, above all, determines what
form of state framework is feasible in a particular place at a given
point in time. Beyond Alpine-type landscapes, the historical and
contemporary situations of Switzerland and Bosnia &
Herzegovina have virtually nothing in common. The Swiss confederation of nineteen predominantly German-speaking cantons,
six mainly French-speaking cantons and one Italian-speaking canton originated in a German-speaking organic core, which then
gradually expanded. There is nothing comparable in Bosnia's historical development. Moreover, the contemporary Swiss state was
built upon, and is sustained by, a definite 'national Swiss patriotism'.[56] Swiss collective experience, overshadowing a history of
medieval and early modern religious warfare, is based above all
upon the necessity of unity against external perils. In the late
modern epoch, as middle Europe repeatedly erupted in flames of
war around them, above all because of Franco-German conflict,

---

[55] From the text of the testimony of Mgr. Ratko Peric, Bishop of Mostar, to the
Committee on International Relations of the United States House
of Representatives, Washington, DC, July 25, 2001. Accessed at
http://www.house.gov/international_relations/peri0725.htm. During
2001, Drazen Budisa, one of post-Tudjman Croatia's top politicians, publicly
advocated elimination of the RS as a self-governing entity and the replacement
of the Dayton state by a cantonized BiH.

[56] Christopher Hughes, 'Cantonalism: Federalism and Confederacy in the
Golden Epoch of Switzerland' in M. Burges, and A.G. Gagnon (eds), *Comparative
Federalism and Federation*, Brighton, 1993, p. 156.

the Swiss banded together to preserve their small country from being engulfed and consumed by the flames. Bosnia's experience has been exactly the opposite. Over the past century and more, the major regional conflicts of the Balkans and between the south Slav peoples have had their most bitter and intense manifestations on the territory of Bosnia & Herzegovina.

However, there are certain elements of the Swiss model that may be relevant to post-1995 Bosnia. For example, in Switzerland, 'there is no acknowledged national capital city; the nation in many-centred', in regional capitals like Zurich, Geneva, Basel and to some extent Lugano, of which the latter three cities effectively 'transcend international frontiers' because of locational proximity vis-à-vis neighbouring countries. And the enduring, stable 'Swiss compromise' between identities and cultures has been described as a 'harmony of reciprocated dislike', 'a sort of compromise, a living apart in the same house', and as a pragmatic model 'worthy of imitation'.[57] Federations are neither meant nor expected to eradicate conflict; indeed, conflicts of perception and interest between the different groups and layers of government are intrinsic to federations and vital to their health. A 'Bosnian compromise' will necessarily be an adaptation to specific Bosnian realities, but it can usefully draw on comparable elements of other experiences.

Ultimately two factors will determine the survival and stabilization of Bosnia's (con)federal framework in the next few years. One relates to the elite level of politics; the other to the level of mass publics. International policymakers involved with Bosnia would do well to be cognizant of both factors.

In a pioneering work on the origins of federations, William Riker, an American scholar, presented a critique of what he called the 'ideological fallacy'[58]—the notion that federations come into being because of elite ideological commitments to federalism as a principle, especially an equation of the federal form with 'free-

---

[57] Ibid., pp. 158-61. On Switzerland, see also Jonathan Steinberg, *Why Switzerland?*, Cambridge, 1991; Jurg Steiner, 'Power-Sharing: Another Swiss Export Product?' in J. Montville (ed.), *Conflict and Peacemaking in Multiethnic Societies*, Lexington, MA, 1989, pp. 107-14; and Daniel Thurer, 'Switzerland: The Model in Need of Adaptation?' in J. Hesse and V. Wright (eds), *Federalizing Europe? The Costs, Benefits and Pre-Conditions of Federal Political Systems*, Oxford, 1996, pp. 219-39.

[58] William Riker, *Federalism: Origin, Operation, Significance*, Boston, 1964.

dom' or 'justice'. Following Riker, later works have urged students of comparative federalism to 'reexamine and reconsider the real motivations which drive particular elites to champion the federal bargain.' Elites who strike a federal compact are usually 'guided by some sense of perceived interest', in particular a calculation that a federal state 'will directly or indirectly entrench their interests and secure their future.' A focus on elite perceptions of self-interest helps us to understand not only 'the origins of federations but also... how they change and develop', because 'the emergence of new groups and interests, or the revitalization of old ones, could provoke fresh tensions and challenges within the federation which might constitute an agenda for reform.'[59]

The Bosnian case is undoubtedly peculiar, in that the (con)federal (and multi-level consociational) agreement is to a substantial degree devised and implemented by external, international elites, albeit in close interaction with the Bosnian segmental elites and leaderships in Serbia and Croatia, and on the basis of historical and institutional precedents in former Yugoslavia. Nonetheless, the history of federative pacts tells us that it will survive and stabilize only if the bulk of Bosnia's segmental elites perceive, or come to perceive, that arrangement as consistent or at least reconciliable with their own interests as political actors. There has been slow but steady progress in this direction in the years since Dayton. But there is still some way to go and unresolved anomalies, such as the Croat question, continue to fester and plague the prospects of stabilization of the (con)federal framework. Similarly, reform to the Dayton framework will only be possible and sustainable if the bulk of Bosnia's segmental elites perceive such change as serving—or at least not damaging to—their own interest-driven concerns.

Any strategy that intends to build lasting, cross-national acceptance of the post-war settlement among the ordinary citizens of BiH must be based on a flexible conception of the meaning and objectives of the (con)federal state. The Bosnian public remains deeply divided on the legitimacy of the single Bosnian state, and mutual distrust as well as distrust of the international

---

[59] Michael Burgess, 'Federalism as Political Ideology: Interests, Benefits and Beneficiaries in Federalism and Federation' in M. Burgess and A.G. Gagnon (eds), *Comparative Federalism and Federation*, pp. 104–5.

community's intentions remain high. The genius of the federal idea is that while it operates within one overarching political framework, by its very nature it calls for something 'less than a comprehensive, monolithic conception of shared identity and citizenship' from citizens. It does require a minimum commitment on the part of all citizens and communities toward federative ties, but its intrinsic flexibility means that different federating units and communities 'do not have to identify with the federal state *in the same way or to the same extent*' (emphasis mine).[60] This charact-eristic of federalism could be a vital asset to the international goal of creating a viable Bosnian state, including limited but functional shared institutions, by the end of its post-Dayton intervention. But it requires that the international community not demand of Bosnians that they identify with the state in the same way or to the same extent. In short, it calls for understanding and respecting the 'different ways' of being Bosnian, as Ivo Andric put it, different ways that have been powerfully shaped by the overlapping yet distinctive national histories and experiences of Bosnia's constituent peoples.

Consociational present, consociational future?

'A consociational system is inherently undemocratic and violates both the rights of non-recognized groups and the rights of individuals... It violates the rights of those groups in being and those that may develop in the future whose existence is not recognized by the state. It also fails to provide protection to and may lead to the oppression of individuals who wish not to be identified with or wish to free themselves from identification with particular cultural groups. The use of particular consociational devices does not necessarily have this effect, but the creation of a system based on rigid segmental autonomy and isolation certainly does.'—*Paul Brass, political scientist*[61]

'Noone, I imagine, would want to flee the abstractions of an undifferentiated humanity only to end up with its opposite; noone would favour

[60] Wayne Norman, 'Towards a Philosophy of Federalism' in J. Baker (ed), *Group Rights,* Toronto, 1994, pp. 79–100.
[61] Paul Brass, *Ethnicity and Nationalism: Theory and Comparison*, New Delhi, Thousand Oaks and London, 1991, pp. 334, 342.

the kind of politics in which people speak only for their own group identity and interests, and never address any wider concerns... [That] would mean shoring up communal boundaries and tensions, which could be as oppressive as any universalist norm.'—*Anne Phillips, political theorist*[62]

The risks of consociationalism worry many democrats—both thinkers and practitioners—even those who are otherwise favourably disposed to notions of group autonomy and group rights. The risks are real. Consociationalism does recognize some collective identities to the exclusion of others, and it does institutionally entrench those cleavages. This carries genuine risks of 'freezing what are [in fact] multiple and shifting identities', and 'validating an exclusive and fragmented politics that leaves little space for the development of a wider solidarity'[63]—in short, the fragmentation of social and political life into enclaves. Consociation also depends heavily on elite will and capacity. It may, therefore, spawn vested interests, claiming to be the spokesmen and protectors of group autonomy and rights, who are inclined to foment 'a politics of grievance... to devote their political energy to establishing a perception of disadvantage, rather than working [constructively] to overcome it, in order to secure' their own interests.[64]

Nonetheless, 'consociationalism... is the solution when all else fails.'[65] The international community's 'inability to achieve a more integrative power-sharing solution for Bosnia', at and since Dayton, indeed 'contains many lessons.'[66] The main lesson, this chapter has explained, is about the constraints and limits to integrative strategies in a deeply divided society emerging tentatively from a civil war. In such circumstances, consociation may be the most viable institutional option, short of formal partition, redrawing of boundaries and exchange of populations. There is a view in comparative political science that a consociational framework

---

[62] Anne Phillips, *Democracy and Difference*, University Park, PA, 1993.
[63] Ibid.
[64] Will Kymlicka and Wayne Norman, 'The Return of the Citizen: A Survey of Recent Work in Citizenship Theory' in R. Beiner (ed.), *Theorizing Citizenship*, Albany, NY, 1995, p. 304.
[65] Reilly and Reynolds, *Electoral Systems and Conflict in Divided Societies*, p. 31.
[66] Sisk, *Power-Sharing and International Mediation in Ethnic Conflicts*, p. 99.

works in moderately divided societies but not deeply divided ones, and it is not necessarily wrong. At the same time, however, a paradox exists: there may be no feasible alternative to consociationalism in deeply divided societies. That is why societies such as Northern Ireland and Lebanon, where divisions are deep but partition is not a feasible course, have opted to institutionalize consociational settlements, despite the manifest difficulties of making the settlements work. The 1998 agreement in Northern Ireland is, like Bosnia's post-Dayton formula, an exemplar of a consociational settlement,[67] and it indisputably represents the most serious chance, ever, of moving beyond a situation of chronic, protracted sectarian strife. In Lebanon the Taif accords of 1989 institutionalized a revised form of the earlier consociational scheme, the National Pact dating to 1943, which broke down in civil war in 1975-6. It is neither accident nor aberration that a consociational structure provides the mainstay of Dayton Bosnia, a transitional democracy in a weak, fragile state with a legitimacy problem among two of the three constituent communities.

In his writings elaborating the consociational model and then defending it against its numerous critics, Lijphart has developed a laundry-list of factors that influence the prospects of consociation in specific contexts. Some—for example the claim that consociation generally works better between groups of roughly equal size—gives us partial insights into why the consociational paradigm of the Muslim-Croat federation, in which Muslims outnumber Croats by four to one, has run into heavy weather. The most important conducive factor, relevant to Bosnia, that he cites is, however, something else—a broadly shared sense of national identity among the segments of the plural society. This can help explain, for instance, why South Africa—where many of Lijphart's other conditions for consociation were non-existent or unfavourable but where an overarching national identity and territorial integrity were not contested—was able to hammer out a consociational pact several years before Northern Ireland, where many of the lesser conditions were more favourable but the key condition was not.[68] It also helps us to appreciate why the implementation of the consociational Dayton settlement has had such a

---

[67] O'Leary, 'The Nature of the British-Irish Agreement.'

[68] I am grateful to Brendan O'Leary for this insight.

difficult career in post-war Bosnia, ranging from the inter-Entity level to conflict management in local sites such as Mostar. The conflict in Bosnia is not about ethnic, linguistic, racial or cultural difference. It is, in the post-Yugoslav context, about antagonistic national identities and an underlying dispute over the legitimate unit of sovereignty. This sort of dispute cannot be solved by any institutional formula or framework. As one analyst puts it, 'the international community can do many things in ethnic conflict management, but one thing it cannot do is force an oath of fealty to a state which many of its inhabitants believe is artificial. Without that… structural agreements for the state are without foundation.'[69] The most suitable structural agreement in such infelicitous circumstances is, however, the consociational pact. To pessimists this may seem like building a house of cards on a foundation of sand, and they are not incorrect. In a more optimistic prognosis, however, even a house of cards can become at least somewhat stronger over time, and the sand can become more settled and stable. Consociation provides the most appropriate basis and the best chance for working towards such an outcome. Its flaws, risks and difficulties are real. But some of those deficiencies are overstated by its critics, while other potential problems can be addressed by constitutional engineers who are alive in advance to the risk of such problems.

The problem of dependence on elite will and capacity is serious but can be overstated. First, all political systems are ultimately elite-centred; this is not a unique defect of consociationalism. Second, in the context of former Yugoslavia, and within BiH, the attitudes and actions of segmental elites during the late 1980s and early 1990s did play a major role in precipitating war, but were far from being the sole causal factor. The cauldron of conflict was stirred by elites until it boiled over—however, this implies the existence of a cauldron, or at least ingredients thereof, that could be stirred in this manner. Elites can provoke and precipitate violent conflict, but they cannot invent or fabricate such conflicts out of thin air. Third, the composition and character of segmental elites is not unchanging; it can and does change over time, including for the better. Simply and concretely put, there is at least some

[69] John Chipman, cited in Sisk, *Power-Sharing and International Mediation in Ethnic Conflicts*, p. 98.

difference between Alija Izetbegovic and Zlatko Lagumdzija, between Radovan Karadzic and Mladen Ivanic,[70] and even, perhaps, between Mate Boban and Ante Jelavic. Astute international policy can obviously play an important role in aiding the emergence and consolidation of better segmental elites, and in nurturing cooperative links between them. Contrary to what one critic of consociationalism, quoted above, has to say, consociation is not co-terminous with the mutual 'isolation' of the respective groups. It actually enjoins the segments and their representatives to have a fair, possibly even substantial amount to do with one another. It merely prescribes certain ground rules and parameters by which those relations are to be conducted.

The most effective criticism of the consociational paradigm is that it fails to 'recognize the variability of ethnic identities, and the pervasiveness of intra-ethnic cleavages in most societies.'[71] Certainly, the salience of ethnic identities varies depending on situational context and over time, intra-ethnic cleavages are the norm not the exception, and every individual has multiple identities, of which ethnic or national identity is only one. But what of cases where, for the time being, ethnic/national identities *are* the most salient identities, exercising a decisive influence on the political outlook and behaviour of most individuals and rendering intra-group cleavages that do exist less significant? The consociational formula responds to precisely this sort of situation. Even the permanent Election Commission of Bosnia & Herzegovina (EC-BiH), the authority which will be the custodian of BiH's democratic framework from 2002 onwards, is constituted on consociational principles—two Croats, two Bosniacs, two Serbs, and one 'Other' member (during the transitional phase, which may last for several years yet, the high representative retains ultimate control over the EC, which will consist of four Bosnian members—one each from among Croats, Bosniacs, Serbs and Others—plus three

---

[70] In late July 1990 the founding convention of the SDS featured two guest speakers. One was Jovan Raskovic, the first leader of the SDS in Croatia. The other was Alija Izetbegovic. Izetbegovic congratulated his 'Orthodox brothers' on the formation of their party and, in his typical grandfatherly style, gently chided them for not having formed their party even earlier. He received an ovation from the delegates. See Tim Judah, *The Serbs: Myth, History and the Destruction of Yugoslavia*, New Haven and London, 1997, pp. 196-7.

[71] Brass, *Ethnicity and Nationalism*, p. 334.

international members, making a total of seven). The EC members will serve for a five-year term, and 'one Croat, one Bosniac, one Serb and the Other member shall each serve as president for one fifteen-month rotation' within that term. The EC's central counting centre will consist of a director and three deputies. 'The director and deputies shall be from different constituent peoples of BiH... one shall be a representative of Others', and none 'shall... be active members of any political party.' The Election Appeals and Complaints Council, nominated by the EC, is to be made up of qualified jurists and constitutional experts and 'shall consist of five members: one Croat, one Bosniac, one Serb, one representative of Others and a member of the EC-BiH.'[72]

Nonetheless, the importance of ethnic/national identities relative to other forms of identity can and most likely will gradually become *less salient* over time, in keeping with the pace and extent of changes in the interlocked situational contexts of Bosnia and its surrounding region. I have argued that it is important that the Dayton settlement not be rashly subjected to major alterations by international fiat or without the concurrence of all parties to the agreement, but for this reason, it is also important that the settlement not be elevated to the status of an eternally valid, cast-in-stone framework. The Lebanese National Pact of 1943 worked as a formula for stability in that country for many years. But some of its provisions eventually turned out to be too rigid to keep pace with demographic and other changes within the country and in its regional environment. In order to remain relevant and useful, all electoral and constitutional frameworks need to be remain notionally open to the possibility of revision and renovation.[73] In Bosnia, of course, this is an inherently sensitive issue, and will require broadly based agreement, which will, in turn, probably require mediation by other parties. The international community,

---

[72] *Election Law of BiH*, Articles 2.5, 2.6, 5.22, 6.8 and 20.1. The Election Law entrusts the bulk of responsibility for the administration of elections to all levels of government to local (municipal) authorities throughout the country. To this end, it authorizes formation of municipal election commissions and polling station committees. It also authorizes the formation of Entity election commissions.

[73]The permanent BiH Election Law in fact includes provisions for review of its regulations by BiH and Entity legislative institutions every four years.

in collaboration with Bosnia's neighbours, can look forward to remaining involved with Bosnia and its problems in some capacity for years to come. The communist solution to the national question aimed to create a complex, multi-tiered institutional structure 'national in form, but socialist in content.'[74] It architects ended up giving rise to a system national in form and nationalist in content.[75] The challenge this time is to overcome the false dichotomy between form and content, and build a system that can simultaneously accommodate national identities and liberal-democratic values.

[74] See Teresa Rakowska-Harmstone, 'The Dialectics of Nationalism in the USSR', *Problems of Communism* 23, 3 (1974).

[75] On the Soviet parallel, see Philip Roeder, 'Soviet Federalism and Ethnic Mobilization', *World Politics* 43, 2 (1991).

6

POST-YUGOSLAV FUTURES

LESSONS FROM (AND FOR)
INTERNATIONAL INTERVENTION

'The external powers making Bosnian policy seem to believe that you can create an all-Bosnian nation and single political community by creating first a Bosnian state... Any... resistance to international proposals that comes from Bosnians themselves is rejected. At the same time as declaring the Dayton accord inviolate and dismissing elected officials if they are seen not to be acting in accordance with Dayton, moreover, the internationals are spearheading radical efforts to alter Dayton in the direction of a less decentralized and more unified, multiethnic set of Bosnian institutions... the Dayton accord institutionalizes the war strategy of the US government to defeat the Serbs. Implementing that agreement is an effort to finish the job. The fact that the international operation is still fighting the war through constitutional means both degrades the legitimacy of constitutions and the law and understandably gives an excuse to Bosnians to continue the war and its nationalist agendas rather than move towards creating a new state and political community... The result of more than five years of Dayton implementation has been to revive... older Bosnian patterns of adjustment to the fact of external rule... Those who might want a modern state... have left the country or want to leave... The political elite compete for spoils and use historically fine-tuned tactics in manipulating the international donors and administrators—with the result of deep corruption, insider privatization, getting internationals to eliminate one's rivals, and plenty of cooperation among leaders of the three national communities if necessary to keep the game going... Domestic politics... revolves around this game of demands and responses between international officials and Bosnian party leaders. Claims of protection in the event of a new war or patronage over local housing and jobs still characterize relations between politicians and citizens.'—*Susan Woodward, scholar*[1]

'Every attempt to make BiH a melting pot of nations and transform

[1] Susan Woodward, 'Milosevic Who? Origins of the New Balkans', discussion paper of the Hellenic Observatory, European Institute, London School of Economics and Political Science, July 2001, pp. 13-14.

these peoples into yesterday's 'Yugoslavs' or the 'Bosnians' of today... has ended in failure. Policy such as this gives us not state-builders but state-dissolvers... Pax Daytoniana... can and must be changed in those areas where it is evidently neither efficient nor just... Dayton's original sin [was]... dividing BiH into asymmetric entities... and granting [one] entity an exclusive national title 'Republika Srpska' with specific attributes common to independent states... The biggest anomaly of Dayton is that 'Republika Srpska'—as a unitary entity on a territory from which 220,000 Croat Catholics and twice as many Muslims were expelled, and the Federation in which 10 cantons have been federated—has become the 'Bible' to certain international representatives... One group, after all the crimes committed in that part of the country, has its own parliament and government, and another group, a victim, ostensibly equal under the constitution, cannot even have its own legitimate voice in the Presidency or in the Houses of Peoples... After the [November 2000] elections, the Serbs are represented [in state and Entity organs] by a coalition that won the majority in their Constituency. The Muslims are represented by a coalition that won the majority among them. The Croats, however, are represented by a handful of parties that received less than 10% of the Croat constituency's vote... I ask you, do the Croat people... have the right to their democratic choice? According to the international authority in BiH, they do not... The current international authority... which is practically functioning as an absolute power, is a curious political machine made up of varying interests, institutions and intentions... Yet one has the impression that the US ambassador in Sarajevo is at the helm, and in full control... The constituent people in the Serb entity are Serbs, and in the Federation entity are Muslims, with Croats having their rights taken away partially at Dayton, and fully by the November 2000 election law change by the OSCE... I am afraid that it is rather useless to build up the state of BiH on the foundation of the current Dayton agreement... Everyone agrees that the outer framework of BiH should remain untouchable, but life within the country must be balanced and harmonized... The international authority has created a protectorate in BiH. The unique element is that it has taken all the rights and freedoms, and has left the obligations and responsibilities to the local politicians... Croat Catholics will not accept the authority's objectives to dissolve their political and economic institutions and subjugate them to the rule of others... My only hope is Christ our Saviour... the people who implement 'the Dayton agreement' in practice operate selectively, tendentiously and unilaterally... Those who consider themselves teachers of democracy cannot evade the law of democracy!... The deaf and wandering international politics in BiH... progressively relegates the Croats to the 'remainder' category... For over 400 years the Catholic Croats of

BiH were on Ottoman plantations or in their prisons... For seventy years in the last century the Croats were either emigrating or in Yugoslav prisons or living in constant fear... [The Bishops' Conference of BiH] distance themselves from all those who would usurp the essential interests of the Croatian people for their own private aims, as well as all those who would reduce this nation to a national minority.'—*Mgr Ratko Peric, Bishop of Mostar*[2]

'[The argument that] the resolution of Bosnia & Herzegovina's underlying political difficulties lies in a fundamental change of tack, with constitutional tinkering aimed at altering the Dayton process, is wrong... the Dayton agreement is not 'kaput'... Dayton can change itself. This is not the time to talk about abandoning the agreement or replacing it with something else... The agreement enshrines constitutional safeguards that were necessary at the end of a terrible and tragic war... Political reorganization, cantons, new entities and such do not have obvious urgency as we apply ourselves to the task of making BiH a self-sustainable state. Indeed, constitutional tinkering diverts political energy away from more pressing objectives. What is needed in BiH is the application of a focused political will to the business of establishing legal and fiscal structures that will sustain a growing economy. This will be done more slowly if political will is sapped by repetitive and redundant arguments about new layers of government or new federal structures... Our priority is to establish the rule of law [and] improve the quality of government... within the context of the Dayton constitution... We have seen for example that those cantons where the HDZ is in power do not enjoy rule of law... Our priority is certainly not to reward incompetent politicians by allowing obsessive preoccupations with constitutional change to set the political agenda... far from seeking to isolate any community, we are doing our utmost to include every community. This will not be done by introducing new cantons or new federal structures. It will be done by ensuring that the existing provisions to secure group rights are effective... The European Union offers to the people of BiH a democratic, multicultural model of prosperity... Trade with, and eventual accession to the EU are priorities of Bosnian politicians and Bosnian business people. Redrawing cantonal boundaries and changing the

[2] These extracts have been culled from Mgr Peric's testimony to the committee on international relations of the US House of Representatives (July 25, 2001), his unanswered letter to the then US ambassador in Sarajevo dated June 29, 2001, his speech at the Mostar assembly of the HDZ-led Croat National Congress on March 3, 2001, and from a press statement of the BiH Catholic bishops' conference issued in Sarajevo, endorsing Peric's views, on March 8, 2001.

nature of federal institutions are not.'—*Wolfgang Petritsch, the international 'high representative' coordinating and overseeing Bosnia's post-Dayton transition*[3]

What a tangled web the international community confronts in Bosnia. This author cannot but feel a reflexive sympathy for Bosnia's international 'viceroy', under an obligation to navigate a Byzantine labyrinth of claims and counter-claims while being subjected to scathing attacks by noted academics on the one hand and mind-numbing ranting by nationalist priests on the other. The texts excerpted above convey, quite starkly, that the debate over Bosnia & Herzegovina's post-Yugoslav future remains not just unsettled but fiercely contested after six years of intensive international involvement.

The underlying cause is that all three of BiH's communities have what might be described as *defensive mentalities*, albeit for different reasons. The Bosnian Serbs, traumatized by the collapse of Yugoslavia[4] and radicalized by the experience of a bitter war, are determined to preserve and protect the entity they ultimately salvaged from a very dark period in their history as a people. Many of them are aware that the Republika Srpska's origins are bloody, even macabre. Yet they consider themselves fortunate in comparison to the other Serb communities outside core Serbia—the Krajina and west Slavonian Serbs, defeated and driven from Croatia in the summer of 1995, or the Serbs of Kosovo four years later. The statelet called RS is thus a minimum guarantee of security and survival in difficult times. BiH Serbs and their politicians are therefore extremely sensitive to any perceived attempts by the international community to undermine the RS, particularly in response to demands for a more centralized Bosnian state ema-

---

[3] Wolfgang Petritsch, 'We Must Stay the Course in BiH', *Wall Street Journal*, June 12, 2001. Petritsch is responding in particular to issues raised by the HDZ-led Croat revolt, but his column can and should also be read as a general statement of purpose. Petritsch, an Austrian diplomat, took over as HR from Spain's Carlos Westendorp in August 1999. He is scheduled to be replaced by the veteran British politician Paddy Ashdown in August 2002.

[4] Just as Bosnian Muslims regard BiH as 'their' state—albeit, of course, shared with other groups—and are consequently deeply distressed by its wartime partition and post-war disunity, Serbs, particularly those in Bosnia and Croatia, regarded multinational, federal Yugoslavia as 'their' state.

nating from the Bosniac community and its leaders. The Bosnian Serbs have, during the post-war years, gradually emerged as stalwart defenders of the post-Dayton *status quo*, in contrast to the other two communities.

The Bosnian Muslims are the single largest national group in Bosnia, at a level probably close to constituting a simple majority of the population. This matters a great deal in a region where the relative numbers (and proportions) of groups provide a basic fulcrum and determinant of politics, so obvious since Croatia and Bosnia first in Kosovo and then in Macedonia, and is sufficient in itself to induce a state of panic among the other two groups of BiH. However, the relative numerical superiority of Muslims in the population of BiH would become a really weighty factor if, and only if, a strong single state were to develop in Bosnia (which, of course, provides Bosnian Serbs and Croats with ample motivation to resist the development of such a state). The Dayton state does not fulfil this condition. It is a loose, decentralized state with very limited jurisdiction for central ('joint') institutions, which expressly gives the RS a right to establish and develop relations with Serbia (and Montenegro), and the FBiH a similar right vis-à-vis Croatia—which supplements, in practice, the *de facto* close relationship of most regions dominated by BiH Croats with Croatia. This downward devolution and outward diffusion of sovereignty is, expectedly, not to the liking of most Bosniac opinion. Bosniacs tend to see themselves, justifiably, as the greatest victims of the Bosnian tragedy, and, not justifiably, as its sole victims. Many expected the huge post-war international intervention in Bosnia to correct the wrongs done to them as a people, above all by establishing a state more consistent with their conception and their interests. Five to six years after Dayton it had become increasingly obvious that the international community in Bosnia has neither the capacity nor the desire to do so. This painful dawning of reality explains, for example, an escalating torrent of abusive attacks in Sarajevo media during the second half of 2001 on HR Petritsch, an international official who otherwise has done a great deal to address core Bosniac concerns such as freedom and viability of minority returns. The fact is that if the defining postwar context is an effectively tri-zonal, tri-national Bosnia & Herzegovina, nominally one but surrounded on all sides by relatively more cohesive states like Serbia (plus Montenegro) and Croatia, the Bosniac plurality within BiH is politically useless. In that wider regional context, the Bosniacs are a fairly small minority, boxed into a few swathes of territory in northeastern Bosnia, central Bosnia, the Sarajevo area, the Cazinska Krajina (extended Bihac) in northwestern Bosnia, and pockets of Herzegovina.

The BiH Croats are, in a way, in the most ambiguous and quixotic position of the three groups, which helps explain the viciously defensive posture of considerable elements of the community. It was Serb-Croat antagonism (not disregarding the basic contribution made by the Slovenes) that broke up Yugoslavia, precipitated civil war in Croatia, and led to war in Bosnia, with tragic consequences for all three peoples, especially the Bosnian Muslims. Within Bosnia, however, the major adversary for the Croats in the armed conflict turned out to be not the Serbs but the Muslims. Yet in an ironic turn of events, purely because of circumstantial forces and the insistence of the United States that a Croat-Muslim military alliance was the essential linchpin of a successful strategy to roll back the Serbs in both BiH and Croatia, the BiH Croats found themselves corralled into a 'federation' with the Muslims, engineered in Washington, DC in March 1994 and confirmed at Dayton, Ohio in November 1995. All the assurances and built-in constitutional safeguards of equality, parity, consensus etc have over the years failed to obviate a dominant perception among BiH Croats that they are the subordinate partner in an accidental marriage which is blighted by mutual suspicion. The BiH Croats, whose proportion of the Bosnian population has declined from 18% in 1992 to perhaps 12% today, share with the BiH Serbs a fear of becoming, in practice if not on paper, a 'national minority'.[5] In their view the Serbs are more or less safe from suffering this fate because of the constitutionally entrenched status of Republika Srpska, but they have no such guarantee. Hence the exaggerated sense of injustice, and the allergic reaction to any move by the international community that can be remotely construed as a step towards a less group-based and more majoritarian federation. The dismantling of the federation and the creation of a Croat entity would represent the optimal solution, from

---

[5] As Julie Mostov has written, 'one of the few things which the opposing forces in ex-Yugoslavia could agree about was that nobody wanted to be a minority in

this perspective. If such a huge change is infeasible because it would mean striking at one of the foundational elements of the Dayton framework and risk re-opening a can of dozing but very live worms, perhaps more limited reform can be undertaken, in this view, such as carving up the two mixed Croat-Muslim cantons of the federation into homogeneous units.

Each of the three Bosnian communities thus has a *minority syndrome,* albeit in relation to different political-geographical contexts—the Serbs within the territory of Bosnia & Herzegovina, the Muslims within the wider region including Serbia-Montenegro and Croatia, and the Croats within the framework of the Muslim-Croat federation. These variants of the minority syndrome result in each community having a guarded, defensive and at least somewhat aggrieved stance towards the very delicate equilibrium created by the Dayton settlement. Even the Serbs, the least revisionist of the groups, have a latent dissatisfaction with the Dayton compromise because it prevents them from separating from Bosnia & Herzegovina, obliges them to participate in limited, but gradually more meaningful tasks of common-state governance, and enjoins their local and Entity authorities to cooperate in key areas such as minority returns. It has frequently been pointed out that the three Bosnian nationalisms are mutually reinforcing in a way that perpetuates a cycle of distrust and division. This, of course, is not incorrect. However, it is incomplete and conceptually inadequate for understanding Bosnia's transition since Dayton to a post-Yugoslav future. Three defensive and reciprocally antagonistic yet mutually dependent particularisms are part of the picture, but not the whole picture. Bosnia's transition is by no means as static, as 'locked in', as the partial picture implies.

The dynamic and fluid character of Bosnia's post-war evolution is better understood through an alternative and altogether more sophisticated conceptual framework. This also posits a triangular relationship, between *a new nationalizing state, its national minorities, and the external national homelands of those minorities.* It has been pre-

another's national state... As majorities in their own states, they have proved arrogant in their blindness to the concerns of other ethnic and national groups; as minorities in other states, they have been militant in their indignation about violations or potential violations of their citizenship rights, and political and cultural autonomy.' Mostov, 'Democracy and the Politics of National Identity', p. 21.

sented by Rogers Brubaker, an American social scientist, as a framework for understanding the new realities of a European continent fundamentally reshaped in the wake of Cold War bipolarity by the remaking of political maps, particularly the break-up of the Soviet Union and Yugoslavia.[6] The formulation of the triadic nexus is in itself not novel.[7] Brubaker's model however represents a theoretical advance on earlier versions, in that he seeks to capture 'the contingency and variability of the relations between national minorities, nationalizing states and external national homelands—*contingency* and *variability* that follow from treating each of these elements as fields of struggle among competing positions or stances, and from seeing relations *between* the three fields as closely intertwined with relations *internal* to [each of] these fields.'[8] The concept of the differentiated field, having dynamic, shifting relations with other, similarly differentiated fields, in turn owes much to the work of French sociologist Pierre Bourdieu. To demonstrate the utility of this approach, Brubaker explains the 'bloody dynamics' of the disintegration of Yugoslavia by focusing on the triadic interaction in the early 1990s between the rise of an aggressively nationalizing state in Tudjman's Croatia, the militant mobilization of Serbs in Croatia's small-town and rural borderlands, and the articulation of a homeland-based nationalism in Milosevic's Serbia.[9] It can equally be a useful device for developing a nuanced understanding of continuity and change in Bosnia after Dayton.

Brubaker emphasizes that 'external national homelands are constructed through political action, not given by the facts of ethnic demography. A state becomes an external national 'homeland' for 'its' ethnic diaspora when political or cultural elites define ethnonational kin in other states as members of one and the same nation, claim that they 'belong', in some sense, to the state and assert that their condition must be monitored and their interests protected and promoted by the state, and when the state actually

[6] Rogers Brubaker, *Nationalism Reframed: Nationhood and the National Question in the New Europe*, Cambridge, 1996, Chapter 3, pp. 55-76.

[7] For example, a similar framework for understanding irredentist conflict is developed in Myron Weiner, 'The Macedonian Syndrome: An Historical Model of International Relations and Political Development', *World Politics* 23, 1 (1970).

[8] Brubaker, *Nationalism Reframed*, p. 59. Emphases mine.

[9] Ibid., pp. 69-76.

does take action in the name of monitoring, promoting or protecting the interests of its ethnonational kin'. Of course, the ethnic co-nationals in the diaspora have to be receptive to this construction of shared brotherhood and interests if the ideologues of the external national homeland are to be successful, and they normally would respond positively only if they felt threatened by a new, 'nationalizing' state. This formulation is more sensitive to the importance of context and contingency, key to understanding the fragmentation of Yugoslavia and the climate within Bosnia (and Croatia) in the early 1990s, than are simplistic evocations of timeless 'Greater Serbia' and 'Greater Croatia' ideologies and agendas, and their alleged reflexive collaborators among Bosnian Serbs and Croats. The generic 'homeland stance' is defined by an 'axiom of shared nationhood across the boundaries of state and citizenship'.

Yet at the same time, 'there is great variation among particular homeland stances, great variation in understandings of just what the asserted responsibility for ethnic co-nationals entails: Should ethnic co-nationals living as minorities in other states be given moral support, or also material support?... What sort of stance should they be encouraged to take vis-à-vis the states in which they live? And what sort of stance should the homeland adopt towards those states?... What weight should those concerns be given in shaping the homeland state's overall relations toward the states in which the co-ethnics live?... These are all contested questions in homeland states.' Thus 'homeland politics takes a variety of forms, ranging from immigration and citizenship privileges for 'returning' members of the ethnic diaspora, through various attempts to influence other states' policies towards the co-ethnics, to irredentist claims on the territory of other states'. Moreover, the variety of 'homeland stances compete not only with one another but with stances that reject the basic premise of homeland politics, or at least set sharp limits on the permissible forms of homeland politics... The field of struggle over state policy is therefore constituted by struggles over whether and how a state should be a homeland for its ethnic co-nationals in other states.'[10]

Similarly, 'a national minority is not simply a 'group' that is given by the facts of ethnic demography. It is a dynamic political stance, or more precisely, a family of related yet mutually compet-

[10] Ibid., pp. 58, 67.

ing stances, not a static ethno-demographic condition'. The core
traits that define this generic stance are: a public claim to membership of an ethno-cultural nation different from the numerically or politically dominant group in the new state; a demand that
the state recognize this distinct ethno-cultural identity; and the
assertion of collective cultural or political rights on the basis of
that nationality. Nonetheless, the rights claimed can 'vary widely
in their specific content', ranging from 'full cooperative participation in the institutions of the host state' to 'a separatist, non-coop-
erative stance'. Thus a national minority is usually not an internally unified, unitary group with an uniform, unvarying political
preference, but a 'field of differentiated or competitive positions or
stances adopted by different organizations, parties, movements or
individual political entrepreneurs, each seeking to "represent" the
minority to its own putative members, to the host state, or to the
outside world, each seeking to monopolize the legitimate representation of the group'.[11]

The third element of the triangle, the 'nationalizing state', is
also a set of stances with a shared 'tendency to see the state as an
'unrealized' nation-state, as a state destined to be a nation-state...
but not yet in fact a nation-state, or at least not to a sufficient
degree, and the concomitant disposition to remedy this perceived
defect, to make the state what it is properly and legitimately destined to be'. Such an idiom is 'virtually obligatory in some contexts' as a matter of political necessity, but a 'wide range of nationalizing stances within a single state' is still possible, and often actual, a 'spectrum of related yet distinct and even mutually antagonistic stances adopted by differently positioned' parties, movements
and individuals.

Brubaker's framework has an additional feature which makes it
particularly useful for understanding the way the triadic relationship played out in Croatia and Bosnia—the centrality of *perception*.
Thus 'to ask whether [certain] policies and practices are "really"
nationalizing makes little sense... A nationalizing state, or nationalizing practice, policy or event, is not one whose representatives,
authors or agents understand or articulate it as such, but rather
one that is *perceived* as such in the field of the national minority or
external national homeland'. Conversely 'one can impose and sus-

[11] Ibid., pp. 60-2.

tain a stance as a mobilized national minority, with its demands for recognition and rights, only by imposing and sustaining a vision', [i.e. perception], 'of the host state as a nationalizing or nationally oppressive state.' This in turn generates a perception among the supporters of that state that the national minority in question is disloyal, separatist or simply unreasonable, and that its external national homeland is a dangerous irredentist power. Thus, it is immaterial whether or not the SDA leadership in early 1992 actually planned a state that would be nationally oppressive to Bosnian Serbs, and Croats (probably they did not have any concrete plan at all in mind, in itself a fatal shortcoming); or indeed, whether hyper-interventionist enthusiasts among the international community really wanted, in the early post-war phase, to change, in the process of implementation, the blueprint for the explicitly multinational state reached at Dayton in a more unitary direction.[12] So long as such perceptions prevailed in other fields, that is what mattered. The essence of the relational nexus between the three fields is 'reciprocal inter-field monitoring: actors in each field closely and continually monitor relations and actions in each of the other two fields.' 'This process of continual reciprocal monitoring' often leads to *selective* attention to and representation of events and developments in other fields, as well as to deliberate, cynical *misrepresentation* of happenings in the other fields. This is because 'a stance to which one is already committed 'requires' a certain representation of the external field, and therefore generates efforts to impose or sustain it through deliberately selective interpretation or outright misrepresentation and distortion'. In this way, 'competing representations of an external field may be closely linked to struggles among competing stances *within* the given field.'[13]

This framework obviously needs to be applied with caution to the Bosnian case. For instance, none of the three groups in Bosnia comprised a majority of the population. At the same time, the

[12] There has in fact been a point of view that has consistently urged a radically interventionist, coercion-intensive international strategy towards this end. See, for example, the International Crisis Group's detailed report-card, *Is Dayton Failing? Bosnia Four Years after the Peace Agreement*, Sarajevo, October 1999, which laments the absence of an 'enforcement mechanism' that can realize such an international agenda in Bosnia. Such views are, however, increasingly relegated to the margins of debates over Bosnia and the international role there.

importance of perception, including *self*-perception, means that Bosnian Serbs saw themselves as being reduced to precisely such a minority—however vehemently they may reject the label, then as now—which helped the most radical stance among them to prevail over more moderate alternatives. Brubaker's triadic model, once filled in with empirical detail, can indeed help us appreciate how the most hardline, uncompromising stances, driven by perception and misperception in a climate of profound uncertainty, came to prevail in each of the three fields of action, and how their conjunction sparked conflagration, first in Croatia and then in BiH. But the most useful element of his model is the emphasis on the *contingent nature* of what eventually did happen. Although 'the relational field in which the national question arises is a highly structured one… what could not be predicted… and what cannot be retrospectively explained as structurally determined, was just *what kind* of nationalizing stance, *what kind* of minority self-understanding, and *what kind* of homeland politics would prevail in the struggles among competing stances within [each of] the three fields'.[14]

The fact that the worst-case scenario did prevail does not mean that this was the only possible outcome. Any serious student of Yugoslavia's twilight and demise will appreciate the argument that there were multiple, competing perspectives in each of the three fields.[15] In Croatia and Bosnia, the three-way interaction between a new 'nationalizing' state, its national 'minority' or minorities, and the external national 'homelands' of those minorities did lead to war with calamitous consequences, but this was a contingent outcome. This is not to deny or downplay the reality that the outcome which prevailed in Bosnia in 1992 and between 1992 and 1995 has left deep scars, and casts a long, dark shadow on prospects of 'reconciliation' in the post-war phase. But the intrinsic contingency of that outcome does mean that relations

---

[13] Brubaker, *Nationalism Reframed*, pp. 63-5, 68.

[14] Ibid., p. 76. Emphases mine.

[15] On the hard dilemmas facing the Bosnian Muslims during the crisis of 1990-2 and competing perspectives within the community on those dilemmas, see Adil Zulfikarpasic, *The Bosniak*, London, 1998. A large portion of this book—effectively the author's memoirs and retrospective reflections—consists of Zulfikarpasic's conversations with Milovan Djilas in March 1994, after Bosnia's fate had been decisively and tragically sealed.

between the three fields are variable over time; they are not fated to remain mired in the catastrophic situation of 1992-3 or 1995-6. In the post-war context of Bosnia and former Yugoslavia, those relations can only improve with time (and international encouragement and facilitation), albeit slowly, cautiously and painfully. In particular, as the dominant stance in any particular field changes over time and more moderate stances come into play, the shift in that field can trigger—given the organic interconnectedness of the three fields—a chain effect of reciprocal movement in the other fields and thus in the nature of the triadic relationship as a whole.

The most significant shift, of course, has occurred in the 'external national homelands'. Regime changes in Serbia and the FRY, and in Croatia, have not produced any dramatic, transformative effects on or within Bosnia. The reason is twofold. The relations between the three elements of the triangle are too complex, and a change in the external field(s) does not in itself solve the internal, endogenous problem of legitimacy of the Bosnian state. Nonetheless, the removal of deeply tainted regimes and their leaders in Serbia/FRY and Croatia unequivocally represent developments with major implications for the Bosnian transition.

Those consequences, generated in dynamic interaction with the fields internal to BiH, are peculiarly mixed. The change of regime in Croatia in early 2000 aggravated the insecurities of the HDZ-BiH. Those anxieties were further heightened when the SDA, until then the leading party apparently representing the Bosnian statist perspective, suffered serious reverses among the Bosniac electorate in local elections in April 2000 and general elections in November 2000. Until 2000 a *de facto* cartel of the SDA and the HDZ controlled the Federation machinery and its institutions, shared out its spoils in the form of political office and patronage resources, and generally cultivated a cosy collusion. The erosion of the SDA among Bosniacs made this arrangement untenable, and this has played a substantial but rarely noticed role in catalysing the crisis of the Federation and the HDZ-BiH's confrontation with the international community. The rise in the strength of the more liberal, non-sectarian SDP among Bosniacs should, intuitively speaking, aid liberalizing trends among Croats and Serbs, but in practice this has been limited and qualified. First, the SDP's growing popularity, not just among Bosniac voters but among international officials and organizations as well, has been seen as a threat by the HDZ-BiH. The SDP has small pockets of support among BiH Croats, and is *potentially* capable of poaching more Croat voters from the HDZ vote-bank in a way the SDA, with its specific Muslim orientation, never could. Second, the SDA has lost support not just to the SDP but also to the SBiH, which stands for a unitary Bosnian agenda radically revisionist vis-à-vis the DPA. Groups like the SBiH reject the changes in Serbia, and the relative liberalization of the political climate in RS, as inconsequential, even farcical. Even as SDP leader and BiH prime minister Lagumdzija meets Kostunica and Djindjic in Belgrade in an effort to restore 'broken ties', and hosts Serbian governmental delegations in Sarajevo, influential voices within the Bosniac community continue to question the existence of RS. This is threatening particularly to BiH Serbs but also, less directly, to the Croats.

Nonetheless, driven by its own logic and compulsions, the differentiation and relative liberalization of the RS's political space has continued. The relatively small but politically crucial party of RS prime minister Ivanic is thus balancing two different stances, tailored to two very different galleries—in Banja Luka a tacit understanding with the strongest party in RS, the SDS; at the level of the 'Sarajevo' institutions, support to the internationally sponsored 'Alliance for Change' which cobbles together the SDP and the SBiH in addition to a host of smaller, mainly FBiH-based parties. The SDS is itself undergoing an evolution, at once superficial and remarkable, given its antecedents. Its elected deputies in the Republika Srpska National Assembly now vote *en bloc* in favour of legislation establishing obligatory cooperation with the Hague tribunal. Its defeated rival, Dodik's 'moderate' SNSD, accuses it of treason and treachery: 'The SDS promises that it will work on strengthening the joint [BiH] institutions and establishing regulatory agencies [for infrastructural and strategic sectors] at BiH level, all of which will strip the RS of its sovereign rights. In their crawling collaboration, they are even ready to arrest Serbs indicted for committing war crimes'.[16] In June 2001, after SDS leader and RS president Mirko Sarovic participated in the (second) ceremony inaugurating the reconstruction of the Ferhadija mosque in Banja Luka, posters appeared in downtown Banja Luka depicting him wearing a skullcap. The captions described him as 'Mirsad Effendi Sarovic'. Around the same time, an inter-party coopera-tion agreement was signed in Belgrade in end-July 2001 between the SDS, represented by RS parliament speaker Dragan Kalinic, and FRY president Vojislav Kostunica's Democratic Party of Serbia (DSS). The agreement called for 'developing the cultural, economic and spiritual unity of the Serb people'. And after meet-ings with his RS counterpart Ivanic, Serbia's prime minister Djindjic announced that 'we want to quickly lift all the econom-ic barriers on the borders and start operating a free-trade zone in the Balkans where it's easiest to do it—between Serbia and RS.'[17]

This bewildering amalgam of continuity and change presents constraints as well as opportunities for a constructive role by the international community, so aptly described by Mihailo Crnobrnja even before Dayton as 'the fourth constituent part' of Bosnia & Herzegovina.

Susan Woodward and Bishop Ratko Peric's perspectives on the Dayton epoch in Bosnia's history have one aspect in common—distrust of the motives and intentions of the United States. Woodward's claim that the Dayton accords merely institutional-ized the war strategy of the US government to 'defeat the Serbs', and that the so-called implementation process is simply an attempt to 'finish the job', sounds strangely similar to a conspira-cy theory that has currency among some circles in Bosnia and in Western countries—that 'Dayton' was the culmination of a sinis-ter plot hatched by powerful Western diplomats and politicians to partition Bosnia & Herzegovina. Of course, the DPA 'was a com-promise, as peace agreements usually are'.[18] This makes it suscep-tible to conspiracy theories of various kinds. Beyond that, Woodward's claim about 'the internationals' scheming to revise unilaterally and radically the DPA to set up a more centralized state is overstated and possibly mistaken, for two reasons. First, what Woodward calls 'the international operation' in Bosnia,

[16] SNSD press release in Banja Luka, December 2000, cited in European Stability Initiative, *Reshaping International Priorities in Bosnia, Part III*, p. 6.
[17] 'Belgrade, Banja Luka to Intensify Economic Cooperation', AFP, Belgrade, August 1, 2001.
[18] Wolfgang Petritsch, in an interview with *Walter* magazine, Sarajevo, September 5, 2001.

allegedly 'still fighting the war through constitutional means', is hardly an undifferentiated, monolithic machine. Instead, as Bishop Peric notes quite correctly, it is 'a curious political machine made up of varying interests, institutions and intentions'. There have always been deep divisions of opinion in the US government about the necessity and efficacy of intervention in Bosnia, and in post-Yugoslav conflict zones generally. Senior members of the military wing of the US establishment have not been the only ones who have consistently harboured grave misgivings about what they regard as protracted and precarious experiments in 'nation-building' in distant places not of high-priority strategic interest to the United States. Second, I believe that at least some international officials who have served in Bosnia since Dayton have undergone a genuine learning experience, a maturing process, as they have struggled on a daily basis with the immense complications of the country. After two years heading the international mission in Bosnia, Petritsch says unequivocally, partly in response to allegations of his personal collaboration with 'genocidal Republika Srpska' by an American lawyer writing in Sarajevo media,[19] that 'the Dayton Peace Agreement is an international, binding agreement. There are no question-marks hanging over it.' Further, the top international in Bosnia visualizes the following:

> The time may come when the peoples of Bosnia & Herzegovina will want to amend the centrepiece of the Agreement: Annex 4, the Constitution, which defines the state of BiH and its institutions. But, it is up to the citizens and peoples of BiH to decide if and how they want to amend it, because they have to find a way of living with each other... in their country.[20]

The conclusion of Chapter 2 argued that debates over 'implementation strategy' actually beg a much more fundamental question: What exactly is the international community trying to implement in Bosnia? And, how far can the Dayton 'mandate' be

[19] This opprobrium was partly occasioned by Petritsch's decision that the March 2001 special-relations agreement between Belgrade and Banja Luka was not in contravention of Bosnia's territorial integrity, its constitution, or the vital interests of any of its constituent nations.

[20] Interview with *Walter* magazine, September 5, 2001.

stretched? During 2001 a feature film titled *No Man's Land*, directed by Danis Tanovic, a young Bosnian filmmaker originally from Sarajevo, won awards at several prestigious international film festivals. The movie uses techniques typical of (post)Yugoslav filmmaking, particularly black humour and tragicomic sequences with a distinct surrealist edge, so effective in such films as Serbian director Srdjan Dragojevic's remarkable rumination on the Bosnian war, *Pretty Village, Pretty Flame*. In Tanovic's film two wounded soldiers, one Serb and one Muslim, lie close to each other in a combat zone. Between them lies another wounded man, who has to keep still because a mine is placed under his body, and if he moves he risks setting it off and killing himself and the two wounded men near him. To Tanovic 'this guy is like Bosnia today'.[21] That artistic metaphor could be a plausible approximation of political constraints and realities.

The clientelistic relations between political bosses and citizens and patronage networks which, Woodward correctly notes, are widely prevalent in Bosnia under the Dayton regime, have a long pedigree in Bosnia, and in former Yugoslavia generally. A few years of an international peace-building presence cannot eliminate deeply rooted practices, nor can it be expected to do so. Similarly, corruption, crony privatization etc are present to a considerable degree in all the Yugoslav successor-states, and in the transitional societies of eastern and central Europe generally, although the problem is worse than average in BiH because of the total collapse of rule of law during the war. However, Woodward has a valid and important point when she observes that Bosnian politics has a long tradition of tactically adjusting to the presence of external powers, and that those historical patterns of adaptation have been revived—and perhaps some new forms born?—under the internationally supervised Dayton regime. The lesson is that international authorities should beware of becoming unnecessarily entangled in the maze of intrigue that is Bosnian politics, and should, in particular, guard against being manipulated into becoming the tools of some factions in their struggle against other factions. Such a lesson would be well taken indeed.

Bishop Peric also has one persuasive argument—that it is

---

[21] Julie Remy, 'Young Exiled Director Says Bosnia Sits on a Mine', Reuters, Toronto, September 9, 2001.

unfair and undemocratic that Croats should be represented in state and Entity institutions, including the BiH state presidency and the rotating presidency of the FBiH, which is nominated by ethnic caucuses in the federation's House of Peoples, by persons and groups who command the support of fewer than 10% of the Croat electorate, as demonstrated by the November 2000 election results. The House of Peoples imbroglio, discussed in Chapter 2, is as yet unresolved. My copy of the BiH Election Law passed in August 2001, electronically downloaded from the OSCE-BiH internet site, says in its table of contents that Chapter 12, Subchapter A, defines the principles of election of the 'House of Peoples of the Parliament of the Federation of Bosnia & Herzegovina'. But this subchapter is missing in the actual text of the document. Since, in the multi-tiered federal model of BiH, the delegates to the state parliament's House of Peoples are nominated by the RS National Assembly and by the Bosniac and Croat caucuses, respectively, of the FBiH's House of Peoples, the impasse extends further than the cantonal and Federation levels. Article 11.1 of the Law tersely states that 'the way of election of the delegates to the House of Peoples in the Parliamentary Assembly of Bosnia & Herzegovina is regulated by the provision of Article 20.16'. Article 20.16 in turn states that 'until the final regulation of the procedure for the election of the delegates to the House of Peoples of the Parliamentary Assembly of Bosnia & Herzegovina, their election shall be conducted in accordance with the Constitution of Bosnia & Herzegovina'. This clause seems to suggest that constitutional provisions take precedence over *ad hoc* changes to provisional electoral regulations, such as the one pertaining to the Federation House of Peoples unilaterally introduced by the OSCE for the November 2000 elections, which so enraged the HDZ, which termed the move unconstitutional. This convoluted issue aside, Mgr Peric's basic point is hard to contest. Given the HDZ-BiH's continuing hold on the Croat population, its exclusion (even if partly self-inflicted) from legislative and executive organs at various levels of the system is simply an unsustainable situation. This is clearly a case where international intervention overstepped limits, needs to find a path for a honourable retreat, and devise a renewed *modus vivendi* with the HDZ and its allies, for they too have constraints and limitations and in their own interest cannot indefinitely sustain a maximalist, rejectionist stance.[22]

Beyond that, Peric's views represent an exemplar of the kind of sectarian, deeply bigoted post-Yugoslav stance that must be resisted. Based on a fantastic account of Croat tribulations over 500 years under Ottoman and Yugoslav regimes, this perverse brand of 'patriotism' alternates between self-pitying hysteria and bellicose rhetoric directed at various 'enemies'. Peric's basic complaint seems to be that while areas 'cleansed' by Serbs were constituted into Republika Srpska, areas similarly 'purified' by Croats were not given over to legal, *de jure* Croat control. Peric justly criticizes the expulsion of hundreds of thousands of Muslims and Croats from territories that eventually became the RS. But there is no mention in his account of the hundreds of thousands of Serbs forced to leave various parts of Croatia between 1991 and 1995, nor of the tens of thousands of Serb civilians cleansed from the Mostar region in 1992. There are, however, dramatic expressions of solidarity with the Croat war-criminals convicted at the Hague for atrocities against Muslims in central Bosnia, and those being tried for similar crimes in the Mostar region. Peric laments the extinction of centuries-old Catholic parishes in Serb-majority parts of Herzegovina. But one would never know from his writings and speeches about the wanton demolition of the beautiful nineteenth-century Orthodox church in the city of Mostar, or about the destruction of the fifteenth-century Orthodox

---

[22] During the stand-off with the international community, HDZ-BiH strategy has alternated between populism and pragmatism. In early May 2001, for example, dismissed BiH co-president and party leader Ante Jelavic stated that 'the time has come to start negotiations between the legitimately and legally elected Croat representatives and all parties in Bosnia as well as the international community', to begin 'the return of the HDZ to parliamentary political life, to the Muslim-Croat Federation and to send a message to Croat soldiers [of the Federation armed forces] to return to their barracks'. 'Bosnian Croat Grouping Seeking to Return to Government', AFP, Mostar, May 4, 2001. In late June, however, Jelavic was quoted by the Croatian weekly *Globus* as saying that he thought 'that the Muslims, that is Izetbegovic, would also rather accept Bosnia-Herzegovina as a federation consisting of three federal units, which means complete demarcation'. *Globus* also published an alleged draft constitution of a BiH 'Croat Republic', and claimed that radical elements in the HDZ-BiH were planning to organize a referendum on a separate Croat entity by the end of the year. 'Bosnian Croat Nationalists Determined to Form Own Republic', AFP, Zagreb, June 28, 2001.

monastery at Zitomislici, a village south of Mostar, by marauders from the nearby Catholic pilgrimage-town of Medjugorje.[23] The roster of Croat 'institutions' this man of religion expressly wants to defend against international interference and assault include the hate-mongering Mostar area TV station Erotel (closed down by international peacekeeping troops in February 2000), the 'ethnically cleansed' enterprise Aluminij Mostar (currently the subject of an independent audit initiated by the OHR), and Hercegovacka Banka, the financial nerve-centre of BiH Croat hardliners which was clumsily raided by international military and civilian personnel in April 2001, provoking rioting and outrage in west Mostar and several other predominantly Croat towns.

As the international operation in BiH gradually winds down, a strategic, focused approach to accomplishing key tasks has become ever more urgent. In this book, I have argued that a clearly defined but relatively modest set of goals may in the end leave the least divisive and most usable legacy for Bosnians themselves, in cooperation with other ex-Yugoslavs, to build on in the future. Wolfgang Petritsch's identification of the areas of highest priority is absolutely on target—'the application of a focused political will to the business of establishing the legal and fiscal structures that can sustain a growing economy'. The real crisis in Bosnia today is the economic crisis, of which the chief symptoms are massively high unemployment, very low average per capita incomes, large-scale financial bankruptcy of firms and government institutions, and levels of foreign investment that place Bosnia at the bottom of all transitional east European states, far below even countries like Albania, Moldova and Macedonia.[24] The magnitude of

---

[23] In June 1981 a few children in this town purportedly sighted the Virgin Mary on a mountain overlooking the town. After this miraculous vision Medjugorje, a sleepy place in western Herzegovina, was transformed into a pilgrimage site for Catholics from all over the world and achieved great prosperity as a result. When I visited the town in 1998, it was swarming with tourists brought in by the busload from the Dalmatian coast. The visitors could confess in any of seventeen different languages, including Spanish, Polish and Gaelic. On Medjugorje's sordid realities during and after the wars of Yugoslav succession, see Mart Bax, 'Barbarization in a Bosnian Pilgrimage Centre' in Halpern and Kideckel (eds), *Neighbours at War*, pp. 187-202.

[24] Drazen Simic, 'Half of BiH Federation on Permanent Vacations: Every Day 30 Workers Out of Work', AIM, Sarajevo, July 9, 2001; 'World Bank Says Bosnia

Bosnia's economic crisis means, unfortunately, that no significant improvement can be expected in the next few years. Nonetheless, constructive analysts have sketched a strategic 'road-map' for the international effort in Bosnia until about the end of 2004, identifying several key points of emphasis:

(1) The 'core Dayton tasks', including continued emphasis on further accelerating property law implementation and minority returns[25]; passage of a permanent Election Law[26]; pursuit and apprehension of high-profile war criminals yet to be brought to justice; and maintenance of a sizeable international security presence,[27] including US participation

(2) Putting in place the basic institutions essential for a viable state, including a professional civil service and a state treasury. Functional integration of key infrastructural and strategic sectors such as energy, telecommunications and mass transportation, which requires intra-Entity and cross-Entity cooperation in the shared interest, and establishment of statewide regulatory bodies[28]

(3) Prioritization of the urgent task of devising and establishing

Ranks Lowest for Investment', Reuters, Banja Luka, April 5, 2001; Nermina Durmic-Kahrovic, 'Economy Fuels Unrest in Bosnia', *Balkan Crisis Reports* 168, Tuzla, September 1, 2000. Between 1996 and 1999, BiH attracted on average only $4.7 million per year in direct foreign investment, much of it from another former Yugoslav republic, Slovenia. This level compares to $56 million per year for Albania, $54 million in Moldova, and $43 million in Macedonia.

[25] According to the latest statistics (September 31, 2001) available from the consortium of international agencies supervising this process, the 'implementation ratios' (actual repossessions, of socially owned and private property combined, as percentage of total claims submitted) are 34% for BiH as a whole, 43% in the Federation, and 24% in RS. The figures for particular regions of the country vary widely.

[26] This was achieved in August 2001. Issues relating to Bosnia's electoral framework are exhaustively discussed in Chapter 5.

[27] After successive albeit gradual cuts, SFOR deployment totals about 19,000 personnel, including approximately 3,200 Americans, as of the autumn of 2001. This is probably close to the minimum level that should be maintained until at least 2003-4.

[28] This entails persuading particularly the RS, but also the Croat-dominated parts of the country, that these are not politically motivated moves intended to progressively strip them of their autonomy and establish a more centralized state, but that the objective is simply limited, strategic cooperation in the shared interest of Bosnia's parts and peoples.

a viable intergovernmental fiscal regime to underpin Bosnia's federal and confederal political structures; in other words, coherent mechanisms for the collection, utilization and distribution of public resources and revenues within and across Bosnia's multiple layers of government.[29]

This is very specific, concrete counsel in a hands-on, somewhat technocratic vein. My own focus in this book has been on the *politics* of international intervention in Bosnia, and specifically the key *norms* that ought to guide this process of engagement. The ultimate goal of international involvement in post–Dayton Bosnia is (or at least should be) to assist Bosnians make a transition from being *subjects* of an international mission to build frameworks of democracy, human rights and rule of law to becoming active, engaged *agents* of their own future(s). At least three key lessons in this regard can be gleaned from the cumulative experience of almost six years of intensive international engagement.

Firstly, Bosnia's future as a democratic country depends on institutions and institutionalization, not on particular individuals or political factions. The sad story of virtually uncritical, unconditional international sponsorship of Milorad Dodik and his failed, discredited regime in Republika Srpska (1998-2000) is a warning against the shortcomings of the latter policy temptation. Individuals and cliques who are given to believe that they are the chosen favourites of powerful Western countries and international agencies tend to rapidly develop a sense of impunity, and degenerate habits of authoritarianism and corruption. In 2001, post-election international engineering of a peculiar political conglomerate called the 'Alliance for Change', cobbled into existence with the sole objective of denying 'nationalist parties' access to power, has enabled the two largest constituents of the coalition, particularly the SDP but also the SBiH, to acquire a range of political offices at the state, Entity (FBiH) and cantonal levels of governance. This type of political alliance, which adopted the objectives outlined by the bi-annual PIC conference held in Brussels in mid-2000 for lack of a programme of its own, is an example, to borrow Donald Horowitz's language, of 'coalitions of

[29] European Stability Initiative, *Reshaping International Priorities in Bosnia, Part III* ,pp. 14-21.

convenience that will dissolve'.[30] That aside, it is noteworthy that as of early 2001, leading SDP politicians in the city and canton of Tuzla, and SDP as well as SBiH leaders in the Brcko District, stood accused of serious charges of malpractice, including award of construction contracts without tender and misappropriation of millions of marks of official funds to purchase 'clothes, mobile phones, jewellery and prostitutes'. As one disillusioned citizen put it: 'Tuzla was always different. We always elected [non-nationalist] social democrats. I guess that is why we now feel so bad when we read that they are perhaps no different from the nationalists.'[31]

Secondly, the transparency and accountability of international officials and organizations, and the opaqueness of their decision-making procedures, is a political issue that cannot, and should not, be ignored or swept under the rug. Regular elections ensure that there is a mechanism for holding Bosnian politicians accountable to their electorates. No such mechanism exists for the vast IC operation, with its web of officials and agencies.[32] The top international official, the HR, is answerable to the 55 governments and organizations that comprise the Peace Implementation Council, but not to the Bosnian people, over whose lives he exerts so much authority through the frequent use of expanded powers of intervention, control and imposition given to the holder of his position in 1997. It is not surprising that many ordinary citizens liken the *modus operandi* of the international community's hierarchy in Bosnia to those of the erstwhile communist elites, who constantly 'fixed' things from behind the scenes while constantly assuring the public that whatever was being done was in their best interest. At the end of August 2001 Croat leader Ante Jelavic appeared before a judge of Bosniac nationality in the Sarajevo canton court

---

[30] Horowitz, *A Democratic South Africa?*, p. 175.

[31] Nermina Durmic-Kahrovic, 'Tuzla Officials Face Corruption Inquiry: Allegations Haunt Ranking SDP Officials', *Balkan Crisis Reports* 227, Tuzla, March 16, 2001.

[32] The lack of accountability can breed serious operational problems. Numerous police officers from different countries who have served since 1996 in the UN-supervised International Police Task Force (IPTF) have been implicated in cases of gross sexual misconduct, as well as corrupt, compromising relationships with sectarian party leaders, police and local authorities in their areas of responsibility. For an investigative report focusing on United States officers, see Colum Lynch, 'UN Police in Bosnia: Who's Watching?', *Washington Post,* May 30, 2001.

to face preliminary charges, instituted by international instigation, of undermining the territorial integrity of Bosnia & Herzegovina. It transpires that 'earlier this year [2001] Petritsch transferred Jelavic's case to Sarajevo from a court in Mostar, a Croat nationalist stronghold, where he [the high representative] feared that the hearings could not be objective.' An aide to Jelavic told members of the media assembled outside the Sarajevo courtroom that 'this court is a farce and reminds us of political persecution [through show trials of dissidents] in the communist era', adding that Jelavic had only come to avoid 'eventual spectacular arrests by SFOR and police'.[33]

The distinction conventionally made by international officials and some Western analysts between good, cooperative Bosnian publics and bad, uncooperative Bosnian elites is questionable at best and false at worst. In November 1999 the high representative summarily dismissed 23 elected Bosnian officials from their posts (nine Serbs, seven Bosniacs and seven Croats), including the mayor of Banja Luka, the governor as well as the interior minister of Una-Sana canton, an overwhelmingly Bosniac area in Bosnia's northwestern corner, the justice minister (a Bosniac) of Sarajevo canton, and the mayors of Stolac, Capljina, Kiseljak, Prozor-Rama and Mostar South-West, all hardline HDZ municipalities. In a joint statement justifying the dismissals, Petritsch, then recently arrived in Bosnia, and the then head of OSCE-BiH claimed that 'these officials have failed the voters who elected them by pursuing anti-Dayton, anti-peace, anti-reconciliation and extra-legal agendas, especially at the local level where their obstructionism hurts the most'. Those dismissed were also barred from standing for or holding public office in future. The sacked officials may indeed have failed to meet the expectations and demands of international community bureaucrats. But it is stretching credulity to claim that they had 'failed the voters who elected them'. The voters who elected these persons to their offices generally did not do so in the hope and expectation that they would toil to promote inter-ethnic harmony and coexistence. To the contrary, in many instances it is likely that these individuals won election because their voters believed that they would strive towards just the oppo-

---

[33] 'Bosnian Croat Nationalist Leader Appears in Court over Breakaway Bid', AFP, Sarajevo, August 29, 2001.

site once elected. Almost two years later, in August 2001, Petritsch the Bosnia veteran noted: 'During my two-year tenure, I removed 66 officials, and passed [imposed] a number of decisions that affected in the most direct way the lives of a large number of people.'[34] Bosnia is a tough work environment, and almost anyone who wants to be taken seriously and achieve results in the public domain has to adopt a tough stance. A policy of *selective sanctions* may have been unavoidable, given the venal, gangsterish disposition of many Bosnian power-brokers. Yet it is important to remember that the use of decree powers to fire elected officials, ban 'undesirable' political groups (for example, the far-right Serb Radical Party, SRS, proscribed in late 1999), and censor or close down 'hostile' local media both in RS and Croat-controlled areas is probably not consistent with the long-term aim of fostering genuine pluralism and rule of law in BiH. Whatever their vices, Bosnian politicians, like all politicians, are generally responsive to the demands and opinions of their constituents. In July–August 2001, three senior Armija BiH officers, Generals Mehmet Alagic and Enver Hadzihasanovic and Colonel Amir Kubura, were indicted for war crimes and crimes against humanity committed against Croats and Serbs in central Bosnia during the war, and transferred to the Hague. Zlatko Lagumdzija, newly appointed BiH prime minister, caused considerable controversy and resentment, especially in the RS, when he made a statement that could be interpreted as being overtly sympathetic to these unsavoury characters. The explanation is that Lagumdzija was behaving not as the prime minister of a deeply divided, multinational country (as he should have) but as the leader of a political party whose vote base, which includes recent defections from the sectarian SDA, is at least 85% Bosniac, many of whom regard the indictees not as war criminals but war-heroes.

This book argues that Bosnia, including the controversies over the legitimacy and the institutional form of its statehood, is best understood through two levels of analysis: *the local level* within

[34] Wolfgang Petritsch, interview to *Ekspres* weekly, Sarajevo, August 23, 2001. By one count, Petritsch imposed 38 laws and binding decisions in a four-month period between November 2000 and March 2001, as opposed to 45 such impositions by the previous HR, Westendorp, in course of his entire two-year term, highlighting the increasingly intrusive nature of international intervention.

Bosnia, and *the supra-state, regional level* which includes but also transcends Bosnia. In relatively settled times, the local context of social relations, characterized by traditional norms of 'good neighbourliness', provided an arena for everyday inter-ethnic accommodation and a cushion against the more exclusive national identities and the potential for conflict inherent in them. That has changed, perhaps irrevocably. The pattern in Bosnia is that local bonds not only proved unable, in times of crisis, to withstand the shock of conflicts generated at a more 'macro' level, but that the locality itself became the site in which those conflicts were played out in the bitterest forms.[35] In the aftermath of the 1992-5 war, most Bosnian localities are either nationally homogeneous (or largely homogeneous, with some barely tolerated 'minorities'), or else flashpoints for tension and sporadic eruptions of conflict, as in Mostar or Brcko.

In the spring of 2000, Strobe Talbott, then US Deputy Secretary of State in the Clinton administration, published an essay in which he attempted 'to define and apply the concept of self-determination in a way that is conducive to integration and not disintegration, in a way that will lead to lasting peace rather than recurrent war'.[36] Talbott's attempt to define the basic principles of a globally applicable solution to a globally prevalent problem rests, first of all, on the premise that existing 'international borders should not be changed by force, either by wars of aggression or wars of secession'. This declaration of principle is, of course, far too late for the extinct country known as Yugoslavia, but it is not too late for the fractured fragment of that country known as Bosnia & Herzegovina. 'The United States is working with its European allies and partners, and with the people of southeastern Europe', Talbott wrote, 'to remake the politics of the region without, this time, having to redraw the map—without splitting up large, repressive or failed states into small, fractious ministates'. Citing the Dayton process in Bosnia as the paradigmatic example, he notes that 'the task is going to take a generation or more' and that even then, the final outcome cannot be predicted with certainty—'after all, citizens of the former Yugoslavia

---

[35] A conversation with Xavier Bougarel helped me to fully appreciate this point.
[36] Strobe Talbott, 'Self-Determination in an Inter-Dependent World', *Foreign Policy* 118 (2000), pp. 152-63.

also had the *accoutrements* of single statehood, but in the end they did not have the requisite sense of common identity.'[37]

Maintaining the territorial *status quo*, however fragile or contested, as still preferable to the alternative—violent fragmentation, civil war, 'ethnic cleansing', permanent partition—is however only the starting point, and quite insufficient in itself. Talbott writes that states which are preserved in this way 'have a responsibility... to ensure that all who live within the boundaries of the state consider themselves fully respected and enfranchised citizens of that state'. In plural societies with multiple ethnic or national segments, this will mean, in my understanding, not just equal citizenship rights but various forms of *recognition and autonomy* for collectively defined groups. The more fragile and divided a state, the more contested its legitimacy, the greater the need for institutionalized forms of recognition and autonomy that will guarantee those rights and protections. Talbott talks in a general way about the 'democratic, federalized, [explicitly] multiethnic state' as the appropriate institutional model for such societies, so that 'self-determination can flourish without requiring the proliferation of ethnically based microstates or encouraging irredentist conflict.'[38] He cites Catalonia in Spain, devolution to Scotland and Wales in the ultra-unitary United Kingdom (omitting to mention the even more dramatic example of Northern Ireland, where devolution from London, power-sharing in Belfast, and a developing confederalization of relations between the British and Irish Isles make up the elements of a far-reaching formula for peace) and Quebec in Canada as examples, however imperfect, of these ideas in action.

But even autonomy, group rights, internal power-sharing and federalism are not enough. The final element of the challenge is 'to make a virtue out of porous borders and intertwined economies and cultures'; in other words, to transform the cultural, economic and other ties that spill across the borders of states from a problem into an asset. An opportunity to realize this is opened up by 'globalization and its subphenomenon, regionalization'. This would be done, in practice, through the institutionalization of 'cross-border economic development and political cooperation' in regional neighbourhoods. 'The most successful

[37] Ibid., pp. 155-7.
[38] Ibid.

states' of the early 21st century, Talbott predicts, 'will be democracies that harness these forces and facts of life rather than deny
them.'[39] It has been argued in this book that renewed regionalism
across former Yugoslavia will gradually ease, although not erase,
the borders erected after 1991 between the former republics and
within Bosnia, not just the IEBL but the *de facto* yet equally potent
'borders' like the one that cuts through the town-centre of
Mostar.

The peoples of former Yugoslavia have long ceased to be
members of a common fraternity of socialist brotherhood. Yet
they remain fated to live next to each other in the same regional
neighbourhood.[40] In a place such as Mostar, where invisible yet
powerful dividing lines literally cut through streets, that challenge
of being neighbours—after all that has happened—is especially
immediate, and enormous. And Mostar is just a microcosm, particularly stark and graphic to be sure, of Bosnia after Dayton.
Yugoslavia is dead, the Yugoslav idea has been consigned to the
history books, and so one common future is no longer possible in
the post-Yugoslav context, whether within Bosnia or in the south
Slav lands as a whole. Bosnia's post-Yugoslav transition, this book
has argued, is leading, quite properly, not to a singular, unambiguous future but to a future which is a compound of hybrid elements and competing influences, laden with ambiguities and contradictions—in other words, plural yet related futures.

A *linked* future for Bosnia's fragmented parts and peoples
remains not just a necessity but an inevitability, as for most of the
parts and peoples of former Yugoslavia as a whole.[41] In this evolution of a post-Yugoslav regional order,[42] post-war Bosnia's
strangely diffuse structure, based on a model of layered sovereignty,[43] multiple citizenships and soft borders (internal and external)
can, with some reform and rationalization, *potentially* be an asset,
not a disadvantage, for the country and its region. Well-wishers
who have some understanding of Bosnia's complexities will not
attempt to privilege and validate any *one* Bosnian perspective over
others, but will typically try to locate a middle ground between
conflicting positions, however difficult and complicated that may

---

[39] Ibid., pp. 153, 156, 161.
[40] A conversation with Dennison Rusinow introduced me to this semantic formulation of the nature of the separate yet inseparable post-Yugoslav transitions.

be. The gigantic international intervention in Bosnia after Dayton, in the framework of understanding advanced in this book, is *not* ultimately about building a *state*. It is about aiding the reconstruction of a broken, divided society which suffered the worst effects of Yugoslavia's demise and about helping its people—Muslims, Serbs and Croats—to get back on their own feet, with an eye also to aiding the normalization and revitalization of the post-Yugoslav region as a whole. Constructing a functional state is a just a means to those ends, not an end in itself. One author has written about the lost Bosnia, that captivating mosaic of histories, religions, cultures and 'nations', in near-poetic terms:

> Bosnia-Herzegovina casts a spell on all who live there or those who were privileged in the past to acquaint themselves with the republic. Sentimentalism plays little part in this—it is through the middle of Bosnia that East meets West, Islam meets Christianity, the Catholic eyes the Orthodox across the Neretva, the line of the Great Schism; Bosnia divided the great empires of Vienna and Constantinople, Bosnia was perhaps the only true reflection of [the essence of] Yugoslavia. It is both the paradigm of peaceful, communal life in the Balkans and its darkest antithesis. Nowhere else does the local culture resonate with so many sounds....[44]

The striking fact is that after the apocalypse Bosnia is still spellbinding, and still profoundly important to our times in so many ways.

[41] Sarajevo was appropriately the venue for the formal launch of the 'Stability Pact' for Southeastern Europe in July 1999.

[42] For interesting speculations on longer-term prospects of the post-Yugoslav region's eventual integration into an incrementally expanding EU, see Michael Emerson, 'Perspectives for the Balkans and a Wider European Order', working paper, Centre for European Policy Studies, Brussels, November 1999.

[43] On the long-term potential of layered-sovereignty frameworks as a basis for renewed cooperation in the post-Yugoslav Balkans, see Carl Bildt, 'A Second Chance in the Balkans', *Foreign Affairs* 80, 1 (2001).

[44] Glenny, *The Fall of Yugoslavia,*, p. 162.

SELECT BIBLIOGRAPHY

This select bibliography consists of a core of works central to the focus of this book. Some provide keys to understanding various aspects of contemporary Bosnia and Herzegovina, while others help situate Bosnia in the context of the region of former Yugoslavia. Yet others are about the comparative and policy debates relating to present-day BiH that are discussed at different points of this book.

Allcock, John B., *Explaining Yugoslavia*, London: Hurst, 2000.

Andric, Ivo, *The Bridge on the Drina*, London: Geo. Allen and Unwin, 1959.

————, *The Damned Yard and Other Stories*, Ed. and Trans. Celia Hawkesworth. Belgrade: Dereta, 2000.

Bakic-Hayden, Milica, 'Nesting Orientalisms: The Case of Former Yugoslavia' *Slavic Review* 54: 4 (winter 1995), pp. 917-31.

Banac, Ivo, *The National Question in Yugoslavia: Origins, History, Politics*, Ithaca, NY: Cornell University Press, 1984.

Bardos, Gordon N., 'The Bosnian Cold War: Politics,Society and International Engagement After Dayton' *Harriman Review* 11: 3 (April 1999), pp. 1-26.

Bart, Max, 'Warlords, Priests and the Politics of Ethnic Cleansing: A Case Study from Rural Bosnia-Hercegovina' *Ethnic and Racial Studies* 23: 1 (January, 2000), pp. 16-36.

Before the Rain, feature film, France/United Kingdom/Macedonia (dir. Milcho Manchevski), 1994.

Bildt, Carl, *Peace Journey: The Struggle for Peace in Bosnia*, London: Weidenfeld and Nicholson, 1998.

————, 'A Second Chance in the Balkans' *Foreign Affairs* 80: 1 (January-February 2001).

————, 'Force and Diplomacy' *Survival: The IISS Quarterly* 42: 1 (Spring, 2000), pp. 141-48.

Bose, Sumantra, 'State Crises and Nationalities Conflict in Sri Lanka and Yugoslavia' *Comparative Political Studies* 28: 1 (April 1995), pp. 87-116.

———, 'Mostar: Microcosm of a Conflict.' web-based multimedia feature at http://www.fathom.com, 2001.

———, 'Bosnia: Origins of the Conflict.' Multimedia interview at http://www.fathom.com, 2001.

———, 'Untangling the Truth: The War in Bosnia' Multimedia interview at http://www.fathom.com, 2001.

———, *Democratization and National Self-Determination: Institutional Structure in post-Tito Yugoslavia, post-Franco Spain and post-colonial Sri Lanka*, Ph.D. dissertation in Political Science, Columbia University, 1998.

✳Bougarel, Xavier, 'Bosnia and Hercegovina: State and Communitarianism' in D.A. Dyker and Ivan Vejvoda (eds), *Yugoslavia and After: A Study in Fragmentation, Despair and Rebirth*, New York: Addison-Wesley Longman, 1996.

Boyd, Charles G., 'Making Bosnia Work' *Foreign Affairs* 77: 1 (spring 1998), pp. 42-55.

Bringa, Tone, *Being Muslim the Bosnian Way: Identity and Community in a Central Bosnian Village*, Princeton University Press, 1995.

Brubaker, Rogers, *Nationalism Reframed: Nationhood and the National Question in the New Europe* Cambridge University Press, 1996.

Burg, Steven and Paul Shoup, *The War in Bosnia-Hercegovina: Ethnic Conflict and International Intervention*, Armonk, NY: M.E. Sharpe, 1999.

Chandler, David, *Bosnia: Faking Democracy After Dayton*, London: Pluto Press, 1999.

Chomsky, Noam, *The New Military Humanism: Lessons from Kosovo*, London: Pluto Press, 1999.

Daalder, Ivo, and Michael Froman, 'Dayton's Incomplete Peace' *Foreign Affairs* 78: 6 (November-December 1999), pp. 106-113.

Daalder, Ivo, *Getting to Dayton: The Making of America's Bosnia Policy*, Washington, DC: Brookings Institution, 2000.

Dani, weekly magazine of news and analysis, Sarajevo. In English translation.

Dimitrijevic, Nenad (ed.), *Managing Multiethnic Local Communities in the Countries of Former Yugoslavia*, Budapest: Open Society Institute, 2000.

✳Donia, Robert J.. 'The Search for Tolerance in Sarajevo's Textbooks' *Human Rights Review* 1: 2 (January-March 2000), pp. 38–55.

Donia, Robert J. and John Fine, *Bosnia and Hercegovina: A Tradition Betrayed*, London: Hurst, 1994.

European Stability Initiative, *Reshaping International Priorities in Bosnia–Part I: Bosnian Power Structures*, Sarajevo: ESI (14 October 1999).

——, *Interim Evaluation of Reconstruction and Return Task Force (RRTF)*, Sarajevo: ESI (September 1999).

——, *Reshaping International Priorities in Bosnia—Part II: International Power*, Sarajevo: ESI (March 2000).

——, *Reshaping International Priorities in Bosnia—Part III: The End of the Nationalist Regimes and the Future of the Bosnian State*, Sarajevo: ESI (22 March 2001).

Federation of Bosnia and Hercegovina, *Constitution of the Federation of Bosnia & Hercegovina*, mimeo (in translation, with amendments), n.d.

Financial Times, *Survey of Bosnia and Hercegovina*, London: FT, 14 December 1999.

Garton Ash, Timothy, 'Anarchy and Madness' *The New York Review of Books* (February 10 .2000), pp. 48–53.

Glenny, Misha, *The Fall of Yugoslavia: The Third Balkan War*, London: Penguin, (rev. edn), 1996.

——, *The Balkans, 1804–1999: Nationalism, War and the Great Powers*, London: Granta Books, 1999.

Greenberg Research, *People on War: The Consultation in Bosnia-Hercegovina—Report*, Sarajevo: International Committee of the Red Cross, 1999.

Halpern, Joel M., and David A. Kideckel, *Neighbors at War: Anthropological Perspectives on Yugoslav Ethnicity, Culture and History*, University Park, PA: Pennsylvania State University Press, 2000.

Hasan, Mushirul (ed.), *India's Partition: Process, Strategy and Mobilization*, Delhi: Oxford University Press, 1994.

Hayden, Robert M., 'Schindler's Fate: Genocide, Ethnic Cleansing and Population Transfers', *Slavic Review* 55: 4 (winter 1999).

——, *Blueprints for a House Divided: The Constitutional Logic of the Yugoslav Conflicts*, Ann Arbor: University of Michigan Press, 1999.

Hoffmann, Stanley, 'The Crisis of Liberal Internationalism' *Foreign*

Policy 98 (September 1995).

Holbrooke, Richard, *To End a War*, New York: Random House, 1998.

Horowitz, Donald, *A Democratic South Africa? Constitutional Engineering in a Divided Society*, Berkeley: University of California Press, 1991.

International Commission on the Balkans, *Unfinished Peace*. Washington, DC: Carnegie Endowment for International Peace, 1996.

International Crisis Group, *Breaking the Mould: Electoral Reform in Bosnia-Hercegovina*, Sarajevo: ICG (March 1999).

————, *Is Dayton Failing? Bosnia Four Years After the Peace Agreement*, Sarajevo: ICG (October 1999).

————, *Bosnia's Municipal Elections: Winners and Losers*, Sarajevo: ICG (April 2000).

————, *Reunifying Mostar: Opportunities for Progress*, Sarajevo: ICG (April 2000).

————, *Bosnia's Refugee Logjam Breaks: Is the International Community Ready?*, Sarajevo: ICG (May 2000).

Jergovic, Miljenko, *Sarajevo Marlboro*, London: Penguin, 1997.

Judah, Tim, *The Serbs: Myth, History and the Destruction of Yugoslavia*, New Haven: Yale University Press, 1997.

Karcic, Fikret, *The Bosniaks and the Challenges of Modernity: Late Ottoman and Habsburg Times*, Sarajevo: El-Kalem, 1999.

Kaufmann, Chaim, 'When All Else Fails: Evaluating Population Transfers and Partition as Solutions to Ethnic Conflict' in Jack Snyder and Barbara Walter (eds.), *Civil Wars, Insecurity and Intervention*, pp. 221-60. New York: Columbia University Press, 1999.

King, Charles, 'Beyond Bosnia: Contextualizing the Politics of Southeastern Europe' *PS: Political Science and Politics* 30: 3 (September), 1997.

Kumar, Radha, 'The Troubled History of Partition' *Foreign Affairs* 76: 1 (January-February 1997).

Lampe, John, *Yugoslavia as History: Twice There Was A Country*, Cambridge University Press (rev. edn.), 2000.

Lijphart, Arend, *Democracy in Plural Societies: A Comparative Exploration*, New Haven: Yale University Press, 1977.

————, *Democracies: Patterns of Majoritarian and Consensus*

Government in Twenty-One Countries, New Haven: Yale University Press, 1984.

————, 'Self-Determination versus Pre-Determination of Ethnic Minorities in Power-Sharing Systems' in Will Kymlicka (ed.), *The Rights of Minority Cultures*, New York: Oxford University Press, 1995.

MacLean, Fitzroy, *Eastern Approaches*, London: Jonathan Cape, 1949.

Mahmutcehajic, Rusmir, *Bosnia the Good: Tolerance and Tradition*, Budapest: Central European University Press, 2000.

Malcolm, Noel, *Bosnia: A Short History*, London: Macmillan, 1996.

Mansergh, Nicholas, *Prelude to Partition: Concepts and Aims in Ireland and India*, Cambridge University Press, 1978.

McGrath, Troy, 'Dealing with Disintegration in the Balkans: Is Partition Such Sweet Sorrow?', *Harriman Review* 11: 3 (April 1999), pp. 27-38.

Mearsheimer, John, and Robert Pape, 'The Answer: A Partition Plan for Bosnia' *The New Republic* (June 14 1993), pp. 22-28.

Mehmedinovic, Semezdin, *Sarajevo Blues*, San Francisco: City Lights Books, 1998.

Mostov, Julie, 'Democracy and the Politics of National Identity', *Studies in East European Thought* 46: 1, 2 (June 1994), pp. 9-31.

Nezavisne Novine, magazine of news and analysis, Banja Luka, weekly edition, in English translation.

Office of the High Representative, Bosnia–Hercegovina, *Bosnia & Hercegovina: Essential Texts,* Sarajevo: OHR, 1997.

————, *Statute of the Brcko District of Bosnia and Hercegovina*, Sarajevo: OHR (7 December 1999).

————, *Arbitral Tribunal for Dispute over Inter-Entity Boundary in Brcko Area: Final Award*, Sarajevo: OHR (5 March 1999).

Organization for Security and Cooperation in Europe, *Election Law of Bosnia and Hercegovina*, Sarajevo: OSCE-BiH, 2001.

Owen, David, *Balkan Odyssey*, London: Indigo, 1996.

Paris, R., 'Peace-Building and the Limits of Liberal Internationalism' *International Security* 22: 2 , pp. 54-89, (1997)

Pinson, Mark (ed.), *The Muslims of Bosnia-Hercegovina*, Cambridge: Center for Middle Eastern Studies, Harvard University, 1993.

Pretty Village, Pretty Flame, feature film, Federal Republic of Yugoslavia (dir. Srdjan Dragojevic), 1996.

Prlic, Jadranko, *Nesavrseni Mir(The Imperfect Peace)*, Mostar: Ziral, 1998.

Pugh, Michael and Margaret Cobble, 'Non-Nationalist Voting in Bosnian Municipal Elections: Implications for Democracy and Peace-Building' *Journal of Peace Research* 38: 1 (2001), pp. 27-47.

Radan, Peter, 'The Badinter Arbitration Commission and the Partition of Yugoslavia' *Nationalities Papers* 25 (1997), pp. 537-57.

————, 'Yugoslavia's Internal Borders as International Borders: A Question Of Appropriateness' *East European Quarterly* XXXIII, No. 2 (June 1999) pp. 137-55.

Ramet, Sabrina P., *Nationalism and Federalism in Yugoslavia, 1962-91*, Bloomington: Indiana University Press, 1992.

Ratner, Steven, 'Drawing a Better Line: *Uti Possidetis* and the Borders of New States' *American Journal of International Law* 90 (1996), pp. 590-624.

Reilly, Ben, and Andrew Reynolds, *Electoral Systems and Conflict in Divided Societies*, Washington, DC: National Academy Press, 1999.

Reporter, weekly magazine of news and analysis, Banja Luka, in English translation.

Republika Srpska, *Constitution of the Republika Srpska*, mimeo (in translation, with amendments), n.d.

Rusinow, Dennison, *The Yugoslav Experiment, 1948-74*, London: Hurst for the RIIA, 1977.

————, (ed.), *Yugoslavia: A Fractured Federalism*, Washington, DC: Wilson Center Press, 1989.

Sadikovic, Cazim, *Human Rights Without Protection*, Sarajevo: Pravni Centar, Fond Otvoreno Drustvo BiH, 1999.

Schaeffer, Robert, *Severed States: Dilemmas of Democracy in a Divided World*, Lanham, MD: Rowman and Littlefield, 1999.

Schmeets, Hans, *The 1997 Municipal Elections in Bosnia & Herzegovina: An Analysis of the Observations*, Dordrecht: Kluwer Academic Publishers for the OSCE and European Commission, 1998.

Selimovic, Mesa, *The Fortress*, Evanston, IL: Northwestern University Press, 1999 (original publication by Svjetlost, Sarajevo, 1970).

Sell, Louis, 'The Serb Flight from Sarajevo: Dayton's First Failure' *East European Politics and Societies* 14: 1 (winter 2000), pp. 179-202.

Silajdzic, Haris, 'The Dayton Peace Accord: A Treaty That Is Not Being Implemented', London: Bosnian Institute, 2000.

Silber, Laura, and Allan Little, *The Death of Yugoslavia*, London: Penguin and BBC Books,(2nd rev. edn), 1996.

Singleton, Fred, *A Short History of the Yugoslav Peoples*, Cambridge University Press, 1985.

Sisk, Timothy, *Power-Sharing and International Mediation in Ethnic Conflicts*, New York: Carnegie Commission on Preventing Deadly Conflict and Washington, DC: United States Institute of Peace, 1996.

Slobodna Bosna(weekly magazine of news and analysis, Sarajevo), in English translation.

Slack, J. Andrew, and Roy R. Doyon, 'Population Dynamics and Susceptibility for Ethnic Conflict: The Case of Bosnia and Hercegovin'; *Journal of Peace Research* 38: 2 (2001), pp. 139-61.

Steil, Benn, and Susan Woodward, 'A European "New Deal" for the Balkans' *Foreign Affairs* 78: 6 (November-December 1999), pp. 95-105.

Stokes, Gale, John Lampe, Dennison Rusinow and Julie Mostov, 'Instant History: Understanding the Wars of Yugoslav Succession' *Slavic Review* 55: 1 (spring 1996).

Stubbs, Paul, *Displaced Promises: Forced Migration, Refuge and Return in Croatia and Bosnia-Herzegovina*, Uppsala: Life and Peace Institute, 1999.

Sudetic, Chuck, *Blood and Vengeance: One's Family's Story of the War in Bosnia*, New York: Norton, 1998.

Talbott, Strobe, 'Self-Determination in an Interdependent World', *Foreign Policy* 118 (spring 2000), pp. 152-63.

Tanner, Marcus, *Croatia: A Nation Forged in War*, New Haven: Yale University Press, 1997.

Thompson, Mark, *A Paper House: The Ending of Yugoslavia*, London: Hutchinson, 1992.

Todorova, Maria, *Imagining the Balkans*, Oxford University Press, 1997.

Underground, feature film, France/Germany/Hungary (dir. Emir Kusturica), 1995.

United States Institute of Peace, *Bosnia's Next Five Years: Dayton and Beyond.*, Washington, DC: USIP (November 2000).

West, Rebecca,. *Black Lamb and Grey Falcon: A Journey Through Yugoslavia*, Edinburgh: Canongate Classics, 1995 (original publication 1942).

Woodward, Susan L., *Balkan Tragedy: Chaos and Dissolution After the Cold War*, Washington, DC: Brookings Institution, 1995.

————, 'Milosevic Who? Origins of the New Balkans', Discussion Paper issued by the Hellenic Observatory, European Institute, London School of Economics and Political Science (July 2001).

————, 'Bosnia and Herzegovina: How Not to End Civil War' in Jack Snyder and Barbara Walter (eds.), *Civil Wars, Insecurity and Intervention*, pp. 73-115. New York: Columbia University Press, 1999.

————, 'Genocide or Partition: Two Faces of the Same Coin?' *Slavic Review* 55: 4 (winter 1996).

INDEX

Abdullah, Sheikh Mohammad, 186, *see also* Kashmir
Aida, V., 97-8
Alagic, Gen. Mehmet, 277
Albania, 172, 272
Alliance for Change, 146, 219, 266, 274-5
Alliance of Reform Forces of Yugoslavia (SRSJ), 15
alternative voting (AV), 221-2, 232, 234, 235, 237, 238
Aluminij Mostar, 131-2, 272
Andabak, Ivan, 141
Andric, Ivo, 38, 95, 246
Andric-Luzanski, Ivo, 229
Armija BiH, 54, 60, 78, 96, 277
Army of Republika Srpska (VRS), 65
Arnaudija mosque (Banja Luka), 154
Austria-Hungary: regime in BiH, 213-14

Babic, Milan, 164
Badinter arbitration commission, 49, 167
Bakic-Hayden, Milica, 12
Banja Luka: 14, 25, 28, 30, 33, 35, 58-60, 74, 75, 93, 94; 2001 riots in 154-61; Bosniac returns to, 159; 200, 227, 228, 231, 266, 276
Barry, Robert, 223
Behmen, Alija, 201
Belgrade, 30, 33, 75, 94, 135, 267
Bender, Ivan, 143, 144
Bengal, 149-50; partition of, 177-9, 187-90, 195-9
Bicakcic, Edhem, 134
Bihac: 15, 23, 37, 60, 209, 228, 276; and Cazin, 169-70, 258
Bijedic, Dzemal, 137
Bijeljina, 34, 35, 169, 172
Bildt, Carl, 1, 26, 53
Boban, Mate, 57, 102-3, 146, 250
Bosanska Gradiska, 159
Bosanski Novi (Novi Grad), 58, 59, 60, 159
Bose, Sarat Chandra: and partition of Bengal, 196-9
Bosnian Cultural Centre (Mostar), 139
Bosnian Party (BOSS), 230, 233-4
Bosnian Patriotic Party (BPS), 229

Bougarel, Xavier, 18, 20
Bourdieu, Pierre, 260
Brajkovic, Mijo, 109, 132, 144
Brass, Paul, 246
Brcko, 34, 75, 275, 278
Bringa, Tone, 17
Brubaker, Rogers, 260-4
Bugojno, 34
Burg, Steven, 194

Calcutta: 150, 188, 197; 1946 communal violence in, 178-9
Canada, 208
Capljina, 101-2, 114, 126, 127, 276
Cavic, Dragan, 156, 230
Cengic, Hasan, 229
Central Bank (BiH), 62, 67-8
Central Bosnia, 23-4, 31, 34, 57, 76, 106, 125, 145, 169, 210, 216, 236, 258, 271; special constitutional regime in, 80-1, 85-6
Chetniks, 99
Christopher, Warren, 11
Citizens' Democratic Party (GDS): 230, 233, 234
'civil war' debate, 18-22
consociational democracy, 42-4, 63-4; in Mostar, 117-18; in Dayton Bosnia, 216-17, 246-52
Constitutional Court (BiH), 65-7
convertible mark (KM), 24, 67, 112
Council of Europe, 9, 32, 219
Crnobrnja, Mihailo, 267
Croat National Congress (HNS), 128, 144, 145
Croatian Army (HV), 39, 54, 105
Croatian Defence Council (HVO), 54, 78, 96, 105, 114, 123, 143, 169
Croatian Democratic Union (HDZ-BiH), 8, 27-9, 31-2, 47, 63, 88, 98, 102, 105, 110, 113, 114, 116-17, 118, 121-4, 129, 138, 142-6, 166, 209-11, 218-19, 229, 238-9, 255, 265-6, 270-1
Cyprus, 46, 180-1

Dahl, Robert, 48, 94

Dayton, Ohio, 2, 60, 146, 168, 258, 263
Dayton constitution (of common state of
    BiH), 61-8
Democratic Party of Serbia (DSS), 267
Diamond, Larry, 204
Djindjic, Zoran, 201, 266-7
Dnevni Avaz, 140
Doboj, 16, 34, 35, 228
Dodik, Milorad, 71, 72, 230-3, 266, 274
Donia, Robert, 13
Dragojevic, Srdjan, 269
Dretelj, 57
Drina Valley, 21, 169, 170
Drvar, 58
Dubrovnik, 74, 102
Dudakovic, Gen. Atif, 60
Duvno (Tomislavgrad), 101
Dzapo, Mirsad, 230
Dzeba, Karlo, 115

Election Commission (BiH), 229, 250-1
Election Law (BiH), 219-4, 270, 273
electoral integration: in Mostar, 118-23;
    in BiH, 215-41
emigration (from BiH), 36-7
Enron, 134
Erotel, 145, 272
European Stability Initiative (ESI), 204
European Union (EU), 33, 146, 255
European Union Administration of
    Mostar (EUAM), 106-10, 116

Fabrika Duhana (Mostar), 133
Federal Republic of Yugoslavia (FRY), 30,
    37, 47, 74-5, 199-200, 265
federalism: different philosophies of, 91-2;
    application to Bosnia, 92-4; and the
    post-Dayton Bosnian state, 241-6
Federation of Bosnia and Herzegovina
    (FBiH): 23, 28-9, 33, 34, 35, 61, 66, 111,
    113, 124, 125, 136, 200, 210, 211, 216,
    219, 220, 224, 226-9, 236, 237-8, 241-
    2, 248, 254, 257, 258-9, 270, 274;con
    stitution and structure of, 75-89; prob-
    lems of, 87-9; crisis of, 145
Feral Tribune, 59
Ferhadija mosque, 154-61, 266
Fine, John V.A., 13
Frasure, Robert, 55
Friedman, Thomas, 29, 41-6

Galbraith, Peter, 58
Gandhi, Mahatma, 197
Garrod, Martin, 110
Gimnazija Mostar, 98, 103, 135-7
Glavas, Branimir, 57

Glenny, Misha, 13
Gojer, Gradimir, 239
Gorazde, 23, 209
Gordon, Leonard, 177-8, 179, 189, 190,
    195-6, 198
Grude, 101, 103

Hadzihasanovic, Enver, 277
Hajrudin, Mimar, 96, 147
Halilovic, Sefer, 229
Hashim, Abul: and partition of Bengal,
    196-9
Hayden, Robert, 24-5, 162, 166, 188, 190-
    4
'Herceg-Bosna', 28, 32, 87, 88, 96, 103,
    132, 134, 146, 163
Hercegovacka Banka (Bank of Herzegovina),
    123-4, 133, 145, 272
Herzegovina, 13, 24, 27-9, 31-2, 39, 56, 57,
    95, 99, 100-2, 106, 143, 145, 159, 169,
    170, 210, 227, 258, 271-2
Herzegovina-Neretva canton: 80-1, 114,
    124; special constitutional regime in, 85-
    7; police reform and integration in, 124-
    9; judiciary reform and integration in,
    129-30; war-crimes trials in, 130-1, 210,
    216, 236; *see also* Mostar
Holbrooke, Richard, 1, 52-60
Horowitz, Donald, 215-18, 221, 222, 233,
    235, 237, 274-5
Hotel Bristol (Mostar), 139
Hotel Ero (Mostar), 107, 109, 138, 145
'House of Peoples' controversy (in FBiH),
    82-3, 254, 270
Hrvatska Banka (Croatian Bank), 147
HVIDRA (HVO war veterans' associa
    tion), 127

Ilidza (Sarajevo), 38, 147
Indian National Congress, 165-6, 197
Institute for War and Peace Reporting
    (IWPR), 29
'integration' debate, 22-38
Inter-Entity Boundary Line (IEBL), 23,
    111, 280
International Committee of the Red Cross
    (ICRC), 20
International Criminal Tribunal for
    Former Yugoslavia (ICTY), 104, 130,
    141, 205, 266, 271, 277
International Crisis Group (ICG), 29, 218,
    222
International Monetary Fund (IMF), 3,
    67
International Police Task Force
    (IPTF), 107, 158

Ivanic, Mladen, 31, 65, 71, 156, 158, 201, 230, 250, 266-7
Ivankovic, Mladen and Jerko, 145
Izetbegovic, Alija, 12, 54, 58, 59, 158, 164, 239, 250

Jablanica, 39, 105, 106, 114, 126, 127
Jajce, 10, 58, 154
Jelavic, Ante, 129, 142-4, 238-9, 250, 275-6
Jinnah, Mohammed Ali, 165, 179, 197
Jutarnji List, 139

Kalinic, Dragan, 156, 267
Kaplan, Robert, 11
Karadzic, Radovan, 14, 40, 57-8, 59, 103, 155, 164, 172, 250
Kashmir, 150, 183-7, 194
Kaufmann, Chaim, 174-89
Kazic, Amra, 140
Kiseljak, 34, 276
Konjic, 106, 114, 126, 127, 170
Koschnick, Hans, 107-10
Kosovo, 162, 213; Serbs of 256; 257
Kostunica, Vojislav, 74-5, 201, 266-7
Kozarac, 36, 159
Krajisnik, Momcilo, 149, 202
Kubura, Col. Amir, 277

Lagumdzija, Zlatko, 2, 156, 201, 250, 266, 277
Laktasi, 231
League of Communists of Yugoslavia (LCY): dissolution of, 214
Lebanon, 46, 248, 251
Leutar, Jozo, 141
liberal internationalism: as ideology, 42, 44; dilemmas in Bosnia of, 89-94
Lijanovici (Siroki Brijeg), 145
Lijphart, Arend, 42-3, 207-8, 212-13, 215-17, 226, 248; see also consociational democracy
Lika, 101
Lipset, Seymour Martin, 207
Lisbon plan (March 1992), 31
Liska street and cemetery (Mostar), 141-2
Little, Allan, 42-7
Livno, 101
Ljubuski, 39, 101

Lozancic, Ivo, 229

M-17 motorway, 101, 143
Macedonia, Former Yugoslav Republic of, 161, 257, 272
MacLean, Fitzroy, 10-11
Mahmutcehajic, Rusmir, 13
Mandic, Dragan, 128-9
Mansergh, Nicholas, 165
Manto, Saadat Hasan, 150-4, 174
Maric, Stipem, 115
Markovic, Antem, 15, 102, 214
Martic, Milan, 164
Martinovic, Vinko ('Stela'), 104
Mearsheimer, John, 29; and Robert Pape, 168-74
Medjugorje, 101, 272
Mehmedinovic, Semezdin, 40
Merlin, Dino, 139
Meter, Dragan, 144
Metkovic, 37
Milosevic, Slobodan, 21, 47, 53-60, 164, 202, 260
minority returns, 33-6; in Mostar and its region, 113-16; 200
Mladic, Gen. Ratko, 57-8, 59, 164
Montenegro: 162; controversy over relationship with Serbia of, 164-5
Mostar: 14, 24, 28, 33, 38, 39, 56, 57, 58, 75, 76, 80, 81, 86-7, 94, 200, 205, 217, 223, 227, 228, 236, 240-1, 249, 271-2, 276, 278, 280; nationalist partition international interention in during 1994-2001, 95-148
Mount Hum: installation of Catholic cross on, 142
Mountbatten, Lord, 197
Mrkonjic Grad, 10, 58
Musa, Josip Jole, 117, 123
Muslim League (India/Pakistan), 165-6, 178, 179, 186; in Bengal's partition, 196-8

Naletilic, Mladen ('Tuta'), 104, 141
National Conference (Kashmir), 186
Nehru, Jawaharlal, 197
Neretva river, 96, 98, 103, 105, 133, 139, 140, 147, 281
Neretva valley, 23-4, 99, 133
Neum, 127, 143

Nevesinje, 74, 100, 115
New Croatian Initiative (NHI), 145, 229, 231
North Atlantic Treaty Organization (NATO), 3, 41, 116, 146, 171, 172, 173, 180
Northern Ireland: conflict and peace process in, 163, 181-3, 248, 279

O'Leary, Brendan, 91-2
Office of the High Representative (OHR), 29, 91, 92, 93, 107, 116, 128, 129, 134-5, 137, 157, 272, 275
Organization for Security and Cooperation in Europe (OSCE), 3, 16, 29, 91, 92, 107, 118, 119, 138, 218-19, 221-3, 226-7, 254, 270, 276
Orucevic, Safet, 109, 114, 118, 123, 132, 144
Owen, David, 49
Paris, Roland, 89-91
partition (of BiH): debate over, 22-38, 149-203; author's criticism of advocates of, 168-94
Party of Bosnia and Herzegovina (SBiH), 26-7, 30-1, 62, 121-4, 170, 209, 211, 218, 229, 266, 274-5
Party of Democratic Action (SDA), 8, 27, 62, 75, 88, 102, 116-7, 118, 121-4, 134, 139, 166, 170, 209, 211, 218-19, 229, 230, 233, 263, 265-6, 277
Party of Democratic Progress Republika Srpska (PDP-RS), 230, 233
party system (of BiH), political implications of, 206-15
Patel, Sardar, 197
Pavarotti Centre (Mostar), 108, 139
Peace Implementation Council (PIC), 91, 218, 236, 274, 275
Peric, Bishop Ratko, 255, 267-72
Petritsch, Wolfgang, 93, 115, 137-8, 157-8, 256, 257, 268, 272, 276, 277;
    see also Office of the High Representative
Phillips, Anne, 247
Plavsic, Biljana, 164
Pocitelj, 101
Poplasen, Nikola, 72

Popovic, Slobodan, 230
Posavina, 23, 75, 145, 169, 210, 227, 236
Praljak, Slobodan, 143
Pretty Village, Pretty Flame, 269
Prijedor, 14-16, 34, 35, 58, 59, 60
Prlic, Jadranko, 88, 143-4
Prozor, 101, 114, 126, 127, 276
Prskalo, Ivan, 110, 118
Puljic, Mile, 113
Punjab, 149-50, 177, 187, 192-3

Quebec, 208, 279

Racan, Ivica, 144
Radan, Peter, 162
Rahman, Sheikh Mujibur, 190
Ratner, Steven, 50-1
Ravno, 114
Reconstruction and Return Task Force (RRTF), 107
referendums on 'self-determination', dangers of, 50-2
Reilly, Ben, 240
Renner Company (Stolac), 132
Republika Srpska (RS), 8, 23, 25, 30-1, 33, 34, 35, 37, 61, 66; constitution and structure of, 68-75; 111, 112, 146, 155, 156, 157-8, 160-1, 163, 199, 200, 201, 210, 211, 219, 220, 221-2, 224, 226-9, 230-5, 237-8, 241-2, 254, 256, 257, 258, 266-7, 268, 270, 271, 274, 277
Republika Srpska Krajina (RSK), 23, 47, 50, 54, 59, 164, 173, 213, 216, 256, 260
Reynolds, Andrew, 240
Riker, William, 244-5
Rokkan, Stein, 207

Sanski Most, 15, 17, 58, 59, 60, 158
Santic, Aleksa, 99, 140
Sarajevo: 14, 17, 23, 28, 29, 33, 34, 35, 37, 38, 39, 40, 45, 75, 80, 94, 126, 127, 141, 143; Serb returns to, 147; 168, 169, 170, 199, 201, 209, 210, 227, 228, 258, 266, 268, 275-6
Sarovic, Mirko, 156, 230, 266-7
Schaeffer, Robert, 166-7, 194-5
'security dilemma' argument: flaws of,

175-83, 187
Selimovic, Mesa, 38
Semberija, 227
Serb Democratic Party (SDS), 8, 102,
  156, 166, 211, 218-19, 229, 230-5,
  237, 266-7
Serb Independent Social
  Democrats (SNSD), 230-5, 266
Serb Radical Party (SRS), 72, 277
Shoup, Paul, 194
Siber, Stjepan, 229
Silajdzic, Haris, 26-7, 30-1, 58, 209
single transferable vote (STV), 234-5,
  237
Siroki Brijeg, 56, 101
Slobodna Dalmacija, 139-40
Slovenia, secession from Yugoslavia,
  164, 179, 213, 258
Social Democratic Party of Bosnia
  and Herzegovina (SDP-BiH), 8, 27,
  30, 62, 117, 121-4, 129, 170, 209-
  11, 229, 230, 233-4, 235, 239, 265-
  6, 274-5
'Sokol' (Mostar), 132
Sopta, Gen. Stanko, 142
South Africa, 248
Split, 33, 57, 58, 127, 132, 138, 140,
  141
Srebrenica, 224
Stabilization Force (SFOR), 91, 107,
  133, 145, 155-6, 276
Stanimirovic, Dragi, 229
Stari Most (Old Bridge) Mostar, 96,
  105, 111, 133; reconstruction of,
  147-8
State Border Service (SBS), 37-8, 200
Steiner, Michael, 88
Stolac, 35, 101-2, 114, 126, 127, 137,
  276
Sudetic, Chuck, 20-1
Suleiman (Ottoman sultan), 96
Susak, Gojko, 56-60, 101, 132, 146
Svilanovic, Goran, 201
Switzerland:,comparison with
  Bosnia, 243-4

Talbott, Strobe, 278-80
Tanovic, Danis, 269

Teslic, 35, 170
Tihic, Sulejman, 229
Todorova, Maria, 12, 14, 44
Toholj, Miroslav, 40
Tomic, Neven, 139, 142, 144
Trebinje, 74, 100; 2001 riots in, 156-
  7; 158, 159
Tudjman, Franjo, 21, 28, 47, 53-60,
  110, 117, 128, 132, 146, 164, 202,
  260; death of, 142-3
Tuzla, 14, 23, 33, 75, 170, 209, 228,
  275

United Nations (UN), 172, 173
United Nations High Commissioner
  for Refugees (UNHCR), 107
United Nations Mission in Bosnia
  and Herzegovina (UNMiBH), 3,
  37, 74, 86-7, 107, 125, 129, 158
Ustashe, 56, 99, 101
uti possidetis juris, 48-51

Vance-Owen plan, 168-9
Vienna, 281
Visegrad, 21
Vitez, 34
Volksdeutsche, 191
Vukovar, 56

Washington Agreement (March
  1994), 75, 104, 258
Whelan, Frederick, 48
Whitaker, Reginald, 241
Woodward, Susan, 253, 267-9
World Bank, 3, 113, 147

Yugoslav People's Army
  (JNA), 16, 95-6, 103, 132, 164, 179

Zagreb, 28, 33, 58, 75, 94, 135, 138,
  201
Zavidovici, 16-17
Zenica, 14, 16, 23, 170, 209, 228
Zenica-Doboj canton, 236
Zitomislici, 272
Zubak, Kresimir, 145, 239
Zvornik, 34, 37, 45-6, 170